France Troubled Ally De Gaulle S Heritage And Prospects

SOME PUBLICATIONS OF THE

COUNCIL ON FOREIGN RELATIONS

FOREIGN AFFAIRS (quarterly), edited by Hamilton Fish Armstrong.

THE UNITED STATES IN WORLD AFFAIRS (annual). Volumes for 1931, 1932, and 1933, by Walter Lippmann and William O. Scroggs, for 1934-1935, 1936, 1937, 1938, 1939 and 1940, by Whitney H Shepardson and William O. Scroggs; for 1945-1947, 1947-1948 and 1948-1949, by John C. Campbell, for 1949, 1950, 1951, 1952, 1953 and 1954, by Richard P. Stebbins; for 1955, by Hollis W. Barber; for 1956, 1957 and 1958, by Richard P Stebbins.

DOCUMENTS ON AMERICAN FOREIGN RELATIONS (annual). Volume for 1952, edited by Clarence W. Baier and Richard P. Stebbins; for 1953 and 1954, edited by Peter V. Curl, for 1955, 1956, 1957 and 1958, edited by Paul E Zinner

POLITICAL HANDBOOK OF THE WORLD (annual), edited by Walter H. Mallory.

THE SCHUMAN PLAN A Study in Economic Cooperation, 1950-1959, by William Diebold, Jr.

SOVIET ECONOMIC AID· The New Aid and Trade Policy in Underdeveloped Countries, by Joseph S. Berliner.

RAW MATERIALS: A Study of American Policy, by Percy W. Bidwell.

FOREIGN POLICY The Next Phase, by Thomas K Finletter.

NATO AND THE FUTURE OF EUROPE, by Ben T. Moore

AFRICAN ECONOMIC DEVELOPMENT, by William A. Hance.

DEFENSE OF THE MIDDLE EAST: Problems of American Policy, by John C Campbell.

INDIA AND AMERICA: A Study of Their Relations, by Phillips Talbot and S. L. Poplai.

JAPAN BETWEEN EAST AND WEST, by Hugh Borton, Jerome B. Cohen, William J. Jorden, Donald Keene, Paul F. Langer and C. Martin Wilbur.

NUCLEAR WEAPONS AND FOREIGN POLICY, by Henry A Kissinger

MOSCOW-PEKING AXIS Strengths and Strains, by Howard L. Boorman, Alexander Eckstein, Philip E Mosely and Benjamin Schwartz.

CLIMATE AND ECONOMIC DEVELOPMENT IN THE TROPICS, by Douglas H. K. Lee

WHAT THE TARIFF MEANS TO AMERICAN INDUSTRIES, by Percy W Bidwell.

UNITED STATES SHIPPING POLICY, by Wytze Gorter

RUSSIA AND AMERICA· Dangers and Prospects, by Henry L. Roberts.

STERLING· Its Meaning in World Finance, by Judd Polk.

KOREA: A Study of U S. Policy in the United Nations, by Leland M Goodrich.

FOREIGN AFFAIRS BIBLIOGRAPHY, 1942-1952 by Henry L. Roberts.

AMERICAN AGENCIES INTERESTED IN INTERNATIONAL AFFAIRS, compiled by Ruth Savord and Donald Wasson.

JAPANESE AND AMERICANS: A Century of Cultural Relations, by Robert S. Schwantes.

THE FUTURE OF UNDERDEVELOPED COUNTRIES: Political Implications of Economic Development, by Eugene Staley

THE UNDECLARED WAR, 1940-1941, by William L. Langer and S. Everett Gleason.

THE CHALLENGE TO ISOLATION, 1937-1940, by William L. Langer and S. Everett Gleason.

BRITAIN AND THE UNITED STATES· Problems in Cooperation, a joint report prepared by Henry L. Roberts and Paul A. Wilson.

TRADE AND PAYMENTS IN WESTERN EUROPE A Study in Economic Co-operation, 1947-1951, by William Diebold, Jr.

France
Troubled Ally

DE GAULLE'S HERITAGE AND PROSPECTS

By

EDGAR S. FURNISS, JR.

Published for the
COUNCIL ON FOREIGN RELATIONS
by
HARPER & BROTHERS
New York
1960

The Council on Foreign Relations is a non-profit institution devoted to study of the international aspects of American political, economic and strategic problems. It takes no stand, expressed or implied, on American policy.

The authors of books published under the auspices of the Council are responsible for their statements of fact and expressions of opinion. The Council is responsible only for determining that they should be presented to the public.

FRANCE, TROUBLED ALLY
De Gaulle's Heritage and Prospects

*Copyright, © 1960, by Council on Foreign Relations, Inc.
Printed in the United States of America*

All rights reserved, including the right to reproduce this book or any portion thereof in any form.

For information, address Council on Foreign Relations, 58 East 68th Street, New York 21

FIRST EDITION

American Book–Stratford Press, Inc., New York

Library of Congress catalog card number LC 59-10582

PUBLISHED FOR THE COUNCIL ON FOREIGN RELATIONS
IN THE UNITED STATES BY HARPER & BROTHERS

COUNCIL ON FOREIGN RELATIONS

OFFICERS AND DIRECTORS

JOHN J. MCCLOY
Chairman of the Board

HENRY M. WRISTON
President

FRANK ALTSCHUL	DAVID ROCKEFELLER
Vice-President & Secretary	*Vice-President*
ELLIOT V. BELL	GEORGE S. FRANKLIN, JR.
Treasurer	*Executive Director*
WILLIAM HENDERSON	FRANK D. CARUTHERS, JR.
Associate Executive Director	*Assistant Treasurer*

HAMILTON FISH ARMSTRONG	GRAYSON L. KIRK
WILLIAM A. M. BURDEN	R. C. LEFFINGWELL
ARTHUR H. DEAN	WALTER H. MALLORY
LEWIS W. DOUGLAS	PHILIP D. REED
ALLEN W. DULLES	WHITNEY H. SHEPARDSON
THOMAS K. FINLETTER	CHARLES M. SPOFFORD
JOSEPH E. JOHNSON	ADLAI E. STEVENSON

JOHN H. WILLIAMS

COMMITTEE ON STUDIES

HENRY M. WRISTON
Chairman

HAMILTON FISH ARMSTRONG	JOSEPH E. JOHNSON
ARTHUR H. DEAN	GRAYSON L. KIRK
BYRON DEXTER	AUGUST MAFFRY
CARYL P. HASKINS	WILLARD L. THORP

JOHN H. WILLIAMS

STUDIES PROGRAM

PHILIP E. MOSELY
Director of Studies

WILLIAM DIEBOLD, JR.	JOHN C. CAMPBELL
Director of Economic Studies	*Director of Political Studies*

PREFACE

As a title *France, Troubled Ally* says too much and too little. Too little, for France more than most Western democracies has been troubled by crises for a long time. Indeed it has been suggested that perpetual crisis, for all it is a contradiction in terms, describes France from 1946, or 1939, or 1914, or 1870, or 1789. Too much, for France, although the recurrent despair of its friends for years, if not for decades, has only rarely permitted its self-generated crises to disturb greatly the course of its national life. Perhaps indeed this has been part of the trouble—the French genius for superficial volatility combined with deep-seated stability. "Plus ça change . . ." is, after all, a French expression, again echoed before the elections of 1958 by the French voter. Even the climactic events of May 1958, as I observed them in France, ruffled only the surface of the deep waters, and many French groups combating for and against De Gaulle strove earnestly to see that this remained so.

One basic theme of this volume is that French foreign policy cannot be understood except in the light of the political, economic, and social setting in which it is shaped. Therefore, French actions on the international scene have been examined as the outgrowth of the domestic demands placed upon the policy-making process. As the Fourth Republic declined into *immobilisme* after 1954, these domestic requirements became at the same time more pressing and more contradictory than they had been before. Consequently, successive governments could do little more than go through the motions of making policy, with individual political leaders hoping that they would escape becoming the personal victims of a "system" which was becoming increasingly divorced from the real life of France. It was this fact which reinforced the faith of French leaders in the value of diplomacy: if diplomacy could not win the day for France, nothing could. Had not sheer diplomatic virtuosity postponed for over six years the appearance of that feared and distrusted phoenix, the West German army?

A second theme the reader will readily discover is the continuity of foreign policy between the Fourth and Fifth Republics. To be sure, there have been changes—in personnel, in procedure, especially in tone, occasionally even in substance. But for the most part De Gaulle seeks to do what the ephemeral statesmen of the Fourth Republic also attempted. Close cooperation with West Germany, acquisition of a nuclear capability, a greater role in NATO, revision of overseas connections to maintain influence over what was once a great empire—the new leader takes up where his predecessors left off. The major difference is that De Gaulle believes he can for the first time since the war mobilize behind a policy of national greatness the many ingredients of French power heretofore antagonistically arrayed against each other. The great question now becomes whether unity and sacrifice can long be imposed on the French people, even by a man endowed with the charismatic aura of twice-over savior of France. At this juncture of history one should neither minimize the obstacles which lie ahead nor underrate the genius of the man. No one who has watched De Gaulle pick his way along the narrow, explosive-lined path between his obdurate supporters and his inveterate enemies would lightly scoff at his feeling that in communion with himself he can find the heart of France and the means to evoke its response. None the less, while the conclusion must be tentative on a record of scarcely more than a year, it is my judgment that in the end De Gaulle will not succeed in restoring France to its past grandeur. Hopefully, his role will be that of supervising the transition of a proud nation to acceptance of an international stature shrunken by the impact of economic and strategic forces outside its control.

Since this volume is addressed primarily to Americans, it is well to emphasize the conclusion that after World War II the United States expected too much of France. It exaggerated the degree and duration of war-born unity within the French body politic, and minimized the effects of the conflict on French society and economy, as well as the consequences of a long-range decline in France's relative power. Through these miscalculations, the United States marked out for France an international role which was beyond its capacity. American expectations encouraged France's leaders in turn to treat its serious domestic problems superficially and to avoid facing the need for fundamental reforms, whether political, economic, military, or colonial. The frustrations inherent in this unrealistic approach led to actions on both sides which often obscured deepset differences in outlook—as over colonial policy or the role of West Germany. Even when disputes broke into the open—as over the European Defense Community, Indo-China, or Suez—the underlying causes were insufficiently understood, hence never completely rectified. In its efforts to support France, official American policy found itself at odds with individual Americans, who became increasingly cynical about the land of Lafayette and the motivation of its inhabitants.

Many Americans, citizens of a newly great power, which believed that the safety of the West lay only in the possession and expression of power on the international scene, tended to believe that Frenchmen who did not feel and act in the same manner must be indulging in some sly form of Gallic immorality. And Americans were encouraged in this judgment by the Frenchmen of affairs who appealed to the Fourth Republic to live up to the lofty role which it claimed. Again the lesson is plain: only at its peril can the United States once more assume that because a new French leader has appeared, suddenly, miraculously all will be different, overnight France will again be a great power. No American statesman can ignore, just because it lies beneath the surface, the forces broadening the French equivalent of the German *Ohne Mich*.

This study is focused on the recent policies of the Fourth and Fifth Republics. The first section sets forth only the principal strains of foreign policy between 1945 and 1954, showing how, with the defeat of the European Defense Community, the period of *immobilisme* reached its zenith. The first nine years after the war fall roughly into three periods of about equal length. In each period French policy-makers devised a strategy designed to win for France a leading place among the nations despite the absence of commensurate ingredients of power. Each strategy won some initial successes; each closed with failures caused by the inability of French leaders to marshall national strength and by their unwillingness to reduce national aspirations and commitments. Thus when Mendès-France was selected as the man to make the painful and long-overdue sacrifices, he prepared the way, not for national rejuvenation or for a new adjustment of aims to means, but rather for the Fourth Republic's last effort to evade history.

The final attempt of the Fourth Republic to retain the position of a world power receives most attention. By a tragic irony, the four years 1954-1958 witnessed the burgeoning of long-delayed economic prosperity, too late to be credited by the French people to their government, too late to enable that government to recapture the loyalty of social groups, especially the army. While most of the military establishment looked on and refused to defend their civilian leaders, a small group of military and civilian conspirators combined to destroy the Republic. They brought De Gaulle to power, not because the Fourth Republic refused to act in Algeria, but because they feared it would act. They sought to prevent precisely the type of conciliatory settlement which more and more Frenchmen believed was inevitable and would save French influence in Algeria and throughout Africa only if it came quickly.

PREFACE   xi

The third section of the book attempts to assess the probable consequences of De Gaulle's initial moves at home and abroad. Certainly his personal achievements have been remarkable. A new constitution has been tailored to his measure. A flood of economic decrees has enforced a rare effort of sacrifice on the French people. By committing France to the Common Market and himself to Adenauer's position regarding Berlin he has brought the country back to a position of leadership among the Six. Swiftly he has created the French Community and to it he has bound all French African territories save one. Yet in a real sense the thrust of his leadership has been strikingly similar to that of Mendès-France. As in 1954, it is doubtful if De Gaulle has at his disposal either the time or the resources to accomplish his positive purposes. Algeria, for which De Gaulle like his predecessors seeks a "liberal" settlement, is not the principal test. It is only one facet of the multiple challenges which a troubled France confronts in the vastly changed world of today.

While my study of French foreign policy had its inception with a Faculty Fellowship of the Social Science Research Council which enabled me to spend the academic year 1952-1953 in France, the present project was begun under a Research Fellowship of the Council on Foreign Relations. I wish to express my deep appreciation to Princeton University for its generosity in granting me a leave of absence for two semesters so that I might be permitted to take advantage of this opportunity. In carrying out this study I had the full cooperation of a Council Study Group which held seven meetings during 1958. I take great pleasure in thanking the members of the Study Group, many of them long experienced in French affairs, for the perspectives and criticisms which they have contributed to my study, while leaving me solely responsible for my conclusions. The Study Group included: August Heckscher, Chairman, John Petty, Rapporteur, George W. Ball, Pierre Bedard, Simon Michael Bessie, Leslie Brady, William A. M. Burden, Cass Canfield,

William L. Cary, Lt. Colonel Arthur R. Datnoff, William Diebold, Jr., Mario Einaudi, Gerald Freund, Henry J. Friendly, Lewis Galantiere, Harmon H. Goldstone, Garfield H. Horn, John Chambers Hughes, Henry B. Hyde, Nelson Dean Jay, Philip M. Kaiser, Edward L. Katzenbach, Jr., Roy Lamson, Jr., Daniel Lerner, Norbert G. Leroy, Larry LeSueur, Harold F. Linder, Philip E. Mosely, Major James Munson, Waldemar A. Nielsen, Justin O'Brien, Henri Peyre, Robert V. Roosa, J. Salwyn Schapiro, Colonel Arthur L. West, Arthur P. Whitaker, Colonel G. H. Woodward, and Colonel Richard Yudkin. I am happy to acknowledge my special debt to the Chairman of the Study Group, August Heckscher, who guided our discussions with great ability and insight.

As a part of the project, I was able to carry on two periods of intensive interviewing in France in April, May, and June 1958, and again in January 1959. None of those with whom I talked has been quoted directly, but their contributions—by Frenchmen and Americans alike—permeate the pages of this volume. Without their aid the result would be far poorer. I wish especially to thank Dana and Jean Orwick for their gracious hospitality in these two periods.

In reviewing and editing the manuscript I have had the able assistance of several people: Percy W. Bidwell, John C. Campbell, William Diebold, Jr., and Wesley Strombeck. My special thanks go to Philip E. Mosely, who helped me from the beginning in shaping my plans for the study, who read the entire manuscript with meticulous care, and who, above all, encouraged me constantly to pursue this difficult task to its completion. I also take special pleasure in thanking Hamilton Fish Armstrong and August Heckscher for their careful reading of my manuscript and their many helpful suggestions. My thanks also go to Lorna Brennan and her staff for their remarkable speed and accuracy in typing and mimeographing the reams of material produced by this project and in the care with which they reviewed the galleys, and to Wesley Strombeck for his efficient preparation of the index. Finally, as is so frequently the case in academic families, only my wife knows how great is my debt to her. Among the more obvious and perhaps less important contributions which she has made have been research in libraries, the organization of interviews, the editing of memoranda and of the manuscript, and a vast amount of typing and retyping of drafts.

At this point it is customary to declare that the merits of the volume belong to others—which should be obvious from the list of acknowledgments—but the faults and errors are mine alone—which the reader will quickly find out for himself. In any case, the opinions are mine, and are not to be attributed to the Council on Foreign Relations or to the members of the Study Group.

This book is dedicated to my father, Edgar S. Furniss, who, for better or for worse, inspired me to follow academic pursuits.

CONTENTS

PREFACE   vii

Part One
The International Position of France: Liberation to Paris Agreements

1. GRANDEUR AND MEDIATION, 1944-1947   3
2. FRANCE AS BUILDER OF "EUROPE," 1947-1950   24
3. INDECISION AND PROCRASTINATION, 1950-1954   60

Part Two
Self-Destruction of the Fourth Republic through "Immobilisme," 1954-1958

4. THE POLITICAL BASIS OF "IMMOBILISME"   113
5. SOME ECONOMIC AND SOCIAL ASPECTS OF "IMMOBILISME"   137
6. THE FOURTH REPUBLIC AND THE FRENCH MILITARY ESTABLISHMENT   165
7. THE FOURTH REPUBLIC AND SUB-SAHARAN AFRICA   179
8. FRANCE AND ITS "DOMESTIC" PROBLEM: THE ALGERIAN WAR   196

9.	TUNISIA AND MOROCCO IN THE ALGERIAN WAR	219
10.	"IMMOBILISME" AND FOREIGN POLICY	236
11.	FRANCE AND EUROPE	251
12.	FRANCE AND NATO	276
13.	UNEASY ALLIES: AMERICA AND THE FOURTH REPUBLIC	291
14.	ALGERIA, GRAVE OF THE FOURTH REPUBLIC	317

PART THREE
Foundations and Prospects of De Gaulle's Fifth Republic

15.	THE CONSTITUTION OF THE FIFTH REPUBLIC	351
16.	POLITICS AND PARTIES UNDER THE FIFTH REPUBLIC	380
17.	ECONOMIC AND SOCIAL PROBLEMS OF THE FIFTH REPUBLIC	403
18.	ALGERIA: PROBLEMS AND PROSPECTS	423
19.	EMERGENCE OF THE FRENCH COMMUNITY	440
20.	THE IMPLICATIONS OF GRANDEUR	456
21.	AMERICAN POLICY AND DE GAULLE'S REPUBLIC	474
	BIBLIOGRAPHICAL NOTE	493
	INDEX	499

Part One

THE INTERNATIONAL POSITION OF FRANCE: LIBERATION TO PARIS AGREEMENTS

Chapter One

GRANDEUR AND MEDIATION
1944-1947

GENERAL CHARLES DE GAULLE's provisional government, triumphantly installed in liberated Paris, directed its first efforts toward a speedy return to the basic lines of France's traditional policy. One of its primary preoccupations was again to attain security against Germany. To bolster the French position, renewed alliances were sought to the East with the Soviet Union and to the West with Great Britain. The Quai d'Orsay also attempted to restore the war-shattered ties with several smaller countries of Central and Eastern Europe. Quite apparently, the objective was to re-establish France's position as the leading power of continental Europe.

The return to prewar policies rested on the belief that the basic conditions of European politics had remained unchanged and thus defined the essential requirements for a successful policy in the years ahead.[1] The third German invasion of France within seventy years had been by far the most disastrous. The very rapidity of the defeat, followed by four years of occupation and humiliating control, had intensified the French determination to eliminate "forever" the menace from beyond the Rhine. In addition, France's failure to withstand Hitler's onslaught was as-

---

[1] A number of French writers immediately following World War II emphasized the unchanging requirements of French foreign policy, e.g., René Pinon, *Les Conditions Permanentes de la Politique Française* (Paris. Cahiers de Politique Étrangère du Journal des Nations Américaines, 1946), especially pp. 37-41.

cribed in part to Germany's having assured itself, as the result of monstrous Western blunders, of Russia's neutrality. Future protection against Germany, still potentially strong in defeat, demanded prompt agreement with the Soviet Union, which after 1941 had fought Hitler successfully and virtually alone for two years. Now the U.S.S.R. was emerging from the war with a greatly augmented relative and absolute power, arrayed in the heart of a devastated Europe. Within France the Communists had played a leading role in the Resistance and would have great influence in determining its postwar policies. The readings of history, the nation's objectives in Germany, realistic appraisals of existing and future strength, domestic experiences and party considerations, all directed French attention toward the Eastern colossus.

As for Great Britain, there was nothing new in the French determination to involve British power as deeply and as inextricably as possible in France's European concerns. Had not Churchill held out to a vanquished France the offer of an Anglo-French union as an alternative to surrender? If Britain before the war had accepted firm and automatic commitments, so French opinion maintained, this would have averted the renewal of German aggression under the Nazis. With the countries of East Central Europe, France had many historic ties—cultural, economic, political and military. Perhaps, in addition, many Frenchmen cherished painful thoughts of what might have been, had France stood fast by its small, prewar allies.

Recognition as a Great Power

There was one prerequisite to the satisfactory pursuit of French policies—recognition by other nations as a great power. To be the initiator rather than the victim of events, France had to obtain a status equal to that of the Big Three. During the war years much of De Gaulle's irritating manner and stubborn intransigence had stemmed from his determination to be treated as the true leader of a great power, unfortunately—but only temporarily—in eclipse. His proximity in London to leaders of other governments-in-exile certainly spurred De Gaulle to emphasize the difference between them and France. On one occasion, when the British War Cabinet complained that "we have ten times more trouble with the Committee of the Free French than with all the other Allies put together," the bearer of the message, none other than Anthony Eden, was reportedly told by De Gaulle, "I have always maintained that France was a very great country."[2]

After the liberation Frenchmen felt the added need to erase from memories at home and abroad the spectacle of a country which, though once more on the winning side, had this time not made any great contribution to the final outcome. National humiliation had been compounded by Hitler's partitioning of France into two zones, each subjected to a different regime. During occupation and liberation, deeply rooted antagonisms had been fanned into something closely akin to civil war. To rally, indeed to recreate, the nation was De Gaulle's mission. He saw himself as both the symbol and the spokesman for the eternal grandeur of France. Once a new and powerful France had resumed its place in the select councils of the world, present miseries would become more bearable, future sacrifices more willingly assumed.

De Gaulle's abrupt refusal to meet President Roosevelt at Algiers, on his return journey from the Yalta conference, was an expression of resentment over being excluded from ". . . a conference in which France has not taken part and about whose various purposes it still does not know."[3] The same desire for equal status led to much pulling and hauling over the status of France at the San Francisco conference of 1945. First claiming the right to be a sponsoring power, it also reserved its freedom to propose amendments to the Charter of the United Nations, only to withdraw at the last minute as a sponsor. At the conference France made some half-hearted efforts to rally the smaller powers

---

[2] Paul Reynaud, "Churchill and France," in Charles Eade, ed., *Churchill, by His Contemporaries* (New York: Simon and Schuster, 1954), p 324. A variation on this theme is told by De Gaulle himself. Charles de Gaulle, *Unity* (New York Simon and Schuster, 1959), p 114

[3] *L'Année Politique*, 1944-1945 (Paris: Éditions du Grand Siècle), p. 130.

against the Big-Three draft, but in the end it accepted for itself all the privileges assigned to the Big Five, including permanent membership and the veto within the Security Council.

A policy of grandeur meant more than salving French pride. Only through achieving equality of status could France participate in building a more secure world. Without its contribution the job might be hopelessly botched. Thus, immediately after the surrender of Japan, France—which had played, if anything, a negative role in the Pacific war—demanded the right to take part in the negotiations. In Europe, only a few weeks earlier, the United States, Britain, and the Soviet Union had adjourned the Potsdam conference, to which France was not invited, only to convoke the London Council of Foreign Ministers in September 1945 to discuss the peace treaties with Italy and with Germany's recent satellites. While Britain and America welcomed France's full participation, the Soviet Union, irked by the French refusal to follow the Soviet lead, publicly reversed its stand at London and tried to limit French participation to the drafting of the peace with Italy. De Gaulle declared that France would consent to no arrangements unless it was consulted "at the same time and in the same manner as the other great powers."[4] The French ambition remained unchanged· ". . . a policy of grandeur, whose ambitions were vast, whose contours were imprecise, whose means were nonexistent . . . again a great power, equal in law to the greatest, consequently associated in all decisions, above all the first power in Europe."[5]

With the wartime Big Three more and more sharply divided, the French pretension gained at least a symbolic acceptance. Not only did France take an outwardly equal part in drafting the peace treaties for the erstwhile German satellites and for Italy, but Paris itself was selected as the seat of the conference, an event hailed by the London *Times* as "the most striking success for France since the

---

[4] Same, pp. 358-359.
[5] François LeRoy, *Les Relations Internationales Depuis 1945* (Paris Cours de Droit, 1951), p. 115.

liberation in the field of foreign policy."[6] The French had won their case for equality because both East and West were now seeking the support of France. Great Britain was as anxious as France to remove the heritage of prewar and wartime conflicts, and it needed a strong and stable partner, albeit a junior one, in Western Europe. With De Gaulle apparently firmly established as the head of a new French government, the United States had also come to terms. The Western powers had willingly carved a German territory for France out of their own occupation zones, although France complained at not receiving from the United States precisely the areas it preferred.[7] On British initiative and with American support France took a seat on the Allied Control Council for Germany, without even being asked to subscribe to the Potsdam Agreement, which laid down Big-Three policies for Germany. If France used its status in German affairs without much attention to the responsibilities of an occupying power—in effect paralyzing the Council for the first year, until the Soviet Union took over the job—this was due primarily to the French government's determination to gain its own distinct objectives toward defeated Germany.

The Soviet Union had nothing against French aspirations to a nebulous status of equality. Quite the contrary: diplomatic smiles and inexpensive gestures were a foreign-policy counterpart to the Communist cooperation in the governing coalition, just as appeals to France's "great Soviet ally" carried weight among nationalist as well as leftist French voters. Russia had been the first power to recognize De Gaulle's provisional government after its establishment in North Africa. Stalin consented to France having an occupation zone in Germany, so long as his own zone was not thereby reduced. Russian gestures, however, did not extend very far. Molotov reversed himself and even broke up the London Council of Foreign Ministers in October 1945 over the question of French participation in drafting the peace treaties for the German satellites. The

[6] April 20, 1946.
[7] J.-B. Duroselle, *Histoire Diplomatique de 1919 à Nos Jours* (Paris: Dalloz, 1953), p. 495.

Russians were annoyed at finding France aligned with Britain and America on question after question. They wanted to show De Gaulle that only Russia could assure France of a great-power status, and they may have believed that France, moving inexorably to the Left, would the sooner find it essential to align itself with Soviet policies.

Mediation between East and West

Once readmitted to the select club of great powers, France was determined that its affairs should be harmoniously conducted. French recovery depended on the rapid weaving of the fabric of peace, and this could be accomplished only if all the great powers were willing to subordinate their differences of view to the larger purpose. In turn, the external harmony of the great powers would promote the internal political harmony of France, expressed in government by coalition.

Immediately after liberation there were in France only three parties that counted. Together the Communist party, the Socialist party, and the Catholic Mouvement Républicain Populaire (MRP) represented more than three-quarters of the electorate. Without any one of them, the other two would be hard put to it to govern; together their strength far exceeded that of any regime during the Third Republic. The ability of three parties to cooperate was put to a severe test by De Gaulle's sudden resignation as Provisional President, on January 20, 1946. The General's obvious intention was to enforce parliamentary obedience to his policies, particularly to his policy of grandeur. The specific issue was the General's demand for large military credits for rebuilding the French army, larger than most of the Constituent Assembly felt France could afford. The answer to De Gaulle's expectation that political chaos would lead to his speedy return was given only two days later. On January 22, 1946, the leaders of the three parties issued a remarkable "protocol." This was in effect a treaty whereby the signers agreed to parcel out executive power among themselves, although without a specific division of ministerial posts. The life of the protocol and the duration of tripartite government in France was thenceforth to be dependent on a foreign policy which avoided making a choice between the Anglo-American and Soviet camps.

As Foreign Minister in successive governments, MRP leader Georges Bidault labored to prevent an East-West split and to avoid actions which could be construed as a commitment to either side. During the first debate on foreign policy in the Constituent Assembly after the liberation, Bidault declared: "An alliance with the West? Of course. How could we do otherwise? But an alliance with the East, also! We are interested in affairs which go beyond the West. France will never permit itself to be limited to the Western part of the world."[8] French relations with the Soviet Union rested on the treaty of December 9, 1944. The alliance placed France in the same position as Great Britain, which had concluded an agreement with Russia two years earlier. The French Assembly took only two days to give its approval, and ratifications were exchanged on February 15, 1945, almost three months before the surrender of Germany.

Formally allied to the Soviet Union and closely linked with Britain and the United States, France entered the year 1946 with the purpose of holding the Big Three together. As André Siegfried put it at the time, "it felt its mission to be that of serving as a moderating element, indispensable to the equilibrium between the great blocs that are trying to divide up the world between them."[9] Perhaps because his own Socialist party was trying to steer the narrow course between a fusion with the Communists and abandoning its traditional Left-wing position, Salomon Grumbach, President of the Foreign Affairs Commission of the Council of the Republic, felt this even more strongly. "It is for the government of the Republic, for French diplomacy," he wrote, "to do all that our international position, all that the influence we have been able to keep in spite of the weakening of our material forces,

[8] *L'Année Politique*, 1944-1945, cited, p. 66.
[9] *L'Année Politique*, 1946, cited, p 315.

allows us in order to promote the reconciliation of the Anglo-Saxon countries and Soviet Russia, without which there will be no certain and stable world peace, no viable solution to the German problem."[10]

The French effort at mediation made itself evident in both the United Nations and the Council of Foreign Ministers. In April 1946, for example, France voted in the Security Council with Russia and Poland and against the United States and Britain in supporting Iran's request that its complaint against the continuing presence of Soviet troops on its soil be removed from the agenda. Secretary-General Trygve Lie also felt that the United Nations should, if possible, avoid being entangled in great-power conflicts, particularly when, as in this case, they seemed on the point of settlement.[11]

A year later, when the Soviet Union sought to have its new satellites admitted to the United Nations, while opposing the West's demand for the admission of Ireland, Portugal, Italy, Finland, and Transjordan, Delegate Alexandre Parodi advanced the only practical solution: blanket approval of all applications regardless of sponsorship, with the exception of Bulgaria, whose execution of Agrarian leader Nikola Petkov had left a widespread sense of outrage. Obstinately, each side wanted victory for itself, defeat for the other, "and France was not strong enough to make its appeal to good sense and to good faith heard."[12]

At the Paris peace conference of 1946, Foreign Minister Bidault tirelessly produced one compromise after another and arranged private exploratory meetings. In order to avoid slights to its newly restored status as well as accusations of joining one side or the other, France's voice was rarely raised in plenary sessions. On no issue did Bidault strive more diligently than on that of Trieste, and the compromises finally adopted in late 1946 owed much to

[10] Salomon Grumbach, "Après Moscou Quelques Réflexions sur l'Échec d'une Conférence à Quatre," *Revue Politique et Parlementaire*, May 1947, p. 108.
[11] Lie's position is stated in his book, *In the Cause of Peace* (New York: Macmillan, 1954), pp 74-88.
[12] *L'Année Politique*, 1947, cited, p. 209.

his unceasing efforts at conciliation. France was less successful in arranging an agreement on the procedure for drafting the German and Austrian peace treaties and on the number and nature of the participation by countries other than the Big Four. By the time this impasse was reached, in February 1947, the gap between East and West was rapidly becoming a chasm. In the same month the Dunkirk Treaty with Great Britain was concluded; in form, it merely balanced the French alliance with the Soviet Union. In May the French Communist ministers, who had been exhibiting signs of increasing restiveness within Socialist Paul Ramadier's coalition, voted with their parliamentary brethren against the government and were forced to resign from office. How much longer could French foreign policy postpone the choice which the French parties had now been forced to make at home?

In March President Harry S. Truman had assumed for the United States the burden of the Greek civil war in words so resounding that they constituted a general statement of purpose. But Greece, unlike Eastern Europe, was a British and American concern, a hang-over of wartime decisions in which France had had no part. Even what was happening in Eastern Europe did not directly affect France until Secretary of State George C. Marshall made his offer, in June 1947, of American aid to Europe. Both France and Britain were vitally interested in translating Marshall's rather vague statement of intent into a tangible American commitment. Foreign Minister Bidault was no less determined to do everything possible to obtain Soviet agreement to a Europe-wide, not just a Western, recovery program. For six days, from June 27 to July 2, 1947, he pleaded with Vyacheslav Molotov to accept the American condition that the European nations work out a common program for reconstruction and modify his position that each country draw up its own separate, independent list of requirements.

Believing that the Russian stubbornness was due solely to their fear of Western interference in the economies of Eastern Europe and the Soviet Union, opening the way to political influence, Bidault proposed a common obligation to avoid any violation of national sovereignty. In vain. The suspicion grew that the Russians were deliberately attempting to forestall any general European agreement which would gain the acceptance of the United States. Isolating a chaotic Europe from American support offered the Communists their best chance to capture the political control which had just slipped through their fingers with the break-up of the tripartite government. On the other hand, the Soviet Union feared lest American cooperation with Europe in economic affairs become the initial step toward political and military agreements. In its impatience to expel American influence from Europe and to prevent any steps toward a Europe unified under other than Soviet auspices, the Soviet government decided that it stood to gain more by solidifying its own control over Eastern Europe while seeking, through the medium of local Communist movements, to prevent the consolidation and recovery of Western Europe.

Even after the failure of the Paris conference of July 1947 on the Marshall Plan, the French government refused to admit that Europe had finally been divided. The National Assembly gave Premier Paul Ramadier unanimous support on July 26 in urging "close association with all the nations of Europe" in "a concerted plan for European reconstruction aimed at . . . avoiding the institution of opposing 'blocs'. . . ."[13]

The postwar international situation had resisted all the efforts of French diplomacy to bring about great-power cohesion through compromise. Worse, from the French point of view, France was unable to step aside from the growing conflict. Forced to choose, France found itself with no real alternative. By geography, by culture, by political and spiritual values, France belonged to the West. By reason of its economic and military weakness and its political discord at home, France needed to draw sustenance from the West. Nor could the tightly organized, broadly based Communist party, the largest in France, prevent an ever-

[13] Same, p. 355.

closer alignment with the West, although it could make the process painful, leaving the French contribution a lesser one, subject to doubt and discount by France's own allies and by France itself.

French Retreat in Germany

France's inability to hold together the allied wartime coalition was measured in the reluctant and piecemeal abandonment of virtually all its initial objectives toward Germany. What France wanted after liberation was clear. Disarmament, demilitarization, trial of war criminals, occupation for a protracted period, represented purposes which France shared generally with the United States, Great Britain, and the Soviet Union. But France had other, more far-reaching objectives which the Big Three talked about a good deal, although vaguely and tentatively. France wished to detach the Rhineland, Ruhr, and Saar areas from Germany, to decentralize the remaining truncated area as a possible prelude to complete dismemberment, and to extract reparations in the form of both plant removals and deliveries from current production, so as to ensure Germany's continued weakness while benefiting France and other victims of Hitler's fury. After so much suffering, the apparent opportunity to attain finally and permanently the elements of European security which had eluded France after 1918 was too precious for any French government to let slip.

These aims of French foreign policy had behind them a broad consensus, forged in the last days of the war and preserved in the ensuing peace, around the theme that the hated enemy must be punished if not actually destroyed as a nation. As the protracted struggle over framing a constitution acceptable to the major parties revealed the strength of old divisions and the existence of new ones, the common hatred of the German enemy became almost the last unifying emotion. If De Gaulle was a positive symbol which could enable Frenchmen to overcome the humiliation of the occupation and the Vichy regime, Germany was the negative symbol of revenge for the years of cor-

for the allegiance of the enemy they had so recently defeated in concert. In the Council of Foreign Ministers, in July 1946, Molotov proclaimed Soviet support for a politically unified Germany, for increases in German industrial production for peaceful purposes, and against the political detachment of the Ruhr. Bidault's hopes for Soviet backing lay shattered around him.

This bitter blow to French hopes was compounded, in the French view, by the steady turn of the United States toward a new and very different German policy. Evidence of this had been emerging bit by bit and perhaps for this reason French opinion was not prepared for Secretary of State James F. Byrnes' address at Stuttgart, on September 6, 1946. Capping Molotov's appeal to the Germans, Byrnes indicated that the war-inspired, negative objectives of Germany's subjugation were to give place to the positive goals of its economic and political rehabilitation and its territorial reunification. "The United States," he declared, "is firmly of the belief that Germany should be administered as an economic unit and that zonal barriers should be completely obliterated so far as the economic life and activity in Germany are concerned. . . . We favor the economic unification of Germany. If complete unification cannot be secured, we shall do everything in our power to secure the maximum possible unification."[18] With regard to the political recovery of Germany Byrnes was equally precise. Construing the clauses of the Potsdam Agreement on decentralization of the political structure as "not intended to prevent progress toward a central government with the powers necessary to deal with matters which would be dealt with on a nation-wide basis," Byrnes continued, "it is the view of the American Government that the German people throughout Germany, under proper safeguards, should now be given the primary responsibility for the running of their own affairs."[19]

[18] Stuttgart speech reproduced in Raymond Dennett and Robert K. Turner, eds., *Documents on American Foreign Relations, 1945-1946* (Princeton, N. J.: Princeton University Press, for the World Peace Foundation, 1948), v. 8, p. 215.
[19] Same.

Hand in hand with economic and political rehabilitation went the principle of maintaining Germany's territorial integrity, except for adjustments in the East in favor of the Soviet Union, a yet-to-be-determined area subject to cession to Poland, and in the West the recognition by the United States of French claims to the Saar. Otherwise, "the United States will not support any encroachment on territory which is indisputably German in origin or any division of Germany which is not genuinely desired by the people concerned. So far as the United States is aware, the people of the Ruhr and the Rhineland desire to remain united with the rest of Germany. And the United States is not going to oppose their desire."

The French reaction to Byrnes' address was dictated by three elements: the domestic economic situation, an outraged sense of justice, and a fear of its implications for the future. In 1946 an especially acute problem for France was its limited supply of coal, and Bidault linked his country's policies closely to this point. "For a long period of time," he warned the three foreign ministers, "we shall demand the certainty of delivery of a substantial and fixed quantity of German coal. In our opinion, this guarantee should be met by reintegrating the Saar into our tariff zone and by internationalizing the Ruhr. . . ."[20] Moreover, by relaxing their grip on Germany the "Anglo-Americans" were apparently showing a preference for the defeated aggressor rather than for France's "most legitimate aspirations."[21] Finally, Frenchmen could predict logically that this first step away from the initially harsh policy would be but the first in a series which would only end with Germany freed of all restraint. The thought had been voiced earlier in Bidault's reply to Byrnes' request that France permit the establishment of central German agencies.

Whatever be the importance, complexity and urgency of the questions posed by the occupation and administration of Germany, the French Government does not think that the occupa-

[20] Quoted in *L'Année Politique*, 1946, cited, p. 596.
[21] Same, p. 391.

tion powers should, to facilitate their immediate task, compromise the guarantees of the future . . . the establishment of central German services having their own right of decision, having ramifications in all the territory actually under control and exercising direct action everywhere by their agents will be generally considered, particularly by the German population, as prejudicing future settlements.[22]

Notwithstanding the logic of its position and the eloquence of its advocates, France was powerless to arrest the drift in the German policies of East and West. The British and Americans went ahead with plans for the economic merger of their two zones, announced on December 2, 1946. Despite official denials, this step was viewed from the outset as foreshadowing the establishment of a political regime in West Germany. The repercussions within France were immediate and violent, with the opposition accusing the ephemeral government of Léon Blum of having given ground faintheartedly. Although the Under Secretary of State for Foreign Affairs, Pierre Schneiter, assured the National Assembly that no modifications had been conceded, his chief, Bidault, plaintively told the American Club only a week later that when France speaks of Germany, "it is a little like a voice crying in the wilderness, and up to now the wilderness has not replied."[23] As late as February 1947, Bidault, declaring that the French government had held steadfast to the national policies first enumerated in September 1945, could receive *unanimous* support from the Assembly "to defend the interests of France and of peace."[24]

Despite official disclaimers, however, the pressure of decisions made elsewhere were forcing the French to make new adaptations in their own attitudes, albeit not rapidly enough to keep pace with events. In January 1947, one French memorandum accepted the principle of economic unity for Germany, while clinging to the theory of political

[22] *Documents on American Foreign Relations,* 1945-1946, cited, p. 204; Bidault note of March 2, 1946.

[23] *L'Année Politique,* 1946, cited, p. 428

[24] *L'Année Politique,* 1947, cited, p. 50; Bidault's speech of February 28, 1947.

decentralization and allied over-all economic control. A second memorandum abandoned the previous French demand for separating the Rhineland from the rest of Germany, advocating, instead, a four-power international supervision of the Ruhr. The Ruhr proposal represented a serious attempt to gain support of the Russians, who could be expected to leap at this new opportunity to gain a foothold in an area vital to western Germany and to Western Europe. For this very reason the British and Americans were, to say the least, unreceptive. At the spring 1947 meeting in Moscow of the Council of Foreign Ministers, the first to deal primarily with the problem of Germany, the isolation of France from both East and West threatened to become definitive. The West was against internationalizing the Ruhr and for a higher steel production quota for Germany; the Soviet Union surprised France very disagreeably by siding with its Anglo-American opponents on the latter issue and also by stubbornly rejecting French demands for more German coal. The Russian attitude must be read in the light of the approaching collapse of the tripartite system of government in France. Clearly the Soviet leaders believed they had nothing more to gain by supporting France in either its international or its domestic affairs. There was nothing more that France could do to perpetuate its role as a mediator.

From now on, the West could offer France compensations for its abandonment of its traditional objectives in Germany, through providing immediate economic assistance and offering long-range guarantees against a renewal of German aggression. At the Moscow meetings the United States and Great Britain indicated their willingness to see the French continue to administer the Saar, and they guaranteed France a specific quantity of German coal, but only for the next six months.

Other Diplomatic Retreats

In addition to impressive external trappings, a successful policy of grandeur required acknowledged internal strength. Lacking the tools of power, France was every-

blame for a deteriorating situation, for actions not taken, policies left unimplemented; upon his successor the task of dealing with the issues he had been unable to settle; upon the institutions of government the necessity of resorting to decree laws and administrative orders in the absence of legislative measures. The parties could make minor adjustments in their political façades, seek stronger control over deputies and ministers, and indulge again in a fascinating game of skill and chance. The National Assembly as an institution could reassert its primacy in government by recapturing an authority it would soon have to delegate again, temporarily, to another coalition. Staying too long in office might deprive a premier of the chance in the near future to form another government or even to assume an important ministerial position. Antoine Pinay, Joseph Laniel, and Guy Mollet were examples of premiers who hung on too long. Laniel and Mollet, whose governments enjoyed particular longevity, formed shifting majorities to win numerous confidence votes; when they finally departed, their very success had alienated practically all the "government groups" in the Assembly, including and especially members of their own parties. Recognizing the danger of manipulating the Assembly once too often, a premier might prefer to seek a propitious moment to step down by forcing a vote which he knew he could not win, by resigning when not actually defeated by a majority of the Assembly on a vote of confidence, or even, as in the case of Pierre Pflimlin in May 1958, by quitting after a vote which he had won.

The delicately poised balance of conflicting forces, once upset, could only be re-created by the skill and political acumen of the President of the Republic. Publicly he had to be in favor of a quick resolution of the crisis, although he knew that it would take time to cajole the disparate political groups, like balky horses, back into the shafts. At least one group could usually be charged with formal responsibility for the crisis, and at the same time shown it had no chance of leading the next coalition, by asking its leader to sound out the situation or even to try his hand

ers were working toward some form of indirect condominium. When France and Britain supported a United Nations resolution expressing confidence that foreign troops would indeed be withdrawn, the Soviet Union interposed the first of what was to become a stream of vetoes, ostensibly because the resolution contained no denunciation of Western colonialism. More probably, the Soviet leaders hoped that the British and French would be forced to leave armed forces in Syria and Lebanon, thus justifying Soviet machinations in Iran. However, France and Britain, announcing that they considered themselves bound by the resolution notwithstanding the veto, continued the evacuation of their troops from both countries until, on December 31, 1946, the French government reported that its last detachment had departed.

In Syria and Lebanon France suffered far more than a temporary diminution of national prestige. Henceforth it could not claim substantial interests in the Near East. Cultural and religious ties were no substitute for the possession of direct power in the form of military bases, or of political influence. Weakness in the Far East and exit from the Near East were making questionable France's ability to act as a great power, one with world-wide commitments which it could fulfill. Abandonment of historic positions under pressure could only encourage those who wished to restrict still further the scope of French action.

As the split widened between East and West, the chance also vanished for France to restore its prewar alliances with the countries of Central and East Europe. Their purpose was to be the same as after World War I: the prevention of renewed aggression by Germany. France, which raised no objections to the expansion of Poland into what had been eastern Germany, saw no obstacles to the conclusion of treaties with both Poland and Czechoslovakia on the model of its Dunkirk Treaty with Britain. Although French overtures were met with official expressions of interest, the Polish and Czech governments never advanced beyond the signing of cultural and economic agreements, which France also concluded with Bulgaria and Hungary.

Chapter Two

FRANCE AS BUILDER OF "EUROPE"
1947-1950

BY THE END of 1947 it was clear to its leaders that France alone was not strong enough either to mediate between East and West or to induce the three great allies of World War II to maintain a tight rein on Germany. Forced to choose the West, which offended French policy most in Germany, as against the East, which was threatening the security of all Europe, around what new focus could France organize its policy?

The path which France marked out for itself in the ensuing years was that of leadership in uniting the countries of Western Europe. By this new route France might yet hope to reach the same goals toward which its earlier policy had been directed. A united Europe would be strong enough to avoid dictation by the United States or subjugation by the Soviet Union. The countries grouped around France would, in fact, become a "Third Force" which could avert war by mediating conflicts between the two opposing powers, ultimately bringing them to some kind of peaceful settlement. André Siegfried, who has often argued that geography and ethnic development cause France to look at once West, East and South,[1] was not slow to support the closely related idea of French leadership of the region in which it was the logical unifying element. In his introduction to *L'Année Politique* for 1949, Siegfried wrote:

[1] As one example, see his *Nations Have Souls* (New York: Putnam, 1952), pp. 45-46.

... Between the two formidable masses—the United States and Soviet Russia—there exists a force, a third force, somewhat loosely connected and amorphous, which, however, is influential by reason of the consensus which it represents. Without doubt the juridical tie seems fairly weak, but the reality lies less in formulae than in the fact that the members of the group come together not through a sense of obligation but because of a desire to create, if they can, a common attitude. What unites them, in addition to an ancient land, is the tradition of a tested association, perhaps, even more the hope of escaping the Communist embrace, if possible without putting themselves under too close protection by the United States.[2]

In addition to enabling France to recover its mediating position, a policy of "building Europe" also offered the only way by which a shared control over West Germany could be maintained. Through the fusion of their zones, Britain and the United States were preparing the way for the political reconstruction of western Germany. German production was being allowed to rise, and Germany was to receive Marshall Plan aid along with other Western European countries. That part of Germany outside the Russian grasp would shortly be once more an important factor in Western European affairs. The question, particularly agonizing for France, was whether or not Germany would be a responsible factor as well. French statesmen were coming to the conclusion that Germany's good behavior could best be assured if Germany were gradually admitted to a strongly organized West European system. Specifically, a West European framework might provide the best guarantee of France's continued control over the Saar, which was fast becoming the only remnant of its original objectives. While Great Britain and the United States had agreed to the detachment of the Saar from Germany and its economic affiliation with France, its political future would nevertheless remain clouded so long as a reviving West Germany failed to accept this new status.

Finally, the policy of seeking to unite Europe met the requirements of the internal French political situation.

[2] *L'Année Politique,* 1949 (Paris. Éditions du Grand Siècle). pp. xiv, xv.

Freed of the stringencies of Communist collaboration, France's new leaders spoke of themselves as a domestic "third force" between the "separatists" of the Left and the "intransigents" of the Right.[3] The anti-Communist, anti-Gaullist third force, stretching from the Socialists on the Left to the Radicals on the Right,[4] had its own central or mediating force in the Catholic Mouvement Républicain Populaire, the party of Foreign Ministers Georges Bidault and Robert Schuman. Robert Schuman, Prime Minister in 1947 and 1948 and successor to Bidault as Foreign Minister from 1948 to 1952, epitomized the principles of an interdependent Western Europe. Born in Luxembourg, he had studied at Metz, Bonn, Munich, Berlin, and Strasbourg. Not only his home and his education, but also his early career as a lawyer had been concentrated in that border region of passage and conflict between France and Germany. After both world wars the Moselle region in Lorraine sent Schuman to the French Parliament. By political affiliation with the national Catholic movement he was closely related to other architects of a united Europe, such as West Germany's Konrad Adenauer and Italy's Alcide de Gasperi.

Steps toward Political Unity

In three related spheres—political, military and economic—the years from 1947 to 1950 saw many new steps toward the goal of a united Europe. The intimate connection among the three aspects of unity was clearly illustrated in the first "European" agreement, the Brussels Pact of March 17, 1948. For Britain, Foreign Minister Ernest Bevin was advocating political unity; for Belgium, Foreign Minister Paul-Henri Spaak was stressing the necessity of closer military ties; and for France, all the French National Assembly except the Communists urged "the prompt conclusion of the contemplated tariff union agree-

---

[3] By the Right of course was meant the newly formed Rassemblement du Peuple Français (RPF), the mass movement above and beyond parties, organized by De Gaulle in 1947.

[4] And later to the Independents and Peasants.

ments with both Italy and Benelux as the first steps toward European economic union.[5] The Communist seizure of power in Czechoslovakia, in February 1948, provided a considerable impetus to translate national ideas into a concrete international engagement. Alluding to this final evidence of the futility of attempts to conciliate the Soviet Union, Foreign Minister Bidault told the National Assembly, "the moment has come to go as fast and as far as possible toward the construction of what remains of Europe."[6]

The linking of political, military and economic strands in the Brussels Treaty placed it at the juncture of three roads. The first was to lead to the Council of Europe and the stillborn European Political Community. The second led to the abortive European Defense Community, as well as to the North Atlantic Treaty Organization. The third has had many branches, beginning with the European Coal and Steel Community. Article 7 of the Brussels Treaty created a Consultative Assembly, which in turn arranged for regular meetings of the finance ministers of the signatories and also created committees of cultural and of social experts. The heart of the defense system was the engagement under Article 4 that, "if any of the High Contracting Parties should be the object of an armed attack in Europe, the other High Contracting Powers will, in accordance with the provisions of Article 51 of the Charter of the United Nations, afford the party so attacked all the military and other aid and assistance in their power."

In the development of all three aspects of Western European unity French initiative played a decisive role, though the imaginative contributions of other continental leaders, especially those of Paul-Henri Spaak, should not be neglected. The short-lived Cabinet of André Marie, in which Robert Schuman, Marie's predecessor as Premier, first made his appearance as Foreign Minister, decided to give official sponsorship to a meeting of nongovernmental groups advocating European union. In these groups promi-

[5] Quoted in *L'Année Politique*, 1949, cited, p. 45.
[6] Same.

nent members of the French National Assembly, among them, Paul Reynaud, Léon Blum, Paul Ramadier, and Assembly President Édouard Herriot, had been active. The French government thus gave its support to a political activity which united many of its adherents in the legislature. It also acted from a fear that the Assembly might otherwise project its action directly into international affairs, as well as from a desire to limit the increasing prestige which was being garnered by individual parliamentarians.[7]

Before the privately sponsored Congress of European Unity at the Hague, Paul Reynaud and Édouard Bonnefous had advocated the drafting of a West European constitution by an assembly to be elected by universal suffrage on the basis of one deputy per million people. For both the French government and the National Assembly's Foreign Affairs Commission, this was moving too far and too fast from cherished aspects of national sovereignty. Yet, when official negotiations were initiated in November 1948, it quickly became clear that the continental powers —France, Belgium, the Netherlands and Luxembourg— had in mind a much closer form of political association than did the British. At this point began the still-unended tale of French disillusionment with British policies toward participation in European affairs. Churchill, the advocate of Franco-British union in the dark, despairing days of defeat, had trumpeted calls for European union as early as 1946. Foreign Minister Bevin had taken the initiative in making a reality of Secretary Marshall's suggestion and had proposed a Western union composed of Britain, France, and the Benelux countries. When the time came to translate talk into documents, however, the British negotiators suddenly began to speak of their ties with the Commonwealth and to dredge up old fears of continental political instability and economic weakness, apparently forgetting that it was precisely that instability and weak-

[7] On the early linking of private and governmental advocacy of European union, see the report of one of the movement's most skillful advocates, Alfred Coste-Floret, "Bilan et Perspectives de la Politique Européenne," *Politique Étrangère*, November 1952, pp. 321-335.

ness for which the cure was being sought in political federation.

To continental proposals for a Consultative Assembly, whose members would be chosen by the various national parliaments[8]—a timid enough plan from the point of view of actually merging national sovereignties—the British countered with a plan for establishing an intergovernmental ministerial committee to be named by the participating nations. Failing agreement by Christmas, the conference broke up with the understanding that it would reconvene in January 1949. When the time came for resumption and Bevin asked for another delay, French fears lest Britain abandon the whole idea of creating a Western European political structure were greatly aggravated. Nor were these fears allayed when Great Britain, finally consenting to attend the conference rather than risk its proceeding without the "benefit" of its own advice, declared its willingness to complement the ministerial committee with a "European parliament." The name "parliament" could only have been selected for its possible propaganda effect, since its members, like the ministerial committee, would actually be named by the various executive branches of government. Again the negotiations among national delegations were broken off, and the whole problem was referred back to the foreign ministers of the five powers.

From this seemingly hopeless impasse the situation was saved by British "concessions" to the "unifiers." After the signing of a preliminary agreement on January 28, 1949, progress toward the Statute of Europe was rapid. Five other governments—Denmark, Ireland, Italy, Norway, and Sweden—joined in preparing the final draft, which was published on May 5. In France the National Assembly with unprecedented promptness voted to join the Council of Europe. On June 17, the Foreign Affairs Commission approved the statute, with some reservations, hailing the agreement as a direct descendant of Aristide Briand's

[8] It should be remembered that many of the negotiators were parliamentarians and as such were not anxious to lose control of the movement in which they were participating.

famous memorandum of almost two decades earlier. After two days of debate the entire Assembly accepted the statute by 423 to 182, with the opposition coming almost exclusively from the Communists and their allies, the Progressives. The statute took effect on August 3, and the first session of the Committee of Ministers began at Strasbourg six days later. Invitations to join were immediately issued to Greece, Turkey, and Iceland, the last named already a member of the North Atlantic Pact, and the first two soon to be.[9]

If the Council of Europe can be regarded as a first step toward the goal of European political unity, from the French point of view it was a very small step and perhaps not even in the right direction.[10] Most of the French criticisms stemmed from the British "concessions." While accepting the continental idea of a European Consultative Assembly, the British ensured its subordination to the Committee of Ministers. Under Article 23 of the statute, the Assembly's agenda is subject to approval by this committee. Article 25 permits representatives to the Assembly to be "appointed in such manner as the government shall decide," thus allowing them to be nominated by the executive if it so chooses. The deliberations of the Assembly are not binding. Its "recommendations" can be made to the Committee of Ministers, "resolutions" to the Assembly's own committees, and "declarations" to anybody and everybody who will read them.

Under the Statute of Europe the directive power lies with the Committee of Ministers, which can reject Assembly recommendations with or without discussion and may, under Article 16, "decide with binding effect all matters relating to the internal organization and arrangements of the Council of Europe." The Committee's deliberations, unlike those of the Assembly, are conducted in private, and

---

[9] The Council of Europe also included all the members of the Organization for European Economic Cooperation except Austria, Portugal, and Switzerland.

[10] See the next chapter for the battle over whether the Council of Europe or the Assembly of the European Coal and Steel Community should draft the constitution of the Political Community.

its votes must be unanimous.[11] The Council as a whole hardly represented the spirit of European political unity at all. The apportionment of seats in the Consultative Assembly by size of population was clearly no substitute for the Bonnefous-Reynaud idea of a popular assembly. The Committee of Ministers was nothing more than an organized, regularized, diplomatic conclave, similar in form—if different in membership—to the corresponding parts of the North Atlantic Treaty Organization and the Organization for European Economic Cooperation. When institutional diplomacy, through the Committee of Ministers, could reach agreement, there was no need for resolutions or recommendations by either the Committee or the Assembly. In fact, agreement among the nations might be reached more easily without having recourse to the "European" machinery.

Since the Council of Europe was neither supranational nor federative in character, the question remained whether the Assembly could use the only power it had, that of publicity and propaganda, to influence public opinion and thus bring pressure to bear for closer political unity. Because the members of the Assembly came from the national parliaments, any advocacy in the Assembly of steps toward European federation would depend on the positions taken by political parties in the participating countries.

There could be little doubt that there was in the French National Assembly extensive support for political unity. In recommending the ratification of the Statute of the Council of Europe, the Foreign Affairs Commission had decried the excessive powers of the Committee of Ministers relative to those of the Consultative Assembly. The Commission wanted the Assembly to have its own separate secretariat, instead of the joint one created by Articles 36 and 37 with its membership recommended by and responsible to the Committee of Ministers. The Commission regretted the omission of a declaration of the rights of man, such as graced the preamble to the constitution of the Fourth Re-

---

[11] In 1951 this provision was somewhat modified to permit partial approval by majority vote if all members should on occasion so decide.

public. Such a declaration, even without obligatory effect on the Council of Europe or the member states, would, it believed, give the peoples of Western Europe a feeling of closer rapport with the new political organization.[12]

The ambiguous nature of the Council of Europe as an embodiment of the political unity sought by French policy was reflected in the problem of West Germany and the Saar. French leaders wanted to build Europe so that international control could be substituted for three-power occupational control over West Germany, and also to prevent the Saar territory from slipping from the French economic grasp. But was the Council of Europe strong enough to do the job? The Foreign Affairs Commission of the French Assembly thought so and hoped that West Germany could be included, along with Portugal, a member of NATO; Switzerland, a member of the Organization for European Economic Cooperation; and Austria, also in the OEEC and, like West Germany, partially occupied by Britain, France and the United States. However, the National Assembly, not for the first or last time, refused to follow its Commission. Its debates found the supporters of the admission of West Germany arrayed against the advocates of postponing the issue until after the signing of a peace treaty. This meant postponing it to a time which might never come and, if it did come, it would signify the end of plans to unify only *Western* Europe. The outcome of the debate reflected both French fears of future developments in Germany and the Assembly's determination to keep a tight rein on the executive in this sensitive area of policy. At the urging of skillful, eloquent Pierre Cot, leader of the Communist-inclined Progressive party, the government agreed to seek the approval of the National Assembly before consenting to the admission of West Germany into the Council of Europe.

Article 1 (d) of the Council of Europe placed national

---

[12] One major result of the activity of the Council of Europe was to be the passage of a European Convention on Human Rights, accepted by a majority of the Council's members.

defense beyond the purview of the Council. Although this provision was later to be negated by discussions of the desirability of creating a European army, in 1949 there appeared to be at least three sound reasons for its inclusion. The Council did not constitute a sufficiently firm organ of political cooperation to be entrusted with the delicate problem of Western rearmament, which, though deemed necessary to meet the increasingly aggressive Soviet behavior, was unpalatable to countries still struggling to recover from the war. In the second place, military defense was the primary concern of the previously negotiated Brussels Pact, which had established a permanent military organization subordinate to a consultative council. The British, who had led in the conclusion of the Brussels Pact but were suspicious of political organizations, would have resisted strongly any attempt to transfer intergovernmental powers over military questions, or even the right to discuss national military affairs, to a body which might yet take the road toward becoming a supranational authority.

The final and most important consideration was the almost complete lack of armed strength throughout Western Europe. If the cooperative system created under the Brussels Pact were to become more than a weak bluff, liable to rude exposure by the next Soviet move, assistance in rearmament was urgently needed from the only possible source, the United States. But the Council of Europe included some members who would remain in it only so long as it was not an instrument for waging a cold or hot war. Sweden and Ireland were determined to remain aloof from the bipolar struggle, and their geographical positions made this policy a tenable one, at least up to the outbreak of actual military conflict. France also did not welcome any ties between the Council of Europe and the United States, particularly ties of a military character. A fundamental objective behind French espousal of European unity was the creation of an independent grouping, with power of its own able to pursue independent policies aimed not at participating in, but at settling, the cold war.

European Military Cooperation

With the Council of Europe deprived of any role in military affairs, the path of military cooperation ran from the Brussels Treaty to the North Atlantic Pact.[13] Even before the NATO Pact was signed, Bidault and Eden had informed Secretary Marshall that the military recovery of Western Europe, like its economic recovery, awaited the assistance of the United States. After the pact had been negotiated, even more pointed urgings were voiced. As Premier Henri Queuille told the United Press:

> The United States could never permit France and Western Europe to be invaded as they had been by Germany. In order for world civilization to be preserved, it is indispensable that this invasion be avoided, and the United States is the only power capable of preventing such a catastrophe. . . . France, the advanced guardian of Europe, cannot stand alone. Nor can it stand with only the aid of the Benelux countries and Great Britain. This is why Western Europe must be able to count on the aid of the United States. To be sure we know that, should Western Europe be occupied, America would come again to our aid, and in the end we would again be liberated. But the consequences would be terrible. The next time you would probably liberate a corpse, and civilization would probably be dead. No, invasion, if against all probability it should arise, must be stopped even before it begins. If we can count on sufficient force to prevent the Russian army from crossing the Elbe, then European civilization can breathe again.[14]

The words of the French Premier reveal a basic and continuing preoccupation of West Europeans: Western Europe must be defended, not used as a springboard to roll back the Communist tide; it must be defended in Western Europe, not from peripheral areas and only after France and its allies have been overrun by Soviet forces; Western Europe can be defended in Western Europe only by committing American military power to that area, not by

---

[13] And hence to the North Atlantic Treaty Organization, the almost-implemented European Defense Community, and back again to the Brussels Pact, retitled Western European Union and linked to NATO.

[14] Declaration reprinted in *L'Année Politique*, 1949, cited, p. 375.

financial or matériel aid or by promises to come running after the attack has been launched.

While the American executive was willing in principle to accept an obligation to aid in the defense of Western Europe, additional steps were necessary to pave the way for Congressional and popular support. First, as in the case of the Marshall Plan, Western Europe had to give clear evidence of its determination to help itself. This test was met, not only by the Brussels Pact, but also by creating under it a Western European Union for the common defense. The new organization began at once to assess the military potentialities and needs of Western Europe, with United States and Canadian military experts taking part informally as representatives of "non-member states."

A second step was to convince key senators and congressmen that the United States could not limit its role to providing matériel. A precedent had been set in 1947 by Congressional acceptance of the Truman Doctrine; "to support free peoples who are resisting attempted subjugation by armed minorities or by outside pressure" the Congress had already appropriated some $400,000,000. However, the same formula could hardly cover Western Europe. Providing military aid, moreover, was a far cry from direct membership in an alliance, and "no entangling alliances" even in wartime was a deeply rooted principle of American diplomacy. In removing this stumbling-block, executive consultations with the minority and majority leaders of the Senate Foreign Relations Committee produced significant results. Both Senator Arthur H. Vandenberg and Senator Tom Connally had been urging the conclusion of the Inter-American Treaty of Reciprocal Assistance, projected by the 1945 Act of Chapultepec, but the negotiations had been held up because of opposition to Juan Perón's regime in Argentina. In 1947 the Department of State withdrew its objections, and both Senators participated actively in the conference of Rio de Janeiro. After the ratification of the treaty, Senator Vandenberg agreed that the treaty provided a precedent for American membership in similar associations outside the Western Hemisphere. On June 11,

1948, with only four negative votes, the Senate passed the Vandenberg Resolution recommending "the association of the United States by constitutional process[15] with such regional and other collective arrangements as are based on continuous and effective self-help and mutual aid and as affect its national security."

The overwhelming support for the Vandenberg Resolution meant that the way was open for the Senate to approve an American military commitment to the defense of Western Europe. Its wording also implied that, rather than associating itself with the Brussels Pact, the United States would take the lead in creating a new and larger regional grouping. In this way countries outside Europe, such as Canada and Iceland, could be brought in. It could also include European countries which were outside the Brussels Pact and whose exclusion might lead the Soviet leaders to assume that aggression against them would not be met by American power. Among them were the Scandinavian countries, Britain's historic ally Portugal, and Italy.

Italy's membership was especially important for France to offset the rejection by the National Assembly of a treaty, signed in January 1949, which provided for a Franco-Italian customs union within one year and for the complete integration of the two economies within six years.[16] In addition, at the end of 1948, France abandoned its previously strong support for Italian claims to hold a United Nations trusteeship over Libya and Somaliland, in the face of the unwillingness of Great Britain, the United States, and the people of the two colonies to see a return of Italian rule. In the final debate in the United Nations France retreated to the position that while both Libya and Somali-

---

[15] This phrase was deliberately introduced to allay Senatorial fears of commitment through executive agreement rather than by treaty requiring the approval of the Senate.

[16] Another significant factor in Franco-Italian relations was the failure of France to take the number of Italian workers anticipated under an agreement of November 30, 1946. Instead of the envisaged 200,000, scarcely 50,000 entered in 1947, and after that year employment opportunities in France declined even further. See Xavier Lannes, *L'Immigration en France Depuis 1945* (The Hague: Martinius Nijhof, 1953), pp. 34-88, especially pp. 49-51 and 65-71.

land might at some time gain independence, the dates set by the majority were premature. The French delegate abstained on the final resolution; which was adopted by 48-1.[17] In seeking Italy's friendship Foreign Minister Bidault had also concluded an agreement, kept secret for a time, to return a part of the frontier territory which France had annexed under the peace treaty of 1947, but this concession was rejected by the Foreign Affairs Commission of the National Assembly in December 1948.

Regarding Italy as a valuable junior partner in European affairs, France proceeded without difficulty in bringing about its inclusion in the North Atlantic Treaty. Even better, so far as France was concerned, was the extension of the treaty to its Algerian Departments. On April 4, 1949, the pact was signed in Washington.[18]

Within France there were two main periods of discussion over the NATO Pact: in March, two months before the signing, and in July, in the process of ratification. The first debates centered around the text, which had been approved by the Consultative Council of the Brussels powers and the French Cabinet. Public discussion served to allay widespread fears, aroused by the Communist seizure of power in Czechoslovakia and the recurrent clashes in the air corridor to blockaded Berlin. The terms of the treaty, said its French advocates, did not violate the Franco-Soviet Treaty of 1944, but, as Premier Queuille stressed, formally committed the United States to the defense of Europe. The vital ingredient missing from the League system of security had finally been added. "We have today," Foreign Minister Schuman told the French people, "obtained what we hoped for in vain between the two wars: the United States recognizes that there is neither peace nor security for America if Europe is in danger."[19]

[17] Direct French interest in the Libyan settlement should not be overlooked. France felt more confident of being able to maintain troops in Fezzan if that territory were separated from Libya or kept as part of a Libyan trusteeship assigned to Italy.

[18] One of the most complete, necessarily official, commentaries on the treaty and its operation is Lord Ismay, *NATO, the First Five Years, 1949-1954* (Paris: North Atlantic Treaty Organization, 1954).

[19] *L'Année Politique*, 1949, cited, p. 54.

Publicity and discussion prior to signature were also important to the French government in winning the support of the National Assembly and in mobilizing popular pressure for prompt ratification. The Assembly at once revealed its worries over Germany. The French espousal of Western European unity had been due in large part to a desire to create organizations strong enough to control Germany, as France alone could not and its allies were unwilling to do. West Germany could therefore become a member of any organization only after that body had proved its effectiveness. The exception of the Council of Europe was only an apparent one; it was precisely the Council's ineffectiveness as an agency of European political unity which had permitted Germany's early inclusion. In the case of a military organization, however, the National Assembly obviously wanted Europe defended on German soil but without Germany's participation. In approving the ratification of the NATO Pact the Foreign Affairs Commission ruled that the consent to the admission of nations other than the original parties could be granted by the President only after legislative authorization. This proviso was clearly due to the fear that France's allies would soon be pressing for the admission of Germany. Notwithstanding this safeguard, Schuman deemed it prudent to give the deputies an unequivocal assurance of Germany's permanent exclusion. "The question cannot arise," he told the Assembly. "There is no treaty of peace: Germany has no treaty of peace and can have none; it has no armaments and will have none."[20] On July 26, 1949, by a vote of 395 to 189, the National Assembly gave its consent to ratification.

A delay, perhaps unavoidable but highly dangerous, intervened between the entry of the NATO Treaty into force and its practical implementation through American military assistance. While the National Assembly was still debating the pact, President Truman followed up the American signature with an immediate request to Congress for aid to specified countries, including France. The

---

[20] Same, p. 138.

Mutual Defense Assistance Bill became law two months later. But over three months then passed before bilateral agreements on aid were concluded with France and seven other NATO members. Finally, on March 16, 1950, the Franco-American agreement was accepted by the National Assembly by a vote of 416-179, a wider margin of approval than that of the pact itself. In the same month the first shipment of American military equipment reached France: aircraft transported by the French carrier "Dixmunde."

Thus American military assistance began reaching Western Europe two years after the negotiation of the Brussels Treaty and one year after the signing of the North Atlantic Treaty. Meanwhile, the countries of Western Europe had not made any significant progress in rearmament. In fact, their position vis-à-vis the Soviet and satellite armies had deteriorated markedly, despite the commitment of two additional American divisions to Germany. Field Marshal Bernard Montgomery reported to the Brussels Treaty powers on June 15, 1950, that "as things stand today and in the foreseeable future, there would be scenes of appalling and indescribable confusion in Western Europe if we were ever attacked by the Russians."[21]

French Policy toward Germany

Against this background of general weakness, the economic recovery of West Germany was all the more striking. As early as the merger of the British and American occupation zones, France had warned its allies that German economic rejuvenation could logically end only in the termination of the occupation and the restoration of German sovereignty. The best hope for French policy now lay in delaying any further concessions to Germany as long as possible, pending creation of a federated Western Europe and the establishment of three-power supervision over the Ruhr. The French view was the subject of protracted discussions among the three Western powers, between February and May 1948. Foreign Minister Bidault did not conceal the fact that he was going to London to meet with his

[21] Quoted in Ismay, cited, p. 30

American and British friends only because it was impossible to reach an agreement with the Soviet Union on Germany. Even under the changed circumstances, French policy, said Bidault, still held fast to its original objectives: control and coal.

If control of Germany was possible only with international supervision of the Ruhr, this in turn required keeping Germany's political structure as weak as possible. For this reason France had refused to join its zone to the British and American ones, correctly assuming that this step, despite American denials, foreshadowed the creation of a central government for West Germany. When later driven to admit that a West German government was inevitable and even desirable, the French still argued for a loose form of association that would avoid prejudicing any movements for autonomy or separation. Obviously, many Frenchmen still longed for the good old days when dozens of small German states had jostled each other across the Rhine and vied for the favor of Versailles. On March 11, 1948, the National Assembly invited the government "to prepare . . . the creation of a federal Germany by the constitution of the *Länder,* which would be invited to merge with a European union, with this new statute taking account of the permanent changes necessary for French security, the reparations to which France has a right, and the international control of the resources of the Ruhr."[22] This resolution said it all, and said it in just one sentence: German political decentralization; European federation, in which many independent Germanies might be separately associated; reparations; control of the Ruhr—and the whole system to be made permanent in the name of French security. If these conditions were met, the National Assembly would be prepared generously to accept the reconstitution of a German government since by then most of the French objectives would have been fulfilled.

There was clearly a considerable gap between what the National Assembly thought to be a desirable and feasible German policy and what the French executive was finding

[22] Quoted in *L'Année Politique,* 1948, cited, p. 47.

it possible to implement. The cabinets regularly fostered new illusions in the Assembly, both to win popularity and to strengthen their hand in negotiating with the two allies. One month after the Assembly's resolution of March 11, 1948, Premier Robert Schuman, subsequently to be an eloquent advocate of Franco-German amity, was declaring to the legislature: "Any plan which resulted in establishing and authorizing a central power would present to Germany a temptation and to us a permanent and growing threat, first of *revanche,* then of bellicose imperialism." On the other hand, "there are several Germany's so strongly divided by their geographic, ethnic, and economic peculiarities that it would be possible to let them separate and organize into autonomous states. These states could then federate for common and limited tasks. Such is our conception of the future Germany, a conception free from all resentment, but inspired by our long experience with men and events. We will not abandon the hope of getting our allies to agree."[23]

But less than three months later, on June 7, 1948, France agreed with Great Britain and the United States on a new course of action toward Germany, one which revealed few traces of the original French proposals. A West German government was to be constituted, and the Germans were to have a major say in deciding on its form. While the delegates to the Constituent Assembly were to come from the *Länder,* as the French had advocated, the local parliaments could choose the way in which the delegates were to be selected, including the way of direct election. With the decision to create a German government, the French refusal to join their occupation zone to "Bizonia" retained only symbolic significance.

On the question of the Ruhr the French position was likewise bending under Anglo-American pressure. After first demanding the outright detachment of the Ruhr, successive French governments had retreated to urging its internationalization, and now what was left was a species

[23] Speech reprinted under title, "La Situation en France." The similarity of French dreams after World Wars I and II is indeed striking.

of control which was neither outright ownership nor complete direction by the occupying authorities. The competence of the new Ruhr Authority was limited to the distribution of coal, coke, and steel. In its decisions, the Authority was to weigh the contributions of the Ruhr to the reconstruction of Europe as against the requirements of European security.

The concessions exacted from the French delegates naturally provoked much wailing and gnashing of teeth in the National Assembly. Before it began its debate, statements from London and Washington blended assurances that Britain and the United States had also made concessions with broad hints that the two would, if necessary, proceed without France. Soft soap and castor oil from abroad notwithstanding, the Schuman government won the Assembly's approval by only fourteen votes. Its resolution admitted ruefully that the agreement could not be rejected, for this would "entail a regrettable loosening of an entente among friendly powers whose close cooperation is today the surest guarantee of peace." Furthermore, "the recommendations reveal a certain progress on the part of the English and Americans toward propositions constantly affirmed by France."

On the slight chance that Great Britain and the United States still did not know exactly where France stood, the Assembly summed up its demands once more: (1) "internationalization of the mines and basic industries of the Ruhr;" (2) "expropriation of the erstwhile magnates," and "extension of control by the international authority to the question of mineral and industrial wealth of the region;" (3) "reparations" assured by "occupation of Germany over a long period of time," after which allied troops would be withdrawn only under precise guarantees backed by the continued occupation of "key regions;" (4) the prohibition of an "authoritarian or centralized *Reich;*" (5) the continued search for a "final four-power agreement on the German problem;" (6) acceleration of progress toward the "economic and political organization of Europe."[24]

[24] *L'Année Politique,* 1948, cited, pp. 335-336.

The separate points of the resolution clearly showed the National Assembly's yearning to turn back the clock. Only the final item represented any constructive thought as to the future of Franco-German relations. The United States and Britain were determined to move forward, and events of the year following the London agreement revealed how far and how fast they were able to pull protesting France. The rate of plant dismantling was further slowed, and the entire reparations program re-evaluated to further Europe's economic recovery. The limits on German production were raised, while the control statute for the Ruhr turned out considerably weaker even than what the French had agreed to in London. Finally, the Germans drafted a new constitution under the supervision of the Western powers, which then replaced their occupation commanders in chief with civilian high commissioners.

On all three points France felt forced to register official protests against Anglo-American policy. In negotiations with Paul Hoffman, director of the Economic Cooperation Administration, French leaders offered to review their own list of German plants slated for dismantling and transfer, and to agree in principle that economic efficiency might be better served by leaving some of them in Germany. However, by October 1948, German pronouncements on their economic and political future became so enthusiastic that the French Foreign Minister had to deny that any abandonment of the plan for restitution to the victims of Nazi aggression was being contemplated. Quite the contrary, further dismantling would proceed promptly, with continued priority being given to plants in fields in which production had been prohibited or curtailed. Even while protesting its adherence to old procedures, France was giving concrete evidence of future retreats. It accepted the inevitable transformation of Bizonia into Trizonia, which meant adopting a common policy toward the German economy and the slackening and gradual abandonment of reparations deliveries.

A more serious crisis arose between France and its Western allies over the drafting of the Ruhr statute. A new

United States-British decree—Number 75—was interpreted by the French as permitting the Germans to resume direction of the Ruhr industries under allied supervision and to determine their final ownership after a German government had been formed. The timing could hardly have been more unfortunate, coming as it did just before Armistice Day. The French official protest was strong, and President Vincent Auriol and Assembly President Herriot took the occasion of the Armistice to warn against another allied abandonment of France. The Foreign Affairs Commission, reminding all and sundry of its resolution of the previous June, was supported by the Assembly, 371-182.

The British and Americans knew in advance of French objections to their Ruhr policies in general and to Law 75 in particular.[25] Being in actual control of the Ruhr, the two powers could later modify the law as a gesture to French sensibilities, while the French government, through its protests, could make itself more popular at home and could enter the negotiations as the representative of a united, aroused nation. Later the French delegates could also argue that final agreement on the International Authority represented a partial victory for their point of view.

An agreement on the Ruhr Authority was reached on December 28, 1948, and four months later the Authority was set up, simultaneously with the completion of the West German federal constitution. To obtain French assent to a political West Germany, the other powers accepted a Ruhr Authority closer to the French concept. It was to control the distribution of coal and steel, enforcing the previously agreed production levels. It was also charged with preventing the return of ownership to Nazis and the recartelization of the only partially decentralized industrial complex. On the other hand, the French failed to secure the "internationalization" of the ownership of the Ruhr industries, an agreement on a definition of decartelization, or a commitment on the permanence of the Authority's control.[26]

[25] See Lucius D. Clay, *Decision in Germany* (Garden City, N.Y.: Doubleday, 1950), p. 332.
[26] The importance of French assent is stressed in Clay, cited, pp. 335-340.

Despite continual difficulties which arose between December 1948 and May 1949, the agreement on the Ruhr Authority meant that the establishment of the new German government was now assured. On May 12, 1949, the three-power occupation was formally over, and the Soviet Union lifted the blockade of Berlin. Like the French, the Russians had been unable to prevent the recovery of Germany. With the occupation officially ended, French leadership was forced to move rapidly to lay the foundations for integrating Germany into Western Europe. In this, the Schuman Plan, made public in May 1950, was a major step, although West Germany had already been a participant in the Marshall Plan, at a time when the occupation authorities were the sole legal representatives of German interests. Consistent with this philosophy was the admission of the new German state to the Council of Europe. In August 1949, at its first session, Winston Churchill, a forceful proponent of European unity, especially when not charged with administering British foreign policy, urged that a united Europe could come about only with the association in it of Germany. Secretary of State Dean Acheson also told a press conference that the admission of Germany to the Council of Europe would be a constructive step toward European integration. By this time "integration" had become the keynote of American policy toward Western Europe, although the meaning and implications Americans attached to it were obscure.

To the French, all this looked like more Anglo-American impatience, with which, as it related to Germany, they had already had unpleasant experiences. Not that France opposed the eventual inclusion of Germany; far from it. "We know that Germany is part of Europe and that she must be given a role which is not conquest but work," replied Bidault to Churchill.[27] But, first, two conditions had to be fulfilled, only one of which was made explicit.

First was the building of support in the French National Assembly, which had ratified the Statute of the Council of Europe only with the proviso that no change in it could

[27] Quoted in *L'Année Politique*, 1949, cited, p. 752.

be made without its approval. Now, while the Council was far from the strong political structure that France had wished to create, its first session had given encouraging signs of future development. The Consultative Assembly, loudly chafing at the subordinate role assigned to it by the statute, had revolted, with claims to broader areas of competence, with a plethora of noble-sounding, sometimes hastily drafted recommendations, and with the clear statement that the goal of the Council of Europe was nothing less than the "creation of a European political authority with limited functions but real powers." In this revolt French parliamentary delegates of the Left, Center, and Right had played leading roles. They now needed time to persuade their colleagues in the Assembly that the Council might yet become strong enough to support the admission of Germany. They might, in fact, go further and seek to convince the Assembly that, through the inclusion of Germany, Britain and Scandinavia might yet be won over to support a European political federation.

The Special Problem of the Saar

The second prerequisite was made crystal clear by Bidault. It related to the Saar, which had been attached economically to France in 1947 as the price for abandoning its objective of detaching both the Ruhr and the Rhineland from Germany. The agreement of November 1947 between France and the Saar had been overwhelmingly accepted by the latter because it did not wish to be treated as part of a defeated and occupied Germany. With the relaxation of occupation controls, however, the new German government inevitably sought to undo as much of the Franco-Saar arrangement as possible. Chancellor Konrad Adenauer lost little time in announcing that the Saar was and always had been German and could not be separated economically or politically from its natural homeland. The new power of Germany forced France in turn to seek a new agreement with the Saar. The best way to prevent its reattachment to Germany and to maintain France's special economic and strategic role was by making the Saar autonomous politically, hence entitled to direct membership in the Council of Europe. The recognition of the Saar's autonomy by other nations, including Germany, would establish a stable situation against the day when a peace treaty would be negotiated with Germany.

The government of France presented its case for Saar autonomy at the first session of the Council of Europe, in August 1949; in the Committee of Ministers in November; in the Permanent Committee of the Consultative Assembly in the same month; and in the negotiations, also in November, between the French, British and American High Commissioners and Chancellor Adenauer. In these last negotiations, resulting in the Petersberg Agreements of November 22, France finally won its point but only after paying a heavy price for a minor victory. Chancellor Adenauer withdrew his opposition to a separate membership for the Saar in the Council of Europe, but on condition that this could in no way prejudice the final settlement of the Saar problem in a peace treaty. On their side, the High Commissioners welcomed Germany to the Organization for European Economic Cooperation and manifested their desire that it be included in the Council of Europe.

Another bargain was struck at Petersberg on the perennial subject of controls over Germany. Adenauer publicly accepted the occupation principles of "demilitarization, democratization, deconcentration, and dismantling." This concession, however, had little concrete value. His government claimed that democratization had been achieved under the Federal Republic; deconcentration of industry was no longer being rigorously pursued; and within the year Germany would be asked to rearm. The Chancellor's polite gesture was rewarded by an allied promise to re-examine (again!) the dismantling program. Germany also stated its intention to request admission to the International Authority for the Ruhr, which would thereby cease to be purely an instrument of the former occupying powers.

Before Germany could participate as an equal member

in European affairs, as signalized by its admission to the Council of Europe, France and the Saar had to reach a new basis of agreement. The negotiations took place amid strident, sometimes provocative, statements from West Germany, which the French felt were echoed in unofficial expostulations from the United States. Germany skillfully combined its publicity campaign with pressure on the High Commissioners to change the recently concluded Petersberg accords. As Franco-German relations deteriorated, the United States finally gave its official support to the French demands. Secretary Acheson's statement that the United States continue to favor a direct economic arrangement between France and the Saar, pending the conclusion of a German peace treaty, was followed by a direct warning to the Germans from the American High Commissioner, John J. McCloy.

If anything was needed to underline for the French their need to maintain an economic hold on the Saar, threats by the new Federal Republic were likely to do just that. Strong opposition to any form of German *revanche* was the one aspect of French foreign policy which commanded unwavering support. Germany's desire to change the Petersberg accords enhanced their appeal to the Assembly regardless of the defeats for French diplomacy contained within them. The French government won a 78-vote majority for the Petersberg accords, whereas the earlier London agreements, which prepared the way for the creation of a German government, had been greeted in the Assembly with manifest hostility and explicit reservations, and had been approved by a margin of only 14 votes.

On March 3, 1950, five principal conventions and seven other agreements were signed between France and the Saar. The conventions revealed that the French were not prepared to insist on the objectives which the United States, not to mention Germany and the Saar, opposed most seriously. Saar railroads were not to be absorbed into the French system, but administered by a Saar corporation under the authority of the Saar government. France also failed to gain a long-term "lease" on the Saar mines, although the French right to operate them until the signing of a German peace treaty was again recognized. A General Economic Convention provided for the free circulation of the goods of each country in the territory of the other and pledged each to seek a common level of prices and wages. The general convention affirmed the autonomy of the Saar government in internal affairs, limiting French power to the protection of Saar security and of the French-Saar economic union. It accorded to France the protection of the Saar's political and economic interests abroad, but also provided that representatives of the Saar could be attached to French embassies and consulates.

The Franco-Saarois agreements led directly and rapidly to the admission of both the Saar and West Germany to associate membership in the Council of Europe, with representation at first limited to the Consultative Assembly. On May 13, the Saar government eagerly accepted, but the West German Federal Republic delayed its reply for two months, in order to show its displeasure. Concrete advantages accruing to Germany, however, dictated its ultimate acceptance. Germany received eighteen seats in the Consultative Assembly, the same number as France, Italy, and Great Britain. Equality in representation, as well as the invitation to membership, constituted direct and striking recognition of the Federal Republic as an independent and important participant in Western European affairs. Germany's status as associate member, it was tacitly acknowledged, would be converted into full rights (participation in the Committee of Ministers) after the conduct of the Federal Republic's foreign relations had been regularized.

The Saar agreements and the Saar's membership in the Council of Europe spelled defeat for German efforts to reverse the decision of 1947 recognizing special French rights in the territory. The French gain, nevertheless, appeared both insubstantial and temporary. German opposition did not subside after the agreements were reached; quite the contrary. Adenauer called the Saar's status worse than a protectorate. He likened its government to national socialism in many respects, and warned its government that it "would have to answer for its deeds to the German people."[28] A German White Book on the history of the Saar reached the conclusion that the agreements of March 3 had no juridical validity. Quite apparently the German government could derive as much popular and legislative support as could the French government by remaining adamant. Such an impasse, however, left the agreements only as secure as French power could keep them in the face of Germany's economic and political recovery.

Economic Integration: the Schuman Plan

If Germany's burgeoning economic power and political competence argued for French attempts at a *rapprochement*, this was made even more urgent by ominous rumors of the need for German rearmament. The question was being brought into the open by three new and interrelated factors. One was the acceptance by the North Atlantic Treaty Organization, in January 1950, of a strategic plan to defend Europe as far to the East as possible. A second lay in the unwillingness, and inability, of European members of NATO to shoulder an armament burden sufficient for this formidable task. Finally, with Germany's recovery of many of the attributes of sovereignty, its government was bound to participate in deciding whether foreign troops would be maintained on German soil and, if so, how many. Eventually, the line between unofficial speculation and official pronouncement of policy was crossed by John J. McCloy. On returning to the United States in May 1950, at the end of his term as High Commissioner, he expressed the opinion that German troops were necessary to the defense of Europe.

France, as we have seen, was already looking to European unification for the solution of German and Saar problems. Chancellor Adenauer was moving along the same path when he suggested to INS correspondent Kingsbury

[28] *L'Année Politique*, 1950, cited, p. 62.

Smith that Franco-German union, the foundation for European unity, would supply the answer to the troublesome Saar question. At this crucial juncture French foreign policy was prepared to make what would perhaps be its most important contribution to postwar stability on the European continent. Unwilling to advocate a complete merger with Germany, France, nevertheless, was ready to suggest concrete measures for a partial economic union between the two countries. Such was the plan advanced by Foreign Minister Robert Schuman for the pooling of French and German coal and steel production and that of other nations under a High Authority.

International events were, of course, not the exclusive determinant of the Schuman Plan. Behind the scenes was Jean Monnet, who had earlier produced a plan for rehabilitating and modernizing France's domestic economy. The Monnet Plan achieved notable results, but by mid-1950 its original term of four years was coming to an end. Moreover, the achievements of the Monnet Plan, though impressive when French production figures for 1946 and 1950 were compared, were far less satisfactory when compared to West German recovery over the same period. When the Schuman Plan was announced, Germany had already begun to threaten France's economic position in Western Europe. German exports in world markets were providing heavy competition for high-priced French products, thus adding to France's difficulties in balancing its external accounts. Extrapolation of production curves appeared to indicate that Germany's economic threat would increase rather than diminish, particularly since France's allies were plainly unwilling to enforce controls on German steel production. For France, a merger of the coal and steel industries—basic elements in a prosperous industrial economy—promised to assist internal recovery by alleviating certain of the disadvantages under which France struggled in competing with Germany. French statesmen, also, had clearly before them the warnings of the American Congress that the Marshall Plan would end on schedule two years hence: at that time the French economy would supposedly have to stand on its own feet, without the massive, annual infusion of dynamic dollars.[29]

To reach its goal, the unification of Western Europe, France was prepared to move ahead in the dark, trusting that faith and imagination would find paths, whereas delay until the ground ahead had been thoroughly explored might reveal the presence of many pitfalls and obstructions. In despair the fainthearted would abandon the project, and the mischief-makers would smother it with chauvinistic slogans. If, however, France took the lead, others would follow. As early as August 1949, Édouard Bonnefous had lectured the Consultative Assembly of the Council of Europe on the need for functional integration. "The different countries, despite their reluctance," he said, "should consent to pool their natural resources under a common, international administration."[30] Nor was Bonnefous alone. "Functional integration" was the watchword of those who had been disappointed in the weakness of European political institutions. In addition to continental representatives, delegates from both the British Labor and Conservative parties also favored the idea, and the Consultative Assembly, in September 1949, passed a resolution reflecting its sentiments. A more precise resolution was drafted in January 1950 by the Assembly's Economic Commission, stating, in part, that ". . . it is necessary to create a public steel authority, made up of delegates of governments, producers, and consumers of steel, an authority endowed with the power to define the general policy of the industry, especially as it concerns investments, volume

---

[29] Jacques Duhamel also claims that domestic political as well as economic considerations lay behind the announcement of the Schuman Plan. See "La Vie Politique: Rêverie . . . de Schuman," *La Nef*, June-July 1950, pp. 167-173 The Plan, says Duhamel, who served in the government which sponsored it, owed its origin to the initiative of Schuman himself. He sprang the idea on his colleagues, and on the world, in order to maintain his own position as Foreign Minister in the face of Premier Bidault's maneuvers to supplant him.

[30] Address quoted in its author's comprehensive survey of plans, progress, and prospects for European integration, *L'Europe en Face de Son Destin* (Paris: Éditions du Grand Siècle, n d., 1952?), p 159.

of production, and prices."[31] Five days before announcing his plan, Foreign Minister Schuman wrote the Secretary-General of the Council of Europe that the French government was interested in the functional integration advocated by the Council.

From the outset the political and economic organization of Europe was a tandem relationship. Foreign Minister Schuman made the connection explicit when, before the treaty for a Coal-Steel Community had been drafted, he asked for a high authority with power to make decisions binding on member states, that is, for the creation of a supranational entity.

British delegates to the Council of Europe had favored functional integration when it was first proposed, and leaders of the ruling Labor party had asserted that close political association could best be assured if it rested on economic unity. It was thus not unreasonable for Schuman to hope that Britain would join the pool. The Schuman Plan also seemed to be in line with American wishes. Basic in the Marshall program was the American desire for a coordinated, intergovernmental plan for the recovery of Western Europe. When the OEEC fell far short of that goal, the United States reiterated with increasing emphasis its hope for Western European "integration." Neither Administrator Paul Hoffman nor other ECA officials defined what they meant by "integration," beyond the creation of "one big common market," but Congress enthusiastically wrote the word into the 1949 revision of the Economic Cooperation Act. French leadership, complemented by American pressure on European waverers and recalcitrants, would succeed, it was hoped, in surmounting the difficulties of converting an idea into an institution.

Foremost in the mind of Foreign Minister Schuman was, of course, the question of Germany. In a much-quoted address to the National Assembly in July he said, "We want to make any war between France and Germany not only impossible, but materially impossible";[32] this objec-

[31] Same, p. 160.
[32] *L'Année Politique*, 1950, cited, p. 169.

tive was still at the head of Schuman's list when he reviewed the Plan three and a half years later.[33] War would be impossible, he said then, not only because neither France nor Germany would control its own coal and steel resources, but also because the agency supervising the key areas of the Saar and Ruhr would include other countries besides the two hereditary enemies.

The transformation of the Schuman Plan into the Coal and Steel Community proceeded fairly rapidly, despite the inopportune French political crisis which lasted from June 24, 1950, when the Bidault government fell, to July 12, when René Pleven succeeded in forming a cabinet acceptable to the National Assembly. Right at the outset, however, French hopes suffered a severe blow, when the British again showed a reluctance to support supranational European organizations. In particular, they were unwilling to accept Schuman's demand that they commit themselves to the new Community in advance of its organization. Even more chilling was the Labor party's blast of June 12. Its pamphlet entitled *European Unity* warned of the danger of British socialism consorting with non-Socialist Europeans, urged intergovernmental rather than supragovernmental measures of cooperation, and asserted that Britain should not sacrifice either its ties with the Commonwealth or its association with the United States in order to undertake commitments to Western Europe.

"There is no more Europe,"[34] bewailed Paul Reynaud, while Maurice Duverger complained that "the entire history of the European idea since the war is the story of concessions made by its advocates to England in order to obtain its consent to participate. Thereby European organizations have been emptied of all content just for the pleasure of having England join."[35] In truth, however, the Labor party's pamphlet contained nothing that the Labor government had not repeatedly made the basis of official

---

[33] Robert Schuman, "Origines et Élaboration du Plan Schuman," *Cahiers de Bruges*, December 1953, pp. 266-287.
[34] At least according to *Revue Politique et Parlementaire*, July 1950.
[35] *L'Année Politique*, 1950, cited, p. 140.

action. French leaders seem to have been misled by the cooperative statements of British delegates to the Council of Europe. They suffered perhaps, as Duverger suggests, from accumulated frustration, from what they regarded as one more betrayal of European hopes. Even as they went ahead with countries prepared to accept the Plan, they feared that the results would fall short of the "Europe" originally envisaged.

While the abstention of Britain was a blow to the deeply rooted French objective of offsetting German power with British support, it did make possible a coal-steel pool endowed with supranational characteristics. The conference of six powers ("the Six" as they came to be known: Belgium, France, Italy, Luxembourg, the Netherlands, and West Germany) opened in Paris, June 20, 1950, on the eve of the outbreak of the Korean War, with Jean Monnet as the head of the French delegation. The treaty was signed on April 18, 1951. The French National Assembly ratified it on December 13, 1951, and it entered into effect six months later. On August 10, 1952, the High Authority began its operations in Strasbourg, a site selected not without difficulty due, ironically enough, to national rivalry in housing this supranational agency.[36]

The treaty on the European Coal and Steel Community established no fewer than five organs—a High Authority, a Consultative Committee, a Common Assembly, a Special Council of Ministers, and a Court of Justice—so intricately related that their respective areas of responsibility would become delineated only as the Community developed. Furthermore, the functions which the Community was to perform could not be separated in advance from those of the participating national economies; hence the over-all competence of the Community likewise depended on its further development.

The idea of the Community as a way station en route toward political unity was embodied in the preamble to

[36] In Schuman, cited, p 282 describes the all-night session which was necessary to wear down rival claimants to the point where Strasbourg could gain acceptance, if not enthusiastic approval.

the treaty: "Conscious that Europe will be built only through concrete actions creating real solidarity, and by the establishment of common bases for economic development. . . . Resolved to substitute for ancient rivalries a fusion of their essential interests, through the installation of an economic community to take the first steps toward a larger and deeper community between peoples long separated by bloody controversies, and to mold the foundations of institutions capable of guiding one destiny heretofore disunited."[87] In other words the Community could not stand still; it would either bring about greater political-economic unity among its participants, or it would decay.

In every respect the Community was independent of the Council of Europe, resolutions of the latter to the contrary notwithstanding. Unlike the Council, which clearly was a substitute for a political union, the Community was designed to meet the demands of effective unity, albeit on a tentative basis. Lines of authority and delimitations of function were either vaguely expressed or omitted altogether, and national governments and national parliaments ensured for themselves a strong position from which to supervise the Community's development. The High Authority's supranational powers were held in check by the close association of the Council of Ministers with all activities of the Community. The Common Assembly, although supposed to represent the peoples of the participating states, was in fact composed of parliamentary delegates. It could censure the High Authority but could neither legislate nor exercise budgetary control. From these and other examples it is clear that negotiators of the treaty intended it to be a controlled experiment in international organization, the results of which could be used as a foundation for more elaborate structures. The implicit conflict between the older, defined, international body—the Council of Europe—and this newer, amorphous, supranational experiment was not long in making itself apparent.

[87] Translated from the French version of the treaty.

The treaty aimed to preserve a balance among nations in the Community. It protected French interests particularly as against the possibility of German control by allocating eighteen members each to France, Germany and Italy. The framers of the treaty expected, moreover, that a non-national, more complex alignment of the delegates would take place as they developed common interests with colleagues representing similar political points of view in other countries. Social Democrats or Christian Democrats from Germany, therefore, would not be able to give the Assembly a nationalistic, Germanic orientation. If they were tempted to do so, French, plus Belgian, Luxembourg, and Italian delegates could make a stronger coalition.

By 1950 the circumstances which in 1947 had given direction to French foreign policy had so altered, in the estimation of French leaders, as to require a new pattern of national statecraft. Already, at the outbreak of the Korean War, the policy of "building Europe" had produced certain striking results. The Brussels alliance had led directly to the formation of the Council of Europe and the North Atlantic Treaty Organization. In both undertakings Great Britain had been a partner of France. The European policy had won for French diplomacy the active assistance and support of its continental neighbors and allies, Belgium, the Netherlands, Luxembourg, and Italy. But another neighbor, West Germany, rapidly recovering strength with the aid of Great Britain and the United States, had introduced into the structure of Europe a powerful influence which the French profoundly distrusted. The concomitant inclusion of the Saar territory in the Council of Europe symbolized the continuation of close French-Saar relations, at least for the near future, despite Germany's increasingly insistent demands. Most important of all in France's European policy was the launching, just before the period ended, of the Schuman Plan.[38] Only a Europe endowed with a supranational au-

---

[38] The Schuman Plan was by no means the only form of functional integration which was proposed; others, such as the "green" and transport pools will be considered in the next chapter.

thority or authorities could, in the French view, be strong enough to enhance the importance of France while controlling the ambitions of Germany. In the Schuman Plan the French had such an institution, one which they hoped would, in addition, constitute a step toward the political integration of Western Europe.[39]

Obstacles to Greater Unity

By mid-1950, however, serious obstacles had arisen to further progress in the direction of European unity under French auspices. In some quarters the first military movement of Communist troops across delimited frontiers was being interpreted as a feint to be followed by the real blow: a Soviet attack on Western Europe. This interpretation threw a blinding light on the military weakness of that area. It had been the basic postulate of the Marshall Plan that economic recovery was not only the prerequisite but the logical source of political stability and military strength. In the North Atlantic Treaty the United States had committed its military forces to the defense of Western Europe. The crisis of 1950 arose before the Marshall Plan had had time to prove its value, and NATO was seemingly not yet strong enough to deter Soviet adventurism. When time was needed, there might be no time. The American solution for the crisis, as we shall see, was to reverse the priority of economic over military aid, to increase the direct American military commitment, to call for far greater armament efforts from other NATO members, and finally to demand immediate large-scale German rearmament.

French and other European statesmen were in agreement with Americans in assessing the nature of the danger; they wanted a deeper American military commitment to Europe, but other consequences saddened them. The Council of Europe, far from being a supranational state,

[39] Organizations associated with the European Recovery Program have not been mentioned because agencies such as the Organization for European Economic Cooperation, the European Payments Union, and the like owed their impetus more directly to American policy, and their membership extended beyond Western Europe.

was clearly incapable of serving even as a bridge to one. The Schuman Plan had been proposed only a month before the North Korean attack; the definitive treaty might be lost in the scramble for national rearmament. Shifting American aid from economic to military forms would hurt France more than Germany. The last straw was the demand that France accept the return to Germany of the final element of national sovereignty, a reconstituted army.

French dependency was deepened as the attitude of Great Britain toward European unity became clearer. By 1950 it had finally been brought home to the French that whichever party in Britain was out of power was only too eager to talk of European unity, but neither party was prepared to commit the British government to any form of supranational association. This left France unable to cope with Germany by itself, unable to create European institutions strong enough to do the job in its place, and unable to enlist British aid in the task France might be willing to contemplate European unification on an economic and political level without Britain. It could not visualize with calm the unification without Britain and *with* a rearmed Germany.

The French, like others, could subscribe enthusiastically to an ideal, particularly one endowed with such a compelling *mystique* as "Europe." Like other peoples they could pledge themselves to hypothetical sacrifices for that grandiose goal. The time would shortly come, however, when the sacrifices would appear all too real, all too painful. Then hitherto unquestioned assumptions on which their support for European unity rested would be subjected to scrutiny and found, in large part, untenable. Among those assumptions were: French leadership in the process of building Europe, the use of Europe to control Germany, concrete economic advantage arising from unifying national economies, political cohesion to be achieved within the French executive by this particular policy. Into these delicately balanced gears was thrown, by mid-1950, the monkey wrench of Anglo-American pressures for German rearmament!

Chapter Three

INDECISION AND PROCRASTINATION
1950-1954

THE OUTBREAK OF WAR in Korea found Western Europe unprepared to face the new crisis. In the year since the North Atlantic Treaty had been signed, its members had adopted a strategic plan calling for the defense of Europe as far to the East as possible, but little had been done to create either the permanent military organization or the national forces which would make the plan more than an idle dream. In its communiqué of May 1950, the North Atlantic Council declared that it had "proceeded on the basis that the combined resources of the members of the North Atlantic Treaty are sufficient, if properly coordinated and applied, to ensure the progressive and speedy development of adequate military defense without impairing the social and economic progress of their countries."[1]

One month before the North Korean attack the NATO countries were clearly operating from two basic assumptions: First, there was plenty of time to build their military strength, and, second, this gradual increase of strength could take place within the context of national social and economic programs, without causing politically unpalatable alterations or dislocations. American leaders had not questioned these assumptions, although they perhaps may have felt a greater sense of urgency than their European

[1] Lord Ismay, *NATO, the First Five Years, 1949-1954* (Paris: North Atlantic Treaty Organization, 1954), p. 183.

allies. The President and his advisers, however, had not taken exception to the Congressional view that European economic recovery took precedence over rearmament.

Faced with the problem of translating "resources" into "adequate military defense," the leadership of NATO could propose only two solutions. The first meant greater American assistance, and greater European efforts. This last, however, met with strong resistance, particularly in France. In June 1950, Premier René Pleven informed the National Assembly's Finance Commission that his government contemplated an increase of 80 billion francs (about $200,000,000) in military spending for 1950. He added, however, that above all he did not wish to upset the French economic balance by making a choice, to date unnecessary, between guns and butter.[2] As Defense Minister Jules Moch put it, France did not intend thoughtlessly to follow the United States down the road to rearmament.

Behind these statements lay a manifest concern to avoid halting the progress of the French economy. In mid-1950 wholesale and retail prices were beginning an unprecedented decline; a favorable commercial balance was in prospect; and some economists were even worrying about potential surpluses of output.[3] Continued advance depended on American economic aid, on restricting French governmental expenditures so as not unduly to unbalance the budget, and on maintaining stable world prices of the primary products which France imported.

The Question of German Rearmament

A second possible solution was to rearm West Germany. As early as 1948 French spokesmen had warned that joining the North Atlantic Pact would lead to re-establishing a German army. As Maurice Duverger wrote in *Le Monde*, "If one speaks of defending Western Europe against possible external aggression, it must be recognized

---

[2] *L'Année Politique*, 1950 (Paris: Éditions du Grand Siècle), pp. 167-168.
[3] See Jean Chardonnet, "Bilan Économique de la France en 1950," *L'Année Politique*, 1950, cited, pp. 327-337.

that these words imply the restoration of the German army at the same time as the French army. For there are only two military peoples on the continent: Germany and France. A European army would be essentially a 'Franco-German army'."[4] On the first anniversary of the North Atlantic Treaty, *Le Monde* reiterated the theme: "The rearming of Germany is contained in the Atlantic Pact like the yolk in the egg."[5] By the end of 1949 German rearmament was being discussed discreetly but persistently in unofficial circles only to be dismissed with equal persistence by government spokesmen in Britain, France and Germany. In France General Billotte found little support for his proposition that an effective defense of the continent must come through creating a strong, unified, European armed force to include, in addition to French and Italian units, contingents from both Spain and West Germany.[6]

The French reaction to the proposal to rearm Germany was like that of a bank president who had been asked to place a notorious thief in charge of the vault. To the trial balloon released by McCloy on May 7, President Vincent Auriol declared that France, which had paid with its blood, would permit no vestige of German rearmament. Defense Minister Pleven, who was to become Premier only two months later, told the Council of the Republic that, if McCloy's suggestion ever became official American policy, he would resign immediately. But when in June the attack on South Korea did make German rearmament official American policy, René Pleven, far from resigning, gave his name to a plan to integrate German troops into a European army.

A session of the Consultative Assembly of the Council of Europe was held just before the announcement of the Pleven Plan. Winston Churchill, still out of power in

[4] *Le Monde*, November 27, 1948.
[5] Same, April 6, 1949.
[6] See Pierre Billotte, *Le Temps du Choix* (Paris: Robert Laffort, 1950). However, the General, a close associate of De Gaulle, did not later support the European Defense Community Treaty, presumably he was advocating associated, national armies, not merged, denationalized units.

Britain, welcomed the newly arrived German delegates and called for the "immediate creation of a European army under the direction of a unified command."[7] French foreign policy was thereby impaled on a three-pronged dilemma from which it dangled from August 1950 until the interment of the European Defense Community Treaty almost exactly four years later. The organization of a politically united Europe was far from complete; indeed it had hardly begun. Lacking political unity, Europe would be endangered if it permitted West Germany to regain its sovereignty, especially that aspect of sovereignty represented by a national army. But, without Germany, Western Europe was virtually defenseless. The need for British support constituted a further problem for French policy. Churchill kept repeating his siren song: Great Britain would participate in a united Western Europe which included a rearmed Germany. As an escape from its dilemma, the French delegation, which included Paul Reynaud, André Philip, and Georges Bidault, joined in sponsoring a resolution in favor of "the immediate creation of a unified European army under the authority of a European Minister of Defense, subject to democratic European control and functioning in cooperation with the United States and Canada."[8]

As the French saw it, the order of business was: first, the creation of a united Europe including Great Britain; second, the formation of a unified European army; and third, the inclusion in it of German contingents. This French scale of priorities was upset just one month later by Secretary of State Dean Acheson at the meeting of the North Atlantic Council in September 1950. When Acheson examined the replies to NATO's query as to how great an armament effort its members were prepared to accept in the light of the Korean crisis, he found that most of them, like the French, had promised increased expendi-

[7] Édouard Bonnefous, *L'Europe en Face de Son Destin* (Paris: Éditions du Grand Siècle, n d , 1952?), p. 180

[8] Quoted in *L'Année Politique*, 1950, cited, p 370. On the French reasoning at this point, see Paul Reynaud, *L'Arbre Allemand Nous Cache la Forêt Russe* (Paris: Flammarion, 1951).

tures and other emergency measures, but also called attention to their domestic economic and social problems. Weighing Western resources against Eastern threats, Acheson called for "the participation of German units and the use of German productive resources" in the defense of Western Europe. French Foreign Minister Robert Schuman was almost alone in pleading that the German issue had been raised far too early, since the rearming of the North Atlantic Pact powers had scarcely begun.

The Council adjourned temporarily to permit its members to consult their governments and also to hold further meetings among the three Western powers in their related capacity as occupiers of Germany and members of the NATO Standing Group. In both rounds of meetings France found itself under familiar pressure. Although the resumed session of the North Atlantic Council revealed no agreement on the size, form, and timing of German rearmament, it was nevertheless clear that the French had made a vital concession, by agreeing, in principle, to the creation of a German armed force. The final communiqué, issued on September 26, 1950, said: "The Council was in agreement that Germany should be enabled to contribute to the build-up of the defense of Western Europe, and noting that the Occupation Powers were studying the matter, requested the Defense Committee to make recommendations at the earliest possible date as to the methods by which Germany could most usefully make its contribution."[9]

The Pleven Plan

In the next month René Pleven's French government moved with speed. It had to. The government rested on a coalition of Radicals, as represented by Premier Pleven of the Union Démocratique et Socialiste de la Résistance (UDSR), Socialists, with Defense Minister Jules Moch, and the Mouvement Républicain Populaire (MRP), with Robert Schuman as Foreign Minister. Any French policy had to be acceptable to these three Center groups. Any

[9] Ismay, cited, p. 186.

policy, furthermore, had to be one which could be simultaneously represented to the United States and to Great Britain as permitting German rearmament, and to the National Assembly and the French people as preventing just that. In solving this puzzle, the government followed the clues provided by the Council of Europe. At the start of a three-day debate, from October 24 to 26, Pleven laid a new plan before the National Assembly: a European army, run by a European defense minister, responsible to a European political structure to be created along with the development of the European Coal and Steel Community; into this army German units of minimum size were to be introduced.

In its provisions regarding Germany, Pleven's plan was not very far from the original American proposal. Neither would have permitted Germany an armaments industry or a general staff. The largest German unit envisaged by the United States had been a division; Pleven hoped to limit it to approximately combat-team strength. Where Pleven's plan differed from those of the Council of Europe and of the American government was not in detail but in its broad conception. It would have delayed German rearmament until after the political unification of Europe. As Premier Pleven told the Assembly:

The French government thought that the creation of the coal-steel pool would allow people to become accustomed to the idea of a European Community before the very delicate question of a common defense was posed. World events do not permit it this leisure time. Therefore, the French government, confident in the peaceful destiny of Europe, and impressed with the necessity of giving to all European peoples a feeling of collective security, proposes to meet this question [common defense] by the same method and in the same spirit [as the Schuman Plan].[10]

In fact the Pleven Plan was shrewdly calculated to prevent the emergence of any German army. The conception of a united Western Europe standing guard over Germany, an idea which had previously inspired French foreign policy,

[10] Quoted by Jules Moch, *Alerte! Le Problème Crucial de la Communauté Européenne* (Paris: Robert Laffort, 1951), p. 133.

was invoked in the Assembly by several orators. To those members who echoed Édouard Daladier in asking what the government planned to do if its proposal were not accepted, the Premier replied that, in that unhappy event, France would uphold its refusal to permit German rearmament. It was in this spirit that the Assembly passed by 343 to 225 (the dissenters being principally Communists and Gaullists) a resolution "approving the government's declaration and *especially its desire not to permit the re-creation of a German general staff*."[11]

Backed by the determined support of both government and Parliament, Defense Minister Moch could then go to the meeting of the NATO Council and present his Premier's plan, take-it-or-leave-it. "I have come here," Moch said on October 28, "to recommend vigorously the adoption of the French plan and *for that purpose only*. I am bound by the instructions of the French Parliament, and I am obliged to follow them."[12]

In addition to a supranational authority, French policy saw two other methods by which the problem of German rearmament could be solved. One was to increase the allied, principally British and American, forces stationed in Germany. This would have the double advantage: (1) of keeping Germany under surveillance; and (2) of committing England and the United States to the defense of Western Europe, not in peripheral areas such as Britain, Spain, or North Africa, but, as NATO had agreed, in Western Europe along a line running through Germany. The second, and bolder, solution envisaged by France was to remove the problem entirely by reopening discussions with the Soviet Union.[13] When Pleven's own newspaper, which went by the euphonious title of *Le Petit Bleu des Côtes du Nord*, opened the campaign, the circumstances were far from promising, but, as that journal asked rhetorically, "If there were only one chance in a thousand

[11] *L'Année Politique*, 1950, cited, p. 227 (italics added).
[12] Same, p. 224 (italics added).
[13] At best the East-West discussions would settle the cold war, of which German rearmament was an integral part; at worst the talks would postpone the evil day when Germans again donned military uniforms.

of a conversation bearing fruit, would it not be the function of French diplomacy to seek to learn the authoritative response to this preliminary question?"[14]

A period of intense diplomatic activity followed. In simultaneous or overlapping negotiations which took place on several different levels and among several different participants, the one common subject was the rearming of West Germany. Inside the North Atlantic Treaty structure the United States pressed hard for recruiting German units immediately, in advance of the creation of a European army. France, continuing to insist on the Pleven Plan, prepared to begin discussions with other European countries. But France did not want to have these discussions proceed too far or too fast, since it still placed first in order of priority the creation of the Coal and Steel Community. Of equal importance to France was the exchange of notes between the three Western powers and the Soviet Union, which led in March 1951 to inconclusive talks at the Palais Rose, on the question of what to talk about at an East-West conference. Over the same period the three occupying powers were negotiating, with West German leaders, a revision of the recently concluded Occupation Statute, which the contemplated German rearmament was already making obsolete. Finally, French representatives to the Council of Europe were essaying the delicate task of maintaining British association in both political and military forms of European unification, notwithstanding the Labor government's firm refusal to accept membership in the Coal and Steel Community.

The United States initially sought German rearmament by means of a new Occupation Statute and gained approval for this procedure by the North Atlantic Council meeting in Brussels in December 1950. The new statute was put into effect on March 6, 1951. By that time, however, French diplomacy had advanced so far toward the European Defense Community that the alternate route to German rearmament was abandoned.

The new Occupation Statute granted the German gov-

[14] *L'Année Politique*, 1950, cited, p. 222.

ernment increased internal autonomy and the right to establish a Ministry of Foreign Affairs. One month later, as part of the agreement on the Coal and Steel Community, virtually all restrictions on German production were removed. Even the theoretical limit of eleven million tons of steel could be breached, if such action would contribute to Western defense. Three months later, on July 9, 1951, the legal state of war between the three Western powers and Germany came to an end. Only two restraints dating from 1945 now remained: the continued presence of American, British, and French troops, and the continued absence of any German military establishment. None the less, the new, quasi-sovereign status of West Germany emboldened the Adenauer regime to renew its agitation over the Saar. The West German Chancellor had been displeased to see Schuman figure as signatory for the Saar in the treaty establishing the Coal and Steel Community. "In the not so distant future," he told the Bundestag in July 1951, "we shall see the Saar question settled on our terms."[15] Adenauer's provocative statement, inspired in part by domestic politics, confirmed the French in their belief that European political unity was the only solution for the German problem.

Negotiations over the European Defense Community continued during 1951, with various interruptions such as the French parliamentary elections, without producing a definitive text. So far as France was concerned, every significant aspect of the international situation was going from bad to worse, with the single exception of the Coal and Steel Community. West Germany, having obtained so much, was demanding more, secure in the knowledge which had nourished its ambition since 1947, namely, that only France was opposed and that France, as before, could not hold out indefinitely against British and American pressure.

After sixty-four meetings in the Palais Rose the foreign ministers abandoned their attempt to frame an agenda for a meeting between East and West. France, and possibly

---

[15] *L'Année Politique*, 1951, cited, p. 173.

Great Britain, might have taken a chance on talks without an agenda, but neither of the two principal antagonists was willing. The focus of East-West diplomatic communications then shifted from Europe to the Far East, where a military stalemate had been reached in Korea.

Equally disappointing to France was the lack of progress in the Council of Europe toward European unity. Ideas, proposals, suggestions, debates were not lacking. Indeed, the Council was throwing off sparks in all directions, but they indicated no more forward movement of the machinery than those of a Fourth of July pinwheel. In November 1950 Foreign Minister Schuman had gained the support of the Consultative Assembly for the French version of a European army by the overwhelming vote of 87-7, with only the German Social Democratic delegates in opposition. Disturbing, however, was the fact that the British Labor party's representatives (nineteen in all) joined the Scandinavian delegates in abstaining.

The basic reasons for the failure of other proposals were to be found in the organization of the Council of Europe. The Consultative Assembly might elaborate projects and pass resolutions until its collective voice gave out, but the Council of Ministers would not listen. And the reason why the Council of Ministers would not listen was the deafness of the British and Scandinavian governments. France had turned from the Council of Europe to negotiate the Coal and Steel Community and was doing the same with regard to the Defense Community. The logical next step seemed to be for France to abandon the Council as a medium for European political federation. Because the Council still symbolized the federative efforts unleashed by World War II, however, an explosion was inevitable just as soon as its record during 1951 was placed beside the text of the European Defense Community Treaty. That moment arrived in December 1951, when Paul-Henri Spaak resigned as President of the Consultative Assembly. The igniting spark, so far as Spaak was concerned, was the advocacy by British Conservatives, again in power, of cooperation between sovereign entities, rather than the creation of supranational authorities. "That is perhaps one way of building Europe," declared Spaak, "although I don't see very clearly just how. But do you really imagine that it was useful to build this palace [at Strasbourg] and to have two hundred European deputies meet twice a year just to support governmental agreements? Don't you think that governments are capable of reaching such agreements without our aid?"[16] Spaak concluded with the French that Commonwealth obligations, on which the British ceaselessly expatiated, were being used as a pretext. But he by no means confined his fire to the British, for complacent continentals were mouthing similar excuses. Before the spectacle of a "Europe which for five years has lived in fear of Russia and on the charity of the United States . . . we are impassive just as if history were waiting for us, just as if we had the time, placidly, over the course of decades and decades, to change our attitude, remove our tariff barriers, abandon our national egotisms. We behave as though we had an eternity before us."[17]

Even as the Belgian statesman spoke, French negotiators were encountering another example of British unwillingness to make commitments to European organizations, in this case to the European Defense Community. The French were also carefully testing American attitudes toward the treaty as its terms became more precise. Premier Pleven, in January 1951, and President Auriol and Foreign Minister Schuman, in March, had journeyed to Washington to assure the United States of French devotion to the Atlantic alliance and to ask reciprocal assurances. The French emissaries wanted to be told that the United States would not abandon the NATO concept of European protection for "peripheral defense," that, consonant with this concept, it would send France increased military aid, and that, even after Germany had been rearmed, France, in the American view, would remain the keystone of Western defense. Finally, the French

[16] Speech of December 11, 1951, reprinted in *L'Année Politique*, 1951, cited, pp. 687-689.
[17] Same.

leaders wanted to impress on the United States the intimate connection between France's difficulties in Europe and its burdens in Asia. In Viet-Nam the war was becoming increasingly painful. This conflict, said the French, was not in any sense "colonial"; rather, like Korea, it was a part of the world-wide defense against communism, and as such deserved a high priority in the allocation of American military assistance.

While the United States officially accepted the French version of the Indo-Chinese situation and promised additional aid, it cannot be said that the French visitors were reassured on the other points. They learned that the amount of military equipment sent to Europe was for Congress to determine, and that the executive could make no firm commitment in advance of legislative action. This the French already knew; what they really sought were reiterations of love and affection. Instead, they heard Herbert Hoover and Senator Robert A. Taft enunciating the doctrine of continental defense. Though the Truman Administration did not espouse these ideas, would not impatience at the lack of progress toward German rearmament make them increasingly attractive? General Dwight D. Eisenhower, newly appointed SHAPE Commander, in reporting to Congress, was emphasizing Western European defense, but at the same time partially clandestine negotiations were going on between the United States and Spain. After diplomatic relations had been renewed in December 1950, Congress had approved a loan of $62,500,000. American emissaries were discussing the use of Spanish naval and air bases in return for military and economic aid, which, in October 1951, was granted by Congress in the amount of $100,000,000. To the French it appeared as though an alternate plan of defense was being developed, in case German rearmament were delayed.

The European Defense Community Treaty

In November 1951, while a draft of a Defense Community Treaty was at long last nearing completion, the North

Atlantic Council, meeting at Rome, tried to give the project one more push by expressing the hope "that a definitive report could be made to the Council at its next meeting."[18] France, however, had paid heavily for this draft, paid on the same account presented periodically since 1947, paid, in short, by accepting still greater concessions to West Germany. Would the Defense Community Treaty serve as the machinery whereby West Germany would recover its sovereignty completely and the occupation era be definitely ended? Such had been the expectations of the French negotiators when they launched the Pleven Plan in February. But in November it appeared that, if the Plan were not adopted soon, Germany would recover its sovereignty anyway, that the United States and Great Britain might act without France to initiate German rearmament. If the Germans could sense such developments in the offing, what would they gain by participation in a supranational military organization? It behooved the French to make haste, at least until Germany had formally committed itself to a defense community. But haste now could only be purchased by concessions to Germany in the treaty. The crux of the dilemma had finally been reached, a dilemma which was to plague and divide the French for three years thereafter. No treaty at all might increase immeasurably the danger to France of a rearmed Germany, but a weak treaty might only plaster over that danger temporarily or, worse, handicap France more than Germany.

In all economic classes except the workers, where Communist influence was the greatest, more Frenchmen approved of a European army than disapproved. Their approval, however, was for a still hypothetical organization, and was by a plurality, not a majority. A public-opinion poll showed that 42 per cent were favorable and 26 per cent hostile; 32 per cent made no reply.[19] Within the National Assembly the tide of opposition was rising in all groups except the Gaullists and Communists (already

---

[18] Ismay, cited, p. 189.
[19] *Sondages (Revue Française de l'Opinion Publique)*, no. 3, 1951, pp. 19-23.

united in condemning the treaty) and the MRP, which was still solidly arrayed behind the European policy of its Foreign Minister. Outstanding among the new opponents was none other than Jules Moch, who as Defense Minister had presented the original Pleven Plan. But, said Moch, there was not now much resemblance between the proposal of October 1950 and the draft treaty of November 1951. In fact the draft made so many concessions to Germany, while retaining so many restrictions on France, that it had become merely a blind behind which the *Wehrmacht* would be reconstituted.[20]

Growing parliamentary opposition to the Defense Community was to lead to questioning the validity of the European unity idea itself, which since 1947 had been the main theme of French foreign policy. The days were passing when a French government could rouse the Assembly to favorable votes by invoking the *mystique* of "Europe." At the same time, as a result of the 1951 elections and the annual crisis over the budget, the executive coalition was shifting, soon it would include individuals and groups lukewarm, neutral, or even hostile to previous French foreign policy. After a four months' absence from office, during the tenure of Radical Henri Queuille, René Pleven on August 10 constituted a government in which the Socialists were conspicuous by their absence. The Section Française de l'Internationale Ouvrière (SFIO) felt that its losses at the polls were a punishment inflicted by the electorate for participation in increasingly rightward-orientated coalitions. On January 7, 1952, the Socialists, despite the pleas of their leader Guy Mollet, took the next step toward political irresponsibility by adding their votes to those of the solid Communist and Gaullist blocs in order to bring down Pleven. During the ensuing two-week crisis a Gaullist, Jacques Soustelle, was for the first time asked to form a cabinet. When he prudently declined, a Radical, Edgar Faure, succeeded in gaining investiture with a coalition which again excluded the Socialists.

[20] Objections to the treaty will be examined below. For Moch's position, see *Alerte! . . .*, cited, especially pp. 132-143, in which the author compares, section by section, the original proposal with the 1952 treaty.

The political maneuvering during the last half of 1951 revealed all too clearly that no firm coalition—firm even by French standards—could be created against the combined opposition of Gaullists, Socialists and Communists. The time was shortly to come when Gaullist groups would abandon their "policy of the worst," thus splitting the monolithic movement created by the General. Until they did so, the Socialists, out of power by their own choice, were the real arbiters of the government's policy, particularly with respect to foreign affairs.

This was the situation which confronted the Faure government when it went before the National Assembly in February 1952, requesting permission to sign the European Defense Community Treaty. The fact of the request and the unusual form in which it was made were proofs of the overwhelming legislative opposition to German rearmament and of the Assembly's power to demand from the executive that ratification should be only preliminary and tentative. At the end of a two-day debate which opened on February 11, the Assembly was presented with two orders of the day: one by the government endorsing the treaty and one by the Socialists favoring further negotiations. Neither side would accept the other's proposal. It was the government which first gave way, modifying its order to emphasize Anglo-American guarantees and the need for integrating national armies, in as small units as possible, into the supranational structure created by the treaty. This order was likewise turned down by the Socialists. Faure then posed the question of confidence, but at the last moment, when his defeat seemed certain, once more gave ground, and substituted a third order of the day. This version proved acceptable to the Socialists, and at 3:40 A.M. on February 17 it was passed by the Assembly by 326-276, a majority of fifty.[21]

Thanks to the Socialists, the Faure Cabinet, which was to last less than two more weeks, could discuss the future of Germany with British, American, and German repre-

---

[21] The debate is summarized in *L'Année Politique*, 1951, cited, pp. 307-312. Practically the entire Assembly for once voted one way or the other on the resolution.

sentatives in London and could then comply with the request of the North Atlantic powers to submit the plans for a European Defense Community to the Lisbon meeting of the Atlantic Council. The "victory" for the Defense Community in the National Assembly, however, was a highly illusory one. As usual, the requisite majority was obtained only by an anti-German appeal. Perusal of the Assembly's resolution reveals this continued preoccupation with the German threat. No German recruitment, said the Assembly, could take place before the actual ratification of the treaty. Despite the demand of Chancellor Adenauer, Germany was not to gain membership in NATO by joining the Community. In no event was Germany to be permitted more troops than France, after measuring the requirements of its domestic economy and the war in Indo-China, was willing to maintain in Europe. The entire European army project was to be subordinated to the creation of a supranational political community. The Assembly once again registered its opposition to the reconstitution of a German national army and a German general staff.

Last but far from least, the Assembly invited "the government to renew its efforts to accomplish the end of attaining *participation* in the European Defense Community by other democratic nations, notably Great Britain; this action, constituting a guarantee fully meeting the concerns expressed by the National Assembly, would lead logically to the study and formulation of institutions and of means most likely to accomplish this result."[22] These words reflected the basic position of the Socialists that Great Britain must be securely tied to the treaty.

In September 1950, the urgings of Secretary Acheson had forced the French to pull a rabbit from a hat quickly. Little wonder that Pleven's animal was a close relative of Schuman's *lapin*. Both were produced for the same purpose—to substitute supranational control for three-power occupation of Germany. Twenty months later, on May 27, 1952, when the European Defense Community Treaty was

[22] The order is reprinted in *L'Année Politique*, 1952, cited, pp. 489-490.

signed, it still closely resembled the Coal and Steel Community. Each was fitted out with an Assembly and a Court. Each was to have a Council of Ministers attached to its directing body. And in the absence of precedent in European federation both communities were essentially experiments.[23]

Can it be said that the Defense Community represented a step toward European unity? The terms of the treaty in and of themselves certainly created no clearly supranational instrumentalities. Integrative tendencies, however, were present. The member states were to have only one army, whose direction was to be unified. The subordination of the military Commissariat to political control was intended to prevent it from becoming an autonomous, irresponsible military hierarchy such as had plagued Germany. While the political control lodged in the Council of Ministers was plainly international, Article 38 of the treaty, concerning which more will be said below, provided for subordination of the Community to unified European political institutions.

On the day before the signing of the Defense Community Treaty an even more complicated agreement was reached, entitled "Convention on Relations between the Three Powers and the Federal Republic of Germany." This was not the separate peace treaty for which Adenauer had fought, but it would do until a definitive all-German treaty could, if ever, be negotiated with the Soviet Union. With the ending of the occupation, allied forces were to remain in Germany as a contribution to European defense. The allies retained control over them and could use them in case of external attack or internal subversion. In addition, the allies retained special rights in Berlin and must approve the terms of any future peace treaty which might reunite divided Germany. With these major exceptions, West Germany obtained direction of its own internal and external affairs. It bound itself to conduct its foreign relations in accordance with the principles of the

[23] For the text of the European Defense Community Treaty, see same, pp. 522-557.

United Nations. It also undertook to contribute financially to European defense on the same terms as other NATO countries, although France stood squarely in the path of its joining that organization.

The Defense Community and the Convention on Germany were of course linked by more than the coincidence of the time of their signing, and linking them together did little to enhance the popularity of the Community with the French. What guarantees now existed to protect France against the misuse of German power? Such as they were, they existed in the terms of both engagements, and in a separate declaration of the three powers. Once more Great Britain and the United States proclaimed that European defense, being in accord with their fundamental interests, would be given their continued support. This support was to be manifested in the future, as in the past, by three related commitments: first, membership in NATO, with which the European Defense Community was to be connected, second, financial contributions to European rearmament; and, third, maintenance of troops on the continent, in Germany as well as in France. Finally, if the Defense Community were threatened from any source, Great Britain and the United States would regard their own security as threatened and would take action under Article 4 of the North Atlantic Treaty.

To Great Britain and the United States, neither of which had previously been so deeply involved in European affairs during "peacetime," these undertakings, especially when read in the light of the development of a progressively integrated North Atlantic Treaty Organization, were certainly serious ones. It still remained to be seen, however, whether France would prefer them to two other, entirely negative, guarantees. The first was that no German soldiers should be recruited before the European Defense Community had been ratified. The second provided that the convention restoring most of the attributes of sovereignty to West Germany should not enter into force until after the treaty had been ratified. Everything, therefore, depended on the reception which the National

Assembly would accord that instrument. Would the Assembly view the Defense Community as consonant with the objectives of French foreign policy? And if the answer to this question was "no," as appeared probable, what should be done then?

Arguments for and against the Treaty

After the signing of the treaty not one of three successive French governments dared submit it to the National Assembly, and the fourth, that of Pierre Mendès-France, finally cast it as a small, decaying fish before a collection of hungry cats. In the two years that elapsed before the officially recorded demise of the European Defense Community, arguments made on its behalf were almost totally negative in character. They were presented with increasing timidity by the treaty's supporters in the face of a rising tide of criticism which ultimately submerged the treaty and swept out of power the individuals who had negotiated it and the party to which they belonged.

Advocates of the treaty defended it in plaintive terms like boys pleading that their torn clothes and black eyes came from opponents bigger and tougher than they. Thus the report of the French delegation: "Psychologically, the fact that the French army must, with the exception of troops destined for overseas territories, 'Europeanize itself' could offend some and provoke reactions. But this is the price we must pay to ensure the advantages of the solution envisaged."[24] And later in the same report: "The French government has from the outset fervently wished Great Britain to participate fully in the European Defense Community. It has never succeeded in obtaining this participation."[25] In the same vein René Pleven wrote in his introduction to a full-scale defense of the treaty by General Edgard de Larminat: "Only a community of defense will permit European nations to make their voice

[24] France, Ministère des Affaires Étrangères, Ministère de Défense Nationale, Conférence pour l'Organisation d'une Communauté Européenne de Défense, *Rapport de la Délégation Française au Gouvernement* (Paris. Imprimerie des Journaux Officiels, 1952), p. 30

[25] Same, p. 24.

heard on a level of equality in the discussion of common plans that affect their security."[26] The General asked: "Is this [the cool reception of the treaty] a manifestation of the debility of which France is today so widely accused?"[27]

Among the "benefits" mentioned by the French delegation was the relation of the Defense Community to the long-sought goal of political unification. The treaty was intended to repair a dangerous omission in earlier institutions, such as the Council of Europe and the Coal and Steel Community, by setting forth a compulsory procedure for progressing toward a European political community. The purpose of the Community was to protect France by continuing the control of Germany. According to the French delegation, the treaty fulfilled the requirements laid on the negotiators by the National Assembly by providing the "best guarantee against the rebirth of German militarism."[28] General de Larminat pointed out, however, that the effectiveness of guarantees, whether in the treaty itself or in commitments accepted by Great Britain and the United States, did not rest on written statements, but rather on a real association of interests Such an association had been achieved in the Coal and Steel Community, was now present in the Defense Community, particularly as it was related to NATO, and would subsequently reach a climax of effectiveness in the organization of a political community.[29] It all came down to this: while France was once more called on to make sacrifices, only by so doing could it ensure its national security vis-à-vis a newly sovereign, newly powerful West Germany.

Was there, then, no alternative to the European Defense Community Treaty? To be sure, much of the opposition to the treaty was factitious. There was much in De Larminat's charge that critics were offering nothing save

[26] General E. de Larminat, *L'Armée Européenne* (Paris: Berger-Levrault, 1952), pp 6-7.
[27] Same, p 62.
[28] *Rapport de la Délégation Française au Gouvernement*, cited, p 28.
[29] De Larminat, cited, p. 73 See also General E. de Larminat and Olivier Manet, "La Communauté Européenne de Défense, *Politique Étrangère*, May-June 1953, pp 149-168, especially pp 155-158.

"fears, hatreds, suspicions, timidities, nostalgias."[30] The treaty was far too complicated, complained some; it would result, said General Weygand, in a "proliferation of organizations, of chiefs of staff, of directors, of bureaus, of commissions, of liaison agents, all costly both in terms of personnel and expenditures which would be much better employed otherwise."[31] Hence no major military figure, it was charged, whether British, American, or French, would dare publicly to support the treaty as an efficient, effective contribution to European defense.[32]

Worse than ineffectiveness, however, were the dangerous implications for national security. The treaty cut the French army in two. The part closest to home would be denationalized, not subject to French control; the other, far away, would remain national but would be engaged in extra-European enterprises.[33] The establishment of the Defense Community would not suffice to protect France, since the controls over Germany were illusory or evanescent. Memories of General Heinrich von Seekt were evoked to remind the French that a German general staff could reappear overnight.[34] Because the Community was weak, demands made upon it in the name of European defense could result only in relaxing controls over Germany and ultimately in abandoning them completely. André Géraud wrote:

If Western relations with Soviet Russia deteriorate, the general staffs of the Atlantic nations will wish to utilize the German military potential fully, whatever the letter of the agreement. This may entail the absorption and destruction of the French army (already handicapped by the high proportion of French troops engaged overseas), since it may be subject to limitations which the Germans may evade.[35]

[30] De Larminat, *L'Armée Européenne*, cited, pp 62-63
[31] Maxime Weygand, "Réflexions sur l'État Militaire de la France," *Revue des Deux Mondes*, October 15, 1952, p 587.
[32] See Louis Salleron, "L'Équivoque de l'Armée Européenne," *Le Monde*, April 11, 1953
[33] See, for example, Weygand, cited, pp. 584-585, Raymond Aron, "L'Unité Économique de l'Europe," *La Revue Libre*, October 1952, p. 10.
[34] Weygand, cited, p 580.
[35] André Géraud ("Pertinax"), "Rise and Fall of the Anglo-French Entente," *Foreign Affairs*, April 1954, p. 381.

If the treaty could not perform the miracle of making the German armed force stronger than the Russian but weaker than the French, what were the alternatives? Opponents of the treaty had at least six suggestions, each of which at one time or another was adopted by French governments as prerequisites to accepting the Defense Community. One idea was to tinker with the terms of the treaty so that only German armed forces would be subject to international control. In order to avoid re-creating a German national army French negotiators had placed their army in a pool with the German. Having taken the Germans in, the French might now be able to take themselves out through a series of modifications and exceptions applying only to them. Such was the approach of Premier René Mayer.

Another suggestion was to consider the treaty only after a new arrangement had been made between France and the Saar, this time a definitive one which West Germany would have to accept as the price of French ratification of the treaty. While seeking to overturn the 1947 decision which attached the Saar economically to France, Johannes Hoffmann's Saar government was urging France to grant more attractive terms, particularly since many of the economic advantages obtained in 1947 by separating the Saar from defeated Germany had now shrunk, or vanished altogether.

Only one solution seemed both acceptable to the Saarlanders and the West Germans, and at the same time not damaging to French interests. It had already been foreshadowed in the separate admission of the Saar to the Council of Europe. Political autonomy under the aegis of a European political community would give the Saar protection against German encroachments, at least until an all-German peace treaty was concluded. In this way a new status for the Saar would be linked to the establishment of a political community, which became one more prerequisite for French acceptance of the Defense Treaty. To be sure, Article 38 of the Defense Treaty had provided for a political statute, but it now appeared that perhaps

French leaders had been going about the business of unifying Europe backwards. Green pools, transport pools, banking pools, all would follow logically from the creation of a supranational political authority. Since the abandonment of a national army represented a serious sacrifice of sovereignty, this step should be taken only after a federal structure had been made ready to receive the transfers of power from the member states.[36]

Another prerequisite to approval of the Defense Community, urged by Socialists and others, was Great Britain's firm commitment to the new organization. For French Socialists the refusal of the British Labor party to accept the Schuman Plan had been a bitter blow. It condemned the French Socialists to a minority position in European councils, where the leadership was too conservative and too Catholic for Left-wing anticlerics. In 1952, when the Defense Treaty was finally signed, the Conservatives were back in power in Britain; their aloof attitude toward European unity remained a painful affront, for without Britain, France was shut up in a small, dark box with Germany. History warned that this situation might have disastrous consequences.

In France [after World War I] not only the Socialists, but all the republicans, all who could be called of the Left in distinction to the reactionary Right, affirmed their faith in the famous formula: security, arbitration, disarmament. By trying to organize first military, then economic, sanctions, they attempted to create a true League of Nations, which would be allowed to take decisions by majority vote. And it was partly because France encountered the bad faith of Britain, because the latter always refused to give to the League of Nations any power at all, that the League remained only a debating society for distinguished men. It was totally ineffective; disarmament was a failure, and finally war came.[37]

---

[36] Socialist party leaders, although not the rank and file, were in the forefront of those who would have made creation of the European Political Community the prerequisite for acceptance of the Defense Treaty See, for example, Guy Mollet, "France and the Defense of Europe," *Foreign Affairs*, April 1954, p. 369

[37] André Philip, *Le Socialisme et l'Unité Européenne* (Paris· Éditions du Mouvement Socialiste pour les États-Unis de l'Europe, 1951), p. 12.

Historically bemused Frenchmen, fearing a fourth German threat within three-quarters of a century, turned again to Great Britain for guarantees of protection.

Because commitments in overseas territories, particularly Indo-China, accounted in large part for France's potential military weakness in Europe compared to Germany, it was argued that the Defense Treaty should be ratified only after affairs in the French Union had been settled. Dissident political factions, however, advocated radically different types of settlement. Some wanted peace negotiated with Ho Chi Minh, although since 1947 Communist advocacy of this course had made most democratic politicians reluctant to mention the possibility above a whisper. Thus no compromise proposal emerged which would uphold French interests and at the same time prove acceptable to the growing Communist forces in Viet-Nam. The issues which had caused the outbreak of the war steadily prevented its termination until in 1954 defeats suffered by French forces made necessary their withdrawal from Indo-China and the cession of the northern half of Viet-Nam to the Communists.

Another form of settlement would have been to mobilize all of French power so as to win a quick military victory in Indo-China. Such was the policy consistently advanced by General de Gaulle and his Rassemblement du Peuple Français (RPF), which had emerged from the 1951 elections as the largest single bloc in the National Assembly. For De Gaulle, as for many others, France was a great power only because it was the center of a world-embracing Union. In his view Robert Schuman and other architects of French foreign policy were, in seeking European supranational unity, neglecting the colonial empire on which French prestige rested in order to surrender French national sovereignty to a nonexistent "Europe."

A third way to end the Indo-Chinese drain on French strength, one not necessarily incompatible with the De Gaulle ideas, was to call on the United States for help. The United States had recognized that the war in Indo-China was part of a world-wide struggle for freedom.

Now, before the Defense Community Treaty was ratified, the United States could be told that, if it really wanted Germany rearmed, it should throw its full weight, except for troops, behind a French effort to win a quick victory.[38]

Some argued that the treaty was unnecessary. Instead of tinkering with it or postponing ratification, why not scrap it altogether? Gaullists wanted to rely on agreements between the French, British, and German governments, which would for the first time create European military strength. To them this seemed the only way to prevent the United States from dominating the North Atlantic alliance, a situation which had given France so many headaches. Others, less critical of NATO, were beginning to say that it would be better able to assimilate a new German army than would a European Defense Community. There was irony in this suggestion, since the Defense Community had been the French riposte to the original American idea that Germany be rearmed under NATO. And, if this were not enough to silence advocates of the NATO solution, they could be reminded that Chancellor Adenauer, just before signing the Defense Community Treaty, had demanded that Germany be admitted to NATO. The Community's control over German rearmament might be dangerously weak, but a remilitarized Germany in NATO might be subjected to no control at all. "More than ever," wrote Michel Debré, Gaullist Senator and outspoken critic of the Defense Treaty, "Atlantic problems are reduced to the preparation of a war in Europe. From the defensive one goes, by force of circumstances, to the offensive." The "national tendencies of the German heart, so dear to the directors of the Pentagon," would have full play in the Defense Treaty, since they would be encouraged by the American leadership of NATO.[39]

---

[38] From 1952 on a steady stream of French representatives, civilians and military, presented a steady stream of plans for winning the war (with American aid).

[39] Michel Debré, "Contre l'Armée Européenne," *Politique Étrangère*, November 1953, pp. 394-395.

French Government: Postponed Decisions

In their search for an escape from their dilemma, the French could not forget the lure of talks with the Soviet Union. At the beginning of the Korean War, American pressure for German rearmament had arisen from a fear that the Soviet Union was about to attack Western Europe. But no attack had come; the Korean War had reached a stalemate, and the Soviets were making sounds like Picasso's dove. A long time had passed since Pleven first advanced the idea of East-West negotiations, but to date the four powers had done no more than argue over what should be argued about. The motive behind Russian overtures, so the United States claimed, was to prevent West Germany from regaining its sovereignty and reconstituting a national army. If this were true, felt the French, so much the better, for here Russian and French objectives were parallel. If East-West tension could be eased, if Russia could be induced to give up its aggressive designs, then the whole rationale of German rearmament would vanish, and France could return to its policy of building European political unity.

The Soviets had launched their "peace offensive" as early as November 1950, and, although no agenda had been framed for an East-West conference, they continued their barrage of notes through 1951. On September 11 they made a separate appeal to France, timed to precede the conclusion of the proposed new arrangements among the powers of Western Europe, the Contractual Agreement with Germany, the Coal and Steel Community, and the Defense Treaty.

While France did not rise to the bait, its attitude toward Soviet proposals was becoming less intransigent than America's, certainly, and Great Britain's, probably. The variance in view was apparent in the responses of the three powers to invitations to the "World Economic Conference," held in Moscow on April 3-12, 1952. The American government labeled the affair a propaganda front, a trap for the unwary, and exerted pressure on private citizens not to participate. But neither the British nor the French governments followed this policy. Lord Boyd Orr led the British delegation, which included several members of Parliament, to the conference. France sent one hundred delegates, including a Radical deputy and erstwhile cabinet member, Paul Bastid.

In June 1952, the three Western powers once more had to reach agreement on a reply to still another Soviet note. Foreign Minister Schuman pleaded that, without some further demonstration that the Russian peace moves were a sham, he would find it difficult to persuade the Assembly to ratify the Defense Treaty. But by this time the American position had hardened into a now familiar line. Before agreeing to East-West talks, the United States demanded that the Soviet Union should give evidence of good faith by moving from kind words to good deeds, by signing an Austrian treaty and agreeing to all-German, free, supervised elections. Secretary Acheson, in direct opposition to Schuman's attitude, asserted that ratification of the Defense Treaty and with it the Contractual Agreement with Germany must precede, not follow, talks with Russia. In this, as in other related matters, the French could see that American and German views coincided. Of what value were American statements of sympathy for France if American policy on key issues consistently favored Germany?

To many Frenchmen, American foreign policy seemed the plaything of domestic politics. The United States was about to abdicate its world-wide responsibilities for half a year while, in their appeals to the electorate, presidential candidates vied with each other in their unyielding attitudes toward the Russians.[40] Other issues added to the anti-American spirit. The French did not enjoy their debtor position and their dependence on their rich creditor. Patently inferior to the United States in economic and military power, France asserted its devotion to nonmaterial values. "There is nothing to be hoped for from

[40] For a French view of the American electoral hiatus, see *L'Année Politique*, 1952, cited, p. 346.

the far too many Frenchmen who blindly admire America and above all admire its faults, putting their feet on the table and chewing gum like ruminating cows; such people worship America's entirely mechanistic 'civilization' . . . a civilization whose deeply rooted materialism, in spite of some religiosity, resembles that of the Soviets."[41] Other Frenchmen also professed to see little difference between the two super-powers. Wrote the distinguished Catholic author, François Mauriac: "Their ideological opposition is perhaps less striking to us than their agreement on human values . . . two technocracies which view themselves as antagonists are dragging humanity toward the same dehumanization."[42]

Minor causes of friction were certain to arise even between friends and allies, issues such as the balance between economic and military assistance, aid to Indo-China, and American economic and ideological interest in North Africa. But the German question remained vital. Since November 1950, the United States had been persistently pressing France to accept German sovereignty and the rebuilding of a German army. This was bad enough, but it was made worse when the United States dogmatically opposed opening negotiations with the Soviet Union, negotiations which might make unnecessary the revival of German militarism. The words of Maurice Duverger, specifically directed at the Far Eastern policy of the United States, had wider implications:

The entire diplomatic tradition of Europe rests on two unwritten principles recognition of reality on the one hand, compromise on the other. If the devil himself should be installed at the head of a nation's government, his neighbors could adopt only two attitudes: either try to destroy him by war or negotiate with him a modus vivendi. The first attitude is military; the second is diplomatic; there is no third. . . . One can almost define the diplomacy of the United States as principles opposed to those which have just been set forth. on the one hand, refusal to

---

[41] Maurice Honoré, "Pour les Relations Meilleures avec les États-Unis," *Revue Politique et Parlementaire*, December 1952, p. 392.
[42] *Figaro*, February 20, 1950.

recognize disagreeable situations, on the other a desire to obtain capitulation pure and simple.[43]

Struggling like a fly in a spider's web, France sought to explore all avenues of escape. In the meantime, the continued delay in placing the Defense Treaty and Contractual Agreement before the National Assembly gave time for the heterogeneous opposition to gather strength and to organize. From the moment the treaty was signed, its architects began to lose the initiative. Once the defenders of the treaty admitted the possibility of improvements being made in the document, their defensive posture was converted into retreat. As soon as proposed reservations were drafted, the retreat threatened to turn into a rout.

Of primary significance in the defeat of the treaty was the changing complexion of successive French cabinets. Those of Pleven and Faure could function only so long as the Socialists abstained from voting against the government. With the advent of Antoine Pinay, a conservative, as Premier, the Gaullist bloc split wide open, and the dissidents, calling themselves the Action Républicaine et Sociale (ARS), supported Pinay. They did not, however, enter his government until Radical René Mayer became Premier, on January 7, 1953. The shift of the Gaullists from adamant opposition to participation was completed some five months later when Independent Joseph Laniel's Cabinet contained both dissident and "regular" Gaullists.[44] When, in the summer of 1954, Pierre Mendès-France, with his "new dynamism," took over direction of policy, the Gaullists continued as a fixture in the coalition.

While the Gaullist groups ceased to represent a parliamentary party of the "opposition," they by no means abandoned their irreconcilable hostility to the treaty. Thus, although in principle Pinay's Cabinet favored the treaty, the Premier could not submit it to the Assembly. For by so doing he would have alienated an important bloc which was supporting his domestic policy, the field

---

[43] *Le Monde*, April 27, 1954.
[44] Both groups were specifically disowned by their former leader, Charles de Gaulle.

with which his government was chiefly concerned. After January 1953 the Mayer and Laniel Cabinets were divided into supporters and opponents of the treaty; submitting it to the National Assembly at any time during this period would have split the coalition upon which each was dependent. The possibility of a different coalition, one favorable to the treaty, vanished when the Socialists, who had been demanding the liberalization of economic and social policy as the price of their participation in government, also became hopelessly split over EDC. Under the political conditions which prevailed from March 1952 to June 1954 it was quite irrelevant whether a majority of the Cabinet favored the treaty, or even whether some kind of majority could perhaps have been found for the treaty in the National Assembly.

The French Cabinet had to give the appearance of approaching a decision on the treaty while actually it was avoiding a decision as long as possible. What was needed was rapid motion of the kind exhibited by a man on a fast-working treadmill. With arms waving, chest heaving, legs moving up and down like purposeful pistons, he gives every indication of grim determination to get ahead; yet his position remains unchanged. The American inventor who devised a complicated machine, wherein wheels turned, lights went on and off, smoke issued, and bells rang—all designed to do nothing at all—could have taken his inspiration from the protracted, useless display of diplomatic pyrotechnics in France between 1952 and 1954.

Postponement of decision was in accord with the requirements of domestic politics. For some the Defense Treaty would be acceptable if Great Britain were associated in the development of a Western European political community. But Great Britain had repeatedly refused to join in this undertaking. For others the solution lay in the association of the French Union in European organization. But for French nationalists the Union was a symbol of French stature as an independent power, not an added element in European federative efforts. Finally, lack of decision was profoundly in accord with a principle of foreign policy with which more Frenchmen were in agreement than any other: that German rearmament must be prevented, or at least postponed, or, when that proved no longer possible, at least limited and controlled. So long as no action was taken on the Defense Treaty, there could be no German army.

A decent respect for the politically deceased requires that we should mention only briefly the painful attempts made by successive French governments to "strengthen" the European Defense Community Treaty. Recurrent conversations with the British brought commitments as concrete as could reasonably have been expected. The British assured the French that they would support the Community in their own interest, that Britain would maintain close liaison with the military staff of the Community, that British troops would be maintained on the continent of Europe, that, together with the United States, Britain would aid France in case Germany should break the provisions of the treaty, or attempt to manipulate it for its own ends. These were substantial, heartening assurances. Every French delegation which heard them returned from London full of encouragement. But reasonable assurances were not enough; France wanted the unreasonable: full British membership in the Community. Was there not also an added reason for the continued pursuit of Britannia, precisely that she never could be caught? Upon a Britain repeatedly found guilty of evasion and faintheartedness the French were able to lay the blame for their own inaction.

Premier Mayer devoted the early days of his brief stay in power to drafting "protocols" to the treaty. He was aided by Georges Bidault, once again Foreign Minister in succession to Robert Schuman. Despite explicit denials by both Premier and Foreign Minister, [45] this shift introduced more subtlety and more adroitness into the negotiations

---

[45] See, for example, the speech of Premier Mayer to the American Club of Paris, as reported in *Le Monde*, March 20, 1953.

on the treaty, thus producing further delays.[46] As finally presented to the other signatories, the protocols were all too clearly designed to placate one group of opponents to the treaty by freeing France from the controls which were to be imposed on Germany and other members. No matter what their respective contributions to the common army, the relative voting strength of the various countries in the Community was not to be altered. Non-German, i.e., French, troops stationed in Germany would have special rights not accorded to German troops stationed in other Western European countries. Only France was to decide what proportion of its armed forces would be part of the international army and what proportion would be reserved for duty in the French Union. The manner of the interchange between the two was also to be a matter for exclusive determination by France. The Commissariat of the Community would be obliged to permit nations with colonies to engage in arms production for use in non-metropolitan areas.[47]

The Germans objected to the terms, as well as the tone, of some of the protocols. Also remaining was the complex question of how the acceptable protocols could be incorporated into the treaty. The official French contention was that no new treaty was needed; since the protocols were in the nature of "understandings," they could be accepted by the other signatories as such. But if they were only "understandings," how could they be made legally binding on other governments, as the French demanded? Most of 1953 was consumed in debating the precise meaning of the protocols and their probable effect, and in discussing their acceptability. Before agreement was reached, the principal author of the protocols, René Mayer, had made way for Joseph Laniel; major French opponents of the treaty had

[46] This interpretation was first aired in the United States in the author's article "French Attitudes toward Western European Unity," *International Organization*, May 1953, especially pp 199 and 210.

[47] The protocols, both lengthy and obscure, have been summarized in the French press, e.g., *Le Monde*, February 15, 1953, and in the Paris edition of the *New York Herald Tribune*, February 14, 1953.

expressed their continued hostility, protocols or no protocols; and French political leaders were off in hot pursuit of another will-o'-the-wisp: talks with the Soviet Union.[48]

In addition to British association the Socialists had insisted, as a prerequisite to agreement on the treaty, upon the creation of a European Political Community with the Saar imbedded therein.[49] The first question was "what group should organize it?" As it became clear that the prior existence of a Political Community would greatly ease passage of the Defense Treaty through the French National Assembly, a good deal of jostling for position began between advocates of the Council of Europe and the Coal and Steel Community. But in the end it was the Assembly of the Coal and Steel Community which drafted the Political Community.

Turning itself into a constituent assembly with the co-option of nine additional delegates—three each from Germany, Italy, and France—the Assembly completed a draft within six months, by March 1953. Five years of intense, sometimes brilliant, often obscure, at times counterproductive work toward the unification of Europe had finally produced not a lion, but a mouse. Furthermore, the mouse was moribund. The new organization was designed less to achieve the political unity of Europe than to serve as a roof over the Coal and Steel and Defense Communities. Not only did the draft fail to create a truly supranational structure, one independent of dictation by the participating countries, but it made movement in that direction practically impossible, since any substantial amendment

[48] What purpose, then, was served by the protocols? They preserved the reputation of Mayer and Bidault as defenders of the treaty, while avoiding a split in the government which would have come if a decision had to be reached. The protocols took off the government some of the pressure emanating from the United States without committing it to an unpopular policy of acceding to American requests. From this point of view, the very obscurity of the protocols with regard to meaning and effect was advantageous.

[49] On Socialist advocacy, see Guy Mollet, "Europe's Most Vital Unfinished Business," *The Reporter*, July 7, 1953, pp. 26-29, as well as "France and the Defense of Europe," cited.

would require unanimous approval of the Council of National Ministers.[50]

Four of the five abstentions in the constituent assembly's vote on the draft came from French delegates, three Socialists and an Independent. In addition, three Gaullist delegates declined to vote at all. Socialist leader Mollet had already quit work on the draft because he opposed the commitment to a common market, insistently pressed by the Dutch delegates. The draft was full of compromises, clearly reflecting the unwillingness of the constituent assembly to advance too fast in international cooperation, thereby risking repudiation by their governments and by popular opinion.

France, the leading light in the search for European unity, was preparing to flash its beam in a new direction. Its disillusionment had many causes: the lack of tangible progress toward European unity, the absence of Great Britain from the proposed Political Community and the presence of West Germany, the undue emphasis which French ministers and parliamentarians placed on the sacrifices required of France and their failure to stress the benefits to be derived from unification. Moreover, the characteristic weakness of the French political structure hindered progress toward European unity. No stable majority could take heart from popular support of the idea and give direction to it. France's economic ills, it appeared, could not be solved by export to an international authority; instead, more, not fewer, nationalistic safeguards seemed needed to protect the high-cost, stagnating French economy.

A strong European Political Community, it had been argued, would solve the vexing problem of the Saar. But the Community was not to be strong; the status of the Saar was still unsettled, and one more supposed pre-

[50] For an examination of the issues which lay behind the final form which the articles in the draft assumed, see Basil Karp, "The Draft Constitution for a European Political Community," *International Organization*, May 1954, pp 181-203. The draft itself has been translated into English and published by the Secretariat of the Constitutional Committee, Paris.

requisite to ratification of the Defense Community Treaty remained unsatisfied. Before the elections in November 1952, with pro-German parties outlawed, West Germany directed a barrage of propaganda at Saarlanders from across the border, urging voters to spoil their ballots. These tactics proved ineffective; less than one-quarter of the voters followed the German advice, and Saar leader Johannes Hoffmann scored a smashing victory. But for France, Hoffmann's victory was costly. Although French negotiators were able to reach a new agreement with him to replace the 1950 conventions, they were forced to grant important concessions in internal affairs of the Saar and to recognize its right to diplomatic and consular representation abroad. France conceded also the Saar's need for greater investments, for higher payments for its coal, and for more control over resources on the Franco-Saar border.

The Saarlanders for a time were satisfied, but not the Germans. From the German point of view, failing the return of the Saar to Germany, only one alternative was acceptable. That was an independent Saar in a united Europe. Thus in its economic relations Germany would be put on a par with France, and its political interests would be protected against the day when the Saarlanders would at last be permitted to choose their permanent affiliation. Part of the attraction of the Coal and Steel Community for Germany was the opportunity to develop closer economic links with the Saar, even though for a long time the French might enjoy a preferred position. If there were established only a weak Political Community, or indeed none at all, the gap between French and German points of view might grow much wider. As in other issues, priority was involved. Would the Germans, as the French wished, bind themselves to an agreement on the Saar before its "Europeanization," or would the French, as the Germans wished, permit new Saar-German relations to be determined after the European status had been attained? Throughout 1953 Franco-German negotiations went round and round on this issue. Hopefully beginning with agreement on the necessity of Europeanizing the Saar, they reached an impasse when the French demand for privileges in the area was countered by the German demand for equal treatment. The failure to reach an agreement on the Saar proved one more obstacle to ratification of the Defense Community.

Stalin's death in March 1953 resurrected French desires for an East-West conference. While *L'Humanité*, displaying a full-page, black-edged picture of the Generalissimo, bemoaned the passing of the "principal guardian of the world's peace," most Frenchmen hoped that with Stalin gone the Kremlin's peace offensive would finally show some sincerity. Ensuing statements by the new Russian triumvirate seemed to support French beliefs that anything was possible, even the dreamed-of modus vivendi, which would make German rearmament unnecessary.

Before France could explore the intentions of the Russians, however, yet another political crisis had to be surmounted. The shaky coalition of René Mayer was falling apart. By the time it was replaced by a government headed by Joseph Laniel, with durable Georges Bidault again Foreign Minister, 1953 was half over. Next the continuing reluctance of the United States to participate in a conference had to be overcome. The British, like the French, were anxious to meet, but Britain suddenly lacked political leadership when Sir Winston Churchill became temporarily incapacitated. Not until December could the Western Three get together to frame a common policy. At Bermuda, amid rumors of cleavages within the French delegation, the United States and Britain once more were subjected to the tale of France's difficulties with the European Defense Community Treaty.[51]

The three allies finally formulated a common approach to the problems of Germany and Austria at the forthcoming four-power meeting of foreign ministers in Berlin. The effect of the Berlin conference of January-February 1954 and its aftermath was to cast a pall over French hopes for a settlement with the Soviet Union. Not only did the foreign ministers make no progress on the subjects of

[51] See the communiqué of December 7, 1953, printed in Peter V. Curl, ed., *Documents on American Foreign Relations, 1953* (Harper, for the Council on Foreign Relations, 1954), pp. 216-218

Germany and Austria, but the Soviet Union proceeded to repeat its familiar maneuver aimed at splitting the Western powers, particularly separating France from the other two. Russia offered to sign a collective security pact with European countries if they would first oust non-European intruders—that is, the American forces of NATO. Reminded that at least one such pact already existed, Russia next blandly asked to be admitted to the North Atlantic Treaty Organization.

In the end it was Asian, not Russian, communism with which France had to come to terms. The site for the settlement was the Geneva conference, which was called to discuss Korea. When the conference convened in April, however, the French plight in Viet-Nam had become the center of attention. As victory plan succeeded victory plan, French fortunes had so deteriorated that its final stand in Northern Viet-Nam, at Dienbienphu, could succeed only through outright military intervention by the United States. The drain on French military strength, the sacrifices accepted as part of the cost of being a great power, the overseas commitment which had prevented acceptance of the Defense Community—all had gone for naught.

From EDC to WEU

It was only logical that, as the possibilities for procrastination and delay became exhausted, the government which had made procrastination and delay a fine art should vanish also. The longevity of Joseph Laniel's government had compensated him somewhat for the rebuff to his presidential ambitions. He had survived domestic strikes amounting almost to insurrection. He had survived German, British, American, and West European pressures to submit the Defense Community Treaty to ratification. He could not survive Dienbienphu. On June 19, 1954, Pierre Mendès-France became Premier, thus carrying on the tradition that every second government should be headed by a Radical. But there tradition stopped. When Mendès-France took over the post of Foreign Minister, he broke the hold the Mouvement Républicain Populaire had on that office, dating from the earliest days of the Fourth Republic. His program presented an even greater break with the past. All Premiers came to the National Assembly with dynamic, far-reaching plans of fundamental reform. Above all, their ideas were beautifully phrased, artfully articulated. This Premier, however, proposed action—clear, precise, related action—set against a specific time schedule. He invited the Assembly to turn him out if he did not produce results when promised. The focus of Mendès-France's decisions was to be acceptance of the inevitable. France could no longer hold North Viet-Nam; let it go. France could not afford the increasing cost necessary to keep a tight lid on Tunisia; grant autonomy in negotiation with the Tunisian nationalists. France would be at a disadvantage vis-à-vis West Germany and Great Britain in a united Europe; turn away from this goal. Above all, France could not play a great-power role when it was economically weak; give domestic economic development first priority in government attention.

It was with the fervor of personal conviction, therefore, that Mendès-France set about giving the sorely wounded Defense Community Treaty its *coup de grâce.* There was not much that was surprising in his Indo-Chinese settlement at Geneva; Laniel was probably correct in pleading with the Assembly before his government fell that he could do the job. Certainly Bidault thought so and argued to that effect with increasing bitterness. But in tackling the Defense Treaty, the new Premier was on his own in two senses. There was plenty of precedent for tinkering with the treaty, but Mendès-France proposed to eliminate from the treaty everything that looked toward establishing a real community. Furthermore, in drafting his changes, he got no help from either the former Foreign Minister or from the Foreign Ministry.

Less than two months after taking office, Mendès-France was ready with a long memorandum setting forth his ideas. Minor revisions included lengthening the time the treaty was to run, to make it coincide with NATO's forty-year span, and a declaration that the signatories desired peaceful coexistence with the Russians. Another change would have solved by fiat the elusive problem of "adequate" British and American guarantees; the terms of the treaty were to remain in effect only so long as British and American troops were stationed in Europe.[52] Other alterations destroyed completely the supranational character of the original treaty. Officers in the European army were to be controlled by the nations which assigned them. There was, indeed, to be no European army at all; integration of national units was to take place only in "forward areas" (that is, in West Germany—there would thus be no German armies in France unless France wanted them there). The provisional period, after the treaty was ratified but before its terms entered into full effect, was to be extended indefinitely from the eighteen months originally contemplated and terminated only by unanimous consent of the states involved. Even after the treaty, as thus amended, became effective, each country had the right to veto its operations for eight more years, during which no appeal to the treaty's court was to be permitted.

The Premier also took care to remove every lingering chance that a Political Community might develop out of the Defense Treaty. The Assembly established under the treaty was to be deprived of its responsibilities in this regard; further steps, if any, toward political unity were to be undertaken by the various national governments. As if afraid that his position still might be misinterpreted, Mendès-France paid his respects to the only functioning supranational organization in Europe, the High Authority of the European Coal and Steel Community, in a provision that no member of that Authority was to be eligible for appointment to the Defense Community until five years after he had resigned his position. (This shot was, of course, aimed directly at the technician of European unity,

[52] At the Bermuda conference Bidault had foreshadowed this change with the suggestion that Britain and the United States must receive approval of the Defense Community states before withdrawing their troops Bidault's proposal met with a cool reception at the time, but later was made the basis of Britain's commitment to the Western European Union.

Jean Monnet.)[53] Three Gaullists, nevertheless, temporarily quit Mendès-France's government because the Premier's alterations did not go far enough.

When Mendès-France took his treaty amendments to Brussels, the other signatories were given a Hobson's choice: a treaty mutilated beyond recognition or no treaty at all. Because Mendès-France clearly was not prepared to patch up any of the damage, the others took their stand on the treaty which they had all ratified. France was alone at Brussels, complained the Premier. French diplomacy had indeed accomplished the not inconsiderable feat of uniting West Germany with Belgium, the Netherlands, Luxembourg, and Italy, leaving France isolated.[54]

On August 30, 1954, the National Assembly interred the treaty with relative calm and dignity. The vote to end debate was 319 to 264, a plurality of fifty-five, with over forty deputies abstaining. The closeness of the vote and the fact that all the parties, except the Communists, were split, gave rise to a flood of speculation. Suppose Mendès-France had fought for the treaty; suppose the Socialist leaders had been able to enforce their pro-treaty position on the rank and file of their party. Entertaining ideas, undoubtedly, but hardly productive. The Radicals were split almost in half, as they had been since their leaders Herriot and Daladier fired withering blasts at the treaty two years earlier. The Socialist party was also split down the middle. This, considering the discipline usually exhibited by its members, attested to the conviction of many Socialists that the treaty contained none of the prerequisites demanded by their party. Almost two-thirds of the members of smaller, independent blocs supported the treaty, as did all but two of the Catholics voting. On the other hand, only sixteen Gaullists cast favorable votes.

[53] Mendès-France's proposed amendments are summarized in the *New York Times*, August 14, 15, 1954.

[54] This applies not only to the government of Mendès-France. After September 1952, when both Radicals and Socialists split over the treaty, French policy-makers were powerless to effect the changes which could have produced Assembly approval, while being unwilling to submit the treaty without these changes.

It is easy, too easy, to say that a non-Communist majority favored the treaty, or even to conclude, with the MRP, that a national referendum would have revealed a popular majority. The narrow margin of defeat of the treaty in truth reflected the depth of the divisions in France on matters of foreign policy.

The discarding of EDC left a vacuum in European affairs. Its fate, said Dr. Thomas Dehler, head of the West German Free Democratic party, "is a sentence of death on the European Coal and Steel Community, which cannot live on as a torso."[55] Something had to be put in its place and speedily, else the French would face a situation far more distasteful than membership in a defense community —the rearmament of West Germany under Anglo-American auspices. The formula was found by Anthony Eden, reportedly in his bath.[56] Like many brilliant ideas, the remedy was simple—to broaden the 1948 Brussels Pact through the addition of West Germany and Italy and to link it with the North Atlantic Treaty Organization. Although the prescription was simple, the details of application were complicated. All the old arrangements, undertakings, and commitments had to be redrawn in new form: American and British guarantees to Europe, German declarations of good intentions, Western rights and duties in Germany, a Franco-German understanding on the Saar, all these in addition to the changes in the Brussels and North Atlantic Treaties themselves.

On hand in London was Secretary of State John Foster Dulles to threaten and to promise, an American posture familiar to France since November 1950. The European Recovery Program and the North Atlantic Treaty Organization, said Dulles, were all part of an American policy of promoting the unification of Europe. In the present circumstances the United States could not see its way to making a commitment such as it had volunteered to the

---

[55] A remark quoted, significantly enough, by the *Bulletin* of the Community itself, High Authority, ECSC, Information Service, *Bulletin from the European Community for Coal and Steel*, no. 1 (Luxembourg, November 1954) pp. 4-5.

[56] *Life*, November 15, 1954, p. 176.

European Defense Community. Then the Secretary produced a sentence which would have earned him the championship in any oratorical marathon. He said:

If, using the Brussels Treaty as a nucleus, it is possible to find in this new pattern a continuing hope of unity among the countries of Europe that are represented here, and if the hopes that were tied into the European Defense Community Treaty can reasonably be transferred into the arrangements which will be the outgrowth of this meeting, then I would be disposed to recommend to the President that he should renew the assurance offered last spring in connection with the European Defense Community Treaty to the effect that the United States will continue to maintain in Europe, including Germany, such units of its armed forces as may be necessary and appropriate to contribute its fair share of the forces needed for the joint defense of the North Atlantic area while a threat to the area exists, and will continue to deploy such forces in accordance with agreed North Atlantic strategy for the defense of this area [57]

Also present in London was Foreign Secretary Anthony Eden, who assured the success of the conference by making what many have described as a history-making pronouncement:

The United Kingdom will continue to maintain on the mainland of Europe, including Germany, the effective strength of the United Kingdom forces now assigned to SACEUR [Supreme Allied Command, Europe], four divisions and the tactical air force, or whatever SACEUR regards as equivalent fighting capacity.

The United Kingdom undertakes not to withdraw those forces against the wishes of the majority of the Brussels Treaty powers, who should take their decision in the knowledge of SACEUR's views.

This understanding would be subject to the understanding that an acute overseas emergency might oblige Her Majesty's Government to omit this procedure.

If the maintenance of United Kingdom forces on the mainland of Europe throws at any time too heavy a strain on the external

[57] *New York Times*, October 4, 1954.

finances of the United Kingdom, the United Kingdom will invite the North Atlantic Council to review the financial conditions on which the formations are maintained.[58]

Careful comparison of what Eden actually said with what professional enthusiasts inferred he meant hardly justifies the appellation "history-making." Rather, the statement was "history-repeating." Britain had already promised to maintain forces on the European continent and in Germany. The present undertaking not to withdraw them was subject to three qualifications adequate to cover every possible contingency. First, the Brussels powers had to take their decision in the light of SACEUR's views. Secondly, an overseas emergency, so declared by Britain, not by the Brussels powers, would leave the former free to re-deploy its troops without obtaining approval from the others.[59] Finally, if the commitment placed too great a strain on Britain, the North Atlantic Council, not the Brussels powers, was to decide what modifications in the assignment of its armed forces Britain could make. The plain fact, of course, was that Great Britain was already as deeply involved in military affairs on the continent as the center of a world-embracing Commonwealth and Empire felt it could afford to be.

Why, then, was Eden's declaration accepted as epochal? By some because they wished thereby to convince the French that one of the uncertainties which had led to the defeat of the Defense Community Treaty had been clarified. By the French because they wished to be convinced. Having done to death the EDC, they had little option, as Dulles made very clear, but to accept the proffered alternative with as good grace as they could muster. If the coating of Eden's words made the pill of German rearmament sweeter to the taste, they would have served their purpose.

The chain of agreements reached in London and Paris

[58] Same.
[59] An early precedent for any British emergency was provided by France when in May 1955 it dispatched to North Africa a division previously assigned to duty in Europe in the emergency created by Algerian unrest.

began with the adaptation of the Brussels Pact to provide for the adherence of West Germany and Italy. Western Europe was returning to its starting point in the search for regional security. Under the changed circumstances the original preamble to the Brussels Pact, which mentioned a possible renewal of German aggression, had to be changed; the new wording could be read as a new path to a familiar destination. Now, the pact had, as one of its purposes, "to promote the unity and to encourage the progressive integration of Europe." The signatories to the Brussels Pact were to set the *maximum* contribution which they would make to NATO, it being understood that the German armament level would be that contemplated under the defunct Defense Community. An "arms control" agency was to be established to supervise the national stocks of various weapons, and to see that Germany fulfilled its promise "not to manufacture in its territory any atomic weapons, chemical weapons, or biological weapons" of the types listed. This unilateral undertaking by Chancellor Adenauer had been necessary to win the consent of Mendès-France to the accords.

In linking the Brussels Treaty to NATO, the conferees granted Adenauer one of his long-standing demands, participation in the North Atlantic Pact. No other course would in fact have been possible without making the Brussels Treaty precisely the instrument controlling only Germany which France had hoped to make out of the Defense Community. The new arrangement extended the authority of SACEUR to all NATO forces except those specifically excluded. SACEUR and NATO were to determine the mode of deployment of these forces, but should NATO decide that more armed forces were needed than the levels established by the Brussels states, it had to obtain their approval. As a slight genuflection to the memory of EDC, the forces were to be "integrated as far as possible consistent with military efficiency."

Related engagements were exchanged between Germany and the three Western powers. The latter promised that henceforth their High Commissioners were to act, so far as possible, as though the occupation were ended and the new statute signed. They agreed also that the Federal Republic, being the only legally constituted German government, was entitled to speak for all Germany and that the achievement of German unity "through peaceful means" remained a "fundamental goal of their policy." Consequently, they would continue to maintain their troops in Berlin and would regard any attack on that city as an attack on themselves. In return West Germany agreed to act in accordance with the principles of the United Nations Charter. More important was its promise to "refrain from any action inconsistent with the strictly defensive character of the two treaties [Brussels and North Atlantic]. In particular the German Federal Republic undertakes never to have recourse to force to achieve the reunification of Germany or the modification of the present boundaries of the German Federal Republic, and to resolve by peaceful means any disputes which may arise between the Federal Republic and other states."

But the French had heard German promises before; they wanted guarantees of good behavior. What they got was a sort of up-dated Locarno Treaty, which was to apply to eastern as well as to western boundaries of the Federal Republic. This was more than they had been able to obtain between the two World Wars; better yet was the return of the United States as guarantor, a position repudiated after World War I. Britain, France, and the United States warned Germany, without naming it, that:

They will regard as a threat to their own peace and safety any recourse to force which, in violation of the principles of the United Nations Charter, threatens the integrity and unity of the Atlantic Alliance or its defensive purposes. In the event of any such action, the three governments, for their part, will consider *the offending government as having forfeited its rights to any guarantee and any military assistance provided for in the North Atlantic Treaty and its protocols.* They will act in accordance with Article 4 of the North Atlantic Treaty with a view to taking other measures which may be appropriate.[60]

[60] This and other quotations given above may be found in the *New York Times*, October 4, 1954.

Finally, Premier Mendès-France was also on hand in London to argue the need for more rigid controls in the new agreements. The French leader, whose protocols to the Defense Community Treaty would have removed all its supranational aspects, now sought to smuggle many of them into the new agreements. He may, with some justice, have reasoned that an Assembly majority against EDC could easily become a majority against the revised Brussels Pact, since opposition to both was based on a single issue: German rearmament. On the other hand, he might ease the Brussels Pact over the parliamentary hurdle by adding a dash of EDC, thus satisfying the supporters of both treaties.

It cannot be said, however, that the Premier's efforts, either in London or Paris, were notably successful. He could argue and complain, but he could not insist. To his plea that the arms-control agency to be established under the Brussels Treaty should have charge of distributing all American military aid, the United States gave a flat *no*. His proposal that this agency should regulate as well as observe armament production, a central feature of the Defense Community, was shunted aside; a committee was set up to look into the idea. Mendès-France also wished to revive the EDC plan for common European military training-schools, but this too was turned down. Lastly, the French Premier sought to resurrect the fundamental principle of EDC, the integration of European arms at a level lower than an army group. At London he obtained only the "military efficiency" formula already quoted, a formula that was repeated in the ensuing Paris negotiations.

One agreement Mendès-France had to obtain before any of the others could possibly pass the French parliament. This was a settlement of the dispute with Germany over the status of the Saar. Its Europeanization was the only basis of accord. Article 1 of the draft agreement, therefore, gave the territory an "international" status, and Article 2 provided for the appointment of a neutral High Commissioner by the expanded Ministerial Council of the Brussels Treaty, replacing the one hitherto named by

France. He was to take over former French responsibilities in the fields of defense and foreign policy. The economic ties between France and the Saar were to continue, but gradually West Germany was to be accorded an equal status. Saarlanders, finally, were to be permitted to accept or reject their new status in a plebiscite. In the campaign for the first time groups advocating reunion with Germany were to be permitted to agitate openly for their point of view.

Significance of the Paris Agreements

While it might be argued that any agreement between France and Germany over the Saar was a step forward, the latest effort was defective in several respects. France had surrendered too much to be happy about the result, and Germany's gains only whetted its appetite for complete victory. So long as France retained some semblance of control over the Saar, trouble was likely to continue. As a solution to the status of the Saar, European federation was still popular; indeed the modified Brussels Treaty was given the title "Western European Union." But in the new series of arrangements the formula was emptied of content, leaving the title bitterly ironic. No organization in which Great Britain was a full participant could hope to develop into a political community.

Thus the European Coal and Steel Community was left all alone, a situation which its founders had never envisaged. It had been designed to be part of a movement toward the integration of Western Europe. So long as that movement continued, it perhaps did not matter greatly that the ECSC control of the European coal and steel industries was far from complete or that its limited powers must remain ineffective until related policies of the participating states had been brought within its purview. The Community, then, was to have been a beginning. Actually it provided a shrine for the ideal of a federated Europe; it was in danger of becoming a mausoleum. Fearing this outcome, Jean Monnet resigned as head of the High Authority in order to use his prestige and influence to rekindle French faith in a united Europe.

It was far from clear whether Mendès-France, in turning abruptly away from the previous policy of "building Europe," was following the desires of a majority of the French people or of their deputies. He had acted, as he explained nine days before his investiture as Premier, in the conviction that economic strength was the indispensable foundation on which to build French influence in international affairs. Having made his choice, however, he still had to place his government behind the London and Paris accords. In doing so he showed none of the enthusiasm necessary to win the support of the Assembly. France, said the Premier, was alone in London as it had been in Brussels. Its Western allies were prepared to rearm Germany, with or without French approval. Later, Socialist Guy Mollet spoke even more precisely. He explained to his Assembly colleagues, and especially to members of the MRP, why he, like they, having voted for EDC, was now, unlike they, about to support the new accords. The United States, he said, wanted Germany rearmed, and the United States was the protector of France in Europe.

France may have had little choice in the matter of German rearmament, but its endorsement of the Brussels Pact brought another strong American guarantee and, above all, British participation. "We shall be seven instead of six," Mendès-France told his countrymen. "We were afraid that the price of *rapprochement* with Germany was the drawing away of England. We shall not have to pay this price. We shall reconcile ourselves with Germany without separating ourselves from England." In any event, putting the best face possible on the whole affair, "the military aspect of European unification is not the essential thing, far from it"; the Brussels Pact contained some economic clauses, half forgotten to be sure, but there all the same.[61] In a final revelation of its true feelings, the National Assembly voted once more against rearming Ger-

[61] *New York Times*, October 3, 1954.

many. But the deputies were trapped beyond possibility of further evasion and knew it. Four years after the Assembly had accepted the Pleven Plan as a scheme to prevent the resurrection of a German army, it accepted Germany's membership in NATO by margins of little more than thirty votes, 289 to 251 and 287 to 256.

The end of the era of procrastination, obfuscation, and vacillation did not come easily. Paul Reynaud, fiery advocate of a united Europe, won more applause than was his wont when he declared that France's retreat from its earlier leadership toward this goal would weaken Chancellor Adenauer's pro-Western position and that France would find Europe controlled militarily by a nationalistic Germany and politically by Great Britain.[62] In the same vein Jacques Soustelle had the day before launched an even more devastating attack.[63] The controls over Germany, he said, were so weak that they would vanish as soon as East-West tension rose. Inside NATO the combination of Germany and the United States would set French policies at naught. Finally, by admitting West Germany, a country with territorial ambitions, NATO had for the first time become an aggressive instrument.[64]

Mendès-France was able to shepherd the agreements past the National Assembly, but he was no longer in power when they were submitted to the Council of the Republic. His popularity with the deputies had been in reverse proportion to his popularity with the United States. In the legislature opposition finally coalesced in the battle over the budget. It focused also on the Premier's failure to fulfill one of his many promises, the negotiation of a settlement with the Tunisian nationalists. It was a new, and more conciliatory government, put together by fellow Radical Edgar Faure, which went before the Council, requesting approval of the London and Paris accords. Significantly enough, the new Cabinet was far from enthusiastic

---

[62] Same, December 22, 1954.
[63] Which might be said to contain elements of hypocrisy, or at least of inconsistency, since Soustelle and his Gaullist group had fought against EDC as too supranational.
[64] Same, December 21, 1954.

about the policy which it was now officially sponsoring. In the vote of December 20, 1954, eleven of its members voted for the admission of West Germany to NATO, six against, and six, including new Foreign Minister Antoine Pinay, abstained. The Faure coalition maintained one strong policy connection with its predecessor, with the National Assembly, and with the Council of the Republic. After ratification of the agreements Mendès-France had declared in Washington and in the National Assembly that there must be new talks with the Soviet. Approval of the agreements will lead directly to new talks with the Soviet Union, echoed Antoine Pinay in the Council of the Republic.

For gloomy French parliamentarians this was perhaps the most appealing note which could have been struck. Perhaps France might be saved at the eleventh hour. Perhaps a modus vivendi with Russia might actually forestall a new German army. A sweet dream in which to forget years of humiliation and defeat!

Part Two

SELF-DESTRUCTION OF THE FOURTH REPUBLIC THROUGH "IMMOBILISME": 1954-1958

Chapter Four

THE POLITICAL BASIS OF "IMMOBILISME"

DID THE SEVEN MONTHS and seventeen days of Mendès-France's regime mark a new beginning, or only an aberration in the general policy of drift under the Fourth Republic? With the advantage of hindsight, Mendès' *Gouverner C'est Choisir*[1] looms up as an attempt to deal consistently with the jumbled mass of France's foreign and domestic crises. By 1954 the situation was such that decisions could no longer be avoided even though the immediate consequences of each decision might be bad. Mendès proposed to cut down on external commitments in order to buy time. By concentrating on domestic reform he hoped to revive national strength so that France could then play the part of a great power. As it turned out, his government paid a heavy price for disengagement abroad, but was unable then to proceed with indispensable reconstruction at home.

The reason was very simple. The "system," which had proved too strong for De Gaulle's Rassemblement du Peuple Français, also dragged down Mendès-France. To the same problems the "system" posed another answer, the reverse of that of the Radical leader. The *immobilisme* which followed his downfall had a certain logic, particularly since the sacrifices which Mendès-France had made provided it with a foundation. The three and a half years

---

[1] V. 1 (Paris: Julliard, 1953), and v. 2, *Sept Mois et Dix-Sept Jours* (Paris: Julliard, 1955).

which ended on June 1, 1958, appear, in retrospect, as the final flowering of the Fourth Republic. The "system," reflecting contradictory aspirations of the French people, balanced or teetered between vested interests, between antagonistic pressures, leading to immobility as the natural, expected, and even desired consequence. The political ingredients of the "system" both expressed and perpetuated the cleavages within France. Seemingly impermeable to intrusion from without, it blew up only under the most peculiar and yet most predictable of circumstances—a revolt by Frenchmen outside the *Métropole*.

In order to understand the French foreign policy aspect of *immobilisme*, and the situation which De Gaulle inherited, we must first analyze the political mechanics of the "system." Since any label attached to three and a half years of a nation's history is necessarily an oversimplification, three important exceptions to *immobilisme* will be noted here, each to be considered later in detail. One of these is the remarkable increase in economic output, fostered by the state investment plan continued during the period. A second is the new policy toward the Overseas Territories which France adopted tentatively in April 1955, and irrevocably in 1956. This exception was, of course, a delayed consequence of changes in approach toward Tunisia and Morocco adopted by Mendès-France and Edgar Faure. A third exception is the French initiative in the drafting and ratification of the Euratom and Common Market Treaties. Ostensibly an unexpected resumption of the movement toward a United Europe, this policy was, in fact, not inconsistent with the basic tenets of *immobilisme*.

The Elections of 1956

The pattern of *immobilisme* was firmly fixed by the elections of January 2, 1956. The electoral battle was particularly bitter because of the split within Radical-Socialist ranks and the sudden upsurge of Pierre Poujade's Union et Fraternité Française (UFF), till then a localized revolt by small shopkeepers against paying taxes. Because of the emotional memories attached to the Macmahon precedent, the dissolution of the National Assembly by Premier Edgar Faure was in itself a dramatic beginning to the campaign. Faure's predissolution maneuvering added fuel to the fire. He had called the elections to prevent Mendès-France, who had now captured control of the Radical-Socialist party, from similarly consolidating his position with the Radical electorate. Faure had also prevented the Assembly from agreeing on any new electoral law, believing that any change would work to the detriment of his wing of the Radicals and of the alliances his followers were prepared to make with other groups of the Center and Right.

These circumstances accentuated the tendency of parties actually close together in political outlook to magnify their differences and to engage in personal vendettas. Poujade's French version of "Know-Nothingism" attacked parliamentary government violently, while the fear of losing a portion of their precious electoral clientele forced other parties, particularly those of the Right, to compete, albeit in more measured tones. Consequently, constitutional revision figured prominently in the political platforms of all groups, whether or not they stood to gain from the continuance of the Fourth Republic, whether or not they were angered by the dissolution of the Assembly. The formation of large Center-Left and Center-Right electoral blocs heightened the illusion that the French voter was being asked to make some crucial choices. Actually, "persuaded that the French electors of 1956, like their predecessors, were concerned with internal policy, that they were little interested in Overseas problems and still less in international politics, [the parties] did not put forth the efforts which were necessary to make them aware of the harsh realities of the present situation."[2]

When the dust had settled, 44 deputies sat in the new Assembly on the antiparliamentary Right (Poujade's UFF) and 145 on the equally antidemocratic Left, a gain for the

[2] Georges Dupeux, "Les Plates-Formes des Partis" in Maurice Duverger, François Goguel, and Jean Touchard, eds., *Les Élections du 2 Janvier 1956* (Paris Colin, 1957), p. 66.

Communists of 50 seats. Badly squeezed on both sides, the diminished center of the political pie had to be shared by groups which, yesterday locked in bitter battle, were today doomed to cooperate in maintaining the system. Although the Gaullist Social Republicans all but disappeared, and the Catholic Mouvement Républicain Populaire suffered some losses, the significant fact was the stability of the electoral base on which the democratic parties rested and hence of their representation in the National Assembly. Individuals, not lists, had figured conspicuously in the competition; as a result there were relatively few new faces,[3] and the average age of the deputies was older than under the Third Republic.[4]

The French voters had elected an Assembly openly committed either to abolishing or to altering the system; at the same time the republican elements within it were exactly the same as those of its predecessor. Mendès-France had not been able to reform France as Prime Minister; as party chieftain he had not succeeded in moving all the Radicals to the Left. *Immobilisme* was the natural product of the mountainous movement of parliamentary dissolution.

The political mechanics of *immobilisme* promptly reasserted themselves after the January 1956 elections. The system continued to rest on the same four pillars: divisions within parliamentary groups, balanced representation of conflicting viewpoints and stable individual positions within the executive, a series of stylized cabinet crises settling nothing, and a permanent administrative apparatus at once all-pervasive and unable to make good the lack of political direction. The erosion of these pillars may be traced through the short-lived coalitions of Maurice Bourgès-Maunoury and Félix Gaillard, which followed the long and supremely immobile tenure of Guy Mollet. It may be measured in the duration and severity

---

[3] See Duverger and others, cited, p. 449, for table.
[4] Mattei Dogan and Peter Campbell, "Le Personnel Ministériel en France et en Grande-Bretagne," pt. 2, *Revue Française de Science Politique* October-December 1957, p. 802.

of the crises which ensued after the fall of each of these three cabinets.

Divided Parliamentary Groups

Because of the large antidemocratic vote in the Assembly, each cabinet had to muster heavy majorities within four groups: Socialists, Radicals, MRP, and Independents. While the Independents, led by Roger Duchet, had built up a loose federation for electoral purposes, most of the deputies remained divided into small cliques, in some instances representing interest groupings, in others personal followings. At one extreme they were close to the antiparliamentary position of the original Gaullist RPF, at the other to the type of support for the Fourth Republic represented by Antoine Pinay. Their common denominator was a determination to prosecute the war in Algeria, their opposition to economic *dirigisme,* and their fear of a revived Popular Front combining Socialists, Communists, and Mendésistes. The rightward drift of the Fourth Republic had brought the Independents to prominence as a source of premiers and ministers without producing in them any unity of positive purpose. *Immobilisme* was for them a necessary objective.

The failure of Mendès-France to impose discipline on the Radicals had left their party even more deeply split. Although at their 1956 party congress Mendès-France had been able, with the aid of Édouard Herriot, to beat down several threats to his authority and force the exclusion of Edgar Faure, André Morice, who had led the fight against Mendès-France, walked out, taking his colleagues with him.[5] The political foundations on which Mendès stood then disintegrated rapidly. By May 1957, having quit the Mollet government, Mendès found himself in direct opposition to those Radicals who were still in the cabinet, notably, to Bourgès-Maunoury, Minister of National Defense and future Premier, René Billères, Minister of National Education, and Maurice Faure, Under Secretary

---

[5] See *L'Année Politique,* 1956, (Paris Éditions du Grand Siècle), pp 91-94, for summary of the Congress

of Foreign Affairs. The main quarrel was over the "hard" line in Algeria, adopted by Mollet after his visit there in February 1956, and executed by his fellow Socialist, Resident Minister Robert Lacoste. After the Radicals' steering committee, also in May, refused by a vote of 17 to 15 to exclude two deputies who had failed to follow Mendès-France in opposing Mollet, once more on Algerian policy, the Radical leader resigned as first vice-president of the party. The shrunken body of Mendésistes, between 12 and 15, retreated into a comfortable posture of opposition and ideological purity, leaving the traditional Radicals to continue their role of providing cabinet ministers. In a few months Mendésisme had declined from a dynamic movement to an impotent clique.

The system was also corroding the MRP and the Socialists. The Catholics had long been torn between the liberal doctrine advanced by the MRP militants and the behavior of rightist governments in which their deputies participated. In the campaign of 1956 the Mouvement Républicain Populaire had had the delicate task of explaining why it had continued to join conservative government coalitions. Its only answer, not a very satisfying one, was that it had done so to protect the Republic against its enemies on the Left and Right, while continuing to press its own social and economic proposals. Forced to the Right by Mendès, cemented there by conservative governments, many members of the MRP were also restive over the same issue which had disrupted the Radicals—the campaign of repression in Algeria. The festering sore was a long time in bursting, but when it came the result was dramatic. On May 23, 1958, for the only time under the Fourth Republic, the members of a political party refused to participate in a government one of their own leaders was seeking to form. After a four-hour discussion, the MRP deputies, senators, and members of the executive committee voted 28 to 25, with two abstentions, not to follow Georges Bidault. Henceforth the MRP was split into two groups: the "regulars" and the supporters of Bidault.

The Socialists were no more united than the Radicals or the MRP in confronting the Algerian problem. If anything, the undercurrent of criticism was even more severe, for the Section Française de l'Internationale Ouvrière (SFIO) was responsible in Algeria for policies hardly compatible with the tenets of French or any other brand of socialism. Contrary to the situation of the Radicals and MRP, party leadership remained in the same hands, those of Guy Mollet, once known as leader of the "doctrinal" wing. However, the pattern of resignations and exclusions was similar. The directing committee of the SFIO underlined the divisions within the party by taking an unusual step: circulation of a memorandum to all secretaries of federations and to all deputies asking them not to collaborate with the *Tribune du Socialisme,* organ of the minority, which included such prominent Socialists as Daniel Mayer and André Philip.[6] After his own ministry had fallen, Mollet undertook to bring about a gradual shift in the Socialist position on Algeria by giving more leeway to his own critics. When the Gaillard Cabinet collapsed, Mollet announced that the Socialists would remain outside the new government, the implied reason being to exclude Lacoste from the coalition, after which the party's "leftist" façade could be restored. In May 1958 Mollet consented to become Vice-Premier under Pierre Pflimlin, ostensibly to protect the Republic against the Algerian rebels and the Gaullists, only, as it turned out, to use his key position to smooth the way to power for De Gaulle.

Under the circumstances government coalitions had to be pasted together, not merely from parties within the Assembly, but from various factions within the parties. As the Fourth Republic evolved, the distinction between "government" and "opposition" became increasingly blurred,[7] with the emergence of overlapping groups of "government men" and "executive supporters." Within the Assembly a potential premier of whatever political color-

---

[6] *Le Monde,* February 25, 1958.
[7] See Stanley Hoffmann, "Politique d'Abord," *Esprit,* December 1957, pp. 813-833.

ation could find deputies eager to form part of his team and even more deputies ready to vote for his investiture. Although four nominees failed of investiture in the crisis between the regimes of René Mayer and Joseph Laniel, 163 deputies had voted for five of the six premiers-designate and 35 for all of them.[8] The existence of a band of potential cabinet members meant that success or failure in forming a cabinet turned less and less on matters of policy and more and more on personal skill in playing the parliamentary game to accommodate slight shifts in clique behavior.

Conflicting Groups within the Executive

The instability of governments was combined with a degree of stability in the composition of their cabinets. Over time certain groups came to have a kind of lien on particular posts, and the same was true of individual deputies. A member of a peasant group was a logical choice as Minister of Agriculture, while Édouard Bonnefous of the Rassemblement des Gauches Républicains became a fixture as Minister of Transport. Several other ministries, such as National Education, Industry and Commerce, and Public Works, also remained outside the range of Assembly gunfire.[9] Normally, deputies chosen for these posts were not party leaders.[10] Party leaders controlling votes, even of only a handful of deputies, were most useful to a cabinet-maker in the offices of the vice-premier or minister of state.[11] The number of these vague posts which an incoming premier found it necessary to create served as a measure of the range of marginal groups he was seeking to conciliate.

Such was the uneasy foundation of division and stability upon which successive cabinets rested. It also set the limits of action to which each government, and especially its

[8] Philip Williams, "Compromise and Crisis in French Politics," *Political Science Quarterly*, September 1957, p. 325
[9] For a study of these points, see same, pp 126-141.
[10] Raymond Aron, "Electeurs, Partis, et Élus," *Revue Française de Science Politique*, April-June 1955, p. 263.
[11] Dogan and Campbell, cited, p 341.

premier, had to conform if it was to survive. One way to avoid disruption was to avoid policy decisions as long as possible; in this art Pinay, Mayer, and Laniel had proven themselves past masters. The National Assembly could harass executives and destroy them. It could not, however, lay down a coherent policy, much less enforce it on the executive. When delay and procrastination gave rise to mounting criticism, another familiar tactic was to apply simultaneously bits and pieces of contradictory policies. One advantage to a hard-pressed premier was that this device gave different segments of responsibility to individual ministers representing divergent points of view. "Pacification and Force" was an attractive slogan for Algeria, as was "Autonomy and Integration," for the problems of Overseas France.

To avoid clashes over the assignment of coveted ministerial posts, a premier could take charge of them himself or entrust them to party members of the same clique. The first of these devices was not one the framers of the constitution of the Fourth Republic had envisaged when they undertook to strengthen the position of the premier as leader of the executive by inserting the provision, later discarded, for the initial investiture of the premier by the National Assembly before he had formed his cabinet. But the crisis of the parliamentary regime mounted, both practices became more common, particularly in the three ministries of Foreign Affairs, Overseas France, and National Defense. Down to 1954 the Ministries of Foreign Affairs and Overseas France had been particularly stable and even the Ministry of National Defense, after the ejection of the Communists from government participation in 1947, relatively so.

However he composed his cabinet, the premier still had to act as conciliator within the coalition. For a premier, as for his American counterparts, it was an advantage not to have been publicly associated with strongly stated convictions. Because of the perennial gap between government income and expenses and the heavy burden of the military establishment, ministers of national defense were constantly at loggerheads with ministers of finance. Only the premier could hope to arbitrate, temporarily easing the conflict. A more attractive alternative was to give way to both demands, resorting to expedients to cover the budgetary deficit.

When intracoalition conflicts could not be avoided, adjusted, or postponed, a premier could turn to several other devices in his efforts to hold on to power. He could appeal to cabinet solidarity against outside pressures, whether by the Assembly, party groupings, or special interests. Obviously, the efficacy of this maneuver depended on whether the premier could forestall intracabinet conflicts before they had actually hardened into firm positions, publicly known, on which individual prestige and reputations had been staked. Executive solidarity was of course a rare and ephemeral plant, but for it, especially in the Fourth Republic's last years, there was the potent argument that the next crisis would be one, not of a particular coalition, but of the system itself.

Alternatively, a premier could attempt to mobilize outside support against positions taken by individual ministers, or he could, like Pinay and Mendès-France, go further by appealing to the country at large against the National Assembly. He could use these tactics only within narrow limits, however, because of the risks to the coalition from inviting the intrusion of outside forces and because of the small number of groups to which the premier could appeal. Relatively cohesive elements like the SFIO and the MRP could, on occasion, temper the behavior of "their" representatives in the cabinet, if not for objective reasons of policy, at least to postpone a crisis from which they saw no discernible profit. The Radicals, after the decline of Mendès-France, were a less dependable body, while the Independents, as their ranks grew in political influence and consequent appetite for office, indulged in active infighting for ministerial advantage.

As a last resort, a premier could dissociate himself and his cabinet from conflicts which he was unable to resolve. If the coalition remained hopelessly divided, he could in effect throw the problem at the legislature, refusing to associate the government with any particular outcome. The ministers, freed from the requirement of cabinet solidarity, which they had not recognized anyway, could then be absent, abstain, or vote their "individual consciences." However, since few legislative actions are self-executing, the number of issues on which the premier could shrug off executive responsibility was limited and tended to result in "do-nothing" decisions. Perhaps the most spectacular example was Mendès-France's decision, taken in the absence of governmental unity, to separate the fate of his government from that of the European Defense Community Treaty, leaving the treaty's burial to the National Assembly.

Within each coalition conflicts arose inevitably out of the nature of the parties and the National Assembly. By definition *immobilisme* concentrated on "resolving" conflicts by tactical means, without taking strategic or long-range action. A premier's investiture address was less a program of intended policy than a device to put together a majority in the Assembly. The same questions persisted from one government to the next. A politically attractive premier was one without strong commitments, a mediator of intraministerial conflicts, a Mr. Micawber, hoping against hope that something would turn up. As problems grew more acute, they also became more tightly intermeshed. Any decision to balance the budget, for example, meant either levying new taxes and collecting the old ones more rigorously, or cutting back expenditures. But action in either direction would have many grave consequences, from reducing the level of government investment to reducing protection for sugar-beet growers. Fiscal action or inaction likewise affected directly the relations between France and its European partners in trade matters and between France and the United States on such issues as the North Atlantic Treaty Organization and American financial and military assistance. Small wonder that increasingly meagre results were hidden by increasingly grandiose promises.

Weighed down by so many complex and unsolved problems, successive governments struggled in a state of perpetual crisis. The coalition presided over by young and able Radical Socialist, Félix Gaillard, offers a typical fever chart. In early December 1957, his Cabinet was on the verge of breaking up from within, over the issue of price increases which were opposed by the Socialist ministers. By late February 1958, his Cabinet again was tottering, this time over the proposed reform of the constitution. But only in April, after having endured as long as the average cabinet under the Fourth Republic, did his Cabinet finally fall over the Algerian issue.

Nature of Government Crises

Since death of any government was foreordained, funeral preparations never waited on its actual demise. One of the least edifying spectacles of the Fourth Republic was the maneuvering of political groups, before and during a ministerial crisis, to extract maximum profit from it. Their behavior assumed such Byzantine subtlety as to defy complete analysis. Four major forces were particularly involved in this intricate game: the Premier, the political parties, the Assembly, and the President of the Republic. Each of the first three had a paramount concern to enter and leave a cabinet crisis with reputation enhanced and position improved, or at the least not significantly damaged. All accepted the premise that any particular government would be brought down. The question was one of timing the crisis so that someone else would have to bear the onus for its fall. A second premise was that a crisis, once produced, must continue for some undefined period before it could be "resolved," thus allowing time for a trial of strength between political groups. The terms of play and the actions of the players had very little to do with the merits either of the issue which had presumably caused the crisis or of proposed solutions.

Although viewed with alarm outside France, the inevitable crisis was not necessarily a "bad thing." It enabled an outgoing premier to force upon the National Assembly the blame for a deteriorating situation, for actions not taken, policies left unimplemented, upon his successor the task of dealing with the issues he had been unable to settle; upon the institutions of government the necessity of resorting to decree laws and administrative orders in the absence of legislative measures. The parties could make minor adjustments in their political façades, seek stronger control over deputies and ministers, and indulge again in a fascinating game of skill and chance. The National Assembly as an institution could reassert its primacy in government by recapturing an authority it would soon have to delegate again, temporarily, to another coalition. Staying too long in office might deprive a premier of the chance in the near future to form another government or even to assume an important ministerial position. Antoine Pinay, Joseph Laniel, and Guy Mollet were examples of premiers who hung on too long. Laniel and Mollet, whose governments enjoyed particular longevity, formed shifting majorities to win numerous confidence votes; when they finally departed, their very success had alienated practically all the "government groups" in the Assembly, including and especially members of their own parties. Recognizing the danger of manipulating the Assembly once too often, a premier might prefer to seek a propitious moment to step down by forcing a vote which he knew he could not win, by resigning when not actually defeated by a majority of the Assembly on a vote of confidence, or even, as in the case of Pierre Pflimlin in May 1958, by quitting after a vote which he had won.

The delicately poised balance of conflicting forces, once upset, could only be re-created by the skill and political acumen of the President of the Republic. Publicly he had to be in favor of a quick resolution of the crisis, although he knew that it would take time to cajole the disparate political groups, like balky horses, back into the shafts. At least one group could usually be charged with formal responsibility for the crisis, and at the same time shown it had no chance of leading the next coalition, by asking its leader to sound out the situation or even to try his hand at forming a cabinet. Because of its influential and negative role in a delicately balanced Assembly, the Social Republican party and its leader Jacques Soustelle were sometimes selected for this thankless task. Another tactic was for the president to entrust a party leader with a "technical mission" or a "mission of information." Ideally, the maximum and minimum demands of each group would thereby become known to the others, while the prestige of the emissary would not be involved in a failure to form a new coalition. In three successive crises, following the downfall of the Mollet, Bourgès-Maunoury, and Gaillard cabinets, René Pleven, whose small Union Démocratique et Socialiste de la Résistance (UDSR) was centrally situated in the Assembly, was entrusted with exploratory missions by President René Coty. While none of them caused Pleven to become premier himself, they did smooth the way for the successful candidate.

As a last resort, the thirst of the Assembly for victims could be slaked by finding politicians willing to seek investiture from its hostile ranks, accepting defeat in advance. At this stage, as in all others, dangerous pitfalls awaited the unwary. A premier-designate who was presented as "constructive sacrifice" to legislative appetites, might actually triumph because some deputies, expecting others to wield the knife, sought to enhance their reputations and availability for future cabinet positions by voting for investiture. As a result, an "accidental" premier, such as Antoine Pinay reputedly was, might emerge. The reverse was also possible. A prospective premier, finally selected because his chances appeared good, might be rejected by the Assembly simply because that body had made a mistake in turning down a previous candidate and now regretted it. This apparently happened in the case of Guy Mollet, who was rejected as successor to Bourgès-Maunoury because the Assembly found out too late it should really have accepted Pinay.[12]

In the complicated search for a solution, the president

[12] "La Vie Politique," *Revue Politique et Parlementaire*, November 1957, p. 268.

had to give the appearance of playing the role assigned to him, which meant having no favorite candidates or policies. Both Vincent Auriol and René Coty were adept at this game, although Auriol was naturally accused by the Right of holding back Socialist candidates until he judged the most propitious moment had arrived for their investiture, and the same was said by the Left of Coty in the case of certain Independent leaders. Toward the end of the Fourth Republic, President Coty, alarmed at the seemingly perpetual crisis, abandoned the practice of designating premiers in stylized order in favor of missions of information and advice.

As cabinet crises continued day after day, week after week, they were supposed to "ripen"—to reach that point where a resolution was possible. The ingredients of solution were: first, communication of information between political groups and individuals; second, assessment of their relative strength; third, reduction and adjustment of their ambitions to a point where trading and bargaining could take place (this was one cogent reason for dropping the requirement that a premier-designate must seek investiture before forming his cabinet, that is, before, not after, the process of bargaining had been completed); fourth, relaxation of tension between groups of deputies to a point where the requisite percentage of those who must support the system were ready to do so; fifth, increased boredom with a game which had gone on too long and for which the end was now predictable; and, sixth, mobilization of extraparliamentary pressure to end the crisis. While some matters of substance were formally associated with the demise of one government and the birth of another, the decisive factors were those of procedure. Clearer statements of intent could be expected from premier-designates confronting an Assembly early in a crisis, for example, those of Mendès-France in 1953 and Paul Reynaud in 1952. Later candidates tended to be less categorical. A commentary on Gaillard's investiture address described it as concise enough not to arouse latent antagonisms by reviewing issues which had brought on the crisis and vague enough not to alarm political groups over possible distasteful solutions to the myriad problems which the new cabinet faced.[18] *Immobilisme* reigned as the policy issues on which each coalition foundered were rarely if ever solved by its fall and the emergence of a new majority. In fact, unless the new majority was very much like the old majority, no government at all was possible.

Centralized Administration

Because the ability and the inclination to take positive action only rarely emerged from a system based on balanced political antagonisms, large antidemocratic blocs, and recurrent crises, the highly centralized administrative apparatus was necessarily responsible for holding the country together. While other Western states have also witnessed a steady growth of administrative power, some peculiar factors have accentuated this tendency within France. Over the past two centuries there has been little experience, comparable to Great Britain or the United States, with local political or administrative responsibility. The efforts of the Pétain regime to promote some measure of decentralization were swept away in the postwar rejection of everything associated with Vichy. It proved politically and ideologically expedient to ignore Chapter 10 of the constitution of the Fourth Republic, especially Article 89, which provided that "organic laws shall extend departmental and communal freedoms." On the contrary, state power was increased, for example, by the Monnet Plan of postwar reconstruction and development. Greater responsibility, direct and indirect, for the national economy was also assumed with the nationalization of enterprises in the fields of coal, steel, gas, electricity, manufacturing, and banking. In addition, under the threat of Communist control of certain geographic regions and sectors of the economy, Jules Moch, the vigorous Minister of the Interior, had instituted a system of "super-prefects." These powerful administrators exercised at the outset emergency

[13] Same, p. 273

police powers, and, after the menace of subversion had subsided, they retained broad responsibilities for regional coordination.

Most important of all, the incapacity of the National Assembly to deal with complex problems led, despite an apparently precise prohibition in the constitution, to an increasing reliance on *loi-cadres*.[14] Under this system, which further blurred the inherently fuzzy line between administrative regulation and legislation, many cabinets were given the power to deal by decree laws with particular situations and for limited periods. As had happened under the Weimar Republic, this practice was easier to start than to halt or control. Areas of action to be covered by decree laws were steadily broadened. Successive coalitions, after hazardous investitures, tended to exact this power from the Assembly as a matter of course in order to escape irrational, contradictory, and destructive legislative interference. Supervision by the Assembly, whether as a unit or as a series of committees, could hardly be continuous or effective. On the other hand, any ex post facto accounting to the Assembly became difficult if not impossible because of the ephemeral nature of the executive coalitions.

As transitory executives came to rely heavily on the centralized administration, they thereby invited the permanent bureaucracy to take more and more responsibility for defining national policy. Two peculiar customs added considerably to the weight of the administrative apparatus in its relation to the political executive. For one thing, established practice called for each minister to hand over his office to his successor without advice and with as little information as possible. This made the incoming minister "almost a prisoner of the ministry which he is supposed to direct...."[15] The influence of the bureaucracy was further enhanced by the important role of the minister's *cabinet*, whose function was to furnish him with information and

---

[14] Article 13 reads: "The National Assembly alone has the right to legislate. It cannot delegate this right."
[15] "The Steadying Power in French Politics," *Réalités*, March 1958, p. 27.

technical advice and to serve as liaison between the minister, the ministry, and the National Assembly. In many ministries the director, or *chef de cabinet*, was supposedly a political expert, while the rest, out of a total of ten to fifteen, were mostly civil servants, predominantly though not exclusively drawn from the ranks of the ministry itself.[16]

The *cabinet* was designed as an instrument of political control over administration and would perhaps have been effective in this role if the executive had been strong, united and stable. In practice, the *cabinet*, under the Fourth Republic, became an element of power, for it partially filled a void in the policy-making process. "For the conception of the *cabinet*," wrote René Massigli, a career diplomat, "as a liaison body between the minister and his agency and between the minister and the Parliament, there has been substituted the notion of a *cabinet* which is simultaneously the brains of the minister and the eye of the master in relation to the agency."[17] The *cabinet's* influence with the minister meant influence over policy decision. Its position in the ministry and in communicating with the National Assembly gave it influence over policy execution. The tendency to change the personal composition of the *cabinet* somewhat with each departure of a minister served to dilute the continuity and consistency of policy without diminishing the power and the crucial role of the bureaucracy as such.[18] The more important the ministry, the greater the relative role of the administrative apparatus, as for example in the Ministry of Finance.

Centralization of administration had some beneficial effects.[19] Efficient prefects often charted local needs in

---

[16] Same. See also Marcel Abraham, "Le Ministre et ses Services," *La Nef*, May 1951, pp. 101-105.

[17] As quoted in *Le Monde*, June 11, 1958, from René Massigli, *Sur Quelques Maladies de l'État* (Paris: Plon, 1958).

[18] The average duration of a member of the *cabinet* was four ministries. "The Steadying Power in French Politics," cited, p. 29.

[19] For a fuller discussion, see, for example, Brian Chapman, *Introduction to French Local Government* (London: Allen and Unwin, 1955), and *The Prefects and Provincial France* (London: Allen and Unwin, 1955).

consultation with local representatives and then pressed the central government to allocate the necessary funds. Under centralized administration the work of reconstruction and development went forward steadily, helping to bring about remarkable advance in economic production, especially between 1953 and the end of 1957.

With the founding of the Fourth Republic, a number of important changes were made in recruitment and training of the civil service. The aim was to open to people of all social and economic groups the avenues leading toward civil-service careers, at the same time improving the opportunities of advancement for well-trained graduates of the National School of Administration. Broadened training programs were devised so that particular ministries, such as Foreign Affairs and Finance, would not be able to monopolize the better candidates. While it is too early to reach any final judgment, the reforms apparently succeeded in maintaining the high prestige of civil-service careers and in equipping entrants with the diverse skills necessary for rapid advancement.[20] The more delicate problem of enlarging the economic and social sources of government servants will be considered below.

However inevitable, administrative centralization was not strengthened without paying a heavy price. The monopoly of competence and responsibility, enjoyed in practice by central authorities, has narrowed greatly the middle ground between the extremes of complete standardization and local independence. For example, one of France's major needs is for rapidly constructed, inexpensive housing. All too frequently central control has slowed down the rate of building without introducing compensating economies of time, labor, and cost. At the other extreme, local initiative without local responsibility has led to the evasion of national control or to the manipulation of central authorities on behalf of special, restricted interests.

[20] For details on the reform of the administrative system see Roger Grégoire, *La Fonction Publique* (Paris: Julliard, 1955) Also Paul Marie Gaudemet, "En Marge de la Réforme de la Fonction Publique," *Revue Française de Science Politique*, October-December 1954, pp 869-875

Inevitably, under any political system strong pressures are brought to bear on the central points of decision and action. Nor is there anything inherently wrong or antidemocratic in the attempts of special groups to influence institutions of government in their favor. Serious evils do arise when those institutions are so weak as to be unable to judge conflicting demands and to single out those policies which are of national benefit, in other words, when statecraft and statesmen are absent or impotent. Unfortunately for France, its political and administrative institutions were particularly susceptible to group pressures at the very time the breadth of their formal responsibilities made them an inevitable target.

Deputies to the Assembly were popularly regarded as spokesmen for special and narrow interests, while the desire for political survival encouraged them to press hard for local needs. The National Assembly to a considerable extent became a congeries of groups bent on using the power of the legislature to attain parochial ends. A formal ban, set forth in National Assembly Standing Order 13, against groups of deputies formed "for the defense of particular, local, or professional interest," was easily evaded by establishing "study groups." The effects of the close links between deputies and extraparliamentary organizations was reflected in many fields of government action or inaction, for example, agricultural protection, import restrictions, and the absence of effective measures against tax evasion.[21]

Surviving by the grace of the legislature, the executive could do little to extricate the national interest from the welter of special pleading buttressed by parliamentary pressures. An extra burden therefore fell on the administrative apparatus as guardian of the general welfare. How well did it carry that burden? While no general conclusion

[21] Bernard E. Brown in "Pressure Politics in France," *Journal of Politics*, November 1956, pp. 702-720, concluded that ". . . pressure groups continue to be of greater importance in France than in Great Britain or even in the United States" (p. 718); see also Georges Lavau, "Note sur un 'Pressure Group' Français: la Confédération Générale des Petites et Moyennes Entreprises," *Revue Française de Science Politique*, April-June 1955, pp. 370-384.

can be drawn with confidence, it is clear that interest groups have many lines of contact and leverage in their dealings with the bureaucracy. As a group *fonctionnaires* are poorly paid, while the tax structure weighs inequitably upon them. Those with experience and technical knowledge can frequently command higher salaries in private industry. This gap between public and private remuneration is widest in the Ministries of Finance and Industry, state companies controlling gas and electricity, and other agencies concerned with the national economy. Probably the personnel of newer state services created by postwar nationalization has been more susceptible to outside influences, whereas higher personnel in the "old-school" ministries have been more attracted to better-paid positions in private enterprises.[22]

Social and professional communication also provide many channels of contact. Despite new postwar patterns of recruitment, top administrative positions are mostly filled by people trained before World War II, when there was an even closer similarity in social and economic backgrounds between public administrators and those in private enterprise. Finally, advisory councils created by the Fourth Republic, including the Economic Council, have not done much in their avowed function of assisting in the formulation of *national* policy, but they have brought representatives from private special interest groups into close contact with the civil servants. Small wonder if administrators sometimes act as advocates of particular interests within their ministries or the government as a whole. Against this tendency stand the traditional independence of the civil service, the prestige which still attaches to it, and the general reluctance of administrators to move from private to government careers.

Administrative power has been subject to few checks by executive or legislative branches. Nor has strong restraint been exercised by the French legal system, which has traditionally recognized and respected a broad area of

[22] Jean Maynaud, "Les Groupes d'Intérêt et l'Administration en France," *Revue Française de Science Politique*, July-September 1957, pp. 577-581.

administrative discretion. Like the administrative tribunals beneath it, the *Conseil d'État* starts with the assumption that the apparatus of the French state acts for the public welfare. "It considers that above formal legality emanating from texts, there is another, higher, quasi-constitutional in nature, that follows from the necessity of maintaining the state and assuring the successful operation of its public services. . . ."[23] It is not necessary to go as far as some French writers and conclude that, because France lacks the legal safeguards built into the British and American systems, it lives under bureaucratic authoritarianism. Rather, Frenchmen, viewing the State, have had the uneasy feeling of living next to anarchy on one side and dictatorship on the other. If the administrative apparatus has prevented a weak executive and an irresponsible legislature from sliding into chaos, the weakness of the executive and the irresponsibility of the legislature have likewise prevented the administrative machinery from becoming an unbearable instrument of oppression.

One road of escape from the dangerous situation in which there was either no government or entirely too much government would be the instillation of a feeling of local responsibility. Unfortunately, administrative units—the communes and the departments—were to a large extent the creatures of central authority, especially of the Minister of the Interior. While neither corresponded to political realities or economic requirements, regrouping of a system two centuries old was beyond the capacity of the Fourth Republic. "The absence of local democracy," said one French critic, "is one of the reasons for the poverty of collective life in France; but national unity is not a mystical force. It rests on concrete communities. It likewise requires a certain homogeneity of public spirit that centralization helps to destroy. . . ."[24]

[23] André Cocatre-Zilgien, "Le Contrôle Juridictionnel de l'Administration en France et en Angleterre," *Revue Politique et Parlementaire*, December 1955, pp. 402-403.

[24] Charles Brindillac, "Décoloniser la France," *Esprit*, December 1957, devoted to "La France des Français."

Some Implications of "Immobilisme"

Bemused and impatient with the dazzling gyrations of French politics, Americans can justly be accused of failing to view French political institutions in their French setting, of failing to examine the values of French life, which lie at the very foundation of political choices. As the Fourth Republic relapsed into *immobilisme,* French critics, Right and Left, also looked abroad, primarily to Great Britain, but occasionally to the United States, in search of ideas and structures which, if borrowed, could transform their government into an efficient and responsive machine. However, France in the mid-twentieth century could not beg, borrow, or steal elements of the British or American systems with any guarantee of success. French institutions are French, not alien forms grafted on the French nation. Reform can succeed only if political change is accompanied by congruent social and economic adaptations, just as Mendès-France recognized, just as De Gaulle argued long before his advent to power.

Pending fundamental reforms, Frenchmen found some very concrete advantages in *immobilisme.* As crisis followed crisis, they withdrew as far as possible from their political system, viewing the cut-throat operations of the Assembly, the impotence of transitory governments, the abortive efforts of ministers of finance, with cynical but relaxed detachment. To repeated summons to greatness they gave slight response. *La grandeur,* like effective government, would cost money. Worse, it would destroy a pattern of life which had proved as resistant to defeat as to victory, a way of life which, if not as rich in material things as that enjoyed in the United States or even in some Western European countries, was both familiar and, in the same years when *immobilisme* flourished, demonstrably better than it had been. Far from being contradictory, therefore, the Frenchman's alienation from the Fourth Republic arose from his traditional distrust of government in general and his desire to have as little of it as possible.

Seeing all around him a centralized administration at work, he avoided some of its effects and negated others by making the political executive weak and the constitutionally powerful National Assembly incapable of defining consistent national policies. Despite an undoubted longing to have a "strong man" at the helm—France is after all the country of Napoleon and Boulanger—much of this longing was a projection of his own aloofness and his preoccupation with his own private needs; it was a desire to create a leader in his own image who would settle conflicts to his own satisfaction.

Chapter Five

SOME ECONOMIC AND SOCIAL ASPECTS OF "IMMOBILISME"

IF THE FOURTH REPUBLIC were to play a significant international role, it needed social cohesion and economic viability no less than political efficacy. In seeking basic changes in the prewar situation the framers of the new republic recognized that the state must assume paramount responsibility. Socialists, Communists, and members of the Mouvement Républican Populaire were later to disagree violently over the direction and extent of governmental power. Initially, however, they joined in writing into the preamble of the 1946 constitution these far-reaching social and economic goals:

It is the duty of all to work, and the right of all to obtain employment. . . . Every man may protect his rights and interests by trade-union action, and belong to the union of his choice. . . . Any property and undertaking which possesses or acquires the character of a public service or of a monopoly must come under collective ownership. The nation guarantees, for the individual and for the family, the conditions necessary to their development. It guarantees to all, especially to children, mothers, and elderly workers, the safeguarding of their health, material security, rest, and leisure. Every human being who is unable to work on account of his age, his physical or mental condition, or the economic situation, is entitled to obtain from the community the appropriate means of existence. . . . The nation guarantees equal access of children and adults to education, to professional training, and to general culture. It is the duty of the State to organize free and secular public education at all levels.

Postwar population increases were changing the setting in which the Fourth Republic's social policies were carried out. The comprehensive program of state assistance to families was partly responsible, and contributing also were an upsurge of marriages and births; recurrent inflation, after 1945, which diminished the already weakened motivation for saving; and the prolonged shortage of consumers' goods. The result was a striking change from the demographic stagnation which had characterized France since the turn of the century. In 1900 the population had stood at 40.6 million; in 1945 it was 100,000 less. In the years that followed, however, the annual surplus of births over deaths brought the 1955 population to 43 million.[1]

Population increase, together with state direction and control over the economy, produced greater urban concentration. Of the two and one-quarter million gain in population between 1946 and 1954, Paris alone accounted for one-third, or 718,000. As much as three-fourths of the increase was located north of a line between Le Havre and Belfort,[2] in that part of France labeled "dynamic" by French sociologists because of its high industrial and agricultural productivity.

With demographic growth the inactive proportion of the French population rose from 48.1 per cent in 1946 to 53.9 per cent in 1954,[3] thus generating new pressures on the government for increased aid to working mothers, family allotments, and old-age assistance. While initially the relatively reduced labor force entailed shortages of some types of labor, forced wages upward in certain industries, and stimulated a search for unskilled workers in both Europe and North Africa, the time was inevitably coming when the millions born after World War II would

[1] Jean-Marcel Jeanneney, *Forces et Faiblesses de l'Économie Française* (Paris Colin, 1956), p 9
[2] Michel Phlipponneau, "Le Déséquilibre Régional Français et la Défense Nationale," pt 1, *Revue de Défense Nationale*, April 1957, p. 545.
[3] André Philip, *La Démocratie Industrielle* (Paris Presses Universitaires de France, 1955), p. 182.

be entering the job market, thereby adding another series of requirements to national policy.

Housing Policies and Problems

Population increases made it more difficult for the Fourth Republic to discharge the responsibility it had assumed in the field of housing. Because of destruction in two World Wars plus progressive deterioration of existing buildings, serious efforts would have been necessary to restore French housing even to the inadequate prewar situation. However, by 1950 the housing problem had worsened as the result of the slowness of economic recovery, the maintenance of rent controls at fantastically low levels, and the inability of the government to spare adequate credits from a chronically unbalanced budget. In the five years from 1945 to 1950 it was estimated that less than 100,000 units were built or rebuilt.[4] Thereafter, as the figures below reveal, there was substantial improvement. The number of dwellings completed increased almost 40 per cent in the years 1953 to 1957 when economic production was registering its greatest advances.

Year	Dwellings Completed[5]
1951	77,000
1952	84,000
1953	115,000
1954	162,000
1955	210,000
1956	230,000
1957	260,000

Of the more than one million dwellings constructed since World War II, about a quarter were built under state programs, thus placing a further strain on precarious government finances. Between 1954 and 1958 public aid to housing mounted from 533 to 900 million francs.[6] Ac-

[4] Louis Henry, "Perspectives Relatives aux Besoins de Logement," *Population*, July-September 1950, p. 505.
[5] Alfred Sauvy, "Le Logement des Faibles Nouvelles Données sur l'Élimination du Prolétariat," same, October-December 1957, p. 599.
[6] See *Le Monde*, May 25-26, 1958.

cording to one survey the French people, if not noticeably enthusiastic, seemed generally satisfied with the government's housing programs[7] while another inquiry reported that 70 per cent of the respondents described themselves as "well housed."[8] Further examination, however, suggests that seeming public acceptance of a situation, described by one commentator as a "classic example of how good intentions pave the way to a living hell,"[9] resulted from faulty questioning techniques or reflected ignorance and long conditioning to substandard dwellings.

Compared with estimated housing needs, with the number of people objectively classified as "badly housed," or with progress in other countries, the French record was far from impressive. In 1950 it was estimated[10] that construction of no fewer than 320,000 dwellings annually was needed if the country were to cover its requirements by 1970, while 210,000 would have to be built yearly in order to prevent a worsening of existing conditions. The table on Page 139 shows that in none of the years 1951-1957 did actual new construction exceed 260,000, with the result that by the end of 1957 a further gap of over one million dwellings had been added to the shortage previously existing.

A 1957 survey indicated that 22 per cent of the French population—40 per cent in Paris—were badly housed.[11] The worst off were those aged twenty to forty, the young people on whom the future of the economy and the preservation of French democratic institutions depended.

Most of France's neighbors had better records. Even counting the years of greatest French construction—1956 and 1957—France still ranked ninth among European countries in its per capita rate of construction. Its rate of dwelling completions—6 per 1,000—was ahead of Great

[7] Alain Girard and Henri Bastide, "Niveau de Vie et Répartition Professionnelle. Enquête sur l'Information et les Attitudes du Public," *Population*, January-March 1957, pp 85-86

[8] "How Happy are the French?" *Réalités*, December 1955, p. 84.

[9] David Schoenbrun, *As France Goes* (New York: Harper, 1957), p. 181.

[10] By Alfred Sauvy and Louis Henry See "Le Logement des Faibles," cited, p. 598.

[11] Same, pp. 594 and 598.

Britain and Italy, but behind West Germany's 11, Norway's and the Soviet Union's 8, and Switzerland's and Sweden's 7.[12]

New Initiatives in French Education

Reforms in French education were as urgent, many French leaders believed, as overcoming the crisis in housing. The urge to act was heightened by the close connection between education and political thinking.[13] In its attempts to remake the French State, the Vichy regime had attacked the prevailing system of education and its patterns of teaching, particularly at the lower levels. In this, as in other areas of policy, the leaders of the Fourth Republic lost no time in nullifying the Vichy decrees. They quickly followed with a purge of teachers who had supported Marshal Henri Pétain. But reforms could not stop there. French education was under indictment as substantially responsible for the ideological divisions and economic weaknesses which had led to the collapse of 1940. Nothing less than fundamental change could satisfy the demand for national rejuvenation.

The new goals included better education, compulsory for a longer period, and equality of access to it. The Langevin Commission, appointed just after the war, recommended that compulsory schooling be prolonged to the age of eighteen. Curricula at the lower levels were to be revised, stressing the relations of abstract concepts to the everyday life of most French pupils, who were not headed for the universities. More emphasis was also to be placed on technical subjects.

According to Jean Bayet, Director of National Education, formalism in French education had produced "signs of senility and a lassitude of spirit among the children. For France it is very grave, as this tendency changes the character of *l'esprit français*, results in categorization of faculties, a Cartesian division, and finally a divorce from

---

[12] "Economic Review," *New York Herald Tribune* (Paris Edition), May 1958.
[13] See, for example, Léon Emery, "L'Université Française et l'Idéologie," *Le Contrat Social*, January 1958, pp. 1-8.

life. We have arrived at the formidable formalism of the *Grandes Écoles* on the one hand and an insufficiency of technical education on the other."[14] The state, he implied, was interested in the training of teachers, a larger place for scientific research in the universities, and revised programs for prospective civil servants. Finally, in fulfillment of the promise contained in the preamble of the constitution—"equal access of children and of adults to education, to professional training . . . free and secular public education at all levels"—secondary and higher education were to be opened to social and economic classes which had been largely excluded before World War II.

As with its housing programs, the Fourth Republic scored some successes and some failures in its educational policies. Two achievements stand out. In 1951 under conservative political leadership, the old, bitter controversy over state aid to Catholic schools was reopened. Despite claims that the Barangé bill violated Article 1 of the constitution, which read, "France is a Republic, indivisible, laic, democratic, and social," the second National Assembly approved financial assistance to parochial schools. Cassandra-like prophecies that the measure would deepen social, religious, and political antagonisms were not fulfilled during the life of the Fourth Republic, although the issue did reappear to plague the Fifth. The alienation of the MRP from the Socialists, and from some Radical groups, stemmed from domestic and foreign issues not involving Catholicism. Although the third National Assembly contained an apparent majority for repeal of the Barangé Law, Guy Mollet, even in the absence of the MRP from the government coalition, did not wish to endanger his Cabinet unnecessarily and used his influence to quash legislative debate and action.

The training of government administrators has been improved in many ways. Despite low salaries, compared to those in most industries, careers in government have retained their high prestige. This has been reflected in the

[14] Quoted by Nicholas Hans, *Comparative Education: A Study of Educational Factors and Traditions* (London: Routledge and Kegan Paul, 1949), p. 298.

stiff competition for entrance into the École Nationale d'Administration, to which only about one-tenth of the applicants are admitted. The continued exchange of ideas among graduates, and between them and the older civil servants, has made the thinking of the École Nationale influential throughout the administrative structure.

In any discussion of French failures in education, it must be acknowledged that comparable criticisms could be leveled against other Western countries. The Fourth Republic was unable to lengthen the period of compulsory education or to broaden sufficiently access to educational opportunities. As late as 1957 Minister of Education René Billères was still seeking legislative action to raise the compulsory age for school attendance from fourteen to sixteen. A 1950 survey revealed that only 10 per cent of the French population had completed secondary education and only 6 per cent higher education,[15] as compared with 18.8 per cent in the United States.[16] Even allowing for the superior quality of French secondary schooling, this was, as French critics themselves admitted, too great a disparity. In a sample of 1,000 pupils attending secondary schools in 1957, 218 came from families where the father was head of a business concern and 124 where the father received an above-average business salary; only 86 pupils came from the "artisan" class, and 65 from the peasant class.[17]

Continued restrictions on educational opportunity are reflected in failure to break the hold of the conservative "haute bourgeoisie" on the civil service by introducing representatives from lower rungs on the social and economic ladder. The following table, covering the years 1945-1951, compares the proportion of various groups in the total population with the percentage of successful

---

[15] "L'Enseignement en France," *Sondages (Revue Française de l'Opinion Publique)*, Summer 1950, p. 10.

[16] André Aymard, "Enseignement et Recherche: des Remèdes Insuffisants et Dangereux," *Revue Politique et Parlementaire*, February 1957, pp. 118-119. The figures are for 1953.

[17] Same. The *New York Times* (July 24, 1957) reported a survey showing only 21 per cent of the children of workers entering secondary education.

candidates for the École Nationale.[18] It reveals that employers, industrialists and professional groups supplied over 60 per cent of the successful applicants, the three groups at the bottom of the socio-economic pyramid 3 per cent.

Group	Per Cent of Total Population	Per Cent of Successful Candidates
Industrialists & Liberal Professions	4	23.2
Higher Civil Servants & Managers	5	41.8
Tradesmen & Artisans	15	11.4
Agricultural Managers	25	3.6
Lower Civil Servants & Salaried Employees	17	16.7
Skilled Workers	22	3.3
Agricultural Workers	10	—
Hand Workers	2	—

Turning from *who* is taught to *what* is taught, one sees another serious gap between objectives and accomplishments in educational reform. In 1957 it was estimated that France needed 50 per cent more skilled workers in the immediate future, 150 per cent more engineers and three times as many scientists and technicians.[19] A report of the French Economic Council emphasized the dangerous consequences of neglecting scientific research. Because of restricted educational opportunity, postponement and neglect of scientific study, and meagerness of state support, France annually turned out only 12,000 scientific research workers, as against 20,000 in West Germany, and 40,000 in Great Britain.[20]

After twelve years of postwar effort French education

[18] Thomas Bottomore, "La Mobilité Sociale dans la Haute Administration Française," *Cahiers Internationaux de Sociologie*, v 13, 1952, p. 169. See also the same author's "Higher Civil Servants in France," *Transactions of the Second World Congress of Sociology* (London: International Sociological Association, 1954), v 2, pp. 143-153.

[19] "La Grande Pénurie de Cadres Techniques en France," *La Nef*, September 1957, pp. 26-27.

[20] See summary of report by Émile Roche, head of the Economic Council, under the title, "La Recherche Est-Elle un Sacerdoce?" *Revue Politique et Parlementaire*, February 1957, pp. 113-118.

was still in serious need of reform. Said François Bloch-Lainé, former Director of the Treasury: ". . . Today's system is very badly suited to the needs of the times, and the abilities of the average Frenchman show this to be true. He understands very little about economic events because he has been badly educated to follow them. This task is all the more urgent because it will take a long time. . . ."[21] Following a detailed study of the French economy, Jean-Marcel Jeanneney concluded that "our educational system, if maintained as it is now, would, in the course of the next twenty years, leave unfulfilled the major needs for qualified personnel."[22]

Indexes of Social Dissatisfaction

The inability of postwar governments to discharge the responsibilities they had assumed in housing and education was a potent factor in destroying the Fourth Republic. Antagonisms between social groups remained unalleviated, many Frenchmen felt little or no loyalty to existing political institutions. Before the 1956 election a public-opinion poll found no one who would admit he was "very satisfied" with the work of the previous Assembly.[23] Although three qualified French voters in four cast ballots, 89 per cent professed to have little or no interest in politics.[24]

Much has been written about the alienation of the French intellectuals and the reasons therefor. Said one commentator, ". . . the most amazing fact about French intellectuals is not their influence, but the way in which this influence fails to be transmitted into action."[25] Cer-

---

[21] "How Strong is the French Economy?" *Réalités*, December 1957, p. 76.
[22] Jeanneney, cited, p. 266.
[23] Georges Dupeux, "Les Plates-Formes des Partis," in Maurice Duverger, François Goguel, and Jean Touchard, eds, *Les Élections du 2 Janvier 1956* (Paris. Colin, 1957), p 66.
[24] *Réalités*, April 1956, p. 13.
[25] "How Right is the French Left?" in same, February 1958, p. 20. Another remarked that "the school was first Radical, then . . . found its center of gravity within the socialism of Jean Jaurès; today it leans toward communism." (Emery, cited, p. 5.)

tainly, continuous criticism by intellectuals of the social and political institutions of the Fourth Republic did not bring about their modification, but this fact did not lead intellectuals to adapt themselves to the system. If the American intellectual of the mid-twentieth century may be censured for exalting conformity, his French counterpart may be described as a cynical bystander.[26]

The intellectuals' view of French society is not dissimilar to that of the workers, for whose love they pine so unrequitedly. One indication of worker attitudes was shown in responses to a question on the degree of injustice existing in France. One-fifth of those questioned made no reply. Of these 79 per cent (15.8 per cent of the total) were members of the Communist-dominated CGT who undoubtedly harbored grievances they did not choose to express. Seventeen per cent of the respondents thought there was not very much injustice, and 63 per cent replied that there was a lot. Most dissatisfied of all appeared to be those groups whose cooperation was essential to continued economic progress: young people, residents of the larger cities, and unmarried persons who did not benefit from state social-assistance programs.[27]

Perhaps even more indicative of social dissatisfaction was the reluctance of those at the bottom of the economic scale to recognize the improvements in the standard of living which had occurred between 1954 and 1957. As the table below indicates, a heavy majority of those who replied thought they were no better, if not actually worse, off than they had been five years previously or before World War II. Almost half—45 per cent—believed that things would get worse before they got better, that there would be an unemployment crisis within the next five years.[28]

[26] A hapless position explored at great length by Simone de Beauvoir in *Les Mandarins* (Paris. Gallimard, 1956).
[27] "The French Worker," *Réalités*, April 1956, pp 9, 14.
[28] Girard and Bastide, cited, p. 41. No sharp distinctions could be found in the attitudes of different age groups.

Social Category	Percentages of Respondents Who Believed that Conditions in France Were:					
	Worse than		Same as		Better than	
	5 Years Ago	Before War	5 Years Ago	Before War	5 Years Ago	Before War
Peasants	23	34	55	37	19	26
Agricultural Workers	15	30	64	40	17	19
Industrial Workers	21	36	51	33	23	22
Artisans & Tradesmen	27	45	48	28	23	20
Middle-level Employees	17	36	41	25	39	29
Higher-paid Employees & Professionals	17	38	39	28	41	25
Retired & *Rentiers*	30	41	47	27	19	27
Averages (unweighted)	22	37	49	31	25	24

Professors Cantril and Rodnick have summarized the "psychological characteristics of the French worker."[29] He shows *apathy*. Only a few workers want the responsibility of elective office in shop councils. "You take it easy and live from day to day, hoping that you will get all minimum pleasures that are open to you."[30] A second trait is his *resentment*. This is an unfocused response, not a strong dislike for any specific thing or person, but a general sense of wrong identified with the owning class, the state and the "system," with no feeling of violence. A *lack of confidence* arises from an unfocused resentment, from a feeling that removal of dissatisfactions is difficult. A factory worker, for example, says: "The workers do not trust the government or the employer. They have no confidence in them. Both are bitter enemies. Also the workers have little use for unions of any kind. . . ."[31] *Lack of hope* is widespread. Workers want much but assume that they can obtain very little, so they feel their lot is hopeless. Seventy-five per cent of industrial workers feel unsure of the chance of improving their situation, and 58 per cent of the white-collar workers and 62 per cent of the supervisory personnel in industry share this view. Finally, the

[29] Hadley Cantril and David Rodnick, *On Understanding the French Left* (Princeton, N J : Institute for International Social Research, 1956), pp. 40-47

[30] Rodnick's summary of a conversation with a group of workers.

[31] The worker, it would seem, feels a need to belong, to be a part of some organization, to take part in action, yet rejects all alternative courses of action perceived by him.

workers display a *lack of faith* "in anyone or anything."

The French, as individuals and in groups, had produced political *immobilisme*, but they refused to acknowledge their handiwork. They denied their government any credit for social and economic improvement. In fact, many refused to admit that any improvement had occurred. They took small satisfaction in their way of life, believing that others were getting an unjust share of the national product. But they did not wish to change places with those who were better off or to exert themselves greatly to change their own lot. They opposed the idea of change, fearing that it would bring not improvement, but setbacks. Their attitude toward the political system ranged from apathy through hostility to sporadic revolt, not against the system, but against the way it affected them personally. At the same time they attempted to use the system as a means of defense, to protect their part of what they viewed as a stabilized national product. "Despite apparent successes it [political mediation] results in a certain social sclerosis, in a crystallization of positions within a system where privilege protects the dignity of the worker and the prerogatives of the employer, but where this equilibrium of preservation does not generate progress. Social distance is maintained, and real initiative by each component is completely stifled. Each of them is only able to block the effort of others, and class struggle ends in the loss of all motion."[82]

The French word for the mingling of revolt and manipulation—well exemplified by peasant groups and small shopkeepers—is *incivisme*. In addition to mass resistance to tax collectors and systematic falsification of tax reporting, *incivisme* takes the form of widespread alcoholism, a problem which derives from social custom, agricultural protection, and pressure politics. Although its unfortunate results have long been evident, the obvious remedies were beyond the reach of governments based on and dedicated to *immobilisme*. "Apathy," say Cantril and Rodnick, "helps ex-

---

[82] Michel Crozier, "Terre de Commandement," *Esprit*, December 1957, p. 789.

plain the fact that the average Frenchman spends 11 francs out of every 100 for alcohol, while spending only 7 francs for his health and 5 for his housing."[33] It has been estimated that the annual per capita consumption in France is 34 liters of pure alcohol (the average French male consuming 54 liters), in the United States, 6 liters, in Holland, 2½, and in Italy, 18.[34] Deaths in France attributed directly to alcoholism have mounted steadily since World War II, from 1.2 per 100,000 in 1946 to 14 per 100,000 ten years later.[35]

The substantial economic cost of alcoholism includes loss of production due to absenteeism and the disability of workers on the job.[36] Furthermore, the cultivation of the raw materials concerned and their distillation employ resources and manpower which could be put to better use. The economic cost is swollen further by the claims by heavy consumers of alcohol for hospital care and other forms of health assistance.

While paying for the effects of alcoholism, the state was simultaneously stimulating both the production and consumption of alcoholic beverages, by propaganda promoting their sale, by purchase of excess stocks, and by award of tax favors to individual distillers. Those who, like Mendès-France, advocated measures of reform were subjected to savage recrimination, their proposals stifled at birth or strangled before they could be implemented. The wealthy alcohol lobby so blatantly manipulated government institutions for its own ends that alcohol, itself a product of *incivisme*, bred more *incivisme*—economic, social, and political. Americans debate whether their country can indefinitely afford to spend billions of dollars in supporting agricultural prices at artificial levels. For France, a much

---

[33] Cantril and Rodnick, cited, p. 42.
[34] Philip, cited, p. 199
[35] *New York Times*, August 6, 1957 Not included in these figures are deaths attributed to cirrhosis of the liver, which in 1956 amounted to 32.5 per 100,000 population.
[36] Philip, cited, gives a figure of 20 per cent for factory workers suffering from alcoholism; p. 200.

poorer country, there can be only one answer to a policy so wasteful of economic, social, and human resources.

Tax Structure

Any separation of the economic from the social policies undertaken by the Fourth Republic is an artificial one. This is particularly true of taxation, since the state used the tax system simultaneously to promote social objectives, including the redistribution of income, and to raise funds for meeting its economic responsibilities. The two aims were in part incompatible, increasing social dissatisfaction while attempts at reform remained largely ineffective. "Our laws," said one critic, "are complex and detestable."[37]

Taxpayers complained that their burdens were excessive. In fact, however, comparisons based on gross national product and net national income show that although the level of taxation is higher in France than in Italy or the United States, it is about the same as in Great Britain and West Germany.[38] The inequitable distribution of the burden of taxation was another source of dissatisfaction. Progressive income taxes ostensibly guaranteed a measure of justice, but these rested most heavily on salaried persons and corporations whose incomes could not easily be concealed. Small businessmen and farmers, on the other hand, found evasion easy. The difficulty of collecting income taxes is, in part at least, responsible for the heavy reliance in the French fiscal system on indirect taxes, especially the general transactions tax. These bear most heavily on persons not reached by income taxes.[39]

The burden of tax assessments and the complexity of the tax code encouraged organized interests to use their in-

---

[37] Joseph Denais, "Une Vraie Réforme Fiscale Est-Elle Possible?" *Revue Politique et Parlementaire*, May 1957, p 115.

[38] Warren C. Baum, *The French Economy and the State* (Princeton, N.J.: Princeton University Press, 1958), p 132.

[39] Same, p. 131. Baum concludes that about two-thirds of the total tax receipts were raised by excise taxes, as compared with 41 per cent in Great Britain, and 22 per cent, including customs duties, in the United States.

fluence on the government to obtain various forms of relief. Wage earners, farmers, and other groups brought pressure on government officials to secure special privileges. Groups and individuals also attempted to defeat the efforts of the tax authorities through bribery, deceit, or open defiance. A notable instance of such direct action was the activity of Pierre Poujade's Union de Défense des Commerçants et Artisans (UDCA), which in 1954 and 1955 advised shopkeepers not to pay taxes and organized mobs to obstruct the work of the collectors. Defiance and evasion were patriotic during the German occupation; their continuance under the Fourth Republic was one indication of its inability to attract the loyalty of French citizens. Twenty-five per cent of the total tax levy, it was estimated, was not paid.

The struggle among various groups for preferred treatment resulted in persistent tinkering with the tax system, but in no fundamental reform. The astonishing success of Poujade's movement in the 1956 elections portended actual insurrection if tax rates were increased. Higher rates also would encourage still greater evasion by small businessmen and farmers, throwing more of the burden on the larger, efficient business concerns. Finally, a thorough overhauling of the complicated tax system might initially reduce total receipts, and several years might pass before the beneficial results of new methods would become apparent.[40] The wisest course seemed to be the path of least resistance; there was always the chance that continued economic progress would produce revenues greater than had been anticipated.[41]

Economic Recovery and Modernization

Despite the inadequate resources at its disposal after World War II, the Fourth Republic undertook both to

[40] Such was the opinion of Edmund Lacourt, "Le Franc Gaillard," *La Nef*, September 1957, p 12

[41] Pierre Locardel pointed out that the state had stumbled on tax windfalls in the past and might under the admittedly defective system do so again if the most dynamic groups in the French economy were not further penalized; *Figaro*, May 16, 1958.

reconstruct and modernize the French economy. The conflict between the two objectives in the allocation of national resources was never resolved, with the result that the rehabilitation program[42] strengthened rather than weakened obsolescent agricultural, industrial, and commercial elements.

For all the state-directed effort in the Monnet Plan and the Hirsch Plan and the large-scale assistance afforded by the United States through the Marshall Plan, French recovery was slow. In 1949 agricultural production was still below the 1934-1938 average. After rising to 111 of the prewar level in 1950, it remained relatively stationary during the next three years.[43] Industrial expansion was more rapid and reached higher levels. In December 1948 the index stood at 117 (base, 1938) and in December 1953 had reached 150. Even so, these attainments fell short in significant sectors of goals set by the Monnet Plan, particularly in coal, electricity, and steel. Among Western European countries only Belgium and the United Kingdom failed to surpass France in general industrial advance between 1945 and 1953.[44]

Upward movement in both agricultural and industrial production was resumed in 1954 and continued through 1957. The Fourth Republic could take pride in this development, since it came after the Marshall Plan had ended. The gains in many sectors were greater than those registered in other countries, including West Germany. Beginning in 1954, French industrial production rose almost 10 per cent each year, as compared to about 7 per cent in the Soviet Union and 3 per cent in the United States. By 1957 industrial production had increased 46 per cent over 1949 and agriculture 25 per cent.[45] Progress was especially marked in two heretofore retarded areas, heavy industry and energy, vital components of a modernized economy.

---

[42] Official estimates of the reconstruction program alone placed the total at approximately 5,000 billion francs. (Baum, cited, p. 19)
[43] Jeanneney, cited, p. 56.
[44] Baum, cited, pp. 25, 41.
[45] "France's Economy Shifts Gears," *Réalités*, January 1958, p. 22.

Within the European Coal and Steel Community, France was the only country to record advances in 1957. In coal, labor productivity by the end of that year had surpassed that of both West Germany and Great Britain, reflecting the results of ten years of investment totaling more than 10 billion dollars.[46] Steel production the same year stood almost 40 per cent above 1929.[47] Led by electricity, which doubled between 1954 and 1958,[48] over-all energy production rose about 50 per cent, reaching a total three and one-half times greater than in 1929.[49] The industrial advance was led by large, modern concerns, both private and government controlled, of the type that were best able to meet new domestic demands and to hold their own against international competition.[50]

During the period of the Monnet Plan, scarcity of goods, low wages, and the government's subsidy to exports had held back French consumption of nonagricultural products. The long pent-up demand, unleashed after 1953, can be seen in a comparison of three major types of expenditures, as envisaged by the Second Modernization Plan and as actually attained in 1956:[51]

	Contemplated	Actual
	(1952 Base = 100)	
Individual	115	132
State	115	144
Investment	135	135

In 1957 the consumption of foodstuffs rose 10 per cent over 1956, fruit juice 30 per cent, beer and unfortified (*doux*) wines 16 per cent, *apéritifs* 8 per cent. More spectacular increases were registered by household appurtenances; purchases of furnishings rose 15 per cent, coal and gas appli-

[46] Report of the Commissioner General of Productivity, quoted in "Economic Review," cited.
[47] *Le Monde*, June 8-9, 1958.
[48] "France's Economy Shifts Gears," cited, p. 22.
[49] *Le Monde*, June 8-9, 1958.
[50] Jeanneney, cited, p. 80.
[51] "Retard et Expansion Économique," *Esprit*, December 1957, devoted to "La France des Français," p. 752.

ances 12 per cent, electrical kitchen appliances 78 per cent, washing machines 40 per cent, hot-water heaters 31 per cent, and refrigerators 25 per cent. An additional indication of the rise in the French standard of living was the shift from motorcycles and motor scooters (production down from 12 to 38 per cent depending on the type) to automobiles (up 4.3 per cent).[52] The released consumer demand was also reflected in purchases of a wider variety of foods and increased buying of industrial products formerly regarded as luxuries.[53] Such were the dimensions of the rising standard of living which most Frenchmen refused to admit had actually taken place.

Inflation and Budgetary Deficits

Government programs after World War II were carried out in an atmosphere alternating between inflation and fear of recession. While the Fourth Republic sought to control price fluctuations, its concern for increased economic production and its assumption of social responsibilities led it to accept as inevitable, if not actually desirable, a certain degree of inflation. Recollections of previous inflationary periods led the French people to regard price rises as a normal part of their lives. Their reactions to anticipated inflation in turn made stability more difficult to attain. Furthermore, experiences during the German occupation caused the French to resist price controls and other measures which the Fourth Republic adopted to limit inflation.

The first inflationary round, which began just after the war, ended only in 1949. During these years of short supply and heavy demand French prices rose about 50 per cent each year.[54] Since inflation continued longer in France than in other Western countries, French prices in 1949 were significantly higher, and the gap was not closed in ensuing

---

[52] *Le Monde*, June 1-2, 1958.

[53] This point is made in more detail by Yves Chaigneau, "Les Français au Travail," in *Esprit's* issue "La France des Français," cited, pp. 740-741.

[54] Jeanneney, cited, p. 98.

years. The brief period of stability which followed had lasted just long enough to cause fear of recession when the onset of the Korean War brought a resumption of the upward spiral. Factors in the new round of increases were greatly expanded military production, the world-wide rise in raw-material prices, and speculation by Frenchmen on continued, large-scale increases. Once again, inflation was more severe in France than in other European nations. By 1952, when the peak was reached, wholesale French prices were about 40 per cent above 1950 levels; in the same period British prices had risen 27 per cent, Dutch 23 per cent, German 22 per cent, Belgian 20 per cent, and Italian 10 per cent.[55] After 1954, the time of greatest economic advance in France, prices resumed their upward movement but at a slower rate than during the two earlier periods.

Budgetary problems and practices contributed to the atmosphere of inflation. Even with large amounts of foreign aid to their military and investment programs, successive French governments had been unable to balance the budget in any single year after World War II. The table below presents the annual situation between 1945 and 1955.[56]

Year	Deficit in current francs*	Deficit in per cent of public expenditures	Foreign aid or loans*	Remaining deficit in current francs*	Remaining deficit in per cent of public expenditures
1945	308	58	59	249	46
1946	353	45	143	210	27
1947	292	31	156	136	14
1948	510	36	124	446	28
1949	611	28	289	322	15
1950	570	23	185	385	16
1951	504	18	150	354	12
1952	872	24	204	668	19
1953	877	23	219	658	17
1954	773	20	109	664	17
1955	780	19	105	675	17

* billions of francs

The colonial and foreign policies of the Fourth Republic weighed heavily on French finances. At the outset, when

[55] *Le Monde*, February 27, 1955, citing data from the Ministry of Labor.
[56] Jeanneney, cited, p. 228.

the French economy was weakest, the war in Indo-China was a serious drain. Into the breathing-spell attained in 1950 intruded the responsibility for large-scale rearmament for the defense of Western Europe. No sooner had the Indo-Chinese conflict ended in the surrender of North Viet-Nam, than the revolt in Algeria demanded attention. As the following table shows, after 1950 military expenditures exceeded civil capital expenditures and absorbed close to one-third of the entire budget.[57]

	1945	1946	1947	1948	1949	1950	1951	1952	1953	1954
(Figures are in billions of francs)										
Operating Expenditures of Civil Services	296	345	414	681	842	1114	1297	1394	1559	1736
Capital Expenditures	52	165	239	578	828	832	755	809	859	812
Military Expenditures	175	171	231	332	377	463	857	1269	1242	1110
Total Expenditures	*523*	*681*	*914*	*1591*	*2047*	*2409*	*2909*	*3542*	*3722*	*3713*

To cover budgetary deficits governments sought advances both from the Bank of France and from commercial banks; these credits were used primarily to continue state investments. Public loans were also floated, but it was becoming increasingly difficult to borrow from the French people. More and more incentives had to be offered, not just in higher interest rates, but also in concessions such as amnesty for past fiscal frauds. Even loans which could be judged a success in terms of the response jeopardized the future, since the money was not used to institute financial reforms, and succeeding regimes were debarred from following one loan immediately with another. As an example, the loan floated by Pinay prevented his successor René Mayer from doing likewise, forcing him instead to obtain advances from the Bank of France.

Efforts to cut governmental expenditures were as fruitless as efforts to raise additional revenues through tax reform. The attempts made by Premiers Bourgès-Maunoury,

[57] Baum, cited, p. 52. Capital expenditures include government housing and economic modernization programs Total expenditures after 1951 include deficits in special treasury accounts, for which prior figures are not available.

Gaillard, and Pflimlin illustrate the predicament faced by post-1954, "immobilist" regimes. Primarily as a result of the deteriorating situation in Algeria, the 1956 deficit was 995 billion francs and that for 1957, 910 billion. Loans were granted by the United States, by European countries, particularly West Germany through the European Payments Union, and by the International Monetary Fund in return for a French promise, among other things, that the 1958 deficit would be reduced to 680 billion francs. While members of the coalition could agree in principle that cuts should be made, repeated and public threats to quit by both Finance Minister and Premier were necessary before those who wished to maintain the existing level of state investments, social-security benefits, and national defense expenditures could be brought to terms. Premier Bourgès-Maunoury, a member of the Radical Socialist party, found himself in the familiar position of arbiter between powerful forces of the Left and Right. The Socialists accused the Independents of abandoning progressive social policies, and only Guy Mollet's personal intervention forced them to accept reductions in this section of the budget. The Independents countered with claims that the Socialists aimed to force capitulation in Algeria by weakening the military establishment. Rightist Defense Minister André Morice, originally in agreement that defense expenditures could be cut, reportedly was the last member of the government to accept the compromise formula, quite possibly because his fellow rightists in the Assembly urged him to remain true to rightist doctrine. In the end it was announced that government investments were to be cut by 20 billion francs, social-security costs by 10 billion, and defense outlays limited to 1,200 billion.[58]

Getting the cabinet to agree on a budget was frequently painful, but this was only the beginning of a French premier's ordeal. He still had to fight the budget, item by item, through any number of National Assembly committees, beating back amendments and even complete substitutes,

[58] *New York Times*, August 1, 2, and 8, 1957.

almost all of which would seek to increase expenditures. Finally, if he had not fallen on some other issue, he had to maneuver for a series of favorable votes in the Assembly, on each of which his cabinet's life was at stake. Bourgès-Maunoury fell on the Algerian question before his budget could come to a vote. Stepping up from Finance Minister to Premier, Gaillard tried to push through the same budget on the theory that deputies will sometimes accept disagreeable policies after a premier has first been sacrificed. As his shaky government tottered toward the abyss, however, pressures to restore the cuts rose rather than diminished.

By the time Pflimlin appeared on the scene, the Right, having caused the collapse of three governments within the year, was all set to attack that portion of the budget allocated to national defense. Against the background of the Algiers revolt, the Right denounced Pflimlin as an arch-appeaser, wrecker of the nation's armed forces. Because cuts in military spending meant curtailment of a wide variety of industries, the unfortunate Premier was also accused of policies calculated to cause an economic recession. Announcement that previously blocked expenditures would be freed was far from enough to save him. In June 1958, when De Gaulle assumed power, the budget had still not been voted in its entirety.[59] Ruling by decree, De Gaulle's government, in the person of Finance Minister Pinay, revealed that the efforts of the previous Premiers to curtail expenditures would be abandoned and no less than 150 billion more francs would be spent beyond the draft budget.[60]

Problems of French Foreign Trade

One of the Fourth Republic's major objectives was to attain international economic "viability," that is, to balance its foreign accounts at greatly expanded levels without resorting to such devices as export subsidies, import

---

[59] See *Le Monde*, June 12, 1958, for the items which had not yet passed.
[60] Furthermore, it should be remembered that, as occurred in 1957, expenses forecast in the first part of the fiscal year frequently turn out to be far below actual expenditures as reported in the annual accounts

restrictions and continual requests for foreign assistance. By both these standards it failed, even though in some years a precarious balance was attained.

Part of the government's program to promote exports included agreements under which French producers reserved a certain proportion of their output for foreign markets. More important were the privileges accorded exporters. They were granted various forms of tax relief, were reimbursed for part or all of their social-security costs, and in the case of agricultural producers were guaranteed profitable prices if they marketed their goods abroad. Government aid at times totaled as much as 12 per cent of the value of all exports, up to 40 per cent in the case of agricultural commodities.[61]

At the same time that it was seeking to augment exports, the French government was acting to reduce imports by recurrently imposing quantitative restrictions and special taxes on nonessential foreign goods. As a consequence France lagged behind other OEEC countries in the progressive lowering of trade barriers, to which all were formally committed. Worse, France's repeated inability to balance its international trading accounts forced it to reimpose restrictions which had been belatedly removed. For example, the stringent trade controls adopted in February 1952 were relaxed very slowly. In April 1956 restrictions had been removed on only 50 per cent of the items falling within the OEEC purview and on only 28 per cent of actual French purchases abroad.[62] Despite its expanding economy, France did not hold even to this limited liberalization. In 1957 when large trade deficits were again incurred, the government was forced to reimpose rigid import controls.[63] Soon after, the Fourth Republic entered its final crisis, and few were surprised when Premier

[61] Marlo Lévi, "L'Évolution de la Structure des Échanges Commerciaux de la France avec l'Étranger de 1951 à 1955," *Politique Étrangère*, November 1956, p. 570.
[62] Same, p 567.
[63] Report of the Administrative Council of the National Bank for Commerce and Industry, printed in *Le Monde*, June 10, 1958.

Pflimlin announced, just before its demise, that still more stringent measures would be necessary.

The deterioration in France's international economic position accompanied that in its political structure. Thanks in large part to American aid, French deficits on current account, which had been as large as 2 billion dollars in 1946, had disappeared by the end of 1950. The impact of the Korean War caused new reverses in 1951 and 1952, but a balance again appeared in 1953 and 1954, and there was a small surplus in 1955.[64] The Suez invasion, however, dealt the *coup de grâce* to the delicately poised equilibrium. In June 1957 the exchange deficit stood at 320 billion francs; in that month exports covered only 65 per cent of French imports.[65] For the entire year 1957 imports totaled 1,635 billion francs, 36 per cent above total French exports.

In addition to the role played by inflation, economic expansion was contributing to the excess of imports. Mounting energy requirements alone accounted for almost half the deficit, with coal imports rising 13 per cent during 1957 despite increased production at home. Elimination of petroleum supplies from the Near East during the Suez crisis emphasized France's reliance on imports. Hence the enthusiasm with which France greeted the discoveries in the Sahara, even before the first trickle of oil came through the Phillippeville pipeline. While progress in chemicals and plastics was encouraging, in this sector of the economy also France still was dependent on imports.[66] Far less heartening for the future was the situation in agriculture, despite government policies of protection.

The gulf between imports and exports was only a partial indication of failure to attain economic viability, since the Fourth Republic's objective was also to achieve a balance

---

[64] Baum, cited, pp. 84-85; Jeanneney, cited, pp. 130-133; J. S G. Wilson, *French Banking Structure and Credit Policy* (London: Bell, 1957), p. 345.

[65] Report of the Administrative Council of the National Bank for Commerce and Industry, cited. It must be remembered that nonmaterial items form a significant part of the French international account.

[66] Same

of trade at greatly expanded levels. The following table contrasts goals set by the Second Modernization Plan and the actual situation at the end of 1956:[67]

	Envisaged by Plan II	Actual, 1956
	(1952 = 100)	
Métropole imports from abroad	100	125
Métropole imports from franc zone	109	100
Métropole exports abroad	135	108
Métropole exports to franc zone	96	72

Deterioration in the trade situation during 1957 and the first half of 1958 caused Clappier, Director of Foreign Economic Relations in the Ministry of Finance, to admit that only heroic efforts could bring France to the goal set for 1961: a balanced trade, with exports at twice the 1957 figure.[68] But heroic measures were not plentiful in a Fourth Republic subjected to powerful protectionist pressures. France preferred the role of mendicant, soliciting alms abroad, now with promises of better behavior, now with accusations of unjust treatment. It was of course primarily from the United States that the Fourth Republic, a pensioner masquerading as a great power, sought help. To the billions of dollars supplied under the Marshall Plan other billions were added after the European Recovery Program officially ended in 1952. Within the framework of the Mutual Assistance Program, American military equipment was provided and French armament supported through "offshore" purchases, which also helped France indirectly in its foreign-exchange balance and industrial investment Smaller programs of "facilities assistance" and "mutual weapons development" had as their objective stimulation and maintenance of particular sections of French military production. In 1952 and 1953 special financial support was granted to the French military budget. All in all France

[67] "Retard et Expansion Économique," cited, p. 753.
[68] *Le Monde*, April 30, 1958.

received more than 40 per cent of bilateral American aid to NATO countries. The United States also contributed a substantial share to NATO's infrastructure program, a network of military support facilities—airfields, pipelines, etc.—most of which were constructed in France. The thousands of American military personnel stationed in France poured millions of dollars into the French economy,[69] as did American tourists. While the Indo-Chinese war lasted, the United States paid an increasing share of its annual cost. By 1954 it was assuming close to three-quarters of the burden, and the abrupt ending of hostilities provided the Fourth Republic with a substantial, unanticipated windfall in aid granted but not yet expended.

The fiscal and foreign trade crisis of 1957 brought France, hat in hand, once more to its benefactors—the United States, European governments, especially West Germany, and international lending agencies. Resulting loans, totaling 655 million dollars, probably exceeded French expectations,[70] with the largest share coming from the International Fund. Despite facile assurances that corrective measures would be taken, April 1958 saw one-fifth of the monetary aid consumed without any noticeable improvement in the prospects for financial stability.[71] *The Economist's* gloomy prediction[72] that the loan would be used to postpone the day of reckoning on the complex of issues involving Algeria, budget balancing, tax revision and institutional reform was proving all too accurate.

A major source of difficulty in balancing external accounts was the high French price level relative to other countries. The differential produced by prolonged postwar

---

[69] Dollar infusions from this source would have been greater had the United States not treated France like an underdeveloped country. Military commissaries and PX's sold American goods to American servicemen at drastically reduced prices, thus making it possible for men in uniform to avoid exposure to French food, French liquor and French clothing, and instead to buy spongy, white bread, bonded bourbon, and American "snuggies."

[70] "Respite for France," *The Economist*, February 8, 1958, p. 462.

[71] According to M. Cloppier, quoted in *Le Monde*, April 30, 1958.

[72] "Respite for France," cited.

inflation had continued to plague France during the period of its rapid economic progress. Efforts to align French prices with those of other European countries by currency devaluation had not produced lasting results. Success in stimulating exports obviously depended on the time which elapsed before internal prices resumed their former relationship with world levels. In this respect the effects of successive devaluations varied considerably. That of November 1945 had won a "breathing-spell" of only about two months, that of January 1948, less than six months. Fourteen months were gained by the devaluation of September 1949. After 1952, French governments resisted any new adjustment in exchange rates, although there were increasing indications that the franc was again overvalued. When in 1957 devaluation could no longer be avoided, it was too little and too late to bring any lasting or substantial improvement in the French foreign-trade situation. Fearing that government action to reduce domestic prices would further slow down economic progress and provoke serious social unrest, French officials took refuge in the hope that somehow foreign prices would rise to meet French levels if they could be held stationary meanwhile.[73]

A second hope, mingled with fear, concerned the decision to enter the European Common Market. "Ability to compete," said one French analyst, "is a state of mind as much as an economic fact." Fear of the costs of adaptation to a new competitive situation, he added, as one of the "great fears" of the twentieth century, born of world wars, chronic inflation, unbalanced budgets, and unstable governments.[74] Over the decades French producers had developed large vested interests in a protected economy, which post-1954 domestic prosperity had strengthened. A report of the Administrative Council of the National Bank of Commerce and Industry emphasized that government actions to promote exports would have only slight effect so

[73] Jeanneney, cited, pp. 156, 65, 167.
[74] André Piatier, "L'Économie Française, Est-Elle Compétitive?" *Politique Étrangère*, April-May 1955, pp. 163-164.

long as the French economy remained closed and protected within its national frontiers. If the economy "chooses expansion and general improvement in the standard of living, it must of necessity accept the discipline of international competition which such a policy implies. . . . The project for the creation of one vast market among the six countries of the European Coal and Steel Community has appeared—provided it is brought about by stages and with the necessary guarantees—as one of the best means for our country to escape this monetary instability from which it periodically suffers. . . . To substitute for traditional and conservative methods the spirit of enterprise and modernization . . . that is the essential change the Common Market must bring about. . . ."[75]

When the Fourth Republic fell before the revolutionists of May 13, 1958, its economic policy was virtually bankrupt. A prosperity nourished by protection and by large infusions of foreign aid had not been converted into living standards recognized and accepted by the French people as adequate. Heavily and inequitably taxed, Frenchmen saw their national resources dissipated in domestic and foreign policies grandiose in conception, but ineffective or contradictory in execution. Their political system had consistently rejected leaders of courage and vision in favor of temporizers and procrastinators. With something akin to relief, governors and governed alike finally allowed responsibility for dealing with France's multiple dilemmas to fall into the hands of one man, a man confident of his own ability to take and enforce decisions.

[75] *Le Monde,* June 10, 1958.

Chapter Six

THE FOURTH REPUBLIC AND THE FRENCH MILITARY ESTABLISHMENT

DURING THE PERIOD of the Fourth Republic, the French military establishment, along with other ingredients of statecraft, failed to respond effectively to the foreign and colonial challenges posed to the international ambitions of its political leadership. Ultimately the republic was destroyed by revolt of a small portion of armed forces against a situation in which once more there was a disparity between objectives the military was required to pursue and resources placed at its disposal. Military inadequacy was the inescapable consequence of France's domestic socioeconomic condition. The "tone" of the military, itself a social group, or rather a complex of social groups, was being influenced by, at the same time it was influencing, the general "tone" of the nation.[1]

After World War II the French army became increasingly conscious of its isolation within French society. "The events of the postwar period, far from regrouping the nation around its soldiers, as had happened after previous adventures, only further alienated each from the other. The city dweller or the farmer regarded the army only as heavy budget charges, as legionnaires or parachutists fighting in far-off Indo-China, as units garrisoned in Germany or in military posts scattered across France. Career military

[1] On this point see Tony Albord, "Il Faut Réintégrer l'Armée dans la Nation," *Revue Politique et Parlementaire*, November 1956, pp. 235-236

personnel thus lived outside French society; for them their country was only a rest zone where they felt disoriented and badly understood. Thus were systematically removed the necessary conditions for impressing on the army its true character and exalting its mission."[2]

Other sources of civilian-military hostility were of longer standing. Following World War I the myth arose that it was not the officers, but the ordinary *poilu* who had really beaten the Germans.[3] In the Second World War, the regular army hardly fought at all before it was overwhelmed and a great proportion made prisoner. Searching for a scapegoat on whom to place the blame for their ignominious defeat, Frenchmen pounced on the generals. The large number of officers, especially in the navy, who supported the Vichy regime added to the antimilitary ferment. And the manner in which France was liberated produced the ideal of the gallant civilian fighter, the "Man of the Resistance." He was envisaged as aided to a degree by a few shining exceptions among the officer class, who, however, came from abroad under the banner of the Cross of Lorraine, not from France itself, and most certainly not from Pétain's *Milice*. For political and ideological reasons, the early leaders of the Fourth Republic completed the destruction of the officers' prestige by purges, demotions, retirements, and by inserting them into the regular civil service, where they regarded themselves as underranked and relatively underpaid.[4] Nor did the conduct of some officers on and off the battlefields of Indo-China do much to restore the social standing of the military establishment.

One sign of the debased position of the military in the social scale, and a force toward perpetuation of that status, was the continuous difficulty in recruiting and training junior officers. The following table shows the number of applications and acceptances at St. Cyr between 1949, when

[2] General André Zeller, "Armée et Politique," *Revue de Défense Nationale*, April 1957, p. 502.
[3] Albord, cited, p. 230.
[4] Jean Planchais, *Le Malaise de l'Armée* (Paris: Plon, 1958), pp. 17-18.

the famous military school, remodeled and refurbished, resumed its role after World War II, and 1955:[5]

Year	Applications	Acceptances
1949	564	274
1950	563	268
1951	586	339
1952	762	413
1953	846	348
1954	888	363
1955	909	283

Acceptances in 1949-1951 were the lowest in the history of the school, except in 1920 when the young men in qualified age classes had already served in World War I. Despite increased enrollment in the years after 1951, due in large part to the addition of options in nonscientific subjects,[6] the desired level of four applications to one acceptance was not attained. Those applying for the difficult scientific option at St. Cyr dropped from 600 in 1956 to 400 in 1957. The École Polytechnique, which specialized in training military engineers, was annually graduating only a handful of officers.

The effects of diminished recruitment were multiplied by losses of junior officers in Indo-China and Algeria. "Each year from 1945 to 1954 a proportion of officers equal to three-fifths of the average graduating class from St. Cyr (323) was killed and the remaining two-fifths wounded."[7] High positions were still held by older officers; advancement, except within the air force, and the special paratroop units particularly, was slow. Bad pay, retarded careers, lack of prestige, dangerous and dirty work explain why many junior officers after the minimum service of fifteen years quit the service and took their pensions. At the same time because of demographic factors, fewer and fewer

[5] General Georges Malgré, "Recrutement des Officiers et Structure Sociale: la Crise de Saint-Cyr et ses Remèdes," *Revue Politique et Parlementaire*, April 1956, pp. 21-22.
[6] Same.
[7] Planchais, cited, p. 10.

young men were available for service either as officers or in the ranks.[8] Hence changes in the social and economic position of the army created a crisis in both its upper and lower echelons, a crisis which could be expected to endure at least for one military generation unless remedial measures were taken.

Military Relations with the Public

As with other problems of the Fourth Republic, the essential difficulty was not confusion over the diagnosis, but failure to apply the prescribed remedies successfully. The military establishment recognized that recovery from the disaster of 1940 depended on its accomplishing the "formation" of youth and the "propagation" of ideas within the civilian society.[9] Its complete failure in both endeavors added to the sense of frustration and alienation of the armed forces. While it felt the need for better public relations and a sympathetic press, the French army, like its counterparts the world over, regarded journalists as a group with a mixture of suspicion and animosity. Although it naturally preferred favorable to unfavorable reporting, no publicity at all was considered best. Press and information sections attached to the military branches were kept small. Consequently individual services were frequently forced to rely on civilian departments for news even of military developments. Canned releases were used wherever possible in preference to guided tours or personal interviews. Although in theory local commanders in France were entitled to their own press officers, most of them attempted to do the job themselves. Bureaucratic supervision encouraged them in this course: only the head of a military region could authorize interviews with representatives of the press and then only if their papers were judged to be favorably disposed toward the armed forces, or one of its branches.[10]

[8] This downward trend would continue until 1960.
[9] See, for example, Colonel Nemo, "La Guerre dans le Milieu Social," *Revue de Défense Nationale*, May 1956, p. 615.
[10] On these points, see Pierre Denoyer, "L'Armée et la Presse," *Revue de Défense Nationale*, April 1957, pp. 533-545.

In France special circumstances aggravated the difficulty, prevalent in many countries, of getting the military point of view across to the public. One was the high degree of centralization in Paris of population, of economic affairs, and of civil and military administration.[11] As had been true before World War II, most of the newspaper space devoted to military affairs, foreign and domestic, was concentrated in the Parisian press. Fallacious though the reasoning might be, it was therefore understandable that the military should believe that the road to influencing public opinion lay through a few prominent journals in Paris.[12] The "politicalization" of the French press, however, caused the military, with good reason, to distrust its objectivity. Despite postwar purges, many journals reflected special interests and were used by politicians as instruments for personal aggrandizement.[13] The military was at a disadvantage in this form of competition, and the very adeptness of a few "political" generals in playing the press game increased the hostility and aloofness of the military as an organization.[14]

Some of the activities in which the army was engaged placed a premium on concealment. In a France suffering from a shortage of consumers goods, the less known about the high style of living of the armed forces on occupation duty in Germany, the better. The less the press could find out about the piaster traffic in Indo-China, in fact the less journalists were able to compare continuously optimistic official military reports with the actual situation in that "nasty war" the better. When after 1954 the spotlight of public opinion focused on North Africa, particularly on

[11] See Michel Phlipponneau, "Le Déséquilibre Régional Français et la Défense Nationale," *Revue de Défense Nationale*, pt. 1, April 1957, pp. 545-559, and pt. 2, May 1957, pp. 714-728.

[12] For example, see Jacques Kayser, "La Presse de Province en France et l'Évolution de la Situation Internationale," *Politique Étrangère*, no. 1, 1955, pp 41-51; same author's "La Presse Française et la Crise de Suez," in same, no 2, 1957, pp 203-214

[13] For a summary of postwar efforts to "purify" the press, see Jean Mottin, *Histoire Politique de la Presse 1944-1949* (Paris Bilans Hebdomadaires, 1949).

[14] See Planchais, cited, pp. 65-73, a chapter significantly entitled "La Grande Muette et le Quatrième Pouvoir."

Algeria, to old reasons for suppressing information were added the acts of torture and reprisal committed by local units and explicitly or implicitly sanctioned by the higher command in the name of military necessity. It must not be forgotten that, while theoretically Metropolitan France was at peace and therefore entitled to freedom of information, actually a state of war existed in Algeria. On this fact censorship affecting both Algeria and the *Métropole* could be justified.

Notwithstanding the perceived need for imparting military views to the public, therefore, avenues of communication were systematically distorted or blocked. To the military, the press and its representatives appeared as either basic components of a detested political system, or as sources of subversive criticism, or both. The army's efforts to inform and indoctrinate the public, far from lessening the sense of isolation within the social structure, actually increased it. From this position of alienation it was but a short step to general rejection of criticism and freedom of the press, both basic rights in any democratic system. This step was taken by the army in Algeria in May 1958, with no illusions or regrets concerning the consequences.

In working with French youth, the military was no more successful. Each year the army received the reluctant services of hundreds of thousands of young Frenchmen. At a minimum these men must be brought to accept for the limited period of their service the discipline imposed upon them. At a maximum they could provide contact between the army and French society, and serve as channels of military influence throughout the nation. Not only was the maximum goal unattained,[15] but military control at times even fell short of the minimum (as when riots by draftees being sent to Algeria took place). The morale of conscripts was not improved by the decision that they should not be called upon to fight in Indo-China. Then, as the Algerian war increased in severity, thousands were transferred from relatively pleasant duty in Germany to

---

[15] Except, of course, in the case of some paratroop units.

confront conditions in North Africa about which they had heard nothing encouraging.

Lack of military influence on French youth and its reasons were epitomized in the brief, frustrating record of the Army-Youth Committee. Created in 1953 by René Pleven while Minister of National Defense, the committee brought together officers and representatives of youth organizations to promote a better understanding of each other's point of view and to offer recommendations for the solution of specific problems. All but ignored by the military organization and by successive governments, the committee quickly became a battleground for the two participants in the "dialogue." The number of officer members was increased in order to bring pressure to bear on youth organizations to tone down or abandon altogether their criticism of military policy in North Africa. But this tactic only aroused the young men to extend their attacks. In January 1957, the major youth groups refused to censure one of their number for opposing the Algerian war and decided instead to withdraw their delegates from the committee.[16]

Far from improving social relations, contact with youth, both in the mass and individually, only widened the separation of the military from civilians. ". . . The primary occurrence [in the alienation of the French military] was the call to arms of our youth, badly instructed in the reasons for that appeal, unenthusiastic from the beginning for the inevitable sacrifices and for their incorporation into a military machine in the process of transformation, with all the consequent improvisations, hesitations and errors. Thus even the blindest clearly saw the bad material and moral organization of our defense system and drew from this experience additional justification for the doubt they already felt toward the men, methods and traditions of the army."[17]

[16] Planchais, cited, pp 62-64.
[17] Albord, cited, pp. 31-32.

Military Relations with Political Institutions

Mutual recrimination, itself the source of increased hostility, consistently characterized the relations between military and civilian groups within the political framework of the Fourth Republic. Blamed for the debacle in Indo-China and for the failure to maintain or restore peace in Algeria, the army felt it had in fact been betrayed. Betrayed, not alone by defeatists, appeasers, traitors, Communists, leftists in the National Assembly and in the government, but by the political system itself, by the skimpiness of its annual appropriations, by the disorganization it introduced to the military establishment, above all by its lack of coherent, consistent, effective policy.

Strictures on the budgetary process in general applied with particular force to that portion allocated to national defense. It was, to begin with, difficult to discover just what the *military* budget included, since certain government recommendations, following NATO criteria, might properly be considered civilian charges, for example, pensions and veterans' benefits. If some conclusion could be reached on the totals authorized by the National Assembly, it was still difficult to correlate these accurately with expenditures actually made by various coalitions. A law of 1951 gave governments the right to transfer funds without legislative approval from one part of the military budget to another. Furthermore, as was an almost automatic practice in a system burdened with chronic deficits, the executive by decree could block expenditures already authorized.[18]

These manipulations enabled the executive to evade responsibility, but they did not make the military any happier with its lot. Since there was never enough money to go around, prolonged, pitched battles within the executive were the order of the day, pitting as primary antagonists the minister of finance and the minister of national defense, who was often regarded by the military as a weak

[18] Jean Godard, "Les Budgets Militaires Français," *Revue de Défense Nationale*, March 1956, pp 321-332. The author was an auditor in the Cours des Comptes

reed to lean upon. Affrays similar to that over the 1958 budget, previously noted, had taken place in previous years. In 1951 the war in Indo-China and pressure for increased defense efforts in Western Europe coincided with the advent of French elections to the National Assembly. The consequence was a limitation on military expenditures which not only resulted in a failure to meet Indo-Chinese and European requirements, but also adversely affected French economic growth in the two ensuing years.[19] And the French army was left to see its inadequate budget allocations burned up in Asia rather than used constructively to build a modern military force of which the nation could be proud, one which would justify its claim to rank as a major power. In the four years from 1951 through 1954 France poured out an estimated 1,447 billion francs to fight the Indo-Chinese war, or just about half the total military appropriations for that period.[20]

Operating on a deficit within a deficit, so to speak, the French army, like the French government, was heavily dependent on American assistance. In 1952, 1953, and 1954 American aid constituted 4.8, 7.3, and 18.8 per cent of the respective total French national budgets.[21] In addition to political and psychological difficulties inherent in this seemingly perpetual debtor relationship, there was a very practical problem involved. Because the American fiscal year did not begin until July, six months after the French, nobody in France could know at the time budgets were being formulated, or even when they were debated in the National Assembly, how much assistance would be forthcoming. Representations, sometimes querulous, sometimes caustic, to the State Department produced the constitutionally correct but politically unsatisfying answer that the President proposed, but Congress, sooner or later, disposed. This reply came all the more readily to American lips when

[19] Thierry de Clermont-Tonnerre, "Les Finances Publiques et la Guerre," *Revue de Défense Nationale*, January 1957, p 48.
[20] Godard, cited, pp 328-329
[21] Jean Godard, "La Contribution Alliée aux Charges Militaires de la France," *Revue de Défense Nationale*, April 1956, p. 443

French actions in the recent past and suspected behavior in the future did not accord with United States expectations.

The army not only felt it was poorly represented in the fiscal battle within the executive; it regarded this situation as just one more consequence of the general failure of the Fourth Republic to establish any logical organization for the military establishment. Ministers came and went, their titles changed, and so did their functions. It appeared to the military chiefs that their civilian peers were chosen as the consequence of the interplay of partisan political forces in a game both incomprehensible and sordid. Through it all the committee structure for national defense planning and decision within the executive branch pursued its chaotic, irrational course, now used for purposes for which it had never been designed, now not used at all.[22]

Shifting, incompetent direction, employing ineffective instruments for politico-military coordination, deprived the cabinet in general and the premier, as final arbiter of disputes, in particular, of the bases for allocating limited resources among competing branches of the armed forces and between the military organization as a whole and the mass of civilian agencies. Although reorganization had often been discussed within both the executive and legislative divisions, some constitutional difficulties stood in the way. The dissolution of the National Assembly in December 1955 prevented legislative enactment of a basic statute which interested and informed groups agreed was essential.

Confronting the political process, the military drew the same conclusions as had other critics: the basic trouble was the lack of consistent, well-directed policy. The Committee

[22] Investigators who have tried to follow Pentagon organizational charts would have a far more difficult time pursuing the records of French national defense organization under the Fourth Republic. Some useful references on French military organization are Edgard Pisani, "L'Organisation de la Défense Nationale," *Revue de Défense Nationale*, February 1956, pp. 158-169, René Sistach, "Défense Nationale et Secrétariats d'État," in same, March 1956, pp. 280-285; A. Lamson, "L'Organisation de Défense Nationale et des Forces Armées," *Revue Politique et Parlementaire*, June 1956, pp. 240-256.

of National Defense of the Council of the Republic expressed its regret that "the Government, almost as much as the press, no longer accords to our army the reverence it deserves and the respect that is its due, the respect formerly accorded it." The Committee emphasized that "the responsibility for the disorganization, for the mistakes, for the reverses suffered by our army is not attributable to officers or soldiers; that if at the top of the political hierarchy there had been more constancy of position, more authority in the definition of our missions, more firmness in the giving of orders, our army would never have known its present difficulties."[23] General Henri Navarre concluded his book, *The Agony of Indo-China:* "The true reasons for the Indo-Chinese defeat are political. The first, from which almost all the others follow, is the absence of policy; from the beginning to the end our leaders never knew what they wanted; or if they did know, did not know how to get it. They never dared tell the country that there was a war in Indo-China. They did not know how to engage the nation in war or how to make peace. They were incapable of defining a line of conduct toward the Associated States, to stick to it, and to impose it on those who represented France out there. They only knew how to take from day to day bastard measures always outstripped by events."[24]

Alienated from the social structure, distrustful of the political process, the armed forces found themselves unable to provide either the military capabilities or the concomitant doctrine to discharge the manifold missions thrust upon them after World War II. Postwar rearmament, retarded for political and ideological as well as economic reasons, took place within the European framework of the North Atlantic Treaty Organization and under the initial requirement of occupying Germany. At the same time, however, the immediate focus of military concern remained the conflict in Indo-China, where equipment and tables of

[23] Pisani, cited, pp. 167-168.
[24] Quoted in Planchais, cited, p. 9.

organization designed for European needs were of only limited use. Thus a wide gap was opened between what France's allies felt its military role should be and the colonial objectives for which weapons and manpower were actually being employed. France's allies, particularly the United States, Great Britain, and West Germany, were well aware of this discrepancy, even though they paid lip service to the proposition that the French fight in Indo-China was part of the West's world-wide struggle against Communist aggression, and the United States supported its theoretical approval with an increasing flow of financial assistance.

As the consequence of its low rate of rearmament and a seemingly endless drain of men and material in Indo-China, France after the outbreak of war in Korea was in no position to counter American pressure for German rearmament with the argument that it was willing and able to meet the need for which German soldiers were now desired. Its only tactic was delay: postponement of the day when the new, potentially powerful Germany, a competitor as well as an ally, would take its place in the system of European defense. Worse, when, with the Paris Accords, the decision to arm this competitor-ally was finally accepted, the outbreak of war in Algeria forced France to deplete that portion of its military establishment best able to meet the German challenge. In spite of the negotiated settlement Mendès-France had reached in Indo-China or because he had encouraged North African nationalism by his Tunisian policy, the army once more confronted the same large gap between military missions outside the Metropolitan area and those designed to meet the Communist threat in Europe. This time, however, France's allies most obviously refused to accept any connection between the two, and France perforce was on its own.

To the question, "what is the mission of the army?" General Ély replied, "The only possible system is . . . one which, thanks to 'flexibility' makes possible the *almost immediate* creation of forces suitable to *any* form of war, able to carry out all sorts of missions, whether in Europe or overseas."[25] But this was patently impossible. Under the Fourth Republic the French army had not been granted the funds necessary for the discharge of any mission at all. Instead, it had experienced failure and, ultimately, disaster in Indo-China, failure and humiliation in NATO, failure and even degradation in Algeria.

The most important cause of the state of "psychological shock" into which the French armed forces had fallen by the spring of 1958 was the Suez fiasco. For the French military, particularly the paratroops who were suffering the most because their pride was the greatest, the invasion of Suez presented a golden opportunity to recapture prestige lost at home, to regain the right "to speak crisply to the Americans, as an equal, and no longer . . . as a surly and humbled debtor."[26] But although military leaders estimated that the invasion was well within French and British capabilities, the French government, representing the same political system that had so often in the past shown itself incapable of making and executing decisions, capitulated to British timidity, American pressure, and Russian threats, thus turning glorious victory into ignominious retreat. Gloating over the frustration of French forces, President Gamal Abdel Nasser was left to increase his moral and material aid to the Algerian rebels.

Suspicious of each other, fearful of the consequences of their distrust, political and military leaders indulged in increasingly intemperate criticism, in increasingly overt attempts to manipulate the other. For the military the antics of the last Fourth Republic governments provided conclusive evidence that fundamental political change was overdue and must come soon, if the hierarchical authority of the armed forces were to escape utter destruction. To be sure, General Zeller declared that political leaders should get over their fear of a military coup, that such adventures either took place long ago (Napoleon) or were pure vaude-

---

[25] General Paul Ély, *Revue Militaire Générale*, October 1957, quoted by Planchais, cited, p 49. Italics added.
[26] Georges R. Manue, "La Leçon de Suez," *Revue de Défense Nationale*, October 1956, p. 1163

ville (Boulanger).[27] But the very fact that he felt compelled to write these words made them seem less a reassurance than a threat, especially since he added that, in any event, the principal cause of military coups was political weakness. Albord restated this theme when he said that danger did not arise from a military threat to constitutional liberties, but rather from an ineffective civil power and a badly informed public opinion.[28] This reasoning led to the same conclusion which some military leaders had accepted much earlier. In May 1951 Guillain de Bénouville had written: "One must not be fooled by a mirage. Military men do not overstep their proper bounds, but these no longer seem defined, nor have they been inscribed in a general system. Is it their fault that the system does not exist?"[29]

If there were no discernible boundaries in military-civilian relations, if in fact the political system was so amorphous that it did not exist at all, action by the military became easy as well as necessary; to motive, opportunity was added. "The army possesses considerable power to influence the French of the *Métropole*," wrote Robert Lacoste, at the time Socialist Governor General in Algeria.[30] His implied advice was hardly necessary, however. While one should not make the mistake of viewing the French military establishment as a monolithic structure, of attributing the same ideas to all officers, in all branches and in all grades, it is none the less significant of the complete alienation of the French military from other political and social institutions that, when the decisive trial of strength between the political executive in Paris and the military rebels in Algeria was taking place, not one single officer in the army, navy or air force (to say nothing of the paratroops) came forward publicly to defend the Fourth Republic and call for military obedience to duly constituted civil authority.

[27] Zeller, cited, p. 516.
[28] Albord, cited, p. 233.
[29] Guillain de Bénouville, "Les Généraux Devant la Politique," *La Nef*, April-May 1951, p. 139.
[30] Quoted in Planchais, cited, p 77.

Chapter Seven

THE FOURTH REPUBLIC AND SUB-SAHARAN AFRICA

HOWEVER ENCOURAGING its economic and social progress at home might be, France could continue as a world power only by building a stable relationship between the *Métropole* and the Overseas Territories. Without these areas, nearly all of which were in Africa, France would be a middle-sized country of Western Europe, locked in an uneasy and unequal partnership with West Germany. Abandonment of its colonial effort (or, as French leaders often called it, its civilizing mission) would be much more than an economic blow.

One could prove that French colonialism, like that of other colonialisms, did not "pay" in crude figures of national income and outgo. However, such figures had little relevance, for they did not measure the social and psychological effects. Millions of "French" citizens, whose livelihood and ambitions were overseas, would turn against a regime which abandoned them They would be joined by many more millions of continental Frenchmen in attacking a system which could only lose territory. For millions more, the logical reaction to the loss of empire would be to put an end to cooperation with the West, which had failed to preserve France's overseas position, and to turn to neutralism or even to overt association with a Soviet-led anti-Western bloc. Neither the foreign policy of *immobilisme* nor that of De Gaulle today can be fully understood without examining the efforts which the Fourth Republic made after 1954 to solve the problems of the Overseas Territories, the trusteeships, the Sahara, and Algeria.

An unexpected combination of factors confronted France in 1955 with the challenge to make a fresh start in its colonial policy in tropical Africa. Its colonial empire was melting away. Indo-China had been lost, Tunisia and Morocco had received their independence, and revolt was spreading among the Moslems of Algeria. Unless something were done, and done promptly, to satisfy the demands of France's African subjects, revolution might be adopted as the common pattern of protest. France was placed on the defensive by the British example in Africa. The Gold Coast had become the independent state of Ghana, and Nigeria was assured of a similar position, although it was expected that both nations would remain within the Commonwealth. Within the United Nations the French position was also deteriorating. Before the Trusteeship Council France was annually forced to justify and even to modify its policies toward the two trust territories of Togo and the Cameroons. Especially after the Bandung conference of April 1955, the voice of anticolonialist nationalism was raised more assertively. The pressure of the Afro-Asian bloc received loud support from the Soviet Union, and even the equivocal stand of the United States was interpreted by France as encouragement to anticolonial forces.

Background of the 1956 Enabling Act

By themselves, external pressures were seldom able to cause profound shifts in French policy. But in colonial affairs, oddly enough, domestic factors supported rather than resisted the forces of change. For one thing, the colonial elites, exemplified by Léopold Senghor, deputy to the National Assembly from Senegal, and Félix Houphouet-Boigny, West African leader of the Rassemblement Démocratique Africain (RDA),[1] were not only products of

[1] Several competing tendencies existed in African nationalism. Boigny, trained as a doctor but also a skillful politician of long standing, broke with the Communists in 1950 and in 1956 became the first Negro accorded a French cabinet position. He has espoused the principle of association of

French education and culture; in 1956 they still sought to use French institutions, such as the French Union and the French National Assembly, to work for African autonomy.

For various reasons the Assembly proved unusually lenient in granting decree powers to the executive under the *loi-cadre* of June 23, 1956. Many of the reforms finally initiated under the *loi-cadre* had been championed for at least eight years by individual members of the Assembly or by the Council of the French Union. Premier Guy Mollet and his fellow Socialist Gaston Defferre, Minister of Overseas Territories, were now able to capitalize on these earlier efforts. More recent precedents further smoothed the way. In April 1955 the Assembly had been brought to accept a reform of the political institutions of Togo. A law passed in November 1955 authorized the extension of local authority within the various overseas possessions and the abolition of separate electoral colleges for "Europeans" and "natives." Also important in the Assembly's assessment of the need for reform was the obvious decline in the control exerted by the parties in France itself over the new political groupings which were developing in the Overseas

---

African territories individually with France. Senghor, political rival of Boigny, is one of Africa's leading intellectuals and a poet of recognized brilliance. He had been the organizer in Africa of Socialist movements affiliated with the French SFIO and hopes for an African federation retaining links with France. Less well known is Sylvanus Olympio. Destined to become Prime Minister of Togo and to lead that territory in choosing self-government within the French Community, he also was forced to consider the problem of association between French and non-French areas In Togo, the largest, most politically aware group is the Ewe tribe, but almost half its people, through the workings of European colonization, lie in Ghana, which in 1956 was emerging from British tutelage. Still a fourth type of solution to the problem of Franco-African relations was represented by Sekou Touré, the vigorous young leader in French Guinea. Onetime civil servant in Guinea's Post Office administration, Touré entered politics by the labor-union route. After the war he was made president of the local affiliate of the Communist-dominated General Confederation of Labor, and has held high positions within the central organization. At one time a close collaborator of Houphouet-Boigny in the Rassemblement Démocratique Africain, and a member of the French Assembly, his impatient nationalism caused him after 1956 to lead the territory whose political life he dominated down the path toward complete independence and separation from France.

Territories. By 1956 the native parties were passing from the clandestine movements which they had been before World War II to open and purely African groupings. No longer was it possible to treat them as pliable instruments of French parties. Deputies of the Center and Right could now see that failure to act decisively would only accelerate the trend toward separation, to the benefit of the Communists and perhaps also of the Socialists, who had maintained better working relations with the emergent African parties. Socialist deputies could see just as clearly that the retention of at least some of their party advantages depended on voting the *loi-cadre*.

Through a painful process of trial and error, the preceding decade of French overseas policy had brought about some measure of agreement on the requirements of the new orientation. Within the territories the French government admitted the need to open in practice as well as in theory responsible administrative positions to qualified local candidates. Heretofore the higher reaches of the territorial civil services had been blocked and positions monopolized by Frenchmen. One result was to inflate greatly the number of inferior posts to which Africans were admitted and thus to strain local budgets. More serious for the future of Franco-African association was the turning of African elites toward political agitation as the outlet for their talents and ambitions. There was therefore a danger that transition toward local autonomy would be handicapped by the dearth of properly trained personnel, while the most ambitious pressed for measures of independence beyond the capacity of the territory to absorb them.

French and African leaders agreed on the inadequacy of the French Union. Created by the 1946 constitution as an assemblage of representatives from overseas territories, the Council of the Union had always lacked any leverage on the decisions of the National Assembly or the French government. Its discussions had attracted little or no public or even official notice; its protests against French colonial policy had gone unheeded. The failure of this supposedly major innovation in overseas relationships would not have been so serious had the simultaneously approved doctrine of colonial assimilation proved successful. But this doctrine, embodied in the post-1946 machinery for the representation of French colonial territories in the National Assembly, was also a failure. While claiming to carry out the provisions of the constitution, postwar governments instituted a system of restricted electorates and double colleges, with the result that, on the average, only one-fifth of the native population was able to vote. Representation in the National Assembly was so far restricted by the law of October 5, 1946, that there were only 38 deputies to "represent" 29 million people of Overseas France, compared with 544 for the Metropolitan population of 42 million. The few adjustments made after 1946 failed to change the situation appreciably. Overseas deputies could hope to influence the Assembly's actions only when the Metropolitan parties were in a precarious balance. Rarely did they hold cabinet positions, and even on those infrequent occasions, their influence was slight. For example, none of the 39 members of Laniel's long-lived Cabinet were overseas deputies, and studied practice of French premiers made the Ministry of Overseas Territories a preserve for deputies from Metropolitan France.

Léopold Senghor of Senegal, a vocal advocate of close cooperation with France, issued a warning on the consequences of this policy of limited assimilation and unlimited centralization: "Parliament is amusing itself. French intelligence and imagination, the most fruitful in the world, is degraded to supply circus performances. Deputies waste most of their time in subtle maneuvers to create a future government or future elections reflecting their party or their personal ambition. Meanwhile, the organic laws, which the overseas people await, gather dust in various committees. While waiting, these people grow impatient and dream. Of what do they dream if not to annul a compromise which has proved so sterile? Of what, if not a statute which would allow them to 'regulate their own affairs' since the Republic 'one and indivisible' is incapable of running them?"[2]

A new form of association had to be found, but it could only grow out of French measures to increase local *autonomy* and *responsibility*. A partial return had to be made to the Brazzaville declaration of 1944, with its promise of a new and cooperative relationship, and to the portions of the constitution of 1946 which reflected its spirit. The Brazzaville conference had, it is true, declared that the "objectives of the civilizing work accomplished by France in its colonies rules out any idea of autonomy, any possibility of evolution outside of the French Empire; the eventual, even distant, establishment of self-government is rejected." However, the declaration had gone on to express a desire "to see them [the territories] led by stages from administrative decentralization to a political personality."[3] Administrative decentralization meant the creation "of administrative assemblies at all levels, which would combine modern metropolitan administration with the traditional institutions of the Overseas Territories."

The attempt to harness together political centralization and local responsibility had been carried over into the constitution of 1946. "Faithful to its traditional mission," reads the last paragraph of the preamble, "France proposes to lead the peoples whose tutelage it has assumed to a state of freedom in which they will administer themselves and conduct their own affairs democratically; rejecting any form of colonial rule based on arbitrary power, it guarantees to all equal access to the public service, and the individual or collective exercise of the rights and liberties proclaimed or confirmed above." In practice, the habit of political centralization had won out over the timid promise of local responsibility. By 1956, however, ten years after the adoption of the constitution, the Fourth Republic was

[2] Quoted in P.-F. Gonidec, *L'Évolution des Territoires d'Outre-Mer depuis 1946* (Paris. Pichon and Durand-Auzias, 1958), p. 15.
[3] "Personalité" is translated as "individuality" by René Massigli, see "New Conceptions of French Policy in Tropical Africa," *International Affairs*, October 1957, p. 408.

proposing to breathe life into the idea of territorial self-government and to re-examine the basis of political association.

In the French efforts after 1956 to create a new system for the Overseas Territories, an important role was played by the distinction, however illusory it may appear to Anglo-Saxon minds, between local administrative responsibility and political independence. Local responsibility was now to be recognized as a legitimate aspiration of colonial areas; political independence was still ruled out. While the new reforms created new political institutions in the territories and endowed them with some authority, these political aspects of the reforms were viewed as merely a special variety of administrative decentralization. The revamped territorial political structures were designed to enable the local populations to run their own affairs, but to run them as part of and within the integral union called France.

The following table shows the wide variations in size, population, and budgetary expenditures among the territories covered by the *loi-cadre*. Political development before 1956 had been just as uneven. In general, French West Africa, with better resources and port facilities, was more advanced than French Equatorial Africa. Of the eight West African territories Senegal and the Ivory Coast were the leaders, their population and economic and political life concentrating on the seaports of Dakar and Conakry.

Territory	Size (square miles)	Population	Budget Expenditures (1956) (thousands of dollars)
French West Africa	*1,820,600*	*18,749,000*	
Senegal	80,600	2,224,000	44,660
Mauritania	415,900	615,000	6,809
Sudan	450,500	3,643,000	23,091
French Guinea	106,200	2,507,000	23,711
Ivory Coast	123,200	2,485,000	43,437
Upper Volta	105,900	3,325,000	17,022
Dahomey	43,800	1,615,000	15,965
Niger	494,500	2,335,000	15,268

French Equatorial Africa	969,000	4,769,415	
Gabon	103,000	383,410	7,751
Middle Congo	132,000	746,193	9,059
Ubangi-Shari	238,000	1,119,959	8,971
Tchad	496,000	2,519,853	10,471

In addition to the twelve territories, reforms were enacted for Madagascar, which since World War II had been agitating for a greater measure of self-government, and two areas—the Cameroons and Togo—administered by France under United Nations trusteeships. Except for Madagascar, the French territories formed a bloc between Algeria and the Belgian Congo, between the Southern Atlantic on one hand and Libya and the Sudan on the other. Sandwiched among the French West African territories, at times exerting considerable influence upon them, were British, Spanish, and Portuguese possessions, as well as the independent state of Liberia.

The New Institutions

Within a year after passage of the *loi-cadre* more than forty-five decrees had been promulgated. They established essentially similar political systems within the African territories, in spite of their vast geographic and ethnological differences and even (in the case of Togo and the Cameroons) in their relation to France itself. Executive functions were to be performed by a Government Council, which included from six to twelve ministers, elected by the Territorial Assemblies and headed by the representative of France. The deputy receiving the most votes was to be Prime Minister and, as such, was empowered to assign ministerial portfolios to the others.[4] In Togo and the Cameroons the Assembly could force from office the elected executive by passing a motion of censure, and in the Cameroons by rejecting a vote of confidence. In the other overseas territories the elected executive was theoretically

---

[4] In Togo the French Commissioner was to name and the Assembly to accept or reject a premier-designate.

responsible only to the French Commissioner, but he could resign if he felt he had lost the confidence of the Assembly. The principle of the separation of powers was further weakened by granting to all the new Assemblies the right of interpolation. The Assemblies were to be elected by universal suffrage, acting through a single electoral college. In Madagascar there were also to be a number of regional assemblies, reflecting that territory's supposed suitability to the federative principle.

Behind this imposing institutional façade, the all-important question was: which powers were to be held by the Assemblies and their elected executives, and which were reserved to the representatives of France? Specified fields generally retained under French control included, in addition to foreign affairs and military defense, the maintenance of internal security, the protection of individual freedoms, and the economic, social and cultural services necessary to maintain the "solidarity of Franco-territorial relations." This vague category was defined more precisely, after debate in the National Assembly, to include customs regulations, postal services, telecommunications, atomic-energy development, and higher education.

A second line of activity was reserved to France through the Commissioners for West Africa and Equatorial Africa. It was their function to assure uniformity within the grouping of the territories under their jurisdiction. Finally, like these "Super-Commissioners," the Commissioners in the individual territories were regarded as representatives of the French State, responsible to it in the person of the Minister of Overseas France. If a Commissioner found that the local Assembly was overstepping its proper boundaries, he could demand a reconsideration of its actions. If then overruled by the Assembly, he could appeal in the case of Togo and the Cameroons to the French Council of State; in that of the Overseas French territories, to the Minister in Paris.

While the division of competence between France and its overseas colonies had been delineated in general terms, in practice the actual balance would depend greatly on how the new relationship actually evolved.[5] The first test of the *loi-cadre* came in the elections of March 31, 1957. The results demonstrated the success of the new dispensation, but they also forewarned of developments which might shortly threaten with dramatic failure the basic purpose of the new French policy, to hold the overseas territories securely within the French Union. Twelve million voters selected representatives to the territorial assemblies from among party lists, all of which included "Europeans." In turn the assemblies chose 127 ministers for the new Government Councils, among them twenty-eight "Europeans." Such self-restraint by the African electorate and its parties allayed French fears that the overwhelming African majority, once it had the chance, would submerge the small European minority.

The elections also recorded the triumph of political amalgamation over the forces of geographical, social, economic, and religious fragmentation. The Rassemblement Démocratique Africain, led by Houphouet-Boigny, captured all or a majority of the legislative seats in seven of the twelve territories: Gabon, French Guinea, Ivory Coast, Upper Volta, and Sudan, in French West Africa; Middle Congo and Tchad, in Equatorial Africa. Another political formation, Léopold Senghor's African Convention, displayed pronounced strength in Upper Volta and Dahomey, as well as in Senghor's own territory of Senegal. A third group, the African Socialist Movement, an autonomous African party linked with the Metropolitan French Socialists and headed by Lamine-Gueye, elected representatives to the legislatures of Senegal, Niger, Sudan, and Guinea.

The successes of the RDA were largely responsible for the decision of the other political groups to band together in a Parti du Regroupement Africain under the leadership of Senghor and Lamine-Gueye. The emergence of these

---

[5] For a more complete description and assessment of the political institutions in territories and trust areas, see Gonidec, cited, pp. 68-126. A brief summary is given by Joseph Perrin, Senator from the Ivory Coast, in "Mieux qu'une Loi, un Cadre," *La Nef*, May 1958, pp. 26-28.

large, united political groups led to the installation of homogeneous executives in most of the territories, with the principal exception of Upper Volta, where an unstable coalition took power. "All in all," Joseph Perrin, Senator from the Ivory Coast, was later able to write, "the governments installed a year ago have demonstrated a stability which is the envy of the *Métropole,* and the least favorably disposed observer is obliged to recognize that territories like the Ivory Coast or Guinea are extremely well governed."[6]

The threat to France from African political movements lay in their growing membership and their ready channels of communication. It was clearly not possible any longer to isolate each territory from its neighbors and to bind it directly to France by separate and strong ties. Through the organized African political groupings, whatever was or was not done in one territory would speedily become known in all the others. The demonstrated electoral strength of the parties, especially the three major ones, encouraged their leaders to compete with one another in seeking further concessions from France. Their demands brought modifications in both the substantive and the administrative implementation of decrees issued under the *loi-cadre.* The African parties pressed for larger responsibilities in a wider range of policy areas. They also asked that the head of the executive branch be an elected official, with the representative of France restricted to technical, coordinating, and arbitral functions.[7]

The New Political Forces

For France, the essence of the problem was that the government in Paris had done only half a job. It had created political institutions for the territories, and had assigned them some powers, but this was admittedly only a first step and essentially a negative one. The old system of centralized administration had been swept away, and

[6] Perrin, cited, p 29.
[7] Same, p. 30.

the ground prepared for some new association. But what kind of association was it to be? "In this dialogue with the *Métropole,* there is one side which remains silent or evasive: the French government, and therefore the parliament, which has not been provided with the programs for constitutional revision."[8] While silence and evasion continued, time was working against the creation of a Franco-African relationship which the territories could accept.

In Togo, immediately adjacent to the new state of Ghana, the territorial assembly in 1955 demanded the end of the United Nations trusteeship and the inclusion of the territory in a French Community. The fact that no such Community existed made it increasingly probable that Togo's evolution under the separate statute of April 16, 1955, would result in its independence, once the trusteeship was ended. The French Cameroons was also drifting away from France. A decree of the Territorial Assembly, of February 24, 1957, declared the area an autonomous state with its own citizenship. As neighboring British Nigeria made its preparations for eventual self-government, the Cameroons Assembly began to seek a union with the British Cameroons and, with that, its own independence from France. Unrest and impatience grew rapidly. In January 1958, an outbreak of violence instigated by the Union des Populations du Cameroun, a reputedly Communist-led group publicly committed to seeking immediate independence, forced the Premier of the Cameroons to request French military support.[9]

Madagascar likewise presented a special problem as it entered the new era of reform. Many of the Madagascan leaders accused France of inventing the device of federation in order to weaken the central assembly of the island, without granting any real compensation by augmenting the responsibilities of the regional assemblies. Behind this charge lay the memory of the 1947 revolt, which had been forcibly repressed by France at the cost of some 80,000

[8] Same, p. 31
[9] *New York Times,* January 6, 1958.

Madagascan casualties. As part of its new colonial policy, France had decreed an amnesty for those rebels still in custody, but its application had then been postponed until 1963. Against this delay, said to be motivated by a desire to influence territorial elections, the Madagascan political leaders reacted with a demand for independence and the subsequent conclusion of a new association between France and Madagascar on a footing of sovereign equality.

Independence *with* France, not separation *from* France, was continually proclaimed by their best-known leaders as the goal of the major political movements in both West and Equatorial Africa. But within these movements younger members, more nationalistic, less identified with France, were making themselves heard. New groups, promising to put an end to all ties with France, were being formed outside the three big parties, as evidenced by the emergence of the Parti Africain de l'Indépendance. The impact of rising nationalism on the older parties was reflected in the cautiously worded declaration of the Rassemblement Démocratique Africain, issued in 1957 by its conference at Bamako: "The Congress, believing that membership by Black Africa in a large political and economic grouping is a factor for power and real independence of all the members of this grouping, propose the realization and reinforcement of a Franco-African Community, democratic and fraternal, based on equality." The Congress went on to declare that the independence of peoples ". . . is an inalienable right, allowing them to manage the attributes of their own sovereignty according to the interests of the general public," but "the interdependence of peoples is the golden rule of the twentieth century. . . ."[10]

In declarations such as this, uncertainty, vagueness, even equivocation were due only in part to internal and external pressures at work in Africa. At least two other factors were exerting a powerful influence. The more immediate one was the policy which France was pursuing in North Africa.

[10] Perrin, cited, p. 30. Also see J. H. Huizinga, "French Black Africa Bypasses 'The Tempest of Nationalism,'" *The Reporter*, June 26, 1958.

The course of the Algerian conflict and its effects on Tunisia and Morocco were putting African leaders elsewhere in an uncomfortable position. It appeared increasingly unlikely that France could hold on to Algeria as a constituent part of the *Métropole*. At the same time, it showed no signs of accepting an autonomous Algeria as a member of a Franco-African Community. By the same unending conflict Tunisia and Morocco were being driven to pose the so-called "Maghreb" solution, a federation of the three North African areas, with or without French participation. A community of France and Black Africa could, it was true, be envisaged regardless of what might happen in North Africa, but the loss of Algeria by France and the complete severance of French connections with Tunisia and Morocco would make the future community far less viable and even less desirable. African politicians desired the association of their territories with France, primarily for economic reasons. They could not, however, take the position that France was right in North Africa and that Tunisia and Morocco and the Algerian rebels were wrong. As North African nationalism was coming to demand a complete separation from France, it was becoming that much more difficult for Black African nationalism to espouse a permanent association with France.

These difficulties might have vanished or been overcome had a blueprint existed for the new French Union. A primary reason for its absence was of course the Algerian war. Another, Africans suspected, was the desire of France to hold the territories of West and Equatorial Africa in a status somewhere short of local autonomy. This suspicion was nurtured by contrasts which existed between the original government project for the 1956 *loi-cadre* and the proposals advanced by the National Assembly's Committee on Overseas Territories. On certain matters, such as the authority allocated to the African executive and his relation to the French Commissioner, the project of the government was far less liberal than that of the Committee.[11] The "hard

---

[11] See Gonidec, cited, *passim* and pp. 109-110.

line" pursued in Algeria and the undeviating insistence by government officials on the *French* nature of the area lent further weight to the argument that French governments were responding only to pressure, not genuinely striving to form a new association which would fully satisfy territorial aspirations.

Under the circumstances there was plenty of room for dispute over the structural form which the Franco-African Community should take. African political leaders were themselves divided over the issue of whether each territory should be a member or whether West and Equatorial Africa should serve as intermediate groupings. Constitutional terms, such as "federation," "confederation," and "union," were freely bandied about in the best French legalistic tradition. Theoretical discussion did not obscure the fact, however, that France lacked any structure comparable to the British Commonwealth. The continued elaboration of "modalities," the French felt, was preferable to running the risk of setting up a structure so loose that African territories could easily break away whenever they so desired. Paradoxically, the longer the *Métropole* avoided a choice between possible institutions embodying the Franco-African Community, the more probable it became that African defections would indeed occur. "The question," wrote René Massigli, "is not what kinds of links tropical Africa will keep with the West; the question is whether any links at all will be maintained on a voluntary basis, and whether Africans, with their Atlantic seaboard, will realize in time that their fate cannot be isolated from the destiny of Atlantic Europe."[12]

The Economic Interests of France

The French stake in Africa was economic as well as psychological and political. Along with France's "civilizing mission" had gone substantial state investments in African territories and trusteeships. Largely through the Fonds d'Investissement et de Développement Économique et

---

[12] Massigli, cited, p 415.

Social (FIDES), established in 1946, an estimated 500 billion francs had by 1955 been poured into the area under the direction of the Ministry of Overseas France. Private investments for the same period totaled perhaps as much as 900 billion francs.[13] After 1955 the war in Algeria and the new independence of Tunisia and Morocco made special cases of those areas, but the French contribution to Black Africa, significantly, increased with the passage of the *loi-cadre*. The figures below for the years 1956 and 1957 show the divisions between French state investments and operating budgets of the fifteen territories:[14]

	Investments		*Budgets*	
	(Figures in billions of francs)			
	1956	*1957*	*1956*	*1957*
Overseas Territories	69.4	77.8	18.3	29.1
Overseas Trusteeships	8.2	8.6	3.1	1.9
Totals	77.6	86.4	21.4	31.0

The French were careful to point out to the Africans that France's contribution in comparison to its national income far exceeded that of Great Britain; hence French African territories had a more substantial interest in continued association with the home country than did their British counterparts. Severance of administrative ties to France would place a heavy financial strain on local resources, even if the territories could somehow succeed in attracting investments from other than French sources.

Minerals constituted the chief objective of French investments. Although the mineral wealth of the territories has not yet been accurately assessed, Gabon is believed to be rich in manganese, Mauritania in copper and iron, and Guinea in bauxite.[15] Increases in French production between 1954 and 1958 and the concomitant foreign exchange

[13] Luc Bourcier du Carbon, "Les Conditions d'Équilibre dans l'Expansion pour l'Union Française," *Politique Étrangère*, December 1955, p 663.
[14] France, Ministère des Finances et des Affaires Économiques, *Statistiques et Études Financières*, April 1958.
[15] Pierre Moussa, *Les Chances Économiques de la Communauté Franco-Africaine* (Paris· Colin, 1957), pp. 226-241.

crisis intensified the drive to discover and exploit raw materials within the franc zone. There was also hope of extracting oil from Gabon and the Middle Congo and bauxite from the Cameroons.[16]

A spur to French investment, both public and private, was the fear that French projects would be submerged when and if the association of the Overseas Territories in the European Common Market opened them to exploitation by other European (primarily West German) capital.

[16] *Le Monde*, June 1-2, 1958.

Chapter Eight

FRANCE AND ITS "DOMESTIC" PROBLEM: THE ALGERIAN WAR

THE PROBLEMS that confronted France in Black Africa, however complex, paled in comparison with that of Algeria. Unless the Fourth Republic could find some way to end this conflict, other African territories might well break away, its foreign objectives be set at naught, and domestic recovery undermined. Last but not least, the rich oil resources of the Sahara might slip out of its grasp. No problem was simple for the "immobilist" political system, but none offered more complex dilemmas than the Algerian problem. Behind the immediate aim of winning the war lay other goals important in themselves and to some extent self-contradictory. Hence the means employed, while possibly consistent with individual ends, constantly worked at cross-purposes. After nationalist agitation had grown to full-scale revolt in 1955 the policies pursued by successive French governments brought their own lethal infection. In the end, the Algerian war killed the Fourth Republic.

For France, the Algerian war was and must remain a domestic problem. Certain parcels of land had been won in blood and glory; they must be considered as sacred as any of the oldest French provinces.[1] Conquered in 1835, Algeria supplied cheap labor to the *Métropole* and laid the foundation for the riches of a few Frenchmen. As the place where De Gaulle's exile movement had coalesced with the

[1] "X", "Réponse aux Partisans d'une Petite France," *Revue de Défense Nationale*, June 1956, p. 684.

forces of internal resistance, Algiers had a special place in French sentiment. Resisting, in the dubious name of "assimilation," nationalist demands for greater autonomy for the Moslem majority, France maintained in the Algerian Departments a political and administrative system which gave effective power to the "European" eighth of the population. As a consequence, after the abortive uprisings of 1946, both sides moved farther and farther apart, with Ferhat Abbas, one-time dentist in Sétif, emerging as the leader of Algerian nationalism. The rapidly increasing Moslem population, with its ever heavier pressure on marginal resources, fed the social and political sources of unrest. In the end, however, it was Mendès-France's decision to grant substantial independence to Tunisia and Morocco, while Algerians were still a subject people, which triggered the full-scale revolt.

If Algeria was, in the French view, a domestic question pure and simple, it followed that international organizations as well as foreign governments should keep hands off. France's allies in the North Atlantic Treaty Organization accepted this position readily enough. Without outward protest from them France diverted to Algeria more and more of the troops it had committed to NATO and more and more of the military equipment that had been supplied to it for the defense of Western Europe.

Retreat in the United Nations

A far more difficult obstacle confronted France in the United Nations, where between 1955 and 1957 it was forced steadily to give ground. Reflecting on the 1955 meeting of the General Assembly, General Marchand described the United Nations as an anticolonial stronghold where ill-assorted countries—like India with its caste system, Saudi Arabia with its feudalism, Libya, a creation of the United States and Britain, and Liberia, controlled by former American Negroes—joined in attacking France.[2] In that session

[2] General Jean Marchand, "Les Puissances Anticolonialistes et l'Afrique Noire Française," same, May 1956, p 577.

the French delegation had effectively defied the Assembly by stalking out when Algeria was placed on the agenda. Although American maneuvering succeeded in having the offensive item deleted, in 1957 France was forced to stand up in the United Nations and debate its position. In February of that year Foreign Minister Christian Pineau outlined at length France's plans for Algeria but rejected the Assembly's competence. "The members of the committee are now informed. This does not mean, however, that we ask them to make their views known to us. I repeat, we are dealing with an internal problem of France, in which the Assembly of the United Nations may not interfere any more than the Political Committee."[3] This retreat from silence to information-without-debate was also ineffective. In a unanimous resolution the Assembly expressed its hope that "a peaceful, democratic, and just solution will be found, through appropriate means, in conformity with the principles of the Charter of the United Nations."[4]

By the next meeting of the Assembly, in November 1957, France had lost more ground. While still rejecting formal mediation by Tunisia and Morocco, it felt compelled to sit down with their representatives to seek a resolution which it could accept. When the Afro-Asian bloc proposed a settlement on the basis of self-determination, France sought the help of its allies, especially the United States, Canada, and Norway in advancing amendments.[5] This maneuver was temporarily effective, for the Political Committee threw out the entire draft resolution by a tie vote of 37 to 37. A final blow, however, fell on France when the Assembly, with France not voting, unanimously adopted a hastily concocted compromise resolution,[6] expressing concern over the Algerian situation, noting the good offices offer of Morocco and Tunisia, and setting forth its wish that "in a spirit of effective cooperation *pourparlers* will be entered into and other appropriate means utilized"

[3] *New York Times*, February 5, 1957.
[4] Same, February 16, 1957.
[5] Same, November 30, 1957.
[6] Same, December 4, 1957.

for a just solution.⁷ France, like South Africa, might continue to insist that the treatment of people within its own territories was none of the United Nations' business, but the organization had shown its determination to go beyond an expression of interest to endorse the principle of negotiation between France and its Algerian "rebels."

The Importance of Saharan Oil

France was fighting in Algeria, not only for the rights and privileges of the European *colons,* but also because a formerly worthless part of the "sacred soil" had suddenly become of incalculable, potential value. Surveys, begun systematically only in 1953, had revealed the presence in the vast desert region of oil and natural gas deposits perhaps second only to those of the Arabian peninsula. Although their full extent could only be conjectured, French hopes soared at the prospect of freeing their country from its dependence on foreign supplies, which the Suez crisis had shown to be unreliable and costly. Two of the first fields detected were at Edjelé, near the Libyan border, and Hassi Messaoud, in southern Algeria. Scarcely had the first trickle of oil started to flow toward France in 1958 when the French public rushed to buy oil shares in an exhibition of enthusiasm rarely if ever equaled by a nation of notably cynical investors.

As the French government was well aware, the entire venture posed risks of failure fully as great as its chances of success. One stemmed from the physical nature of the area. The intense heat was an ever-present danger to Europeans, as well as the sudden fluctuations in temperature. The supply of water was insufficient, and much of it unfit to drink. Also ". . . the isolation, in spite of newspapers, recreation, and the makings of modern comfort, was a most terrible enemy."⁸ It was hard to find people willing to go to such unattractive spots or to remain there long enough to be useful.

---

⁷ Same, December 10, 1957.
⁸ Roger Brunet, "La France et le Pétrole Africain," *Revue Politique et Parlementaire,* February 1958, p. 125.

Financial problems were much in evidence. Everything must be brought in over long distances: men, water, food, clothing, housing, reading and recreational material. Air transport was very expensive, and trucks did not last. Vast sums must be spent on research and exploration in an area whose potentialities were still largely unknown. Equipment had to be bought and put into operation to recover oil once it was found. Then the oil had to be transported to great distances. The total of these costs was staggering. It has been estimated that a drilling apparatus cost between 250 and 500 million francs, and its use 2 to 3 million francs a day. On this basis the French calculated that 75 billion francs would be needed for the Sahara alone for the year 1958. Of this amount 32 billion would go for research, 43 billion for transportation and exploitation. The forecast for 1960, when it was hoped the exploitation of Saharan oil would really have begun, was 250 billion francs.[9]

Along with the money needed to get at the oil, the French had also to consider the extent to which they could control its exploitation. Clearly, French governmental and private investments alone would not suffice. And France was short of both equipment and technicians. On the other hand, foreign companies constituted a potentially economic threat, particularly if they were such giants of American industry as Standard Oil and Caltex. While French officials remained silent, the matter was being settled by an association of foreign and French capital which transposed the problem to a different level. Unless French saving was greatly increased, France could hardly avoid becoming a very junior partner in the near future.[10]

Administrative organization for the Sahara posed grave problems with many political implications. There were drawbacks to any course France might choose. The area could not be left as part of Algeria, for to have it drawn into that conflict would discourage both French and foreign investors. Yet, its separation from Algeria was resented by

[9] Same, p 127.
[10] J. M. de Lattre, "Sahara, Clé de Voûte de l'Ensemble Eurafricain Français," *Politique Étrangère*, no 4, 1957, p. 352.

Algerian nationalists, and indeed by French administrators as well. Those who hoped to come to terms with the rebels on some form of association with France saw a very high trump card—the Sahara's potentially great contributions to Algeria's economic development—disappearing from their hand. A separate political organization for the Sahara made little sense and would be vehemently opposed by all the neighboring territories, yet a purely administrative apparatus might not be powerful enough to control operations in the area and protect its one million inhabitants.

The ultimate decision of the French government, as embodied in a law of January 11, 1957, was not without ambiguity. The Organisation Commune des Régions Sahariennes (OCRS) was established with participation by France, Sudan, Niger, Tchad, and, belatedly, Mauritania. Those who viewed the organization as primarily a managing and coordinating bureau feared it would not be adequate to supervise activities in the 2 million square kilometers of the Algerian Sahara and the 1.6 million of the neighboring territories.[11] But the representatives of participating territories saw in the organization a possible instrument for taking away the richest portions of their land. They pointed to Article 10, which read: "The delegate general can receive by decree of the Council of Ministers, after having, in appropriate instances, received the advice of the Minister of Overseas France or the Minister charged with Algerian affairs, all or part of the powers actually exercised by the governor of French West Africa or French Equatorial Africa."[12] Nevertheless, there were many, including Houphouet-Boigny, who supported OCRS as an essential element in any Franco-African community. Through the organization, they point out, France might share with the African territories its profits from Saharan oil. If other major obstacles were surmounted, these profits could provide a foundation for their own political and

[11] Brunet, cited, p. 132.
[12] See Pierre Cornet, "L'Aube se Lève sur le Sahara," *Revue Politique et Parlementaire*, February 1958, pp. 119-120; the author was Secretary of the High Commission of OCRS.

economic progress. At the same time, they maintained, collaboration with France would strengthen the bonds of the community. Tunisia and Morocco, as well as a restabilized Algeria, could be drawn into the mutual-benefit enterprise, thus realizing the fondest dreams of Eurafrican enthusiasts.[13]

French Efforts to Isolate the Rebels

The success of this vision depended on France's ability to accomplish its military objectives in Algeria. One of them was to isolate the rebels from the mass of the Moslem population and from outside help and encouragement. This was a prerequisite to other goals, because it would give backing to the official thesis that the rebel forces were not supported except under duress, by the overwhelming majority of Algerians and that they constituted only a small minority dependent on foreign assistance. ". . . The vast body of Algerians do not want to be severed from France," wrote the prominent Socialist Marcel-Edmond Naegelen. "I say that, not because I wish it, not in support of a thesis, not even because I believe it. I say it because I know it and daily receive mounting proof of it. To grant Algerian independence would be tantamount to handing over Algeria and its Moslem and European populations to a few agitators who serve other interests than those of that country. It would involve condemning them to oppression and opening wide the doors to Communist influence which has so quickly been able to implant itself in Egypt and the Middle East."[14] The government's view was in distinct contrast with that of Germaine Tillion, a close student of Algerian affairs for more than twenty years, who had lived much of that time in Algeria. Most Moslems, she said, watched the insurrection during its initial stage "with benevolence, with curiosity, with anxiety, but from the outside."

But, beginning in December 1955, the masses allowed themselves to be enrolled by nationalist networks, and beginning

[13] De Lattre, cited, pp. 373-378
[14] Marcel-Edmond Naegelen, "A Waterloo for the West," *Western World*, October 1957, p. 36.

in February 1956, the movement became with incredible speed a general one. . . . During this second phase, the directors, the men who act, are no longer only revolutionary cadres (isolated from the masses by the necessary secrecy of their action); on the contrary they represent the entirety of the notables of the Algerian population. Hence to imagine that one is going to remove this population from the force that influences it is pure myth.[15]

It was precisely this myth, however, that the French rebels of May 13, 1958, sought with a high degree of success to induce the *Métropole* to believe.

If the Algerian nationalists were in fact only "a few agitators," it followed that they must always be losing to the French. An aura of optimism continued to surround French military reports on Algeria, just as during the Indo-Chinese war. In October 1957, French communiqués spoke of increased rebel surrenders, with the added insinuation that the nationalists might be getting tired of the war.[16] "Comparative French military figures tell a 1957 success story in Algeria confirmed by the current calm atmosphere in all major cities," wrote *New York Times* reporter W. H. Lawrence in January 1958.[17] At the end of the following month French officials, although admitting that the nationalists were stronger than ever, claimed that their forces had killed over three thousand rebels in February alone.[18] Less than a week later General Raoul Salan had raised the estimate of nationalist losses to eight thousand for the first two months of 1958.[19] The real purpose of this optimism and its attendant juggling of statistics at that point became clear. French military figures were trying to convince Metropolitan political leaders that the war could be won, provided enough money and support were forthcoming from the government. The bombing of Sakiet was then being defended as justified interdiction of outside aid to a

---

[15] Germaine Tillion, "Algérie 1958 ou les Ennemis Complémentaires," *Preuves*, May 1958, pp 5-6
[16] *New York Times*, October 13, 1957.
[17] Same, January 5, 1958
[18] Same, February 28, 1958
[19] Same, March 5, 1958.

nationalist cause on the verge of defeat. The *Métropole* was being warned not to abandon an enterprise in which so much had been invested, an enterprise within sight of successful completion.[20]

Policies adopted to isolate the rebels within Algeria included "pacification" of the population and sealing off the frontiers. "Pacification" in Algeria meant establishing and deepening French contacts with the Moslems for the purpose of convincing them that their own best interests rested with the French, who should therefore command their sympathy. Thus, the army was assigned two difficult and potentially conflicting missions. These were repeatedly emphasized in the "directives" issued by Minister for Algeria Robert Lacoste.

You are compelled by the facts of the situation to a line of political and military action which forces you to expand your efforts simultaneously in two directions [he told the army in August 1957]—the elimination of contacts between the rebels and the population by destroying the armed bands, and by wiping out the hostile political and administrative network wherever it already exists . . . the resumption of normal relations with all the Algerian populations by gradually establishing new institutions calling for new men who really represent these populations. The struggle against the rebel bands must be conducted with unremitting vigor and with constant concern for maintaining that dynamism and mobility of action which alone will make it possible to obtain substantial results. . . . You must always remember, however, to avoid unnecessary violence. Do not make the mistake of considering a priori a whole village, a whole "mechta" uniformly guilty. On the contrary, know how to distinguish the terrorist and those who help him from the innumerable friends whom France numbers among the Moslem masses. . . . You must make every effort to assist this population in tearing itself free of the rebel hold. All attempts, all initiatives, even if they seem revolutionary, must be tried.[21]

---

[20] W. H. Lawrence reports such a warning in the *New York Times*, March 8, 1958.

[21] Ambassade de France, Service de Presse et d'Information, *General Directive No. 5*, French Affairs no. 39b: Algeria (New York, September 1957), pp. 4-5.

Special military units, popularly known as the "Black Commandos," were established solely for the job of pacification. However, military training and organization were formidable obstacles to their success. "To turn an entire military system against its nature, by converting it into an instrument of permeation and pacification, takes iron will, scrupulous daily supervision, and tireless missionary zeal."[22] These rare qualities could certainly be found among French soldiers and officers, but not in abundance. "The way to promotion and pay" lay in fighting. Those who did establish contacts with the Moslems were put under heavy pressure by their fellow officers to reveal all they may have found out concerning the identity, location, size, and plans of Algeria's nationalist units. It was as difficult for the French to distinguish among a friendly Moslem, a terrified Moslem, and a nationalist Moslem as it was for the Arabs to tell a friendly "Commando" unit from a *ratissage* ready to shoot on sight. Political and military leaders in Algeria believed only half-heartedly, if at all, in the value of pacification. By lending only lukewarm support or none at all, they helped to make their prophecy that pacification would fail come true. As the war continued and acts of violence increased on both sides, middle-ground positions became increasingly untenable. Moderates on either side were gradually forced to adopt an extreme position or lost their influence. "Pacification, isolating the rebellion and stamping it out, that's all over," Servan-Schreiber reported an officer in the "Black Commandos" as saying. (That officer continued, none the less, to dedicate himself to this ideal, ultimately at the cost of his life.)[23]

It was no easier to isolate the rebels from foreign contacts than to cut them off from Algerian Moslem support. Electrified barbed wire entanglements were constructed along the Moroccan and Tunisian frontiers, the latter extending about 185 miles. On the Moroccan side geography helped,

---

[22] Jean-Jacques Servan-Schreiber, *Lieutenant in Algeria* (New York: Knopf, 1957), p. 155.
[23] Same, p. 55.

and the barrier was officially labeled "effective."[24] The Algerian-Tunisian frontier was a different story. There, plans to strengthen the long barricade were coupled by Lacoste with reassertion of the "necessary and legitimate exercise of the right of pursuit."[25] The bombing of Sakiet was an admission that the frontier remained highly permeable despite French efforts. This fact was crucial to the conduct of the war. Differences in activity on the two frontiers were caused by more than topographical distinctions. One factor was that Habib Bourguiba's Tunisia had become enmeshed in the fortunes of the Algerian nationalists. Further, the continued espousal by France of the "right of pursuit" converted the Algerian war, in military as well as political fact, into an international engagement. Its logical end could be only an enlargement of the battle zone or a forced settlement.

Algeria as Part of Metropolitan France

The French hoped, not only to win the war, but to win it in such a way that both Algerias—the "French" million and a quarter and the "Moslem" eight and a half million—would remain an integral part of the Metropolitan territory. Both groups had to be prevented from seceding or dividing Algeria between them Here also policies to implement this goal contained potential contradictions. The agricultural economy of the *colons* was supported both directly and indirectly by France. Physical protection had to be afforded some 19,400 settlers, 7,432 of whom held less than ten hectares and only 300 of whom could be called "rich."[26] The importance of the Algerian wine industry, which is dependent upon purchases by the *Métropole*, is apparent in trade figures for 1957. Of 144,260 million francs of exports listed by specific product, 82,881 million

---

[24] *General Directive No. 5*, cited, p. 3.
[25] Same.
[26] Germaine Tillion, *L'Algérie en 1957* (Paris Éditions de Minuit, 1957), p. 16.

francs, or 57 per cent, were accounted for by wine, almost six times the value of the second leading product.[27] Some $280 million of the $600-million Algerian budget was furnished by Metropolitan France. Of this $115 million went for equipment, $51 million to make up the Algerian deficit, and $23 million to the National Solidarity Fund.[28] In addition, loans were made for farm machinery and advances granted to soldiers who wished to take up residence as farmers or businessmen in Algeria. This aid was justified on far more substantial grounds than help to French settlers caught in a war-torn land. It made economic progress in Algeria seem both necessary and possible, a claim officially expressed despite the ravages of war and a land-population ratio which was, to say the least, becoming more and more unfavorable.

It was estimated that the Algerian population was doubling every twenty years and would reach the incredible total of 40 million by 1995.[29] To meet the minimum needs of this, one of the most rapidly expanding populations in the world, France had carried through one four-year modernization plan from 1949 to 1953, a project which had cost the government $714 million, or about four-fifths of the total $871 million invested in Algeria during this period. Concerned with maintaining or recapturing the allegiance of Algerian Moslems, France interrupted a second four-year plan with a ten-year program of modernization and development having the proclaimed goal of raising the Algerian national income by 6 per cent per year. Government contributions under this new program would be gradually increased to almost $429 million after 1962, a 75 per cent increase over 1956.[30] This long-range assist-

[27] France, Ministère de l'Algérie, *Bulletin Mensuel de Statistique Générale*, February 1958
[28] Ambassade de France, Service de Presse et d'Information, *Algeria* (New York, August 1957), p. 4.
[29] Tillion, *L'Algérie en 1957*, cited, p. 45.
[30] *Algeria*, cited, pp. 4-5. Readers will recognize the outlines of De Gaulle's later, highly publicized, "Constantine Program."

ance was to be in addition to French aid in public health, education, and housing.[31]

Clearly, France was prepared to offer Moslem as well as French Algerians a great deal of money to help develop a French Algeria in which both groups would have an expanding interest. Quite probably these contributions were all or more than France could afford, and there was every reason for French officials to be aggressively proud of them. But were they enough to meet the economic requirements of the population, to say nothing of its political and ideological needs? Quite probably not. ". . . I will dare to state," said Germaine Tillion, "until all Algerians are at the minimum *French* standard of living, no capital can be invested with any security in their country."[32] Although the Minister for Algeria estimated that two and a half million Moslems had in 1957 attained a European standard of living, the Budget Minister estimated the total at only 560,000.[33] This discrepancy of almost two million could be accounted for only in part by the ambiguity of the term "European" (or French) standard of living. But, even accepting the professional optimism of the Minister for Algeria, the task of attaining a minimum acceptable level for the increasing number of Moslems was enormous. Perhaps as much as a billion dollars in investments would be needed annually for five years.[34]

Moreover, doing only part of the job might be worse than doing nothing. As modern medical and health facilities helped more people to live longer, concurrently mounting pressure on limited land resources might leave the majority in a worse rather than a better situation. The relatively few who benefited from assistance programs might receive only enough to heighten their aspirations, to make them fight that much more intensively because their frustrations

---

[31] Same, p. 6. Housing for Algeria alone cost $57 million in public funds in the single year 1955.
[32] Tillion, *L'Algérie en 1957*, cited, p 77.
[33] "J B.," "Note sur le Coût de la Guerre et du Développement de l'Algérie," *Cahiers de la République*, May-June 1958, p 84.
[34] Tillion, *L'Algérie en 1957*, cited, p. 118.

were that much greater. "Revolt lies midway between hopeless despair . . . and the balanced response of those for whom conditions permit a belief in the future."[35]

If economic aid, bounteous though it was by French and other Western standards, showed signs of being too little and too late, what can be said about the proposed political reforms? For years the double-college electoral system had operated in Algeria to discriminate against the Moslem majority. In the first, or "European," college, 570,000 Europeans and 350,000 Moslems were grouped; in the second 1,450,000 electors represented all the other eight million Moslems. Thus a European's vote had six times the weight of a Moslem's. Although the 1956 *loi-cadre* established universal suffrage and one electoral body for the Overseas Territories, it proved all but impossible to accomplish the same for Algeria. In 1957 the Mollet government, in cautious public statements, began to prepare the way for a bill designed to introduce the same pattern into Algeria while protecting the Algerian "French" by gerrymandering the country into districts, each of which has substantial responsibility for administering its own affairs. The response was almost totally negative. The Left condemned the plan on the ground that it did not go far enough to hold out any hope of weakening Algerian nationalist resistance. The Right echoed the fears of the Algerian *colons* that, decentralization or no, the single college and universal suffrage would end their domination.[36]

Pushed by the imminence of the United Nations debate on Algeria, Bourgès-Maunoury tried to ram a much-amended, much-confused bill through the National Assembly. On this issue, André Morice threatened to quit as Minister of National Defense, even though few thought that the Algerian nationalists would accept any political reform, however generous, which began, as this bill did, "Algeria is an integral part of the French Republic." Once more a French Premier was caught squarely in the middle

[35] Same, p. 53.
[36] *New York Times*, January 11, 1957; *Le Monde*, January 9, 1957.

of opposing Assembly forces, with the usual result. The reform bill was defeated, and the Premier was out. However, having combined negatives, the Assembly again had nothing different to offer. No more did Gaillard, Bourgès-Maunoury's successor. On January 31, 1958, virtually the same plan was passed by 296 to 244.[37]

This belated legislative action was possible because the issue as such no longer mattered very much. From the first, French governments had insisted that a cease-fire must precede elections. While the cease-fire was called an "unconditional offer" by Foreign Minister Pineau in addressing the United Nations General Assembly,[38] what it actually amounted to was an insistence that the Algerian nationalists abandon their struggle. On March 27, 1957, Premier Mollet likewise informed the French National Assembly that "within three months after the restoration of calm, elections will be organized in a single electoral college, whose freedom will be strictly supervised."[39] The Algerian nationalists could no more lay down their arms on this basis than the French could accept the nationalist demand for independence as the prerequisite for ceasing hostilities. Under the circumstances the *colon* could let the nationalists do their work for them; they could avoid assuming a position of intransigent opposition, even though the double-college system was one of the things they were determined to maintain. No one was surprised, therefore, that Resident Minister Lacoste could find but few Moslems to enter his municipal administrative units. The severity of the conflict made a mockery of sincere efforts and Machiavellian maneuvers alike. As time passed, both the cease-fire offer and the contemplated political reforms became less and less relevant to the real situation in Algeria, less and

---

[37] *New York Times*, February 1, 1958; a description of the election and decentralization measures may be found in Ambassade de France, Service de Presse et d'Information, *Transformations of the Recent Political Institutions of Algeria—the Loi-Cadre and the Electoral Law*, French Affairs no. 52 (New York, February 1958).

[38] *New York Times*, February 5, 1957.

[39] Ambassade de France, Service de Presse et d'Information, *Speeches and Press Conferences*, no 91 (New York, April 1957).

less viable as policies to preserve the "French Presence" there.

Costs of the French Military Effort

What counted was the military effort pure and simple, stripped of the sham of pacification. And although this effort did prevent the nationalists from winning, it did not give France its victory. As in Indo-China, military power was substantially dissipated in chasing after phantoms. The French army confronted an enemy which could be considered both an army of the people and a people in arms.[40] In its despair the army, supported by French civil authority in Algiers, resorted to two self-defeating "military" measures: *ratissage* and torture. *Ratissage*, literally a "scraping" or "raking," meant attacks on entire Moslem villages suspected of harboring or aiding the nationalists. It was a policy that did not discriminate between communities legitimately suspect and those merely handy for retaliation against nationalist attack. Its effect was to drive survivors into the arms of the nationalists, or cause them to flee across the Tunisian border, or both. *Ratissage* and torture alike were instrumental in spreading conflict on both the national and international planes, and they made even more remote any settlement based on negotiation.

Systematic use of torture was originally denied by the French military and civilians, but the realization of its existence was forced on the French public in such books as Jean-Jacques Servan-Schreiber's *Lieutenant in Algeria*,[41] and Henri Alleg's *La Question*. It is impossible to say with certainty how many hundreds of Moslems were secretly tortured, how many were killed in the process, or shot "while trying to escape." Whatever the number, these measures produced among the Algerians the same reaction as that exhibited by the French when Nazi occupation forces used torture tactics. For every leader betrayed under torture ten

[40] For the analogies between Indo-China and Algeria, see Colonel Nemo, "La Guerre dans le Milieu Social," *Revue de Defense Nationale*, May 1956, pp 605-624.
[41] Cited, French edition published by René Julliard in 1957.

others were found; for every Algerian killed or maimed in the secret chambers a hundred others sprang to take his place. "Without any doubt the executioners are not the colonizers, nor are the colonizers the executioners. . . . But hate is a magnetic field: it has crossed over to them, corroded them and enslaved them."[42]

What were the political costs of these measures? It would indeed have been a miracle had the poison infecting Algeria not spread to the mainland. That it did spread can be seen in the painfully slow progress toward enactment of the reform bill. Like EDC, the Algerian question divided parties and embittered the already tense relations between Left and Right. Because a war was going on in Algeria while France itself was officially at peace, political figures such as François Mitterand and Mendès-France, theoretically free to advocate solutions based on negotiations and compromise with the nationalists, were sharply attacked as defeatists, appeasers, and even traitors. In February 1956, French *colons*, howling and throwing stones at newly invested Premier Guy Mollet, succeeded in frightening the Socialist leader into following a "hard line" in Algeria, abandoning any previous leaning toward compromise. Thus, at a time when some faint chance of compromise with the nationalists may yet have existed, the French executive came under increasing influence of the extreme Right as represented by National Defense Minister Jacques Chaban-Delmas, and his assistant, Léon Delbecque. Legislative support for severe policies came from other extremists such as Jacques Soustelle. French political institutions became a prisoner to policies which most French leaders privately believed could not succeed. However, those who dreaded the worst were forced, with a few exceptions, to remain silent, unable to seek the support of public opinion for compromises which they believed France would one day be compelled to make.

Economic losses sustained during the period of political

---

[42] Jean-Paul Sartre, introduction to Henri Alleg, *The Question*, translated by John Calder (New York. Braziller, 1958), p 34.

deterioration were as substantial as they were difficult to measure. Resident Minister Lacoste was quite logical in adding to the strictly military cost of about 200 billion francs yearly the decrease of national production caused by the presence in the army of men who would otherwise be working in agriculture and industry. The number of such displaced employees he estimated at 133,000, or .7 per cent of the active French population. Assuming that this group would contribute an average of 18,200 billion francs to the 1956 total national revenue, Lacoste calculated this additional loss at some 125 billion francs. Thus for 1956 the Algerian war was said to represent a national drain on France of about 325 billion francs. Of course, this calculation does not attempt to include indirect losses such as uneconomic shifts in production and consumption, slowing down of investment, and the like.

In military terms, the Algerian war was close to becoming a national disaster. The French army of 408,000 included 295,800 conscripts as of October 1957.[43] Of them, a substantial percentage had no desire to fight in Algeria, as recurrent draft riots in France demonstrated. Lack of morale among enlisted men was matched by that among junior and senior officers, who either had no stomach for the kind of war they were forced to engage in or, conversely, resented concessions made by military effectiveness to civilian softheadedness. Some officers, like the draftees, went home as soon as their tour of duty was up—or just about at the point where the investment in their training was beginning to pay off.

Evidence of disagreement within the officers' corps could be seen in two actions of early 1957. In January the Ministry of National Defense acknowledged that "sanctions" had been taken against an unnamed French officer in Algeria for "verbal imprudence" and "observations" made to some other officers. The French press, identifying Brigadier General Jacques Faure, reported that he had been confined to quarters for a month. His "imprudence"

[43] *New York Times*, October 19, 1957.

was said to have been far more than verbal, having in fact consisted of nothing less than an attempt to gain supporters for a plan to set up military rule in Algeria. Those subjected to "observations" were reported to be Lieutenant General René Frandon, in charge of French aviation in Algeria, and Brigadier General René Dumesnil de Malicourt, air force commander.[44] Two months later General Jacques Marie Roch Paris de Bollardière, who had led the French paratroopers in Indo-China, resigned his Algerian command. According to the government, the resignation was tendered because the command had been downgraded; according to the French press it was a protest against the extreme measures, including torture, being employed against the Algerian Moslems.[45] More than a year before the French army rebelled it was clear that the crisis in morale was in large part the result of a moral conflict inevitable in a military establishment which was fighting for France, but with some of its members violating all the human values to which France was traditionally committed.

The moral position of France was further weakened by Metropolitan restrictions of civil liberties, shocking in a country reputedly dedicated to freedom. Even while the government was establishing, in response to public pressure, a commission of jurists to inquire into alleged violations of human rights in Algeria, it was preparing a bill to take over extraordinary powers in France proper. As presented to the Assembly in July 1957, this bill gave the government the right to detain suspects for an unlimited period, to institute police visits and searches at night, and to restrict the movements within France of alleged sympathizers with the Algerian nationalists. In fact, the French police had already been conducting night raids for some time, rounding up, questioning, and detaining Algerians by the hundreds. Although many groups in the Assembly were seriously disturbed by the implications of the measure,

---

[44] *Le Monde*, January 7, 1957.
[45] Same, March 28, 1957. Jean Planchais contrasts the careers of Generals Faure and Paris de Bollardière in *Le Malaise de l'Armée* (Paris Plon, 1958), pp. 39-45.

outright opposition came only from the Communists and Poujadistes. Those on the Left and Center sought guarantees against abuse of the powers, while the Right attempted to push the government even further.[46] The measure passed after the government had accepted a Socialist amendment to restrict the period of detention to thirty days.[47] "For the first time in the history of the Republic a government has asked Parliament, at a time when there is no foreign war, for the right to open concentration camps in which to lock up Frenchmen," wrote Maurice Duverger.[48]

To restrictions on individuals France added censorship of the press and of periodicals and books. French authorities in Algiers seized publications opposing French military policy on the grounds that the nation was at war in Algeria. Principal victims were the neutralist *Observateur*, Mendès-France's *Express*, for which Servan-Schreiber wrote, and even, occasionally, the respectable, conservative, if neutralist-tinged *Le Monde*. Censorship also spread to the mainland. Henri Alleg's book *La Question* was suppressed and copies confiscated.[49] On one famous occasion when *Express* was confiscated in France, the entire front page of the next issue, that of March 13, 1958, depicted a sheep holding in its mouth a copy of *Express*, with "Vive Gaillard" emblazoned across it.

If it was not actually physically dangerous for Frenchmen in France to oppose the official line of *guerre à outrance*, it became at least imprudent and costly. A wish to be safe rather than sorry led many French journals and journalists to follow the example of most political leaders and avoid overt criticism; in other words, they added a much more pervasive self-censorship to that imposed by the government. "A large part of the press," wrote Françoise Giroud in *Express*, "has for two years chosen, sometimes for hon-

[46] *New York Times*, July 17, 1957.
[47] Same, July 20, 1957.
[48] *Le Monde*, July 18, 1957.
[49] Notwithstanding which, it quickly sold about 150,000 copies according to publisher, George Braziller, in the preface to the American edition, cited, p. 10.

orable reasons, not to print the truth that it knew when it had occasion to know it. To preserve Algeria, so they believe, they have abandoned France."[50] When the events of May 1958 took place, the French people were largely ignorant of the attitudes of the French army and civilians in Algeria. Unaware of the extent to which their freedoms had been eroded by a system they had deliberately kept weak in order to guarantee those freedoms, they were caught without any alternative to a Republic from which they had been systematically alienated and an authoritarian regime sprouting from issues of which they had not been fully informed.

France's inability to decide on consistent objectives in Algeria, to define them in clear policies and enforce them on Algerian Moslems, European *colons,* and civilian and military authorities meant international isolation. This might not have occurred had France quickly won the war or accepted a negotiated settlement. France's inability either to find a compromise solution or to win a prompt victory threatened to separate it from its partners in Western Europe, estrange it from the United States and Britain, destroy the last vestiges of its influence with the Arab states, alienate its erstwhile protectorates, Tunisia and Morocco, and bring about secession by Black Africa. French incoherence over EDC had resulted in a "France Seule," and French divisions over Algeria reinforced its solitude. It was a heavy, perhaps fatal, price to pay whatever the reasons—grandeur, civilization, Western ideals, French *colons,* economic investment, or any combination thereof. As an ultimate irony, France's claim to sole competence with Algeria led in the end to internationalizing the conflict.

French leaders saw or suspected several different sources of foreign intrusion into Algerian affairs. Soviet ideology and Soviet ambitions naturally favored the triumph of the Algerian nationalists. Russian policy made common cause with and worked through Arab nationalism, especially

[50] May 29, 1958.

through Nasser's Egypt. This form of intrusion, complicated by the weakness of Tunisia and Morocco, especially the former, tended to involve these two countries in the struggle. Finally, as Tunisia and Morocco became committed to an FLN (Front de la Libération Nationale Algérienne) victory, they involved Great Britain and the United States. Therefore, in the French view, while the connections between the outside countries might at times be indirect, all—United States, Great Britain, Morocco, Tunisia, and Egypt—were consciously or unconsciously playing in Algeria the Soviet game.

Despite repeated denials by FLN leaders, France maintained that the Algerian nationalist movement owed much to both Algerian and international communism. Communists, the French said, had shown the Algerians how to organize revolutionary cadres, had supplied leading activists for those cadres, and had fomented purges of those willing to come to terms with France. Finally and most important, Communists had shown the rebels the military and psychological techniques of revolutionary war, including the use of terror.[51]

This internal collaboration, France claimed, was supported by outside assistance. The Soviet Union provided themes for the Cairo Radio in its steady incitement of the Algerians to violence and murder. Through Egypt guns, ammunition, medicines, food, transport, and supplies were funneled from Communist-dominated countries to Algeria. Military shipments were also attempted by other means, as was shown when the French seized a Yugoslav ship outside the Algerian port of Oran. Reputedly bound for Casablanca and New York, the vessel was carrying 3,286 cases of arms and ammunition.[52]

The involvement of Egypt in the Algerian war began with Nasser's accession to power. It was more to eliminate him than to win back the Canal that French troops were landed at Suez. Their failure left Nasser free to use his

[51] *Rébellion et Communisme*, no date, no author, but bearing "special imprint of Government-General, Algiers," pp. 42-73
[52] *New York Times*, January 20, 1958.

greatly enhanced prestige to aid the nationalists. In addition to his use of the Cairo Radio for propaganda purposes, he sent money and military supplies to Algerian rebels. Cairo became the seat of the nationalists' political committee. Though Bourguiba may have hoped to win them away from Nasser by making Tunisia a haven for rebel leaders, the rebels, in fact, made use of both centers. Along with Nasser went the rest of the Arab world. Through the medium of the Arab League assistance and propaganda poured into Algeria. Whatever the disputes and intrigues among its members, the Arab League was united on two issues—support of the FLN and destruction of Israel.

Objectives of the Arab League in time conditioned French policy in the Near East. France took no stock in the Baghdad Pact, which, in its view, tended to exacerbate Arab nationalism and to give Near Eastern neutralism a pro-Soviet tinge. In the French view, the pact was worse than useless as a defense against Communist expansion; it positively encouraged it.[53] On the other hand, French friendship with Israel was in the interest of both countries, since Israel was the only power in the Near East able and willing to stand up to Nasser. Awakening to the possibilities of this friendship, France reversed its rather lukewarm attitude and proceeded to supply the Ben Gurion regime with arms, planes, and, some said, pilots. The collapse of the Suez venture left Israel and France closer together than ever before, each facing a prolonged and serious challenge against common external enemies.

---

[53] See Metellus, "Politique de la France au Proche-Orient," *Politique Étrangère*, December 1955, pp. 686-687.

Chapter Nine

TUNISIA AND MOROCCO IN THE ALGERIAN WAR

TUNISIA'S ENTANGLEMENT in the Algerian conflict was virtually inevitable. For one thing, there had not been time for the new state to emerge in a firm pattern. In his Carthage Declaration of July 31, 1954, Premier Mendès-France declared that "the self-government of the Tunisian State is recognized and proclaimed without reservation by the French government, whose intention it is both to confirm this principle and to enable Tunisia to carry it successfully into action."[1] But more than a year elapsed before the various conventions entered into force.[2] The basis of the Franco-Tunisian relationship was then modified by the protocol of March 20, 1956, in which "France solemnly acknowledges Tunisia's independence." "In mutual respect of their sovereignties," the protocol continued, "France and Tunisia agree to define or elaborate further the means by which interdependence may be freely achieved between the two countries, by organizing their cooperation in those fields in which they have common interests, in particular defense and foreign relations."[3]

Breakdown of Franco-Tunisian Relations

The negotiations promised in the protocol had not led to any agreement by the time the controversy culminating in

[1] Quoted in "Tunisia Faces the Future," World's Documents Series, *Le Monde Économique*, special issue, June 1956, p. 56.
[2] The texts may be found, in English translation, in same, pp. 172-204.
[3] Same, p. 169.

the French bombing of Sakiet broke off contacts between the two governments. France and Tunisia were left with conventions which both agreed had become, in part at least, outmoded. In them a special position had been granted to France and to Frenchmen in Tunisia with regard to (1) foreign affairs and national defense, (2) special guarantees to French citizens, (3) French administrative responsibilities in Tunisia, (4) economic unity and French assistance. These privileges implied a considerable diminution of the independence which had been acknowledged but not implemented in the protocol. Special security zones in south Tunisia and in the north around the French naval base at Bizerte were defined. French troops remained in Tunisia, and the Tunisian government accepted an obligation "to take, at the request of France, all measures necessary for ensuring in Tunisia a constant adaptation to the general system of defense and security implemented by France as part of her own responsibilities and of her responsibilities in the defense of the Free World."[4]

In the draft conventions, special guarantees covered French property rights, the continuance of French courts over a period of twenty years, and the application to Frenchmen in Tunisia of French laws covering such matters as inheritance, marriage, and divorce.[5] A part of the French administrative apparatus was to remain in both Tunisian central and local governments for a ten-year period.[6] During that time Tunisian administrators were to be trained, but for twenty years certain national positions were to be reserved for French officials. Frenchmen were also to comprise at least one-third of the police force in certain cities containing most of the French nationals. Finally, an Economic and Financial Convention provided for a customs union between the two countries, supervised by a Franco-Tunisian Joint Committee, and for French economic assistance to Tunisia.[7]

[4] Article 10, Paragraph 3, of General Convention, in same, p. 173.
[5] Convention on the Status of Persons, same, pp. 180-182.
[6] The positions are listed in Annexed Protocol no. 4 to the General Convention, same, p. 176.
[7] Same, pp. 201-205.

As relations between the two countries deteriorated over the Algerian conflict, the special position of France, accepted by Tunisia, remained vague and poorly adapted to Tunisia's evolution toward full sovereignty. The lag was especially significant in economic and military affairs. There were approximately four million people in Tunisia, an estimated 180,000 of whom were French. "Of an active [French] population of 62,500 persons . . . roughly two-thirds are directors or managers in industry, agriculture, or commerce, members of the liberal professions or civil servants."[8] After the Carthage Declaration the French began to leave; 60,000 were gone by the end of 1957. With them went about 10 per cent of the Tunisian national revenue and about one-third of the bank deposits in the areas of French concentration.[9]

This was only one aspect of French influence on the Tunisian economy. In May 1957, the Mollet government cut off economic aid to Tunisia, a move which was followed by President Bourguiba's denunciation of the entire Economic and Financial Convention. Tunisia was thereby denied 12 billion francs in assistance promised by France for 1957.[10] Moreover, until its abrogation the customs union had acted in Tunisia to maintain a preferential market for French goods despite their high prices. On February 6, 1958, two days before the bombing of Sakiet, President Bourguiba acknowledged the parlous economic condition of his country. There were, he said, 400,000 unemployed, and the rapidly growing population required the investment of 35 billion francs a year for ten years to provide employment. But, he added, "one cannot abandon our sovereignty and our Algerian brothers for some 30 billion francs."[11]

Far from causing Tunisia to be more amenable, French policies were threatening to undermine its Western orientation, especially since other countries, particularly the

[8] Same, p. 46
[9] Louis Chevalier, "France et Tunisie," *Population*, October-December 1957, pp. 609-610.
[10] *New York Times*, May 24, 1957.
[11] Same, February 7, 1958.

United States, were not moving in to replace France as a source of economic assistance.

On the other side, Bourguiba was being pressed by the Front de la Libération Nationale Algérienne (FLN) and Arab nationalists. Not yet fully master in his own house, he was maneuvering to moderate the aims of the Algerian rebels. To this end he had run the risk of bringing the FLN directorate from Cairo to Tunis in order to remove it from the extremist influences centered around Nasser and the Cairo Radio. He had also conducted what amounted to continual negotiations with Libya and Morocco, since the monarchs of both nations were known to favor an Algerian settlement at some point short of independence. To balance on this high wire, however, he needed economic and diplomatic support from France's two major allies, Britain and the United States. Hence their decision, in November 1957, to send arms to Tunisia far transcended in importance the quantity or firepower involved.

France suspended deliveries of military equipment in the summer of 1957 when it cut off economic aid. On September 4, 1957, Bourguiba requested arms from Great Britain and the United States (having failed to get them from Italy and Belgium, said the French).[12] According to American sources, the Mollet government, rather than see Great Britain and the United States make the shipments, agreed to supply arms jointly with other European countries. This decision, however, promptly placed the Premier in jeopardy because of rightist attacks. He therefore formally denied the existence of any such arrangement, but denial did not prevent his fall. His successor, Félix Gaillard, then proposed to resume French arms deliveries to Tunisia. Again, because of opposition within the government and the National Assembly, the proposal was not carried out. Unwilling to wait any longer, the United States and Great Britain first notified France of their intention to ship the arms if France did not act and subsequently

[12] Félix Gaillard address of November 15, 1957, to the National Assembly, reprinted in NATO Information Service (Paris), *NATO Letter*, December 1957, pp. 11-12.

announced the shipments, on November 14, 1957.[13] The amounts were small indeed: 500 MI rifles and 50,000 rounds of ammunition from the United States, 350 Sterling submachine guns and 70 Bren guns with ammunition from Great Britain.[14]

The Tunisian arms incident had serious consequences for the Algerian conflict, for Anglo-American relations with France, and, in fact, for the entire Western alliance. The immediate effect was that relations between France and Tunisia were all but broken off. Bourguiba demanded that French troops in Tunisia, some 15,000 men, be removed from the country before March 15.[15] It was his contention that these troops, and French citizens in key areas, constituted a menace to Tunisian political, military, and economic stability. France was equally certain that the opposite was true. Arms ostensibly assigned to the Tunisian army (which numbered only 4,000) might well wind up in the hands of the Algerian nationalists. Furthermore, said France, Bourguiba wanted French troops moved north and then evacuated so that the border area might more easily serve as a sanctuary for the rebels and a staging area for their re-entry into the conflict. The French were of the opinion that the Tunisian President had gone so far down the road with the Algerians that, even had he wished, he could not now retreat.

The suspicions of both sides were unpleasantly confirmed in January 1958, when President Bourguiba refused to accept a French mission bearing a message from Premier Gaillard until its military member, Brigadier General Georges Buchalet, was withdrawn. To the Tunisians, his presence was a not very subtle military threat.[16] On the other hand, Bourguiba's action was interpreted by Gaillard as a pretext for disavowing all responsibility for the increasing number of incidents along the Tunisian-Algerian border, especially the capture of four French soldiers by the Algerians in an

[13] *New York Times*, November 14, November 17, 1957.
[14] *NATO Letter*, cited, p. 11.
[15] *New York Times*, December 26, 1957.
[16] Same, January 17, 1958.

ambush near Sakiet-Sıdi-Youssef. "There are questions," Gaillard told the National Assembly, "that M. Bourguiba does not wish to discuss on any account; there are choices that M. Bourguiba does not seem to wish to make. When the evidence is against him, he turns the problem around with consummate skill."[17]

The Bombing of Sakiet-Sidi-Youssef

The last act in the drama of Tunisian involvement occurred on February 8, when twenty-five French planes attacked Sakiet-Sidi-Youssef. From the official French point of view the attack was the tragic but logical consequence of Bourguiba's inability and unwillingness to stop the Algerians from using his territory as a base of operations.

> For months now [declared Gaillard] the French Government has repeatedly warned the Tunisian Government of the considerable risks to the relations between our two Governments inherent in the fact that increasingly large forces and a logistic center of the FLN have been established in Tunisia.... Whether it wants it or not, whether it has been led into it more by events than by its will, Tunisia has, nevertheless, gradually placed itself in a state of belligerence with regard to France. We have been unable to find any indication to show that it has made any great effort to avoid this situation.[18]

For many people in France, however, and for most of the outside world, the attack on Sakiet was further evidence that the Fourth Republic was falling into chaos. French civilian and military leaders in Algeria appeared to have lost control over extremist units, or to have given a blank check to field officers to retaliate across an international frontier, an indication of reckless irresponsibility Quite possibly the Gaillard government had not even been informed in advance of the attack, much less asked for permission.[19] If such were the case, the Premier's subsequent

[17] Speech of February 11, 1958, quoted from Ambassade de France, Service de Presse et d'Information, *Speeches and Press Conferences*, no. 105 (New York, February 1958), p. 6.
[18] Same, pp. 7-8.
[19] *The Economist*, February 15, 1958, p. 588.

wholehearted defense of the action on February 11 signified that he was becoming a prisoner of French extremists in Algeria and the *Métropole*.

Many facts concerning the attack are in dispute, including the size and nature of the FLN position in Sakiet, the character and extent of the casualties which resulted from the bombing. There can be no doubt, however, that the raid led directly to the internationalization of the Algerian conflict, a step which French governments had adamantly opposed.[20] Immediately after the attack Tunisia notified the United Nations that the raid "constitutes armed aggression by France against Tunisia in flagrant contradiction to the spirit of the Charter of the United Nations and particularly to Article 2, Paragraph 4, of the Charter." (This article binds member states to refrain "from the threat or use of force against the territorial integrity or political independence of any state, or in any other manner inconsistent with the purposes of the United Nations.")[21] Three days later Tunisia requested a meeting of the Security Council to consider "an act of aggression" by France against Tunisia.[22] France, like the United States, had been hoping to keep the entire matter out of the United Nations, and therefore out of the hands of its twenty-nine Afro-Asian bloc members, to say nothing of the Soviet Union. But, as a result of Tunisia's second move, France was forced to submit a counterclaim, asking the Council to look at "the situation arising from aid from Tunisia to the Algerian rebels, permitting these to conduct from Tunisian territory operations directed against the integrity of French territories and the security of persons and property."[23]

Meanwhile Bourguiba used the Sakiet affair to renew his demand that all French troops be withdrawn. Roadblocks were thrown around the military bases near Tunis, and at Gafsa, Gabès, Sfax, and Medjez-el-Bab. France was warned not to send its naval craft into Bizerte, which was

---

[20] See *Le Monde*, February 10, 1958.
[21] Text of the Tunisian note in *New York Times*, February 11, 1958.
[22] *New York Times*, February 14, 1958.
[23] Same, February 15, 1958

a NATO as well as a French base. Tunisia demanded that five of the ten French consulates be closed immediately; France refused to comply and made this the basis of a new protest to the United Nations. Finally, French residents in Sbeitla, Souk-el-Arba, and Moktar were told to pack up and move out. France regarded this as a form of property confiscation contrary to its 1955 agreement with Tunisia.[24] Bourguiba then informed the world that the controversy could be liquidated and Franco-Tunisian relations restored only when all French troops had left the country and the Bizerte base had been surrendered.[25]

The Anglo-American Good-Offices Mission

Whether the establishment of an Anglo-American good-offices mission was a deliberate overture or, as the *New York Times* reported,[26] just an accident, it provided another form of internationalizing the conflict. Tunisia welcomed the idea of a mission because Bourguiba saw it as a vehicle through which to attain his five primary and related goals: a Western commitment to an Algerian settlement; the settlement itself, based on Algerian autonomy; the evacuation of French troops from Tunisia; an escape from the risks of extremist Moslem nationalism; and a resumption of relations, including economic ties, with France.

As for France, or rather the Gaillard government, there were equally strong reasons for accepting the Anglo-American offer. France did not wish to isolate itself completely from its allies. It already knew what the United States thought, officially and unofficially, of French behavior; Secretary Dulles had summoned French Ambassador Hervé Alphand to his home on February 9 to tell him. In the second place, France hoped to avoid a difficult debate in the Security Council. (It succeeded; on February 18, the Council adjourned without setting any date for meeting again on the Sakiet-Tunisian question, despite the plea of the

[24] Same, February 12, 1958.
[25] Same, February 13, 1958.
[26] February 26, 1958.

Tunisian representative.)[27] The Anglo-American mission looked like the best, if not the only, means of resuming its negotiations with Tunisia so that French economic, political, and military interests might be recovered. Finally, outside intrusion could relieve domestic political pressures on the Gaillard government. The Left and even the Center and moderate Right were insisting that some gestures had to be made to appease Tunisian and, above all, foreign opinion. At the same time, the obdurate Right was insisting that any concessions at all would encourage Bourguiba to ask for more, and would inspire the Algerian rebels to greater violence. The Gaillard government, which had already decided that some relaxation of tension was necessary, could satisfy the demands of the Left by allowing the good-offices mission to do its work. Subsequent attacks by the Right could then be diverted from the Premier himself to the United States and Britain, which were already suspected by conservatives of wishing to eliminate French influence from North Africa.

So the Robert Murphy-Harold Beeley team was launched on the Paris-Tunis road, but it was far easier to start the shuttling process than to bring it to a successful end. One fundamental obstacle lay in the varying interpretations of the term "good offices." Under international law, "mediation" involves positive suggestions by a third party for settlement of a dispute and "arbitration" of a judgment as to who is right and who is wrong. "Good offices," however, only implies the carrying back and forth of messages between disputants, in the hope that they can be brought together to settle the dispute themselves. This definition was precisely the one, and the only one, accepted by France.[28] From such a minimal interpretation stemmed the other French positions: that the entire question of Algeria was outside the mission's purview, that freedom and security of movement should be restored to French nationals and military personnel before resuming Franco-Tuni-

[27] *New York Times*, February 19, 1958.
[28] *Le Monde*, February 25, 1958, reporting a decision of the Council of Ministers of February 22.

party were initially able to work together to maintain close economic and political ties with France, ties based on a long record of French assistance and on Franco-Moroccan solidarity in two World Wars.

Friction between France and Morocco was further reduced by the fact that Moroccan nationalism was directed outward, toward territorial expansion. In opening negotiations with France in February 1956, Embarek Bekkai, head of the Moroccan government, had clearly indicated the course his country intended to follow. "Gentlemen," he declared, "exceptional circumstances early in this century had led to the demarcation of zones of influence in our country. Such circumstances are no longer consistent with historical factors. The independence of Morocco would be truly significant only if our country regained its territorial unity, to which the Moroccan people have been and remain unanimously and strongly attached. . . . We are convinced that in this field France will not fail to help us."[36]

The French support in which M. Bekkai professed such conviction was not realized, but Morocco unilaterally set out to attain its territorial objectives. In October 1956, eight nations—of which the United States was one—transferred the international zone of Tangier to Moroccan control. In this instance Morocco acted slowly and with restraint in giving effect to its sovereignty. The administrative apparatus was not drastically altered, and the international character of the police force and legal structure was retained. Tangier remained a free port and a free-currency market, although its economic situation rapidly deteriorated. Foreigners left the city and took their bank balances with them, joining in the flight of the French from Morocco and Tunisia, with the same results.

The next objects of Moroccan expansionist ambitions were the small enclave of Ifni and the so-called Southern

[36] Address of February 22, 1956; English translation in Ambassade de France, Service de Presse et d'Information, *Documentary Background of the Franco-Moroccan Agreements of March 2, 1956*, Moroccan Affairs no. 12 (New York, March 1956), p 12.

Protectorate of Morocco, both controlled by Spain. Spain's difficulties with Morocco over these bits of arid real estate serve as an object lesson in how a nation may be rewarded if it supports Arab (or any form of) nationalism. Moroccan irregular troops began fighting in Ifni in November 1957.[37] They soon received the official approval of the Moroccan government and of Jordan, Syria, Saudi Arabia, Lebanon, and Tunisia. Several Arab League states offered to "mediate the conflict,"[38] and mediation was indeed needed by both sides. Spain saw the Moroccans rapidly extending their pressure from Ifni to include the Southern Protectorate and the places still under Spanish control in Northern Morocco. For its part the Moroccan government found nationalism a force easier to unleash than to restrain. The outlawed Moroccan Communists proclaimed their approval of anti-Spanish moves in both south and north,[39] while other extremists began to eye the undefined, long border with France in the Sahara. Morocco was especially interested in the Sahara region because of the prospects for petroleum development, and France for the same reason had delayed any direct comment on Morocco's elastic interpretation of its historic jurisdiction.[40]

The way was opened for settlement when Spanish military action demonstrated that a precarious hold could be maintained over the Protectorate and Ifni but that the effort was actually not worth the trouble. Spain and Morocco agreed in April 1958, reputedly at the instigation of the United States, that the sparsely inhabited Southern Protectorate should go to Morocco. Although Morocco claimed that this cession did not constitute a definitive border agreement with Spain, Spain was, temporarily at least, left in control of its enclaves in Northern Morocco, the most important of which is Ceuta, directly opposite Gibraltar.

[37] *New York Times,* November 30, 1957.
[38] Same, December 6, 1957.
[39] Same, December 4, 1957.
[40] Same, November 13, 1957.

Territorial ambitions have undoubtedly contributed to Morocco's relative aloofness from the Algerian conflict, but there are other reasons too. The border between Morocco and Algeria is relatively short and relatively easy for France to police. Morocco, on the far-side of Algeria, is more remote than Tunisia from the Egyptian-North African conduit. While the Istiqlal party sympathizes officially with Algerian nationalist ambitions, Moroccan conservatism has placed considerable value on close association with France and has favored Algerian autonomy within a Franco-African community. This position, like Tunisia's Western orientation, has caused Moroccan leaders to clash with Arab extremists, particularly with Egypt. In March 1958 Morocco accused Egypt of harboring and even supporting Moroccans whose aim was to otherthrow the Sultanate. The same representations included a sharp denial that Morocco, in advancing the idea of a North African federation, was supporting the aims of French and American imperialists.[41]

Morocco's quarrels with France, even those related to Algeria, have been quite specific, and thus less disruptive of relations between the two countries. In October 1956, France forced down a plane flying five Algerian nationalist leaders from Morocco to Tunisia, and imprisoned them. After a lengthy correspondence, Morocco and France agreed in July 1957 to submit the dispute to a commission of inquiry made up of Belgian, Lebanese, and Italian representatives. At a crucial point in the investigation, when the Belgian and Italian members supported the French refusal to seek direct testimony from the arrested Algerians, the Moroccan delegate withdrew from the commission, which was thereupon adjourned indefinitely.[42]

In another incident which likewise resulted in a stalemate, two French officers, along with an Algerian and a Moroccan, were sentenced to death *in absentia* by a Moroccan court for subversive activities against the Moroccan State. Whether or not French protests and warnings were the cause, the Moroccan Supreme Court in April 1958 de-

[41] Same, March 14, 1958.
[42] Same, February 28, 1958.

clared a mistrial on the technical ground that a written statement of the charges had not been filed initially.[48]

These samples of Franco-Moroccan friction contrast sharply with the steady crescendo of bitter charges and countercharges passing between Paris and Tunis. Economic and military issues were more serious, but here also Morocco's particular situation enabled it to steer clear of any substantial entanglement in the Algerian conflict. Into both issues the United States was introduced as a third party, softening the Franco-Moroccan dialogue. American installations in Morocco are important, perhaps in the short run essential, to the retaliatory capacity of the Strategic Air Command. Major bases are located at Sidi Slimane, inland from Rabat, and at Ben Guerir, forty miles north of Marrakesh. In addition, there is a fighter strip at Boulhaut and a supply depot at Nouaseur, both near Casablanca, naval facilities at Port Lyautey, and a naval air base at Kinitra. American military personnel at these installations totals about 12,000.[44]

The long-term status of the bases has been uncertain. They had been leased by France to the United States before Moroccan independence, and after the Franco-Moroccan agreements of March 1956, French troops continued to maintain responsibility for their "security." Moroccan authorities, although not necessarily opposed to a temporary American military presence, have not been eager to sign any long-term agreement, since this might imply the continued presence of French armed forces. From the outset, therefore, they have insisted that Moroccan sovereignty be recognized before negotiating a defense agreement. American military leaders, on the other hand, desiring base rights for as long as twenty years, have hesitated to accept Moroccan sovereignty before the rights were secured for fear that Morocco would, to get rid of the French, demand that all foreign troops leave. Thus the French claims, which the Fourth Republic had no intention of abandoning, have prevented any firm decision on the future of the bases. In

[43] Same, April 2, 1958
[44] Same, March 24, 1957; April 1, 1958.

November 1957, King Mohammed V visited the United States, but a direct discussion of the problem with the American chief executive was impossible, President Eisenhower having suffered a cerebral occlusion a few hours after he had welcomed the King at the Washington airport. The communiqué issued after the King's talks with Secretary of State Dulles indicated that no final agreement was as yet in sight, but that both sides desired to work out a "provisional solution."[45]

Military relations involving Morocco, France, and the United States could not be separated from the question of economic aid. France had promised both Tunisia and Morocco economic assistance along with their independence. In both cases, however, the actual arrangements for assistance were left unsettled. At issue with Morocco was the recognition of French property rights, which control more than 80 per cent of the economy.[46] Although Morocco has benefited by its membership in the franc zone, particularly from currency transfers following France's devaluation of the franc,[47] it was nevertheless forced to turn to the United States for additional help. This was regarded with suspicion by France, which already blamed the United States for having done much to arouse Moroccan nationalism through President Roosevelt's meeting with the Sultan in 1943.

In the communiqué following the base discussions in 1957, Secretary of State Dulles assured King Mohammed of the "readiness of the United States to assist the Kingdom of Morocco in its efforts to stabilize and expand its economy. For this purpose, the Government of the United States will continue to undertake in Morocco programs of economic and technical assistance agreed upon between the two countries."[48] One such agreement had already been signed in April 1957, under which the United States was to make available such badly needed products as sugar

[45] Same, November 28, 1957.
[46] Same, August 10, 1957.
[47] Same, December 9, 1957.
[48] Same, November 28, 1957.

and edible oils, using the local funds realized by Moroccan purchase primarily for agricultural programs, including irrigation, soil agronomy, and erosion prevention.[49] In November 1957, it was estimated that American aid to Morocco since that country's independence had totaled some $20 million.[50] This was a vivid contrast to France's failure to deliver promised loans and grants-in-aid.

The lesson of Morocco could hardly escape native leaders in the French Overseas Territories. They envisaged a very real possibility that independence from France would bring more material rewards than France was willing or able to grant its dependencies, provided the United States became convinced that it had a strategic stake in those areas and provided also they were able to avoid, as Tunisia had been unable to do, entanglement in the Algerian imbroglio. Hope for continued American interest burgeoned after Vice-President Nixon's publicized tour of Africa, while the growing weakness of the Fourth Republic dimmed any hopes of its putting an end to the Algerian war by either force or negotiation.

[49] Same, April 3, 1957.
[50] Same, November 28, 1957.

Chapter Ten

"IMMOBILISME" AND FOREIGN POLICY

ALTHOUGH, as we have seen, post-1954 governments did little indeed with the time bought at so great a price by Mendès-France, it is unjustified to say that no reforms were attempted, or even that none succeeded. Yet, the political requirements of executive coalitions fluctuating around the unstable center ultimately made it impossible to build the internal strength and cohesion that was needed for positive action on the international scene, despite burgeoning economic prosperity. As in the period 1950-1954, foreign policy consisted of a series of ingenious schemes designed to manipulate the international environment in order to evade as long as possible the fundamental domestic changes that French political leaders could not and would not introduce within a system that had produced those leaders. As with most reckonings, postponement added to the total bill. When finally presented in May 1958, the bill could be settled only by forfeiting the system and, along with it, the Fourth Republic.

Foundations of Foreign Policy-Making

The premier tended increasingly to set the course in foreign policy because the coalitions he headed never really coalesced and because the problems he inherited from preceding governments became more and more intertwined and more and more crucial.[1] At times he was, in fact, his own foreign minister, as under Edgar Faure; or else the foreign minister was a close party associate, as was the case with Christian Pineau in Guy Mollet's government.

The fortunes of the MRP, which until 1954 had provided the only two foreign ministers known to the Fourth Republic, reflected the decline in the status of the foreign minister. By 1952 Robert Schuman, who had followed Georges Bidault in that office, was under heavy attack for his strong advocacy of European unity, allegedly to the neglect of colonial problems. After his displacement Schuman complained that North African officials and *fonctionnaires*, supported by powerful *colons*, had sabotaged Foreign Office directives.[2] His complaint showed how far the government in Paris had by that early date lost control of the situation in North Africa; it also indicated the political desirability of a less determined foreign minister, one better suited to the spirit of *immobilisme*. For a time this need was met by Bidault, whose position on European integration and, in particular, on the European Defense Community Treaty was more ambiguous than Schuman's. In turn, Mendès-France removed Bidault to make possible the liquidation of the war in Indo-China and the interment of EDC. If Schuman was thought too "European," Bidault was tainted with old-fashioned colonialism, a judgment proved accurate by his role in the crisis of 1958. Thus the hold of the MRP on the Foreign Ministry was broken largely because the requirements of the office had become not the generation of policy but rather adjustment to the needs for executive survival.

The Spread of Administrative Autonomy

The absence of strong political direction at the top set certain limits to the actions of the Quai d'Orsay, while its

[1] This trend was discernible earlier. See the author's *The Office of the Premier in French Foreign Policy-Making*, Princeton University, Organizational Behavior Section, Foreign Policy Analysis Series no. 5 (Princeton, N.J., October 1954); mimeographed.
[2] Charles Ledré, *Robert Schuman—Pèlerin de l'Europe* (Paris: Spès, 1954), pp. 210-213.

autonomy was simultaneously enhanced by its continuing prestige and high competence. As one of the "Grandes Administrations," the ministry was able to recruit able graduates of the École Nationale. As its officers progressed in the service, they maintained highly important, if informal, channels of communication and coordination with other graduates scattered in other ministries. This function was especially significant in the face of a relative lack of high-level administrative coordination independent of the Council of Ministers. The continued emphasis, moreover, upon the importance of diplomacy as a means of compensating for the lack of tangible power further increased the administrative autonomy of the ministry. Logically, then, senior positions in the foreign service were, to a greater extent than in the United States, held by professional personnel, and there was far less turnover. Administrative autonomy at home provided much greater freedom to the heads of French missions abroad than was enjoyed by their counterparts from the United States or Great Britain, to say nothing of those from the Soviet Union.[3]

The reverse side of the coin shows the serious limitations of the French procedure. The nature of the task assigned to the Foreign Office and the absence of strong political direction made it extremely difficult to reorganize the office for effective action.[4] Especially neglected were planning for long-range policy and coordination within the agency and with other ministries. Not only did policy-planning appear useless, since there was no answer to the question of what to make plans for except "disaster," but also planning seemed incompatible with the traditional French "style" of skillfully articulated, individual impro-

[3] J.-B. Duroselle, "L'Élaboration de la Politique Étrangère Française," *Revue Française de Science Politique*, July-September 1956, pp. 516-517

[4] On the persistence of the heritage from the eighteenth and seventeenth centuries and the relative lack of internal realignment, see the articles by Amédée Outrey, "Histoire et Principes de l'Administration Française des Affaires Étrangères," *Revue Française de Science Politique*, April-June 1953, pp. 298-319; July-September 1953, pp. 491-511; October-December 1953, pp. 714-739. Instructive also on this point is Ambassador Jacques Dumaine's chronological, anecdotal account of his experiences, *Quai d'Orsay* (Paris Julliard, 1955)

visation. As for coordination, it was regarded as a function of political direction, misdirection, or lack of direction. Administrative autonomy was a game others could play, and the Foreign Ministry was recurrently coming up against actions by agencies that it could neither dictate to nor win over, even though the success of French foreign policy ultimately depended on the ministry's ability to create consistency in both formulation and execution. Outstanding opponents of the Foreign Ministry were the Ministries of French Overseas Territories and of National Defense.

The Foreign Ministry over time lost many foreign policy functions.[5] Some became centered in the premier's own administrative staff when he came to play a crucial role in bringing internal and external policies into some rough sort of balance. Other functions were assumed by so-called "technical groups," as far removed as possible from political interference. It was, for example, Jean Monnet and his technical staff, rather than the Quai d'Orsay, who planned and developed the idea of a Coal and Steel Community; after the defeat of EDC, Monnet's group then charted the new course toward economic and functional, rather than military and political, integration.

A final limit was set to administrative autonomy by its responsiveness to vigorous political direction whenever and wherever such direction might appear. In the absence of a core of basic and coherent French foreign policy, a political figure powerful enough to develop new ideas would meet with little resistance. Should the apparatus of the Foreign Ministry prove inflexible and unyielding, other channels, including the ministers' personal staffs, could readily be improvised. The ease with which Mendès-France liquidated the Indo-Chinese war and buried EDC revealed how slight a hold these supposedly fundamental policies had on either the administrative or the political apparatus. Later, General de Gaulle, who logically chose a professional

[5] It is the opinion of Duroselle that the role of the Quai d'Orsay in policy formation has been declining since 1900 See Duroselle, cited, p. 522

diplomat, Maurice Couve de Murville, to head the Foreign Ministry, duplicated the experience of Mendès.

Executive-Legislative Colloquies on Foreign Policy

In its search for a foreign policy the executive could obtain little support from either Parliament or the people. The former was irascible, the latter did not care. Since Assembly debates were the culmination of a disorderly and risk-strewn process, cabinets tried to avoid discussion of foreign policy whenever possible. They fought shy especially of debates over concrete issues that might eventuate in a vote which was as likely as not to go against the government of the day. Equally important, both debate and balloting served merely to reveal the extent of divisions within each political party, including those which made up the coalition—as in the classic case of the EDC Treaty. Because foreign policy by its nature tended to escape from legislative control, debates which could not be avoided or side-stepped ascended to the realm of platitude, leaving ample room for individual exchanges, following which "orders of the day" would instruct the government to pursue vigorously some unidentified course of action.

The debates in the National Assembly at the time of the Suez crisis offer a striking example of this tendency. There were previous signs that the Assembly was drawing away from the government, just when the government gave indications of acting tough as well as talking tough. In October 1956, however, Premier Mollet had won a vote of confidence by 330-140, with 49 abstentions; the opponents included the Poujadistes, some Independents, and some MRP members who were still miffed at being out of office.[6] After the Franco-British ultimatum to Egypt and Israel, the last step before the invasion, there was no real debate at all on the new policy. Under the rules only one reply could be made to the government's statement, and this task fell to the able dialectician Pierre Cot, member of the Progressive group, closely allied with the Communists. Although Cot prophet-

[6] *L'Année Politique*, 1956 (Paris. Éditions du grand Siècle), pp. 374-385.

ically warned "we won't profit by adopting Charles Maurras' slogan, 'France alone,' " Mollet's call to grandeur gained him a vote of 368-182, with only 11 abstentions. This time the MRP backed the government's stand, as did the Independents. Apart from the Communists, the opposition centered on Mendès-France, who annoyed his fellow deputies by calling once more for a new policy in North Africa.[7] After the fiasco over the Canal, for the first time some speakers began to attack the government—for failing to take into account the low reserves of oil and for ignoring what were now called the perfectly predictable reactions of the United States.[8]

The "order of the day" which closed the debate over Suez was a masterpiece of the draftsman's art, reflecting the issues smothered in the debate, just as the debate itself reflected the melancholy fortunes of France. Establish general peace in the Near East, internationalize the Suez Canal, make the United Nations more effective, strengthen the Atlantic Pact, complete the treaties for European integration—this bag of multicolored candy contained flavors for many tastes, as was reflected in the vote, 325-210, with 36 abstentions.[9] So ended the colloquy between executive and legislature at a crucial moment in French history.

Two issues, however, did produce frequent and serious debates. Elections were fought, governments were made and unmade over Algeria, Tunisia, and Morocco. The main reason was that these areas were hardly regarded as foreign at all; instead they evoked the same manifold economic, social, political, and military pressures which played on the legislature and the executive. To avoid legislative criticism and indeed its own overthrow, the government depended on its skill in mingling expressions of fierce determination with excoriation of "foreign intervention" in the internal affairs of France. We shall see how Félix Gail-

[7] Same, pp 382-383.
[8] Actually, perhaps one of the fatal attractions of the Suez venture was the conviction that, as in the case of a forbidden cigarette, mama was sure to raise her hands in delicious horror over the bad behavior.
[9] *L'Année Politique*, 1956, cited, pp. 428-430.

lard won support by demanding a steadfast posture after the units of the French air force had attacked the Tunisian town of Sakiet-Sidi-Youssef. His fatal error was to welcome and cooperate with the Anglo-American good offices mission, which proved to be, after all, a form of foreign intrusion.

The second exception concerned the ratification of the European treaties. Approval of the Common Market and Euratom depended on a positive blend of benefits, however distant, with a negative avoidance of immediate costs. These treaties were to be a neat solution to all problems, from Germany's dominant role in Western Europe to the economic development of French overseas territories under French political control. They were to cost nothing, for French prosperity would be guaranteed and French producers would continue to be protected against competition.

In the government's search for a foreign policy the committees of the legislature provided more hindrance than help. The assignment of deputies to committees on a basis of proportional representation only sharpened the divisions within political groups. Membership on the Foreign Affairs Committee was a prize much sought after by potential and past ministers, naturally concerned more with their careers than with the aspirations of the government. Government proposals were subjected to intense and frequently confused study, after which the matter was apt to be buried or a report issued far more reflective of the committee's than the government's views. A cardinal principle of executive behavior was to give the Committee on Foreign Affairs as little information as possible. The committee's influence was further limited by its lack of financial sanctions; unlike several other Assembly committees which controlled appropriations, it had no means to compel governments to dance attendance upon it. Consequently, issues vital to France's foreign relations often escaped altogether the Foreign Affairs Committee.

The situation in the Council of the Republic differed somewhat. The Council could not destroy governments, and its conservative composition more closely approximated that of the post-1954 governments. Some of its committees carried out studies on French foreign policy and occasionally stimulated a general if somewhat academic debate. Perhaps the Council's committees, on balance, helped French cabinets by serving as a source of ideas and as a point of leverage, however weak, on the rambunctious Assembly.

The crucial importance of foreign policy for Western countries since the onset of the cold war has led national legislatures to seek to enhance their role. The superior position of a strong executive usually enables it to limit or direct the ambitions of the legislature in determining and executing foreign policy. But the converse is not always true—that when an executive is weak, the legislature inevitably moves into the power vacuum. In France, the weak executive could capitalize on the many divisions among and within political groups and exploit the Assembly's disorganized procedures to achieve as much independence as a strong executive.

The Role of Public Opinion

An appeal by the executive to the "people" over the head of the Assembly could at best only temporarily prolong its hold on life. Both Pinay and Mendès-France were "popular." Both tried to trade on that popularity when they tangled with the Assembly. And both went down to defeat about as quickly as the average coalition. With the possible exception of Guy Mollet in the few, euphoric days of the Suez venture, the premiers of *immobilisme* never enjoyed the same public support as Pinay and Mendès. Clearly, the degree of a premier's popularity was no real index to the probable longevity of his government.

It was, moreover, extremely difficult for a premier to mass public opinion behind an issue of foreign policy. Inured to expect the worst from inflation and taxation, despite a remarkable spurt in prosperity, the French public could hardly confront realistically a foreign policy that, like a "Perils of Pauline" movie scenario, consisted of wriggling out of one defeat after another. It has been suggested that a weak political system, like France's, had to depend on public shock to get things done.[10] But a public shock could only be instilled by painting an image of past failures and potential disasters, and this would unavoidably work against the government. On the other hand, there was a natural tendency on the part both of a government and of the permanent bureaucracy to maintain maximum freedom of action by soothing, not alarming, public opinion. In France, where the amount of information proffered the public could be equated roughly with the amount of its potential opposition, the prevailing inclination to say as little as possible was reinforced.

Public opinion sampling in France repeatedly revealed attitudes that were contradictory and hence unreliable guides to action. The French public, for example, responded favorably to the catchword of "European union," even to such extensions of that slogan as *a* European Defense Community. Yet, opponents of *the* European Defense Community Treaty aroused widespread popular resistance to its acceptance without altering greatly the proportion of those continuing to favor "European union." A poll of opinion on this issue in 1957 showed support for it in all social and economic groups, rising in proportion to the cultural level.[11] However, 60 per cent of those favorable to European union believed that Britain must be a member.[12] Even more discouraging, the French public put "European union" last among several goals, behind increased standards of living and social justice, "general disarmament," the French Union, and French "prestige."[13]

The confusion common to any definition of mass opinion is illustrated by the responses to two questions. "Do you think France could remain neutral in a war?" was asked in

[10] Duroselle, cited, p. 521.
[11] *Sondages (Revue Française de l'Opinion Publique)*, no. 3, 1957, pp. 12-13, naturally this proportion did not apply to the Communists.
[12] Same, p. 14.
[13] Same.

1952. "No," was the gloomy answer of respondents of all political affiliations, from Communists to members of the RPF. "Do you think France should remain neutral if it could?" simultaneously received an affirmative answer from all the same groups.[14] The combined response was either an invitation to extreme neutralism or a counsel of despair. In either event, it was no help whatsoever to policy. Five years later, on a more specific subject, public opinion was equally contradictory. While only 8 per cent thought there would be an atomic war in their lifetime and 64 per cent thought peaceful uses of atomic energy more important than military uses, 51 per cent thought a nation could not be a first-rate power without atomic arms and a plurality, 42 per cent, believed national security was impossible without possession of the atomic bomb.[15] Political leaders could cite this sample of public opinion both for and against deciding to produce atomic weapons. Naturally, inconsistencies, irrationalities, and new hysterias are no monopoly of French opinion and politics, but their effect, added to the institutional obstacles to clear-cut action, was to encourage French leaders to manipulate public moods for purposes of foreign policy. Two deepset currents of emotion were always readily at hand. The first was insistence on France's unimpaired status as a great power, the equal of the United States and Great Britain in the councils of the West—in other words, the sentiment of prestige and grandeur. A second was public resentment over national failures. If objective analysis of the causes of those failures was dangerous to the political institutions of the Fourth Republic, if the adoption of new policies was undesirable or impossible in the context of *immobilisme,* public attention, when properly handled, could be diverted from culprits at home to perfidious friends and implacable enemies abroad.

This executive view of the uses of public opinion was, of course, akin to the "immobilist" concept in seeking the

14 *Sondages,* no 2, 1952, p. 12.
15 *Sondages,* no. 3, 1957, pp 15-20 The results were of course published after and in the light of the brief, non-atomic conflict in the Suez area

appearance of action, the pyramiding of glittering gestures in preference to action itself. Like *immobilisme,* the relation between foreign policy and public opinion had the further advantage of being consistent with the nature of French society. But it contained the fatal flaw of casting policy adrift; should a determined hand seize the tiller, few could say him nay, few mark the limits of his course.

French Insistence on Great-Power Status

The main goal of French foreign policy between 1954 and 1958 was, as we have seen, to compensate for the nation's internal weaknesses, or at the very least to postpone the evil day when those weaknesses, fully exposed, would shake France to its foundations. Although by 1954 France was far less vulnerable than immediately after World War II to the pressure of external events, the mainspring of its policy remained the insistence on its status as a great power, with all the attributes and perquisites pertaining thereto. While some other nations, such as the Soviet Union and Communist China, might try to shoulder their way into the exclusive club of great powers on the basis of national accomplishment. France claimed original membership, acquired at the beginning of the modern state system. Hence it was bad form to examine French credentials. The implications of the policy of prestige were mainly negative. Since France's status was beyond questioning, protests had to be made automatically at the slightest infractions of the code of equality. The forums of protest were groups within which France felt its role was being disparaged.

One such forum was the United Nations. Frenchmen looked at the world organization, in which Arab-Asian countries had the temerity to question French actions in that strictly "internal" problem, Algeria, and they found the position of France to be declining. In United Nations debates France was inclined "to follow, rather than lead."[16]

[16] Ernest Pezet, "Le Fonctionnement Dirigeant de l'O.N.U. et la France," *Revue Politique et Parlementaire,* July 1956, p 40 The author was Vice-President of the Senate and of its Foreign Affairs Committee.

In the administration of the United Nations French nationals held fewer and fewer top posts, a trend which had begun as early as 1948 and which was accelerated by the reorganization undertaken by the second Secretary-General, Dag Hammarskjöld. Of twenty key posts, Ernest Pezet found that France, at the end of 1955, held just two.[17] The fact that it was the Anglo-Americans who dominated the United Nations apparatus made the situation even less palatable. Because, French critics charged, their own delegation to the United Nations was poorly trained,[18] it tended blindly to follow Great Britain and the United States in raising both the number and the importance of non-Western nations within the world organization. French interests demanded that the United Nations maintain a clear view of reality and not base its actions on illusions and ideological preoccupations.[19] Reality meant more than maintenance of the great-power veto, as defined in the Charter; it entailed further protection of internal affairs from outside interference by drawing up a specific list of problems expressly excluded from United Nations jurisdiction.[20]

Another "court of protest" was the Anglo-Saxon conclave. Ever since the war the French had felt uneasy and made disapproving noises whenever British and American leaders went off into a corner and talked by themselves. The March 1957 meetings in Bermuda between Eisenhower and Macmillan was just one example of this deplorable tendency. To be sure, the American President had earlier completed conversations with Premier Mollet, and the French, as always, were pleased to have Franco-American bilateral ties reinforced. However, the Bermuda meeting, coming so soon after the British had "deserted" the French in Suez under heavy American pressure, seemed to constitute a special effort by Washington and London to

---

[17] Same, p. 47.
[18] Same, p 40.
[19] Georges Fischer, "Quelques Réflexions sur la Position de la France à l'O.N.U." *Politique Étrangère*, December 1955, p. 712.
[20] Same, pp. 716-718.

undertaken if France were to find itself in practice on a footing of equality in the interdependence which has been approved in principle by the NATO Conference." The Premier then went on to stress the new understandings among France, West Germany and Italy for pooling their efforts in the field of nuclear research and manufacture, "so that they can benefit from a position of equality in NATO."[26]

As the months of 1958 went by, however, the United States clung to its position, formulated in the very beginning of the atomic age, that it would not carry other nations through the door into the atomic club and would not hand over nuclear weapons to the exclusive jurisdiction of any other country. The French government then retreated perforce to the position that its prestige and equality could best be safeguarded if it backed up diplomatic representations with a demonstration of its own nuclear capability. But would the testing of a single device be sufficient? With its limited nuclear capability had the British position been greatly improved? Such thoughts must have disturbed the sleep of the advocates of a policy of prestige and grandeur.

---

[26] *U. S. News and World Report,* January 3, 1958, p. 63.

Chapter Eleven

FRANCE AND EUROPE

THE DEFEAT of the European Defense Community Treaty led inevitably to the lowering of French prestige in Western Europe. That decline was matched by a sharp sense of national defeat when Mendès-France, certainly an accessory to the burial of EDC, so quickly accepted the Eden plan for the rearmament of West Germany within the Western European Union. For every Frenchman satisfied with this alternative to the quasi-supranational features of EDC, there was at least one other who felt just the opposite, and perhaps two for whom the basic objective of the entire EDC battle had been precisely to prevent or to control and retard the re-creation of the German *Wehrmacht* When Mendès-France left the government, he took along his alternative strategy: to retreat from any further schemes for European integration until the establishment of domestic economic reforms could enable France to hold its own in, if not to dominate, emergent European institutions.

Subsequent French governments about-faced and plunged again into "Europe," hopeful that with careful planning European organizations could perform their traditional function of compensating for and assisting in the correction of France's internal weaknesses. Negotiation and ratification of the Common Market and Euratom Treaties represented two of the most important undertakings of "immobilist" regimes in the post-1954 period. In addition, French leaders used Western European Union to assist them in forging a diplomatic and military partnership with West Germany and, to a lesser extent, with Italy.

Background of the Common Market Treaty

With the demise of the Defense Community, the Coal and Steel Community was left lonely and exposed. On November 11, 1954, Jean Monnet, a major contributor to the creation of ECSC, resigned as head of its High Authority to form an Action Committee for a United Europe. His purpose was to build support for renewed efforts at European integration in all six European member countries, particularly in political parties, such as those of the French and German Socialists, which had been either badly divided or downright hostile to the Defense and Political Communities.

In advising the French to work toward new and more far-reaching forms of economic cooperation, Monnet's arguments were not limited to the negative conclusion that ECSC could not for long remain viable by itself. The High Authority had not proceeded precipitously and radically, as some had feared. On the contrary, it had acted with measured deliberation, relying on patient persuasion and the balance of forces within the Community to gain agreement from economic groups or national governments. Moreover, despite progress toward a united market for coal and steel, including the abolition of tariffs and quota restrictions, countries could still protect themselves by limited exceptions or other means. The French, for example, had retained certain import and price controls on coal. The development of both the coal and steel industries had in some measure been assisted by the organization, thus contributing to the economic advance enjoyed by France in 1955.

French leaders could conclude, therefore, that further economic efforts would be slow enough in their application to allow time for adjustment by the French economy, thus minimizing opposition by entrenched interests. Also, they expected exceptions to be permitted both in administration by a central authority and in action by the national governments. Finally, they felt that French industrial and agricultural sectors seeking external markets, as well as producers requiring materials imported from other European countries, would benefit.

The Coal and Steel Community apparatus was equally important as a prototype for any organization to be established to supervise other aspects of economic cooperation. Skill and experience were available to help draft what would be a detailed treaty, combining general goals with rather specific procedures and machinery. It had also been shown that this machinery need not be heavily weighted on the side of supranationalism, or that it need be part of an encompassing federal system. On the other hand, there was room for exponents of political unification in Western Europe to continue to argue the merits of a functional approach, rather than limit, to integrative efforts. Thus the chances of success would be increased by enlisting in the cause two potentially antagonistic groups.

But from the beginning of negotiations leading to the Common Market and Euratom Treaties, France looked beyond the five other Western European countries to the two nations on which its status as a great power especially depended. The United States had vigorously and repeatedly supported European integration, going so far as to write this objective into both the Economic Cooperation Act of 1948 and its successor, the Mutual Security Act. Discouraged, disillusioned, and disgusted with the denouement of the EDC drama, the United States could be expected to be so enthusiastic over renewed French efforts toward European cooperation that, as with the Coal and Steel Community, financial support would ultimately be forthcoming.

Before long France again would play off Great Britain against the United States, but now it sought to bring the weight of the United States to bear upon Britain in successfully resolving the problem of Britain's relationship to the Common Market. Experience had shown that the British either remained aloof from European organizations, thereby making it more difficult for certain continental groups to accept them, or used their membership to empty the organizations of any real integrative power. Clearly needed in the future was a form of association which would bring British policy into line with that of the European Six while eliminating the possibility of Britain's disrupting the internal working of the machinery.

French Objectives in the Common Market Treaty

One basic French objective in the Common Market involved the association with it of French Overseas Territories. Imputed neglect of nonmetropolitan France had formed, after all, an integral part of the attack on Foreign Minister Schuman; the EDC Treaty had crept toward its grave accompanied by cries that its ratification would cut France off from its colonies and associated states, particularly in North Africa. The bitterness of the internal fight over this issue clearly indicated that the question of the French Overseas Territories would appear prominently in the Common Market negotiations from the outset. "Immobilist" governments were increasingly dependent for their survival on satisfying the demands of groups with interests overseas, especially in Algeria. It was also becoming apparent that continuation of French economic growth and strength depended on enlisting outside assistance in new programs for African development. Carefully established, the Common Market could greatly help in satisfying simultaneously a whole range of economic and political requirements.

As France entered the negotiations for the Common Market and Euratom Treaties, the government's view of what was necessary to gain Assembly ratification was far better defined than it had been with the Defense Community or even the Coal and Steel Community Treaties. While the details of the several meetings, official and unofficial, among the six Western European countries need not be examined,[1] the manner and persistence with which

[1] They may be found in "Le Marché Commun et l'Euratom," *Chronique de Politique Étrangère*, nos. 4-6, July-November 1957.

the French expressed their viewpoints deserve attention in order to evaluate the extent of their ultimate success.

From the initial conference at Messina, in June 1955, France insisted that the institutions of the Common Market be under the direct influence and control of the participating governments. At first, it had demanded a structure completely separate from the Coal and Steel Community, and, as late as July 1956, Premier Mollet had bowed to Assembly wishes in this regard.[2] Although the legislature eventually failed to have its way, the principle of national cooperation rather than supranational authority was faithfully reflected in the treaty. To be sure, a European Commission, with a degree of initiative on such matters as economic aid and national exceptions to treaty clauses, was to be appointed by the Council of Ministers upon nomination of the various governments. The Commission, however, was to be far less influential in the Common Market than was the High Authority of the Coal-Steel Community. Major responsibility was to rest instead with the Council of Ministers, representing the member countries. Although decisions in principle were to be taken by majority vote, on the important issues of economic policy a qualified majority or a weighted majority was required. French and other delegates agreed that there should be neither political integration in the form of a powerful Consultative Assembly, nor a supranational body of technicians, like the High Authority of the Coal-Steel Community. The experts, said Foreign Minister Pineau at Brussels in February 1956, were "more realistic" than in the past,[3] meaning of course more obedient to the dictates of national policy.

The attainment of other French objectives designed to give maximum protection to its internal economy required national control of Common Market institutions. France advanced the principle of graduated stages toward the Common Market, the concomitant admission of national exceptions, special measures for agriculture, and the har-

[2] *L'Année Politique*, 1956 (Paris. Éditions du Grand Siècle), p. 323.
[3] Same, p. 264.

monization of national social charges and wage rates. The principle of stages was accepted by all countries involved at the outset. The resultant provision in the treaty stated that the second step toward a Common Market should not be taken unless all members agreed that the first had been satisfactorily completed. Lacking consensus, postponement was in order, and another extension could occur at the end of the third stage. This meant that the Common Market *could* not be reached in less than twelve years and *might* not be reached until seventeen (or more if action were brought successfully by a particular nation in the Court of Justice).

France got its way with more difficulty in the matter of national exceptions and special treatment for agriculture. For a long time French negotiators clung to the position that French participation would be only "experimental." They abandoned the right to secede when and if things did not go well only in February 1956,[4] when France's "partners" had agreed to allow indefinite continuance of special import taxes and aids to export—in effect a form of national discrimination. Quantitative restrictions were also made permissible until and unless the Council of Ministers specifically disapproved. Special treatment for agriculture involved primarily the establishment of minimum prices, preferential buying, and a possibly lengthy transition period before accepting the institutions of the Common Market as competent to deal with the problem of agriculture on a community, rather than a national, basis. Wrangling on this point and on the nature of the majority which would be required continued to the very end, with the result that last-minute Dutch objections forced postponement of the scheduled signing of the Common Market Treaty from February to March 1957.[5]

French negotiators persistently maintained that a major reason for higher costs in France was liberal social-security provisions and equal pay for men and women. Rather than abandon these welfare measures, France said it would aban-

---

[4] "Le Marché Commun et l'Euratom," cited, pp. 442, 443.
[5] *New York Times*, January 28, 1957.

don instead the idea of a Common Market. At a crucial moment in the argument, emergent opposition to the treaty within the French National Assembly strengthened the French negotiators' position. Mendès-France warned that circulation of goods within the Community would penalize France because of its unusually high social charges, as well as its special military and overseas responsibilities. A draft resolution submitted by four former premiers—Reynaud, Faure, Pinay, and Laniel—and signed by Deputies Jean Médecin, Camille Laurens, and Marcel David, better reflected the thinking of the National Assembly. Harmonization of social changes, said the resolution, should be completed before the end of the first transitional period and tariff reductions made only after this goal had been reached.[6]

In the final draft, the principles of equal pay for men and women and paid vacations were accepted.[7] In addition, a special protocol recognized the need for other countries to approximate French practice in the matter of overtime pay; France was promised appropriate safeguards against failure to reach this objective during the transitional period.[8] Beyond these provisions it was impossible to go, unless other countries actually adopted the French social-security system. The French, furthermore, were well aware of the impossibility of isolating, let alone equating, the various ingredients of production costs. Pending complete political unification, which the French most certainly did not want, France would have to rely on stipulations permitting national exceptions to Community price structure and on the statement in Article 118 that the European Commission "has as its mission the promotion of close cooperation between the member states in the social field, notably in matters relating to . . . social security."

In the mode of associating its Overseas Territories with the Common Market, France gained its essential objectives. First, while its colonial areas were to participate in the Common Market and France agreed gradually to increase

---

[6] Same, January 19 and 20, 1957.
[7] Articles 119, 120.
[8] For text, see "Le Marché Commun et l'Euratom," cited, p. 634.

imports from its partners into these areas, their participation was to be provisional, limited to five years, after which the form of association would be again examined by the Council of Ministers. Second, the overseas Departments of France—Algeria, Guadeloupe, French Guiana, Martinique, and Réunion—were to have access to funds from the European Investment Fund. Third, Algerian labor was not to be guaranteed freedom of movement within the Community or equality in wages and social benefits, in spite of Algeria's formal status as a Department of Metropolitan France. Fourth, the Investment Fund would allow France to tap the financial resources of its European partners, particularly West Germany, which had no overseas dependencies. The assets of the Fund in the first five years were to total 581 million dollars, of which France and West Germany agreed to supply 200 million each. During this period French territories would be potential recipients of $511,250,000, over 300 million dollars more than the contemplated French contribution. The non-French investment schedule was to follow an accelerating pattern, beginning with $30,250,000 the first year and reaching $120,-250,000 in the fifth.[9]

That the Common Market Treaty could be signed on March 25, 1957, was due primarily to Belgium's Foreign Minister Paul-Henri Spaak. He successfully calmed the fears of other Western nations, especially the Netherlands, caused by the numerous concessions which had been made to France. By the same token this treaty and the one establishing Euratom slid rather easily through the French National Assembly. Following favorable preliminary votes, the Assembly approved both 342-239. Unanimous support came from those two political antagonists, the Socialists and MRP, and near unanimity from the Independents. A majority of the Radicals followed their Premier Bourgès-Maunoury in approving, but, as expected, Mendès-France and his handful of followers voted against ratification.

[9] See Ambassade de France, Service de Presse et d'Information, *A New Step in Building Europe, a Common Market for 175 Million Consumers*, European Affairs no. 10 (New York, June 1957), pp. 9-11.

Sixteen Gaullists joined their enemy, Mendès, in opposition, and the rest of the negative ballots were cast by the antidemocratic Left and Right, the Communists and Poujadists. Ratification of the two treaties by the last country—the Netherlands—in December enabled the Common Market to begin to function officially on January 1, 1958.

Implications for French Policy

On the surface it seemed that the Common Market Treaty represented a major success for French foreign policy. Further analysis, however, points to the conclusion that, like other ventures of the Fourth Republic, this also was a brilliant failure. Even with the safeguards written into the treaty, the General Society to Promote the Development of Commerce and Industry in France concluded in June 1958 that France was no better prepared than it had been the year before to enter the Common Market.[10] The reason for this judgment in the face of continued economic progress was that "immobilist" governments, under whatever guise they might appear, were forced to protect economically weak, politically strong groups whenever and wherever their interests conflicted with those of the Common Market.

For all its ingenuity, the policy of opening the back door to international power and prestige through associating Overseas France with the Common Market quite obviously depended on the areas remaining *French*, or, at the very minimum, under strong French influence. Should some fight their way and others negotiate themselves free of French control, the policy would prove futile. The clauses provisionally extending the Common Market to French dependencies were, therefore, in reality a minor part of another fundamental policy whose two goals were to satisfy African demands short of independence from and exclusion of France, and to settle the Algerian conflict on terms acceptable not only to Algerian and French groups, but also to Tunisians and Moroccans. French colonial

[10] *Le Monde*, June 6, 1958.

policy was plainly part and parcel of French foreign policy.[11]

A final spanner in the Common Market works was the familiar problem of Great Britain. To the increasing annoyance of the French the British led other members of the Organization for European Economic Cooperation in assembling a ramshackle, splotchily painted, slow-moving vehicle labeled with typical British wit the "Free Trade Area." The primary purpose of this invention was to protect and enhance the position of Britain, the British Commonwealth, and Britain's continental trading partners in their relation to the more tightly knit Europe of the Six. Neither side openly questioned the need for some form of association. What irritated the French was that, after ratification of the Common Market Treaty, problems of relating it to a Free Trade Area seemed to multiply, almost as though the British were deliberately employing vagueness and flexibility to oppose the French desire for exactitude and predictability. ". . . What safeguards will the free-trade zone as it has been proposed bring us?" asked Paul Reynaud rhetorically at the Council of Europe. "If by some unthinkable chance a French minister should come to accept the free-trade project as it now is presented, the French Parliament would unanimously reject the agreement."[12]

Advocates of the Free Trade Area matched criticism by the European Six. Reporting on whether the Common Market created a customs union (permitted) or a preferential system (prohibited), the General Agreements on Tariffs and Trade (GATT) pointed to proposed high duties on agricultural products imported from outside the area covered by the Common Market.[13] Alarmed by the entire question of Common Market tariffs, in fact, GATT wanted to see them publicly announced as soon as possible, certainly by July 1, 1959, so that outside countries could learn what they were up against and judge for themselves whether or not it was

---

[11] See Chapters 7 and 8.
[12] As quoted in *Le Monde*, May 2, 1958.
[13] "Economic Review," *New York Herald Tribune* (Paris edition), May 1958.

a preferential system in fact, if not in name. Hostile opinion within GATT, for the same reason, increased over the inclusion of France's Overseas Territories in the Common Market. GATT favored instead a series of agreements negotiated product by product, a process which might produce a transition period lasting ten years. The organization feared, too, that if one of the Six—and it would probably be France—found itself in difficulties, the others would use the machinery of the Common Market not to rescue that country within the scope of the Market, but rather to transfer its troubles outside the Community, onto prospective members of the Free Trade Area.[14]

Delegates of eleven major employer and industrial groups from six countries—Britain, Sweden, Norway, Denmark, Austria, and Switzerland—in signing an appeal for the Free Trade Area, criticized the "dirigist" and "centralist" tendencies of the Common Market and demanded that the Market's transitional clauses not be used merely to prop up nonviable enterprises. They also concluded that the French position favoring the harmonization of salaries and social charges was untenable.[15]

Although much of the long negotiation over the relations of the two plans was hidden from the public, the major points of conflict were clear. They involved such questions as the nature and level of external tariffs; general agreements versus product-by-product agreements; that old devil, Imperial Preference; the place of agriculture in both systems; the nature of the majorities required to proceed from one stage to the next; and tariff reductions both between the two areas and between them and outside countries. Compromises which were advanced and national positions which were adjusted did not break the fundamental deadlock, largely because the basic problem was political, not military. Just as Anthony Eden had sought to delay definition of Britain's precise relationship to EDC by advancing what was ironically called a "grand design," so Selwyn Lloyd

[14] *Le Monde*, May 4-5, 1958.
[15] Same, April 23, 1958.

had come forth with a Free Trade Area whose outlines were deliberately kept vague. By evading a final agreement embodying substantial concessions, while at the same time continuing the dialogue with the continent, the British could logically anticipate that one or both of two things would happen. The French, by insisting too long on too much, might alienate the other five and weaken the Common Market to a point where it ceased to be a door closed to the British. Or the French, under allied pressure and in order to attain the desired objective of British association, might modify their position to the point where an arrangement satisfying major British interests could be achieved.

So the British waited, but time was one commodity French "immobilist" governments did not have. Before either development could take place, France's larger role in Western Europe was brought into question by the accession of General Charles de Gaulle.

Euratom

Although there were occasions when such did not appear to be the case, France had fewer difficulties with Euratom than with the Common Market.[16] For one thing there was no problem of British association. The British had had their own nuclear production program in operation for some time, and it was, indeed, this very fact which provided some of the incentive for European countries, including France, to push ahead in this area. Moreover, France was not starting from scratch. Since 1945, it had spent $342,-800,000 on atomic research and development,[17] enough to show the practicalities as well as the obstacles to nuclear production, and to ensure French leadership in any Western European program. Finally, like every other proposal for European association, Euratom was supported on the

[16] For text of Euratom Treaty, see "Le Marché Commun et l'Euratom," cited, pp. 645-699.

[17] Ambassade de France, Service de Presse et d'Information, *Euratom: Six Nations to Pool Atomic Research and Development*, European Affairs no. 11 (New York, June 1957), p. 3.

grounds that it would help free Western Europe from dependence on Great Britain and the United States.

American assistance was, of course, desired and actively sought. In fact, the prospect that the United States in this instance would do more than stand on the sidelines and politely applaud considerably enhanced the appeal of Euratom for the French as well as for other West European countries. Before the treaty was signed, three experts who had previously drawn up production goals for Euratom went to Washington to see what help would be forthcoming. A communiqué issued after five days of talks clearly forecast American aid in the form of information, trained technicians, and nuclear fuel.[18]

The French found Euratom attractive, too, because, unlike the Common Market, other European countries did not stand aloof from the Six. Here France was able to settle the "eternal discussion between advocates of the Europe of six with those of a Europe of seven or even of fifteen,"[19] without having to make a choice between a small, closed system and a large, loosely knit one. The Euratom Treaty permitted agreements with outside states to be negotiated directly by the Commission or by individual members if approved by the Commission.[20] After ratification of the treaty by all six members, the OEEC established a European Nuclear Energy Agency and at the same time signed a convention designed to prevent the use for military purposes of materials coming under the purview of the Agency.[21] This action was designed to facilitate a close working relationship among the six members of Euratom, who were also members of OEEC.

Naturally domestic affairs also entered French calcula-

[18] The three experts were Louis Armand, Director-General of the French Railways and President of the Industrial Equipment Committee of the French Atomic Energy Commission, Franz Etzel, Vice-President of the Coal and Steel Community's High Authority; Francesco Giordani, President of Italy's National Research Council. Text of the communiqué is in the *New York Times*, February 8, 1957.
[19] *L'Année Politique*, 1956, cited, p. 323.
[20] Articles 101-103
[21] *New York Times*, December 20, 1957.

tions. There were no vested-interest groups in the nuclear field demanding special protection against foreign competition, in contrast to both the Coal-Steel Community and the Common Market. Moreover, France was heavily dependent on foreign supplies of conventional sources of energy, particularly oil. Events surrounding the Egyptian seizure of the Suez Canal proved how precarious and costly these supplies could be. The average price of oil c.i.f. European ports jumped 40 per cent by April 1957 over that prevailing before the seizure of the Canal. Concomitant increases in coal and freight charges intensified the adverse effects. To get necessary oil France spent an additional 150 million dollars above its "normal" level as the direct result of Near Eastern developments.[22] Development of atomic power would, it was hoped, ultimately free France from uncertain, outside sources.

To be sure, the production of atomic energy was bound to start slowly and at considerable cost. A goal of 3 million kilowatts was envisaged for 1963 and 15 million by 1967, at an estimated expenditure of 6 billion dollars. However, without a nuclear program, perhaps two-thirds that amount would have to be invested in conventional sources of energy. Estimates indicated, moreover, that nuclear power in Europe could come close to competing in price with conventional power, as it could not in the United States, since existing continental rates were about twice those in America.[23]

The Question of Atomic Weapons

The atomic-weapon problem was probably the most difficult one confronting the French in their decision on Euratom. Was the system of ownership, allocation, and control established under the treaty to be used to prevent the development of nuclear armaments, to advance it, or to leave

[22] European Payments Union, *Seventh Annual Report of the Managing Board: Financial Year 1956-57* (Paris: OEEC, July 1957), pp. 23-24.

[23] Louis Armand, Franz Etzel, and Francesco Giordani, *A Target for Euratom: A Report Submitted . . . at the Request of the Governments of Belgium, France, West Germany, Italy, Luxembourg, and the Netherlands* (Washington: ECSC Information Service, May 1957).

the question open? Each of the three answers was possible, and the French had difficulty in making their choice. Patent disagreement existed within French leadership over the advisability of creating a French nuclear-weapon capability.[24] At the same time there was a strong desire to maintain existing restrictions on German rearmament. To use the atom exclusively for peaceful purposes and to rely on the Euratom machinery to force others to do likewise might well weaken France in a period when its conventional military equipment was being siphoned off to North Africa. But to leave the question unresolved created the danger that the West Germans might acquire nuclear material from outside the Community, perhaps from the United States, and thus overtake France in nuclear weapons *research*. If this happened, it would soon make obsolete the restrictions concerning *production* which were written into the Western European Union as revamped in 1954.

France's conclusion, after discussions with the negotiators of the other five countries and with domestic political and technical groups, was both logical and complicated. First, Euratom should not be given powers which would retard French work on nuclear weapons. During the National Assembly debate on the emerging treaty in July 1956, Premier Guy Mollet said: "France commits itself not to explode an A-bomb before January 1, 1961. Taking account of the delays necessary for study and manufacture, this moratorium can entail no slowdown. At its expiration France will recover its full freedom, unrestrained by any Euratom provision or any agreement . . . I can therefore state that at the end of the moratorium France will have the legal and material capacity to start military production immediately."[25]

This elusive statement of policy and intent was representative of Mollet, whose party's ideology was strongly oriented toward peace, disarmament, and the avoidance of the horrors of nuclear war, but whose personal decisions in both Suez and Algeria had demonstrated a penchant for

[24] *L'Année Politique*, 1956, cited, p. 277
[25] Same, p. 323.

military force. Bourgès-Maunoury, future premier, whose Radical party had neither doctrine nor discipline, could afford to speak more directly: France "has the choice, not between conventional and nuclear arms, but between the possession of nuclear arms and the abandonment of National Defense."[26]

The powers of the nuclear agency to be established by Euratom incorporated a second ingredient of French policy. Countries (meaning France) that had already developed their own programs and sources of supply could maintain them on a national basis. To protect its unique position even further, France had proposed that only the Community be permitted to import material.[27] After West Germany objected, however, the final draft allowed national imports if Community supplies were inadequate and if the Commission gave its approval.

The third element of the French stand on Euratom envisaged the revival of the Western European Union as a system of cooperation and control in continental military matters. Within the Union close ties would be sought with West Germany, regardless of the risks. Despite the exception previously suggested, Euratom implied a high degree of French cooperation in future atomic development. Western European Union was related to this development, since WEU could serve as a device for negotiating unified policies on military aspects of nuclear production. Common membership of France and West Germany in both Euratom and WEU would ensure that France was informed of and participating in West Germany's atomic progress, both peaceful and military.

European Political Cooperation

The Common Market and Euratom Treaties represented the new trend in European cooperation—toward technical structures devoid of federative characteristics and supranational powers. But many still hoped that political

[26] Same. Indications are that Bourgès-Maunoury may have reflected final French decisions more accurately, not only on the development or nondevelopment, but also on the urgency of the first French nuclear test.
[27] *New York Times,* January 12, 1957.

unity would be the ultimate result. Only a political community, Alfred Coste-Floret wrote, could make contemplated economic cooperation successful. Real unity, going beyond federation or confederation, he contended, must come quickly, before economic measures led to international disorder.[28] Pierre Gerbet, also advocating political union, envisaged the reverse possibility. Difficulties within the Common Market, he said, might cause member governments to demand that greater powers be given to international authorities, a step which could in turn lead to the creation of a federal political authority.[29] These two statements only hint at the dangers in leaving technical experts unfettered, but others were explicit. "... The besetting political peril of such schemes of integration [as the Coal-Steel Community]," declared the London *Economist*, "is technology; a bunch of brilliant 'European' mandarins, whose imaginations leap ahead of their fellow citizens, tend to run the show; to counter this danger, live parliamentary bodies are needed, deriving political power from the electorate itself."[30] Similar sentiments were present in continental countries, including France.

Added to arguments concerning the nature of economic cooperation were reprises on a theme familiar since the postwar movement for European integration began: Western Europe as a "Third Force." Senator André Armengaud had led the fight in the Council of the Republic against the Coal-Steel Community and continued to criticize it, but he now wrote: "To the East and to the West, two enormous worlds, with philosophies rather closer to one another than usually is appreciated, squeeze the countries of Europe and threaten in different but none the less significant fashion to expand overseas."[31] One could consider Armengaud's outburst an expression of nationalism as much as European-

[28] Alfred Coste-Floret, "Pour une Coopération Franco-Allemande," *Politique Étrangère*, December 1956, pp. 713-715.
[29] Pierre Gerbet, "Common Market and Foreign Policy," paper read at Franco-American conference, Paris, April 1958.
[30] "Lessons of ECSC," *The Economist*, February 8, 1958, p. 475.
[31] André Armengaud, "L'Avenir de l'Économie Européenne. Organisation Raisonnée ou Décadence," *Politique Étrangère*, no 2, 1957, p. 151.

ism, for indeed the two are quite close together. But the desirability of a Third Force was also stressed by indisputable advocates of European unity. ". . . Only a united Europe can permit the construction of a true Third Force able to make its voice heard in the U.S. and U.S.S.R.," wrote Coste-Floret.[32] Denying that the French rejection of EDC was a rejection of the policy of European integration, Guy Mollet argued that "the cold war necessitated a military Europe; the *détente* brings with it the need for a political Europe."[33] While the *third* aspect of the Third-Force idea is muted, as usual, by Mollet, the interesting vision of a strong France leading a strong Western Europe certainly persisted at the very time Mollet's government was negotiating with others of the Six on the Euratom and Common Market Treaties.

The continuing appeal that political unity held for the French electorate could not be ignored by parties and their leaders, whether their sentiments lay on the Right or on the Left. The defeat of EDC meant that after 1954 the European movement ceased to be dominated by the Socialists and the Catholics, the former criticized as promoters of international "dirigisme," the latter denounced as advocates of Papal predominance. European unity became almost as respectable as Home and Motherhood. But this brought its own risks. Continued public support masked public indifference and nowhere more strikingly than in France. The decline in the overt military threat by the Soviet Union to Western Europe, coinciding with the economic recovery in various Western countries, turned official and unofficial attention more to the possibilities of national progress. It was only logical to view international cooperation, institutionalized in Euratom or the Common Market, as desirable ends in themselves, rather than as way stations to a further goal.[34]

This lack of a sense of urgency caused a clearly observ-

[32] Coste-Floret, cited, p 717.
[33] Guy Mollet, "The Moral Leadership of France in Europe," *European Atlantic Review*, Autumn 1955, pp 17-18.
[34] See B. Landheer, "Sociological Aspects of European Integration," *European Yearbook* (The Hague: Martinius Nijhoff, 1957), v.3, pp. 53-70.

able loss of momentum at the Council of Europe. In the old days, the Assembly could hardly wait to convene in order to resume its drive onward and upward toward political unity. The very first Assembly had before it no fewer than twenty-four proposals, including those of Schuman and Bidault, looking toward the "creation of a European political authority with limited aims but real powers." By 1954, however, the Council of Europe had passed from the idea of a "political authority," through integration of institutions developed by the Coal-Steel and other communities, to general discussions of whatever European problems happened to attract attention at the moment. By 1958 the Mackay Protocol to make the Council of Europe into a quasi-federal organization, able to pass "European Acts" binding on all members had been dead at least seven years If European political unity were ever to come, it would certainly not be via this instrument.[35]

Since the Council of Europe could not be the locus of moves toward political integration, where was it to fall? Indeed, where was to be the political center of the smaller and supposedly more closely knit "Little Europe?" The initial proposal that it wander across the map of Europe is indicative of the strength that nationalism still held in the international institutions that many hoped would some day become truly supranational. The Ministerial Councils created by the Euratom and Common Market Treaties very early appointed a commission of six "experts" to decide on a "European Capital," a common seat for the various institutions. To be helpful in the search, Coudenhove-Kalergi, president of the Pan-European Union, sent a questionnaire to 2,995 parliamentarians in the six countries, inviting them to choose among Brussels, Luxembourg, Paris, and Strasbourg. Less than a quarter (695) cared enough to reply. If the "European" spirit inhabited those who did respond, it was not revealed in their choices.

[35] See A. H. Robertson, *The Council of Europe Its Structure, Functions and Achievements* (New York. Praeger, 1957), especially pp. 85-113 The Council had become what the British had always wanted it to be, and what the continental representatives had reluctantly come to accept.

All the Belgians voted for Brussels, *all* the Luxembourgers for Luxembourg, and the French were divided between Paris and the French Alsatian town of Strasbourg. As for the Germans, Italians, and Dutch—deprived of the chance to vote for Bonn, Rome, and the Hague—they preferred the city closest to home.[36]

Coudenhove-Kalergi proceeded to pour more oil on nationalistic flames by stating that if Strasbourg were chosen, the resultant rebirth of Alsatian demands for autonomy would poison Franco-German relations once again. This maladroit remark reached Parisian ears in the middle of a political crisis. Gaillard was out; Pleven was involved in a long, desperate search for a coalition which Pflimlin would ultimately—and briefly—find. Now, Pflimlin was an Alsatian and could neither resist nor avoid a reply. "This affirmation constitutes an insult and a calumny against my compatriots, which I reject with all my power. From this moment I break off all relations with you."[37] In effect, the last "Queen for a Day" of the Fourth Republic was saying that every nationalist in Alsace would arise to call a liar anyone who dared say there was nationalism in Alsace.

Franco-German Cooperation

A long time seemed likely to pass before action would support the lip service paid to political unity. France's policy toward Euratom and the Common Market reflected the inability and unwillingness of "immobilist" governments to reform fundamentally the domestic economic pattern. This same resistance to change helped account for hostility to supranational political controls. To these motivations another closely related one may now be added. Earlier we have seen how the United States and Great Britain had systematically frustrated France's postwar attempts to keep West Germany weak, at least until it could be absorbed into a European system controlled by France. The rapid recovery of sovereignty by the Bonn government caused French leaders to fear that Germany could now re-

[36] *Le Monde*, April 26, 1958.
[37] Same, April 27-28, 1958, quoting *Dernières Nouvelles d'Alsace*.

verse French expectations and use a European system to itself dominate Western Europe, including France. The remarkable strides made by the West German economy between 1948 and 1953, while French production was relatively stagnant, exacerbated this fear. Extrapolations of future German growth, nurtured by continued Anglo-American assistance, played a major part in the ultimate defeat of EDC. "Let us not deceive ourselves," wrote Max Richard. "In spite of a policy tenaciously pursued by France from 1948 to the summer of 1954, if Europe has very recently capsized, it is because of a very understandable revival of mistrust toward Germany."[38]

But with the substitution of the Paris Accords and German membership in NATO for the European army proposed by EDC there went glimmering the last underpinning of France's initial postwar policy toward Germany. Now a new direction had to be sought. Executive control over foreign policy helped to smooth the quick transition from hostility to cooperation and even intimacy with West Germany on both multinational and bilateral levels. Thus was born one of the most striking features of French "immobilist" foreign relations.

For firmly based cooperation between France and Germany, the Saar had to go back to Germany, notwithstanding the consequent sacrifices to the French economy and to French prestige. The Saar's resources were important to French domestic economy and to France's ability to hold its own with Germany in European trade. From 1950 to 1954 between 62 and 70 per cent of the Saar's exports went to France, and 84 to 87 per cent of its imports came from France In 1954 the Saar's favorable balance of trade with West Germany covered the French trade deficit with West Germany. While measures isolating the Saar from Germany and uncertainty over that area's political future held down foreign investment, by 1954 France alone had spent about 30 billion francs in cooperation with Johannes Hoff-

[38] Max Richard, in Introduction to Jacques Tessier and others, *Dix Ans d'Efforts pour Unir l'Europe, 1945-1955* (Paris Bureau de Liaison Franco-Allemand, 1955), p. 1.

mann's pro-French government on developing the Saar mines and about 20 billion additional francs on other branches of Saar production.[39]

French defeat of EDC had invalidated the initial proposal for solving the conflict between German demands for return of the Saar and French desires to hold on to its substantial investment. Tireless efforts by France's European allies, notably by Holland's Marinus Van der Goes Van Naters, had finally resulted in agreement by France and West Germany that the Saar should be "Europeanized": administered by the European Political Community so that French advantages would gradually be replaced by a policy of nondiscrimination against Germany (and other European countries). Despite a provision for a "European" Saar contained in the agreements of 1954 for revising the Western European Union, Saarlanders realized that there could be no "European" Saar if there was in fact no "Europe." They accordingly buried the idea in a referendum.

Now the only alternative left French negotiators was to get as much as possible in exchange for allowing the Saar to become a part of Germany once more. The task occupied much of 1956, and on January 1, 1957, the Saar became a state within the German Federal Republic. Detailed agreements set forth French rights to Saar coal, solved the knotty foreign-exchange problem, outlined the manner in which the Alsace and Moselle canals would be built, and allotted France three more representatives to the Common Assembly of the Coal-Steel Community as compensation for the three who were passing from the jurisdiction of the Saar to Germany.[40]

Undoubtedly, German support of the French positions regarding Euratom and the Common Market made easier French acceptance of the inevitable. Especially were the Germans thoroughly in accord on the importance of associating French Overseas Territories in the Common Mar-

[39] Henri G. Rathenau, "L'Union Économique Franco-Sarroise," *Politique Étrangère*, August-September 1955, pp. 439-443. The author was Councilor for the Foreign Commerce of France.

[40] On the culmination of the negotiations, see *L'Année Politique*, 1956, cited, pp. 359-366.

ket.⁴¹ With the Saar problem out of the way, cooperation could expand from the economic to the political and military areas.

Although dismissed at the time as a face-saving gesture to France, Western European Union actually proved of great value in the development of Franco-German military cooperation. Its terms gave reassurance to France by the unilateral ban on German production of the so-called A-B-C weapons (atomic, biological, and chemical). Moreover, they set not a minimum, but a maximum size to European armed forces to be placed at the disposal of NATO. This comforted France at a time when its forces were being transferred from West Germany and Metropolitan France to Algeria by providing grounds for resisting any pressure by the United States to raise the levels of German armament in compensation. In spite of Great Britain's membership in WEU and its "guarantee" that substantial British forces would remain on the continent, the essential meaning of the institution was military cooperation among the European Six.

France could use WEU as a tent to cover military cooperation with West Germany and, to a lesser extent, with Italy. Coordination among the three countries—including such activities as the operation of a rocket experimental station in Alsace—had been under way at least a year⁴² before the French, German, and Italian defense ministers announced on January 21, 1958, "that research and common production would be undertaken in the armaments sphere in accordance with NATO principles and with the aim of the standardization of weapons."⁴³

This terse statement was of paramount importance. As a third partner Italy softened the direct confrontation of France and West Germany, so laden with tragic memories. Moreover, the use of WEU enabled France to avoid a choice in the military field between a southern and an

---

⁴¹ See the general communiqué issued after the Franco-German agreement was reached June 5, 1956, on most Saar issues, in same, pp. 311-313
⁴² *New York Times*, January 21, 1958; February 10, 1958.
⁴³ NATO Information Division (Paris), *NATO Letter*, February 1958.

eastern orientation, just as the Coal-Steel, Common Market, and Euratom Treaties had enabled it to do in the economic and nuclear-energy fields. But even more lay behind Italy's inclusion. France was pushing its own atomic weapons program, and the West German government was striving to get the German people to accept the proposition that although it could not (temporarily?) produce nuclear weapons, it could and should under certain circumstances be prepared to use them. In contrast, Italy was cooperating closely with the only contemporary Western supplier of atomic arms, the United States. Far from boggling at the implications of nuclear arms, the Italian government welcomed American missile bases. The third partner thus provided a channel for continental nuclear relations with the United States during a transitional period fraught with difficulties for both France and West Germany.[44]

Great Britain, as conspicuous by its absence from European military cooperation as Italy was by its presence, might not like the three continental nations going off by themselves, but there was little it could do. In fact, Western European Union forced Britain to adopt toward these tripartite undertakings an official attitude of "benevolence" as Britain phrased it at the March 1958 meeting of the organization.[45] In truth, the French and British were embroiled in a number of disputes, including the Free Trade Area and arms for Tunisia. In contrast, West Germany, itself involved in a fight with Britain over who should pay how much to keep the British "watch on the Rhine," was giving steadfast support to French policies.

Based on strong mutual interest, Franco-German military cooperation continued as long as there was an "immobilist" government to uphold the French end. In January 1958 plans for a "European" light tank were announced,[46] followed a month later by plans for a unified continental air-defense system in which, hopefully, a "European"

---

[44] See *New York Times*, December 15, 1957.
[45] Same, March 6, 1958.
[46] Same, January 21, 1958.

fighter aircraft would ultimately play a central role.[47] In the midst of the final convulsion of the Fourth Republic, the French went through with exercise "Foudre" in Germany, designed to test strategic ideas and the requisite new tactics for the employment of nuclear weapons. One of the chief results of "Foudre" reported to the public was to cement "the good relations existing between the officers of our [the French] army and those of the *Bundeswehr*. The barracks were shared, matériel transferred and, in each sector, army commanders entered into the same relations with the German authorities as exist in every garrison town in Metropolitan France."[48]

Not far beneath the surface of French cooperation with Germany inside and outside Western European Union lay the hope that the welding together of a continental bloc could increase French bargaining power against Britain and America. As a direct affiliate of NATO, WEU might be useful in obtaining support for French ambitions in NATO, thereby diminishing the adverse effects of troop transfers to Algeria. Adenauer, to be sure, had always avoided obvious bloc alignments, and was openly worried about France's North African policy. However, the French could still hope that a solid Franco-German front would emerge as a logical consequence of developments in Euratom, the Common Market, the Overseas Territories, and the pooling of military production and deployment. At the least, France would have less cause to fear that Great Britain and the United States would continue to manipulate West German policy to their own benefit and to the further detriment of French power and prestige. While the Fourth Republic moved from impotence through incoherence into dissolution, the Germans appeared to be the only people of consequence who felt confident that France should and could remain strong.

[47] Same, February 11, 1958.
[48] Charles Haquet in *Figaro*, May 24-25, 1958. The fact that this operation, the first such activity for the French army operating on its own, was carried out on schedule constituted a denial to rumors that there were hardly any French troops left in Germany and that those still there longed for an excuse to participate in the Algerian revolt.

Chapter Twelve

FRANCE AND NATO

FOR FRANCE, the main impact of the North Atlantic Treaty Organization has been its inability and unwillingness to assist materially in solving France's most crucial problems. Even though NATO agreed officially that France's struggle in Indo-China was an integral part of Western defense against Communist aggression, this verbal support was not, perhaps could not be, translated into material assistance except through direct United States support. And French warnings that a Korean cease-fire would result in Communist China's military power being turned on Indo-China proved only too accurate. NATO none the less remained dedicated to its major purpose, defense against a Soviet invasion of Western Europe. The Organization, therefore, pressed France for military contributions at the very time France was unable to meet its other commitments. The war in Algeria, following on the heels of the Indo-China settlement, was part of the same pattern. France's NATO allies now, however—in striking contrast to the Western European Union members, who officially supported France's position on Algeria—regarded with increasing concern its unending involvement in a costly and indecisive war.[1]

The French view of NATO as unsympathetic to and restrictive of French policy in Algeria surely provided motivation for French conduct in the Suez affair. Although the Franco-British invasion almost blew the North Atlantic alliance to bits, the French adamantly maintained that

[1] *New York Times*, September 22, 1957.

eliminating Nasser was of overriding importance. France aimed, at one and the same time, to restore the French position in the Near East, repair the tattered prestige of French arms, cement relations with Great Britain in direct opposition to the United States, remove the primary source of outside support for the Algerian rebels, and reinsure French access to the area's vital oil resources. With the project accomplished, France could re-enter the councils of NATO in a central and powerful position. The question, in the meantime, of whether NATO held together was one for the alliance, not France, to answer.

The Organization did not disintegrate, nor, of course, did France succeed at Suez. The result left the earlier relationship basically the same, only with France in an even worse position. NATO was like an arch with its keystone missing. Since French military withdrawals had all but eliminated French power from the continent, the emphasis on West German rearmament continued, both as a logical extension of the NATO purpose and as a substitute for France's missing contribution. The appointment of a German general as commander of Central European ground forces reflected the fact of Germany's assumption of the role forecast since the North Atlantic Treaty was signed, a role which France could neither delete from the play nor act out itself. Finally, French military weakness increased Europe's reliance on nuclear strategy and on American air power stationed around the periphery of the continent.

French policy regarding NATO thus became one of postponing as long as possible the decline of France. Continuation of the Organization, entrenched over the years in its members' national policies, made neutralism an impractical alternative. The lack of results, furthermore, of the Summit Conference at Geneva in 1955 and the *rapprochement* between France and West Germany ruled out a settlement with the Soviet Union. No alternate system of security, under existing circumstances, was to be found.

Could France compensate for its weakness in NATO by strengthening its ties with other European countries? If the Common Market and Euratom Treaties worked out as planned, the Six would develop integrated policies on a wide range of matters. Possibly such agreement in economic areas would lead to extended political coordination. We have seen that France could, if desired, channel into NATO certain common continental positions reached through Western European Union. France used WEU, for example, to add military cooperation to the economic and nuclear arrangements forecast in the Common Market and Euratom Treaties. Finally, the presence of Great Britain as a seventh member of WEU did not prove disruptive, and there was always the chance that through closer association with the continent Britain would give greater support to continental policies advanced by France. Here, then, was no formal bloc. Each member preserved full individuality within NATO, while simultaneously committing itself to the progressive abandonment of its freedom of action in matters vitally affecting its position in the Organization.

Extension of NATO's Scope

Even before the Suez crisis, France had argued for broadening the scope of NATO to include concern with developments occurring outside the treaty's geographical limits. The French reasoned, and they were increasingly hard to dispute, that NATO might succeed in keeping Western Europe out of Soviet clutches and still fail resoundingly should the Sino-Soviet axis come to dominate Asia and Africa. Moreover, were NATO to become a source of Western decisions on non-European affairs, France would have available an instrument for the enhancement of its own policies outside Europe. Suez, among other failures, had shown it did not possess this power on its own.

The French did not want NATO as a military alliance to intrude into extra-European problems. Rather, they felt, political agreement and economic policies ought to advance general Western objectives. Demonstrably weak in military power outside Europe, France believed that its contribution to the nonmilitary aspects of Western strategy consisted in diplomatic skill, assessment of political realities, the supply of technicians, and long experience in economic development. From this assessment emerged the so-called Pineau Plan to place aid to underdeveloped areas within NATO's purview, even though final arrangements might be made under United Nations auspices or through bilateral agreements.

Why did this effort to widen the scope of the NATO alliance fail? First, France, necessarily preoccupied with more immediate matters, could not bring to NATO councils sufficient pressure to overcome American and, to a lesser extent, British objections. American leadership combined statements of its desire to broaden the alliance with qualifications recalling obvious American interests outside Europe that could not be handled through NATO. Also, the logic of the French argument that NATO would be fatally weakened by Communist encroachments in Asia and Africa was matched and possibly overtaken by the counterargument that an active concern by NATO with these problems might actually weaken the alliance without proving effective For Italy, West Germany, Belgium, Holland, Denmark, and Norway, Europe was the sole reason for the existence of the alliance. Some of these countries had even regarded the inclusion of Greece and Turkey with suspicion, as dangerous extensions of NATO's commitments outside Europe. They had reacted strongly to the Franco-British adventure in Suez out of fear that NATO would be dragged into areas and problems beyond its proper sphere. Insistence on a NATO bloc for non-NATO matters would, a majority of its members felt, not only arouse opposition of non-European nations; it would also deepen the already serious cleavages between the Western allies.[2]

Finally, French policies and objectives in Africa weakened its own desire to extend the scope of NATO. If NATO were to involve itself in non-European problems, a logical area of concern would be Africa. This continent needed economic and political far more than military help if it were not to fall prey to Communist infiltration. To this

[2] See Gardner Patterson and Edgar S. Furniss, Jr, *NATO: A Critical Appraisal* (Princeton, N J · International Finance Section, Princeton University, 1957), pp. 65, 77, 83.

France agreed, but at the same time rejecting outside intrusion in its own African affairs. It already regarded American military and economic interests with distrust, and any action by NATO in Africa might well lead to their further growth. France greatly preferred to exploit its association with the five continental countries in order to get needed capital into its African territories, while disinfecting that capital from political consequences. Therefore, while one part of French policy was seeking a ride into the Near and Far East on a NATO chariot, a much stronger part was trying to hold that chariot back from Africa.

Another aspect of France's relationship to NATO involved the Organization in assurances of France's indispensability. Without France, the French argued, there could be no NATO. Admission of West Germany and frequent Anglo-American conclaves made it all the more important to French prestige that there was one unit, the Standing Group, where only the French, British, and Americans were represented. Although the Group was essentially a continuation of the wartime Anglo-American partnership, and France had never attained a position of real equality, there was some compensation in its official representation in the agency of military planning and coordination for NATO.

Because of its central role in NATO, France felt that Great Britain and the United States owed it maximum assistance. The British contribution and part of the American could take the form of specific guarantees—never too often reaffirmed for the French!—to maintain troops in Europe, particularly in West Germany. These guarantees were not subject to bargaining or conditional on French behavior. The same attitude existed toward the other form of American contribution—military assistance in money and matériel. How could the United States, Congressional prerogatives notwithstanding, make such aid dependent on French ratification of EDC, when ratify or no, France remained the senior continental partner? In this relationship of mutual dependence, France contributed geographic position plus as much financial and military power as was not urgently needed in stopping leaks in its dikes. Having done this, France had done all that it could, all that could be expected of it. Its position could not be determined by any assessment of the adequacy of the French contribution.

Actually, then, France sought to transcend its European partners at the very time it sought to submerge parts of its sovereignty in arrangements with them. In this Gallic counterpart of Britain's Commonwealth relationship, France would benefit in a wider sphere from its position as leader of a continental group of nations. And, like Britain, France's status must not be defined as merely one of a group. In and of itself France remained important, entitled to a senior ranking within the Western alliance.

This posture might succeed so long as everyone agreed that the Emperor was appropriately attired. But let some one impolitely suggest that no clothes were visible—indeed that this bare creature was not an emperor at all—and France would have only the diplomatic courtesy of others to cover its embarrassment.

French Criticisms of NATO

As France became weaker, it became more sensitive. The ordering of NATO's military affairs afforded much cause for complaint concerning both form and substance. NATO appeared to France as an American or an Anglo-American show. French feelings of inferiority, arising from the minimal part France played in World War II, were accentuated by its tardy start toward rearmament and reached new heights with the diversion of French troops and equipment to Algeria. General E. Combaux's indictment, while possibly extreme, certainly went to the heart of the military conception of NATO:

From its origin NATO, in which the European spirit was not present, tried to model itself on the American army, an army of debarkation, technically overequipped, extraordinarily costly. Many reasons made this inevitable: the existence on our continent of "surplus" materials, our admiration for the victor, a very lively taste for the technical miracles of modern armament. But it was in error not to ask what modifications would be made in this armament or in its apportionment (*dosage*) to adapt it to our continent. The American organization was so costly that the available financial resources of the European countries were absorbed in equipping ridiculously weak forces. When this disequilibrium in numbers became evident, strange theories resting on nuclear arms—large strategic empty spaces, for example—were invented to erase this disparity.[3]

If NATO were conceived as an instrument of American policy and tailored to American capabilities, it followed that Americans (with British help) controlled the Organization. So long as France remained unable and unwilling to maintain substantial military power on the continent, it could say little publicly on the assignment of top positions. And it was not disposed to quarrel with the American monopoly of SACEUR, a guarantee, after all, of America's military presence in Europe and of its close working relations with the strategic deterrent force, SAC, the basis of NATO's effectiveness. But privately the French felt that the consequence of American military power was the appointment of a disproportionate number of Americans to key positions within the Organization. "Under his [Lauris Norstad's] 'reign,' SHAPE has largely become what the public thinks it is: an American general staff. Certainly the same number of positions of the same importance are still reserved for officers of the fifteen nations of NATO. But the major decisions and the most significant information remain in American hands. . . ."[4]

The French further alleged that American monopoly of decisions was strengthened by the paucity of information made available to the representatives of other countries. Some major documents, the French contended, were marked for very restricted circulation—for "American eyes only."[5] True or not, this charge expressed the feelings of a country which was extremely aware of its declining military position in Europe.

[3] Engineer General E. Combaux, "Armes Atomiques et Non-Atomiques dans la Défense de l'Europe," *Revue de Défense Nationale*, January 1958, p. 64.
[4] Jean Planchais, *Le Malaise de l'Armée* (Paris: Plon, 1958), p 53.
[5] Same.

France and NATO Military Concepts

Rather than concentrating on the intangibles in the relations between France and NATO, French leaders might better have studied NATO military planning for the defense of Europe. As General Combaux indicated, such examination is part and parcel of any criticism of the American role in NATO. With very few exceptions, however, French thought on this complex yet literally vital problem was cursory. Few French writers achieved the integrated approach of Raymond Aron, and even he was more inclined to take a broad or astral view than to examine the problem from close range.

Why is this so? Answers may be found in the same domestic and international factors which both caused and were perpetuated by "immobilist" governments. One of these was the system of French education, with its neglect of science, technical training, and the social sciences. Another was the existence of certain barriers to information and communication concerning atomic energy. Nuclear research had been in progress since World War II, but members of the government and the Assembly—to say nothing of the public—knew little of the activities or indeed of the existence of the French Atomic Energy Commission. In this, as in other matters, political parties failed in their role of informing the electorate and allowing it to select alternative courses of action at the polls. Instead, stress was laid, particularly by the Socialists and Communists, on the horrors of nuclear war, with the ideological insistence by the Communists that these horrors were due solely to American policy. Political discussion was also discouraged by the initial postwar reluctance to reconstitute a strong French military establishment. The realization followed that French resources were inadequate for the attainment of both its military objectives and its pressing domestic economic and social goals. Consequently, French leadership, after several false starts, found itself wavering down the road toward atomic armament, without full knowledge of its prospects or implications. There seemed to be little option; the course of events inside and outside France had already defined the path it must take.

None of the tasks of the French army—occupation duty in Germany, the war in Indo-China, the insurrection in Algeria—had demanded much thought about the implications of atomic armament. While European defense progressively shifted to nuclear means of defense, through NATO decisions dating as far back as 1954, coincidentally French military forces left Germany, and the Algerian conflict became the overriding preoccupation of the armed forces and of French politics. The decision for nuclear defense had been an American decision, for it was the United States which had initially possessed the Western monopoly of atomic arms Great Britain's entry into the atomic picture did not greatly change the situation, since, despite American restrictions on information and matériel, Britain remained closely linked to the United States on nuclear policy. France, on the other hand, reflected some of the mingled ignorance and fear of small countries such as Denmark, the Netherlands, and Belgium.

Finally, the French, correctly or not, interpreted NATO's decision to use atomic weapons if necessary against a Communist attack as applying "over there," across the Rhine in West Germany, not in France. If NATO concepts were to succeed—or indeed if they were to fail—they would do so in West Germany, an impression heightened by German furor over the consequences of any nuclear combat on their territory. Under the circumstances military exercises like "Foudre" necessarily took place in a kind of limbo. Few cared enough or were competent to interpret their results for French audiences because few believed that they fundamentally affected either French military structure or decision-making. All too frequently French writers discussed various and partly conflicting strategic doctrines with little introspection, applying them to the United States, Great Britain, or any other nation—but not to France.[6]

To convince the public of the advantages to be gained from nuclear weapons, French authorities repeated an ar-

[6] As an example, see J. Pergent, "Les Principales Conceptions Stratégiques Atomiques," *Revue de Défense Nationale*, March 1956, pp. 306-321

gument familiar to Americans and Englishmen: these weapons would give a bigger bang for a franc. "Possession . . . very probably permits the attainment of national defense while at the same time realizing tangible economies as compared to the costs of classical weapons systems"[7]—a potent argument indeed in a country where perpetual governmental deficits were created in large part by military expenditures and brought few palpable indications of satisfactory military power. No one alluded to the experience of the United States, where the argument of defense "on the cheap" had proved dangerously fallacious. Recognition that atomic armaments might not provide the answers to all missions assigned to the armed forces—certainly the case with the United States and quite probably with Great Britain—left the French unruffled. They simply added conventional forces and organization to the nuclear necessity, with no mention of consequent costs.[8]

The "advantages through adversity" or "smiling-through" argument was also advanced. With the spread of nuclear technology, the time would come when smaller as well as larger countries could make nuclear weapons if they so chose. France must, then, manipulate the future to its own ends: the possession of atomic weapons would give France a strong bargaining position Then, but only then, could it push hard for international control of armaments and for the restriction of nuclear energy to peaceful purposes.[9] Indeed, at that stage it might actually be feasible to create a true collective security system encompassing all Europe. This peculiarly French construction, redolent of 1922 mothballs, defined aggression so that an automatic, and above all impersonal, decision could determine its existence and then guarantee its defeat by H-bombs. With hydrogen

[7] General Charles Ailleret, "De l'Euratom au Programme Atomique National," *Revue de Défense Nationale*, November 1956, p. 1321. See also Colonel P. M Gallois, "Limitation des Armes à Grand Pouvoir de Destruction," in same, December 1956, p 1486

[8] And often by the same person who was arguing the cost factor See General Ailleret, "L'Organisation de la Sécurité et les Progrès des Armes Nouvelles," *Politique Étrangère*, no. 1, 1957, p. 61.

[9] Paul Guérin, "Conséquences Politiques en Europe du Développement des Armes Nucléaires," in same, August-September 1955, pp. 491-492.

weapons spread about Europe, overtures could be made to the Soviet Union to join a revamped NATO, formally independent of the United Nations. A Soviet refusal to accept the invitation would—by proving the good faith of the West and the bad faith of the East—bestow psychological credit in the event of a future holocaust.[10]

These projections savor of never-never land, because their authors avoided coming to grips with the problem of what would follow an actual test of NATO's defense strategy. Viewed at close range, the French saw a fine or hopeless or confused situation, depending on the observer. General P. M. Gallois was the prototype of the "just-fine" school—persistent, hard-headed, analytical (within defined bounds) and atypical. What was the true implication of nuclear technology? The time had come, said Gallois, when one could adapt the means of combat to the nature of the struggle. Atomic forces could both deter aggression and defeat it through general, all-out response or by selected, limited response, as the case might warrant. Atomic war, however initiated, would not inevitably deteriorate into indiscriminate slaughter of soldiers and civilians. On the contrary, the matching of great destructive power to clear and precise political and military objectives could prevent undesirable extensions of the conflict. The essential factor so far lacking in French policy, therefore, was determination —determination to use all available weapons if necessary. With determination, even forces numerically inferior to those of the enemy would prove powerful deterrents to aggression.[11]

Perhaps pessimism born of long experience caused Frenchmen to accept more readily the opposite, or hopeless, interpretation, of which General Combaux's was one of the clearest expositions. What was wrong with NATO strategy? Practically everything, the General answered. Reliance on nuclear weapons was both dangerous and useless

---

[10] Jacques de Maupéon (Vice-President of the National Defense Committee of the Council of the Republic) and Georges Kitcheev, "O T A.N. et Sécurité Collective," *Politique Étrangère*, April 1956, pp. 143-165.

[11] Gallois, cited, pp. 1485-1497.

—useless because the strategy was not geared to the real problems. In any attack on Europe, the last thing the populations involved would want would be the use of nuclear weapons. An organization predicated on just such a development was one that in time of crisis neither peoples nor governments would support. Moreover, exclusive reliance on atomic armament precluded the West from effectively protecting the Near East or even Austria and Yugoslavia, let alone aiding the Soviet satellites should they revolt.

General Combaux was not proposing that the West discard nuclear weapons altogether. Rather did he contend that their proper role in possible crises both inside and outside Europe was to provide support for conventional forces and protection if they failed to deter all war. Nuclear strategy, in his view, should concern only non-NATO forces, such as the Strategic Air Command. ". . . All technical and psychological conditions are . . . united in causing atomic armament, no matter what its power, no matter what use one wishes to put it to—strategic or tactical—to be indissolubly linked with total war."[12] "A military system endowed with atomic power but giving it too much importance, a military system so mechanized and so costly that it ends by confiding to a few meager professional legions the task of defending the nation, a system insufficiently supported by the masses and which pretends to replace absent divisions by big bombs cannot cope with all situations. Faced with an enemy which is a past master at revolutionary strategy, such a system forces governments toward a tragic dilemma: to give way or unleash general conflict."[13]

The rather sudden revelation that the United States was, like Europe, vulnerable to Soviet attack further complicated an already complex situation. How now to remove European doubts that the United States would risk casualties on the order of 50 to 100 million of its own people by coming to the defense of Europe, especially if Soviet aggression were

[12] Combaux, cited, p. 63.
[13] Same, p. 71.

initially limited in area and classical in the type of weapons employed? One of the few to assess possible answers to this problem was Jacques Vernant, Secretary-General of the Centre d'Études de Politique Étrangère. He found none satisfactory. The proposition that the menace of total war was the only way to prevent local attacks was all right until proved all wrong. And because SAC was charged with this mission, it could hardly be called the NATO answer. But NATO's reliance on tactical nuclear weapons to deal with both classical and limited aggression ran head-on into the difficulty (some would say the practical impossibility) of drawing operational distinctions between tactical and strategic atomic weapons, distinctions acceptable to and recognized by both East and West.

Vernant considered, too, the proposal advocated by many in both Europe and the United States that members of the alliance be given atomic arms or develop their own. Assurances by European countries of their will to resist aggression, presumably a fundamental factor in the decision of Great Britain and the United States to risk Soviet attack by coming to Europe's aid, would then be more persuasive. Greater equality among its participants, furthermore, would strengthen the alliance. Vernant, however, went on to note disadvantages in the spread of nuclear capability to Europe. Europe, he pointed out, would still be greatly dependent on the United States. (After all, how much independence had been won by Great Britain just because it had a Strategic Bomber Command equipped with nuclear weapons?) Europe would still be a vulnerable and tempting target for Soviet expansionism. Strong opposition by neutralists and the various Communist parties to the whole policy of military commitment against the Soviet Union would continue to exist. Finally, European atomic armament, far from increasing mutual trust between Europe and the United States, might push America once again toward isolationism.[14]

[14] Jacques Vernant, "Stratégie et Politique à l'Âge Atomique," *Review de Défense Nationale*, May 1958, pp. 855-863, especially 859-860.

French Conclusions Regarding NATO

Despite confusion and conflict, several clear elements emerge in the French view of NATO. Algeria was specifically covered by the North Atlantic Treaty. French military leaders professed to find evidence of Soviet attack against the West through assistance given to the rebel forces. It remained France's position, none the less, that Algeria was solely a French concern and that NATO should keep its hands off. The positive contribution of NATO then remained to deter a Soviet aggression in Europe, even though this was not considered nearly as likely in 1958 as it had seemed in 1950.

Equally important, perhaps, NATO formally bound together Great Britain, the United States, West Germany, and France. As British commitments under the Western European Union proved fragile, the more comprehensive, if less precise, NATO commitment assumed greater significance. With regard to the United States, the North Atlantic Treaty not only obliged it to defend Europe, but the treaty and the Organization also implied the continuation of American military assistance for an indefinite period. American aid was indispensable in buoying up what French strength remained on the continent and was perhaps equally indispensable to France's ability to continue the Algerian war. In the future the French army would need American help in equipping its forces with nuclear weapons, whether by direct transfer or by multilateral control through NATO, or both. The alleged use of the French armed forces as "pousse-caillou" (literally "kick-pebble") accounted for much of the French resentment against NATO's military strategy. But if the tie to the United States through the Organization might mean perpetuation of this status, it was simultaneously the major hope of transcending it. And if (or, as the French would say, once) the Algerian war could be ended on terms satisfactory to France, its military prestige in Europe would soar with the return of its seasoned veterans. French influence could then be brought to bear upon the adjustment, if not the revision, of NATO conceptions of the proper strategy for the defense of Europe.

The North Atlantic alliance also joined the Western Big Three in a common relation to Germany—in fact, the only link remaining after the end of the occupation era. Within the political section of NATO, France could restrain Britain and the United States from sacrificing Western interests in bargaining with the Soviet Union over German unification. Supported by other European countries, notably Benelux, the French maintained that West Germany's integration into the political and economic affairs of Western Europe had gone so far that it must not be destroyed by reunification on the basis of neutralization. All agreed that this would destroy NATO and with it almost all prospects for the successful defense of Western Europe. For France, West Germany was at last an accepted, indeed a necessary, partner in the construction of European economic institutions. At the best, unification would have serious and unknown consequences; at the worst it might undermine the new European institutions, burying France under the rubble.

Last, and probably least, France considered NATO a more acceptable form of international organization than the United Nations. Its fifteen members were all to a degree Western-oriented. Despite dissimilar interests and unequal power, experience had proved the possibility of attaining a measure of unity on policies generally aligned with those of France. If agreement were ever to be reached with the Soviet Union, it could only be by the concert of the three Western powers, buttressed by the North Atlantic alliance. In contrast, the West was declining as a factor in the United Nations as the importance of former colonial territories increased. As a colonial power, France viewed the evolution of the United Nations with suspicion. Ineffective as an instrument to maintain international peace and security, its discussions of French policy in North Africa and its action in establishing an "international police force" in the Suez area threatened not only France, but Western solidarity as well.

Chapter Thirteen

UNEASY ALLIES: AMERICA AND THE FOURTH REPUBLIC

WHEN WE TURN to those issues which shaped the relations between the Fourth Republic and its American ally, it is important first to distinguish issues which arose between the two governments from popular views held in each country about the other and, likewise, from the opinions of informed but unofficial commentators. Popular views and critical commentaries can, of course, become factors in relations between governments. Through their influence on the executive branch, legislators bring both types of opinion to bear on the policy-making process. Members of the executive arm, responsible for formulating and executing national policy, may utilize popular or informed views to justify action or inaction. Furthermore, the rapidity of international communications has increased the sensitivity of governments to popular or critical foreign opinion. Although we are concerned here primarily with official issues between France and the United States, we cannot ignore the connection between official action and unofficial attitudes.

New Trends in Franco-American Relationships

By 1955 France's postwar relationship to the United States had entered a new phase. Certain new factors were making the earlier feelings of inferiority and superiority less significant, and there was less public mention in France of American interference with French foreign and domestic policies. As successor to the multibillion dollar Marshall Plan, from which France had been the largest beneficiary, the Mutual Security Program, as its name implied, was devoted to military-related *cooperation,* not to economic relief and rehabilitation. By 1955 the French economy had clearly recovered from its war-born pauperization and had entered a period of increasing vigor and prosperity. No longer was it possible for the Communists to gain power by capitalizing on social and economic issues. Though still strong in voting strength, as attested anew in the 1956 elections, their grip on French labor had been loosened and their political representation isolated from positions of control, if not of influence. A major dual objective of American postwar policy—recovery of France and prevention of Communist control—had been achieved.

On the military level, by 1955 French reliance on the United States was also less conspicuous. One year after the United States, through the North Atlantic Treaty Organization, had committed itself to defend an all-but-helpless continent, the Korean War suggested that international communism was again striking out for easy gains. The NATO members responded with a "crash program" to create maximum military strength in minimum time. This meant European dependence, not merely on American promises to rescue Western Europe in case of attack, but also, for France especially, dependence on United States aid to reconstitute armed forces debilitated by defeat, occupation, and purge. Failing to achieve the projected goals of armed strength, the NATO countries decided to settle for less military power over an indefinite period.

By 1955 France had bowed to the collective desire of the West that Germany make a military contribution to the defense of Europe and to do so within the framework of NATO. Anticipated advantages from this strikingly new feature of French policy included a lessening of American concentration on West Germany, from which France believed it had earlier suffered, and a new escape from Franco-American bilateralism, in which France was obviously the junior partner, into a broader multilateral setting.

The completion of the first phase of the NATO infrastructure program eliminated another source of irritation. The network of bases was largely located on French soil, though subsidized mainly by American dollars. Americans not infrequently built installations with American equipment, and both their construction and their use brought large numbers of Americans directly into France, in daily touch with its citizens. Misunderstandings and frictions inevitably accompanied this intimacy. American military activity, like American economic activity, emphasized to the French their inferior status. Only with the completion of the first program could a second begin, one more modest in scope and hence offering less of an affront to French sensibilities.

While there were certainly increasing difficulties between France and the United States over Algeria, the French made their decisions on the conduct of the war in North Africa outside the framework of Franco-American cooperation. From the denouement in Indo-China, French leaders had learned, or thought they had learned, a sorry lesson. Blaming American inaction immediately after World War II for the onset of French difficulties, French leaders then were forced to the realization that the American involvement in the Indo-Chinese conflict would be followed by the ending of French influence. Had the war been won, the United States would have replaced France as the economic and military leader in the area. As it turned out, Frenchmen argued that the United States had given France just enough to enable it to lose with maximum difficulty and humiliation; and in the upshot the United States was forced, whether it liked it or not, to bear the main responsibility for bolstering South Viet-Nam, Laos, and Cambodia and thereby to replace France as the dominant factor. The lesson for the future was that reliance on other countries in its colonial wars spelled political defeat for France whatever the military outcome. French leaders now insisted on exercising sole responsibility in Algeria, and American leaders strove with equal determination to keep the United States unengaged.

In general, then, after 1954 France was less acutely aware of an inferiority of power in the conduct of its economic, military, and colonial affairs. There was also less emphasis on direct bilateral relations, as multilateral organizations grew stronger. Earlier, France had simultaneously desired and dreaded a close bilateral relationship. On the one hand, it feared that, if it became submerged in the operations of international institutions, the United States would regard France as just one more, and perhaps not the most important, member of the larger unit, rather than as a direct partner in world politics. Specifically, the Coal-Steel Community and the Defense and Political Communities might develop into a unified Western Europe monopolizing American attention. On the other hand, France needed the new European institutions in order to gain sufficient power and prestige to deal with the United States on a basis of actual as well as juridical equality. The demise of the Defense and Political Communities and the adoption, after 1954, of a new conception of European unity partly resolved, partly evaded, this painful dilemma. There was now to be no Political Community within the foreseeable future. As substitutes for the abortive Defense Community, NATO and Western European Union would serve as international, not as integrative bodies. In both the Common Market and Euratom, primary responsibility rested on national representatives in the Council of Ministers. Thus France could conclude that the new institutions would reduce the strains in bilateral Franco-American relations without submerging French national identity. If only the problem of associating Britain with them could be solved, France would have found a way to eat its cake and have it too.

Another shift in France's relationship to the United States occurred in 1957. Suddenly it appeared that the American economy was not immune to setbacks. At almost the same time Sputnik I demonstrated that the United States was not so powerful militarily vis-à-vis the Soviet Union as had been assumed. French leaders viewed the American slump with uneasiness, recognizing that, if prolonged, it would undoubtedly have serious, adverse effects in Europe. However, France also felt that it could now take even greater pride in the rapid advance of its own national production. Was not the French blend of the new with the old, of agriculture with industry, of small plants with large establishments, of private ownership with public control, justifiable on more than social and historical grounds? Perhaps it represented an economic system as effective for France as American capitalism was for the United States. If the pupil was not yet qualified to teach the master, at least he no longer had to accept the master's condescending pose of omniscience.

Similarly mixed feelings characterized French reactions to the revelations of Soviet military advances. The American leadership's handling of Sputnik—in one breath deprecating its significance, in the next calling for renewed American scientific efforts—led to popular French amusement at the spectacle of Uncle Sam, self-styled Samson, both embarrassed and confused. But French leaders could not long afford the luxury of amusement or cynicism. Instead they had to count on the United States to maintain, or recapture, a weapons superiority sufficient to prevent Soviet advances in either military or ideological fields. They hoped furthermore that, in meeting a challenge that gave every prospect of continuing indefinitely, the United States would reflect on the nature of its alliance with Western Europe and reassess the balance of responsibility. Was it not now clearer than ever that the United States needed and would continue to need France and Western Europe in other ways than just as a piece of real estate to be denied to the enemy?

French and American Views of World Problems

In the past, leaders in both France and the United States had paid glowing tribute to the alliance as reflecting the common aspirations and goals of both peoples. Now these salutes were more convincing. The two nations were drawing together in their interpretation of the power and implacability of the Soviet Union. Earlier French weakness had bred considerable self-deception regarding

Soviet intentions. After Stalin's death, the fight over the European Defense Community Treaty had led France to glimpse opportunities for coming to a settlement with the Soviet Union. It was France, even more than Great Britain, that dragged a reluctant United States toward the summit in 1955. After the Geneva conference, where, in truth, nothing was settled at all, these illusions wore thin. Whether the question was German unification, disarmament, or relaxation of Communist control over Eastern Europe, Khrushchev and his associates had proved more skillful in diplomacy than Stalin, but no different in ambitions or in methods of pursuing them.

While the Soviet Union was gaining power and holding fast to its positions in Europe, France was acquiring a greater vested interest in maintaining West Germany as an integral part of Western Europe. French governments had found it not only possible to deal with Adenauer, as in the settlement of the Saar issue, but also very advantageous. Though France's traditional enemy might yet prove to be an uncertain friend, German reunification would present the far greater risks of a powerful nation in the heart of Europe, uncommitted to alliances or other pledges of cooperation with the West. Even French Socialists could not agree with their German Social Democratic comrades that the West should be ready to pay a high price for a united Germany. To a Frenchman generally, almost any price was too high. Behind official pronouncements the United States had for some time been of the same opinion. Thus, after the Paris Accords and the Saar settlement both countries joined in insisting that a united Germany must be free to join the Western alliance, that any neutralization of Germany was dangerous, and that the Rapacki Plan for an atom-free zone in Central Europe was unacceptable. When Khrushchev began to talk of yet another summit meeting, the leaders of the Fourth Republic were just as reluctant as the United States to heed his call. The only foreseeable result of such talks was one detrimental to France. Possibly Great Britain and the United States, with their stockpiles of atomic weapons, could agree to suspend nuclear tests. Itself on the verge of joining this exclusive club, France would hardly choose to help slam the door in its own face, unless it could first make some compensatory deal with the United States.

France and the United States agreed, too, on the need for European integration and the preferred way to achieve it. After the fall of Mendès-France, the United States wholeheartedly supported France's "return to Europe." The Americans also approved the French approach of concentrating on economic rather than political and military relations. This emphasis neatly fitted American diagnoses, dating back to the Marshall Plan, that Europe's economic health depended on forming one large market which would lead to a better allocation of productive resources. They also welcomed the French proposals for the common European development of nuclear energy for peaceful purposes. Euratom held out the promise of reducing Europe's dependence on distant petroleum supplies at a time when the United States was once again beginning to worry about their long-term availability and sufficiency. Far from competing with the United States in the production of energy, Western Europe under Euratom would open up attractive areas for American private investment. Equally important, American companies would have a much-needed opportunity to test and perfect techniques for producing and utilizing atomic power before applying them within the United States.

Plans for implementing the Common Market Treaty enhanced the desirability of close relations between France and Great Britain. While the United States had not indicated any clear preferences concerning the form of British association, certainly the American government did not want to see Britain remain entirely aloof. It hoped, along with leaders of the Fourth Republic, for a reconciliation of the Common Market with the Free Trade Area under terms that would protect legitimate British interests without endangering the progress of the six West European countries toward economic unity.

The public controversy over French colonial policy and the contrasting views of France and the United States toward the Near East have obscured the basic agreement between the two countries on the place of neutralist and underdeveloped lands in the world scheme of things. Both recognized that the emergent states of Asia and Africa were rapidly breaking into what had been a bipolar configuration. Both agreed that, for their own sake and because the Soviet Union was a powerful and attractive competitor, the Western powers had to assist them. Both concluded, therefore, that the outcome of the West's struggle with Soviet and international communism might well depend on the speed of economic and social progress in underdeveloped lands and on the West's ability to find a new and durable pattern of political relationship to replace the rapidly vanishing colonial system. The question of *how* these objectives could best be achieved lay at the crux of the serious disagreement between the two countries.

There were signs that France and the United States were coming closer together in their views of the future relations between the new African units and the West and also on their importance for Europe's future. In Africa as well as elsewhere, American executive leadership was moving away from its previous insistence on outright alignment with the West as the price for assistance. At the same time France was seeking a new form of association with its Overseas Territories, one which would not bind them to all the obligations assumed by France as a senior member of the anti-Communist alliance. This somewhat tentative groping in both countries for a new policy did not mean that either was ready to give its approval to neutralism; rather, it suggested their growing awareness of the limitations inherent in the Western alliance system and a recognition that they might have to settle for nonalignment of Asia and Africa with the Soviet bloc as a tenable alternative.

Behind this common view of emergent states, there was agreement that Western Europe still deserved top priority. With Europe secure, the Soviet Union might, of course, still win world domination by attracting the nations of Asia and Africa into its orbit. But while greater attention should therefore be directed to extra-European affairs, Europe must continue to have first claim. In the United States, in 1942 or in 1959, both Republicans and Democrats reached the same conclusion: although the Far East, the Middle East, the Near East and Africa should be kept from Communist control, Western Europe remained the focal point of American statecraft. And French leadership, in spite of the clamor over its African colonies, was well aware that its fundamental interests were at home. This mutual concentration did, upon occasion, produce disagreements, but emphatically not the irreparable cleavage that would have ensued had either country radically lowered its estimate of the central importance of defending Europe.

By 1954 each country had grown more familiar with the other, and if familiarity bred some dissension, it also smoothed certain rough spots. After their inevitably confused relationship following World War II, when the Fourth Republic was just beginning, when America had only recently accepted its new responsibilities in the world, and when the true nature of the postwar international environment was only dimly discerned, France and the United States were learning about each other's limits of tolerance and of possible policy changes. Continuing problems became familiar, and even new problems could be fitted into a predictable pattern of statecraft. The United States gained new insights into the nature and extent of the influence it could productively exert. For its part, the French government began to distinguish between annoying, but immutable American policies and those that it might hope to modify. When interacting policies now struck sparks, it was less accidental than formerly, more from design or from unavoidable clashes of interest.

Finally, time tended to mute recriminations over the past. Immediately after World War II, France was prone to blame the United States for many things—the presence of Soviet power in Eastern Europe, for example, and, along with Britain, the elimination of France from the Near East, not to mention the widely publicized animosity of Franklin D. Roosevelt and Cordell Hull toward De Gaulle. Postwar

American actions had added to this list of resentments, notably the policy of rebuilding Germany. By 1958, some of the earlier differences had been settled. Others were coming to be accepted as unavoidable accompaniments of French-American relations. No longer was it a startling discovery that the United States was by ideology anticolonialist, militarily powerful, or a devotee of free-enterprise capitalism.

Conflicts Arising from French Dilemmas

The spread of better mutual understanding could not of course eliminate conflicts of interest or of basic approaches. To appreciate the nature and extent of the divergent viewpoints of the two countries, they should be traced to their sources so that each does not appear as a rootless, isolated phenomenon.

One cluster of issues developed from the nature of the French policy-making process. Neither the American public nor its leadership appreciated sufficiently the genius of French governments operating under the conditions imposed by the Fourth Republic, especially after the elections of 1951. Because a long-lived executive seemed less possible to achieve than ever before, Americans valued it more. They equated longevity with stability and stability in turn with progressive policies. Yet political crises in France were inevitable; they were also sometimes actually productive, and in certain cases halted at least temporarily a deteriorating situation.[1] Moreover, despite mounting American impatience as crisis followed crisis, a premature solution ran the risk of producing a weaker coalition than the one that might finally emerge from a prolonged process of cabinet-building.

The United States did not sufficiently understand the degree to which domestic and foreign problems had become inextricably intertwined, despite the lessons of the abortive European Defense Community Treaty. Because the system operated inefficiently—a fact acknowledged by all—delays in

[1] As indicated in Chapter 4, governments, like those of Henri Queuille, Joseph Laniel, or Guy Mollet, which lasted a long time, tended to become less and less able to deal with national problems.

changing it were deplored, and, conversely, each slight alteration, for example, the reforms of 1954, was painted as having far more significance than it deserved. The United States failed to understand the pervasiveness of *immobilisme* in France, its causes and its implications. American policy, consequently, heightened the effects of *immobilisme* by making unrealistic demands on French policy growing in turn out of its unrealistic conception of France's position in world affairs.

Behind this disregard of the intricacies of French policy-making lay an unawareness of the sources of support for American policy within France. ". . One may say that between 1947 and 1957 anti-Americanism in France passed from the Left to the Right," wrote Alfred Grosser.[2] While the Left continued to harbor certain resentments against American policy in general and the Eisenhower-Dulles actions in particular, the new antagonism of the Right was a reaction to American failure to support two of its favorite programs—the policies toward Suez and Algeria.

The Suez invasion commanded substantial popular and political support in France, but its failure brought to light many hitherto silent critics, particularly after almost all of France's allies in Western Europe had echoed the strong American disapproval. The same was true of Algeria. Few except the Communists advocated abandoning Algeria to the rebellious nationalists. On the other hand, there was an undercurrent of disapproval of the methods which were being used by the French government and of its intransigent rejection of all possible channels of settlement. On both policies leftist support of—or at least absence of disagreement with—the United States was part and parcel of the leftist battle against the forces of the Right, whose influence over executive policy-making was growing clearly and rapidly.

The position of the United States was indeed a difficult one. In supporting an existing system that in certain respects ran counter to American preferences, it was acting

[2] Alfred Grosser, Professor of Political Science at the École Nationale des Sciences Politiques, in *Témoignage Chrétien*, May 3, 1958.

against the very groups then out of power, which sought to impose new French policies, policies more in line with its own preferences. But any other course would have been extremely delicate for the United States and dangerous to the alliance. Certainly, too transparent American support of the Left would only have increased the anti-Americanism of the Right. Nor could the United States take responsibility for jarring the already shaky balance of the French system; the net result might be an even more difficult situation. Nevertheless, during the last years of the Fourth Republic, American statecraft may have tended to see in leftist criticism of some of its actions an adamant opposition to all of its purposes, whereas conservative expressions of official politeness were construed as indicating a genuine harmony with American hopes.

The influence of anti-American sentiments on the political operations of the Fourth Republic was not a negligible one. At crucial moments French governments used anti-Americanism to create sympathy and rally support within the National Assembly. Weak governments were more prone to invoke the slogan of French independence from "American dictation." In part, vociferous popular approval of the Suez landings stemmed from the knowledge that the action had been taken against Secretary Dulles' wishes and advice. Gaillard made political capital out of his prompt and public protests against the token Anglo-American arms shipment to Tunisia. Conversely, he might have hung on to power longer after the bombing of Sakiet had it not been for his welcoming the good offices of the United States and Britain and his apparent willingness, at their suggestion, to resume negotiations with Tunisia. France's decision to proceed with the manufacture of atomic weapons was forced by the insistence of groups in both the National Assembly and the government that France would thus be equipped to speak up more firmly to the United States.

The French yearning for more independence from the United States was commingled with a more general sentiment of anti-Americanism. Although United States policies could count on some support from these or those political groups within France, an exploitable opposition was never lacking. So long as it avoided overplaying its hand, a skillful government could blend ideological antipathy to America on the Left with specific resentments on the Right. This kind of effort came naturally to coalitions in their daily struggle to find some meeting ground among many clashing groups in order to survive at all. The early postwar years of economic and military dependence on the United States had left behind the belief that a strong French government, by definition, was one that opposed the United States. Since all French executives wished to give the appearance of being strong, here was an added incentive to anti-American posturings.

The deliberate manipulation of this antagonism for domestic political purposes sometimes verged on irresponsibility and irrationality, especially since France was simultaneously looking to the United States as its *deus ex machina*. France sought equality with the United States and wanted to lessen its dependence in order to attain this status, yet it deliberately confused hostility with independence, while looking to the United States to rescue it from the consequences of its own actions. *Immobilisme* could persist as long as it did because the United States was paying a part of the price. What would French troops have done if they had been allowed, without protest, to complete the occupation of Suez? How long could France have gone on without oil from the Western Hemisphere, or without dollar credits to pay for it? What if America had insisted on France shouldering its promised share of the burden for Western European defense instead of transferring men and equipment to Algeria? And how prosperous would the French economy have remained if the United States had not paid a part of the cost of the protective barriers insulating it from outside competition?

These questions are not asked to suggest that the United States *should* (or even that France *could*) necessarily have followed a different course. Rather they point to a growing French anxiety over the nature of the policies which seemed regularly to emerge from the political process. If France continued to see its own situation, according to the Viennese saying, as "hopeless but not serious," might not the United States shift its support to nations where it found both hope for success and seriousness of purpose? France had not forgotten Dulles' threat of "agonizing reappraisal." American-German cooperation had become a mainstay of American policy. Defense of Europe from bases on the periphery of the continent was a basic feature of the Strategic Air Command, while German divisions provided the core of any land defense NATO would be able to mount against attacks. In the Near East the American hope of propitiating Arab nationalism continued strong. The customary candor of the French in discussing the weaknesses of French leadership and the irresponsible character of some French actions only heightened their extreme sensitivity to American attitudes and actions.

Economic Issues and Conflicts

Though lessened and less obvious, France's economic dependence continued even after the completion of the Marshall Plan. France needed, first, direct financial assistance from the United States; second, economic support for Euratom and eventually perhaps for the Common Market, and, finally, favorable trade arrangements. Although all these types of assistance were forthcoming in varying degrees, the French were not completely reassured. How long could the United States be expected to come to the financial rescue of France? Would it some day reject the French view that aid without return was a French right? As the twilight of the Fourth Republic came, the conditions it had to accept in order to secure the new international loan fed the sense of alarm. What, asked French commentators, would be the American response at the end of 1958, when the money had been spent without ameliorative measures having been taken?

Although American help was needed to integrate the European economy and develop nuclear energy, this support, by its very nature, gave rise to new apprehensions. Aid from the American government might delay real European independence. Large-scale private American investment might also bring adverse effects, perhaps condemning European nuclear production to be a subsidiary of American enterprise. Might not Europe become a mere testing ground for American techniques and end up with obsolescent plants inadequate for its needs? Or, if American capital entered wholeheartedly into atomic-energy development in Europe, might it not come to dominate the capital structure, especially in view of the relative scarcity and timidity of French private investment? Finally, for those Frenchmen who were still working for the political integration of Europe, the necessity to look to American support, whether private or public, raised up very real political hazards to the realization of their hopes.

Even the carefully safeguarded economic integration of Europe was complicated by the problem of trade relations with the United States. How would it view the still unresolved question of arrangements between the Common Market and other areas, especially the sterling and dollar zones? The OEEC was fearful that the Common Market would turn into a highly protectionist bloc, and the difficulties France encountered in bringing its prices into line with those of its European partners gave reason to this fear. Failure to overcome this obstacle even within the elastic time limits set by the Common Market Treaty might all too easily lead to raising rather than lowering the common tariffs. Furthermore, if the association of Great Britain and the Free Trade Area with the Common Market also remained unsettled, both Britain and the United States, along with other countries in the dollar and sterling areas, would face a difficult decision within the framework of the General Agreements on Tariffs and Trade. How many exceptions to the progressive liberalization of trade arrangements would they accept for the sake of fostering the economic integration of Western Europe? Britain's trade with Western Europe was particularly vulnerable to discriminatory tariff walls surrounding the Common Market. Hence, some accommodation between the two might be expected ultimately. On the other hand, the United States might react rather strongly against discrimination, even though, in its zeal for promoting European unity, it had come to accept some forms of regional discrimination since World War II. Because the Common Market created potentially large openings for American goods, some of its domestic producers were certain to press for protection, and, if they succeeded, American manufacturers would in turn demand new restrictions on imports into the United States.

Here was the second part of the trade problem. Along with many other countries, France complained that the United States had not fully accepted the necessity for greatly increased imports if the trade of the free world was ever to be placed on a sound basis. The American government's so-called liberal trade program, they felt, fell far short of its announced intentions. Removal of import restrictions, especially those other than formal tariffs, was limited and slow. The program was at the mercy of political pressures that caused sudden reversions to controls, especially on agricultural products, where protectionist sentiment was particularly strong, but also on specialized manufactures such as watches and bicycles.[3] If a highly integrated European economy, with a strong interest in protecting its producers against American imports, began to develop the capacity to export to the United States large quantities of manufactures, such as automobiles, the American government might be driven to adopt even more drastic import restrictions. The American reciprocal trade agreements program faced a long legislative battle each time it came up for renewal, and, when passed, contained escape clauses and other requirements to protect American producers—facts of United States political life not reassuring to Europeans.

French concern over economic relations with the United States was marked by vague uneasiness rather than particular disagreements and by far from optimistic prognoses. Many Frenchmen had real misgivings over the character

[3] Percy W. Bidwell, *What the Tariff Means to American Industry* (New York: Harper, for the Council on Foreign Relations, 1956), and also his *Raw Materials: A Study of American Policy* (New York. Harper, for the Council on Foreign Relations, 1958).

and inner compulsions of American society. American economic assistance, to be sure, had saved Europe after the war. "If one looks at the past, one will not find a comparable act of human solidarity," declared Premier Robert Schuman in 1948.[4] Although economic aid was a recurrent necessity for France, there were inevitably doubts over the motives of a materialistic civilization. It was not necessary to question the generous intentions of individual Americans and their leaders to conclude that they were acting as exponents of American interests. American aid to Europe, wrote the conservative André Armengaud, was recognition that a country in full economic expansion could risk government deficits to create new markets for American products and buy political support.[5] Other critics were more specific. "The disinterestedness of the Americans is only an illusion. The fear of industrial and agricultural overproduction, the fear that internal and present external markets cannot absorb American products arouses leaders to search for new markets and to try to force the solidly bolted doors of our overseas possessions."[6] These and similar views were symptomatic of a continuing fear of the threat of "Americanization" to France's economic and social values. As the Fourth Republic sought to find its place in an economically united Europe and in a reconstructed French Union, and thus to enhance France's own strength and independence, it was inevitably concerned over the prospect of an aggressive American economic expansionism that might undercut these objectives.

The Conflict over Nascent Nationalisms

The issue of French colonialism was a continuing source of serious and often emotional friction. "There would be less anti-Americanism in the world if America would put

[4] Speech at Poitiers, April 18, 1948, printed under the title "La Situation en France."
[5] André Armengaud, "L'Avenir de l'Économie Européenne: Organisation Raisonnée ou Décadence," *Politique Étrangère*, no. 2, 1957, p. 159.
[6] General Jean Marchand, "Les Puissances Anticolonialistes et l'Afrique Noire Française," *Revue de Défense Nationale*, May 1956, p. 571.

aside its philanthropic aspirations, its Santa Claus inclinations, its transcendent international morality, all its missionary paraphernalia, all its boy-scout equipment, if it would openly and intelligently follow a policy of its own interests." So wrote Raymond Cartier in *Paris-Match* under the provocative title, "Why Are Americans Detested Throughout the Entire World?"[7] "Let us underline the contradictions," declared General Marchand. "At home the Americans uphold the doctrine of white supremacy; in North Africa they strive to oppose its application in order to gain the sympathy of the colored populations and dominate their future despite the absence of racial discrimination in our territories. They support with all their power indigenous nationalism but condemn our own nationalism, judging it regressive. . . . There seems to be a flagrant hypocrisy in wishing to emancipate the Bantus of the equatorial forest while in Mississippi and Alabama young men are killed whose sole crime was to look at a white woman."[8]

Such views may be extreme, but they reflect a climate of feeling which has prevented France and the United States, despite their general agreement on the emerging importance of the non-European world, from reaching a consensus on specific policies. To the American sympathy for nationalist movements France has opposed its own concept of a carefully controlled and narrowly limited transition. The objective, they have insisted, is not to gratify every form of nationalism for its own sake or to create a status of sovereignty for every group able to attract attention by its clamor. Rather, it must be to promote stable political and economic development within an international system that will keep the peoples of Asia and Africa in a constructive relationship with Europe and prevent their becoming, wittingly or unwittingly, tools of international Communist expansion.

This goal is shared by the United States. The differences crop up over the ways and means of reaching it. The French put primary emphasis on the maintenance of close ties with the West. If, contend the French, the United States does

[7] March 24, 1956.
[8] Marchand, cited, pp. 569-570.

indeed accept the primacy of Western Europe in its international statecraft, and if European security depends on maintaining an economic or even a military presence in overseas territories and newly independent countries, then the United States should logically support its European allies, not undermine them in their efforts. Frenchmen can point to what they consider to be the disastrous consequences of American anticolonialism—in Viet-Nam, in the Near East, and above all in North Africa. When the United States sacrifices its ideological support for the West to its anticolonial sentiments, it is far more than hypocritical—it is downright destructive. France's experiences with emergent nations since World War II have convinced it that premature sacrifice of political control ultimately leads to the loss of economic, diplomatic, and ideological influence.

The "retreat of the West," to the French, was turning into a rout under the leadership of a country that apparently still believed that the upsurge of nationalism anywhere and everywhere would inevitably lead to good. The increasingly assertive political stands taken by the Afro-Asian bloc were a crude but pointed measure of the extent of Western decline. Great Britain also suffered great losses insofar as it accepted or followed American policy. The sacrifice of British positions in Egypt and Iran had been a major factor in the spread of Soviet influence throughout the Near East and its intrusion into North Africa. It followed logically that American opposition to British and French attempts to recapture lost positions, as in the Suez crisis, only compounded the felony.

As a business civilization, the United States sees in economic expansion a method of compensating for the loss of political influence. This theory, in the French view, has no foundation in fact. American economic assistance to colonial or newly independent peoples has not only been inadequate but has actually created new resentments against the West. "The American or British formulas, consisting of installing an industrial complex in a theoretically free country, are as inhuman, as tragic in their consequences, and therefore finally as stupid and as costly as the colonialist formula. In installing an industry or a single-crop economy in a region (whether colonial or free matters little), you should first put the people of the country in a position to defend themselves against the system in which you are obliging them henceforth to live, and for that you must first of all bear the costs of their adaptation."[9] These spectacular costs the American government or private concerns are not willing to assume.

Point Four, said General Marchand, is an "illusion."[10] By sowing the seeds of rising demands and expectations, the West, through the inevitable frustration will reap a harvest of angry discontent. The large share in economic development marked out by the United States for its private investors would in all likelihood further retard necessary adjustments. The native leaders' resentment against the price which must be paid for the intrusion of American capital and business would be fanned into general hostility toward the West. These leaders, finding it necessary to govern by authoritarian, if not totalitarian, means, would become increasingly receptive to offers of assistance from the Soviet Union, believing it would be less disruptive to their rule.[11] On the other hand, those countries which tried to remain aloof from both East and West, like Burma and Indonesia, would be risking their prestige and ultimately their control because of their inability to satisfy or guide the forces of nationalism.

Crucial in the French view was the American attitude toward the struggle in Algeria. While maintaining officially that the conflict was France's sole concern, the United States government was actually lending support to the Algerian nationalists through its policy of favoring Tunisia. Its unreasoning insistence on placating the Arab-Asian bloc was encouraging Algerian nationalists to reject out-of-hand the solutions offered by France and, indeed, any solution short

[9] Germaine Tillion, *L'Algérie en 1957* (Paris: Éditions de Minuit, 1957), pp. 109-110.
[10] Marchand, cited, p. 571.
[11] One-party rule in new African states was defended at a Congress of West African intellectuals and politicians held in Ibadan, Nigeria in March 1959 (*New York Times*, March 17, 23, 1959.)

of independence. Responsible leaders in France were convinced that France could not abandon Algeria and the more than one million Europeans living there. Any retreat, moreover, would frustrate vital plans for France's economic development, in which Saharan oil holds such a large place. And so American anticolonialism, whatever its motivations, was, in the French view, encouraging a march of events which, if unchecked, would inevitably wipe out many French accomplishments of the past and many French hopes for the future. France could not agree to confine its power and its interests to its European homeland. The psychological shock alone would be too great. The whole foundation of France's international position, which the United States professed to regard as indispensable to Western strength, would crumble.

In the question of the best policies to follow toward dependent peoples the French view of American society and the nature of American politics colored both official and popular attitudes. The French saw anticolonialism as a deeply ingrained conviction of the American people. Since public opinion had more importance in policy formation in the United States than in France, the French discounted measured statements by responsible American leaders, while reacting vehemently to the idealistic oratory of frequently irresponsible politicians. The inevitable result was to heighten French fears and resentments.

Disputes Over Military Strategy

It is deceptively easy to list the specific military issues between the Fourth Republic and the United States. One was the large-scale transfer of French troops to Algeria and France's inability to reach or maintain the agreed NATO force levels. Then there were the legal restrictions on transmitting to the French (and others) information on the production of nuclear weapons. These limitations, in themselves damaging to French *amour-propre*, also forced the French government to proceed with its own costly program of developing and testing an atomic bomb. Finally, there was the American proposal, submitted to the NATO Council in December 1957, for installing intermediate missile sites on French soil.

These concrete differences reflected a more fundamental dilemma of French leadership: how far could and should France accept the American emphasis on the military element in Western strategy? ". . . Leaders and opinion in the United States," wrote Raymond Aron, "are inclined to point out that military preparations are as indispensable today as yesterday; European leaders and opinion are inclined to take the opposite view, for the smiles and speeches of the masters of the Kremlin have encouraged them to abandon their belief in a genuine Soviet menace."[12]

French views were by no means rigidly held. The Soviet suppression of the national uprising in Hungary, the failure of the Geneva and disarmament conferences, the revelations of Soviet military advances, all combined to bring most Frenchmen closer to the American view that indeed "military preparations are as indispensable today as yesterday." "Personally," Foreign Minister Pineau told the National Assembly on January 22, 1958, "I can understand better the logic of those who propose that France remain neutral, who wish to lead it out of a system of collective security, in other words, who wish to allow France to leave itself open to invasion or subversion, than I can the logic of those who contend that we should be content with obsolete military material."

The clash of opinions was over the purposes of these military preparations. To Frenchmen, American policies in Asia carried inadmissible risks of bringing on a nuclear war in which Europe would be the main sufferer. Their reaction was to disassociate France publicly from American action in the Formosa area and to suggest politely that the Communist government of China was entitled to receive diplomatic recognition, if only because it so firmly controlled such a vast area and so many millions of people.

[12] Raymond Aron and August Heckscher, *Diversity of Worlds* (New York: Reynal, 1957), p. 22. The authors report discussions by French and American officials at a conference held in 1956.

In Europe, on the other hand, the Russian threat to France was a direct one. France was also well aware that NATO doctrine called for using nuclear weapons if necessary to repel a Soviet attack. This made it all the more imperative for French views on both deterrence and defense to receive adequate attention in allied planning. To this end French leaders took certain steps. They insisted repeatedly on equality with Britain in all dealings with the United States. After some fumbling they decided to go ahead with the independent development of French nuclear weapons. They demanded the right to decide on the use of American weapons located on French soil. Finally, they re-emphasized the political role of NATO as a forum in which the risks and uncertainties involved in American statecraft could be curbed by common policies advanced by America's allies, including France.[13]

When it came to negotiating with the Soviet Union, French policy faced a dire quandary. On the one hand, too great Western rigidity might increase the risks of war.[14] On the other hand, too flexible Western positions might cause the United States to deal directly with Russia, bypassing America's allies. The ups and downs of the disarmament negotiations illustrated this dilemma. The indefatigable Jules Moch pressed for disarmament within the United Nations Disarmament Commission, and France genuinely feared the consequences of an unrestrained arms race with the Russians. France was also worried about any direct

[13] "As it has been presented," Pineau continued in the same address, "the problem of the launching sites is . . . a false problem, at least as far as installing them on French soil is concerned. Conversely, the question of their use can justifiably be raised. The French government is firmly attached to the principle that such missiles cannot be used without the authorization of the country on whose territory they are installed. I wish to assure you that this particular point will receive our careful attention." Address of January 22, 1958, quoted in Ambassade de France, Service de Presse et d'Information, *Speeches and Press Conferences*, no. 104 (New York, January 1958), p 8.

[14] One purpose of Foreign Minister Pineau's visit to the United States in June 1956 was reportedly to remind the United States of the danger of too great rigidity of policy toward the U.S.S R. *L'Année Politique*, 1956 (Paris: Éditions du Grand Siècle), p. 315.

Soviet-American arrangement, for this would hurt France at a time when most of its conventionally armed troops were tied down in Africa and its atomic capability was still unproven. It was natural, therefore, for France to oppose any inspection system that excluded Europe or involved the "neutralization" of Europe and the withdrawal of American troops.

Whether or not the United States and Britain agreed to end testing atomic weapons, France was not prepared to concur. Defending his country against the charges of negativism, Foreign Minister Pineau explained the French position:

We are not opposed to the prohibition of these tests, on the contrary; but on condition that the manufacture of fissionable material for military purposes be also banned. Otherwise what would have been gained? Countries that have not as yet carried out any tests would be prohibited from doing so, while those that have achieved sufficient progress in the field would be continuing to stockpile atomic or thermonuclear weapons. Then do not speak of disarmament, but of the creation of a club, open to two or three powers and closed to all others. This would force all countries of the world to join one bloc or the other, without ensuring world peace—quite the contrary.[15]

French Doubts Concerning American Leadership

If lack of American understanding of French political processes caused certain problems, French misgivings over American policy-making provoked others. Many Frenchmen felt that American leadership was lacking in stability and too often was influenced by irresponsible and irrational public pressures. The change of administration in 1953 seemed to point up this basic defect in the American system of government. Whereas President Truman had come to

[15] Address of January 22, 1958, *Speeches and Press Conferences*, cited, p. 9. Clearly implied by the Foreign Minister was a favorable view toward the spread of nuclear military technology to "fourth countries," on which issue American policy, seemingly divided, was drifting aimlessly. Equally clear was the prospect of nuclear capacity decreasing French dependence on the West meaning Great Britain and the United States, as well as security from the Soviet threat.

be well liked in France, President Eisenhower, despite his role in the liberation of Europe and the building of NATO, inspired no similar degree of admiration. Still less did Secretary of State Dulles. In its early years the Eisenhower-Dulles Administration was viewed by French critics as an impotent if unwilling prey of "McCarthyism," which was denounced throughout Western Europe as an extreme expression of a widespread American callousness toward domestic liberties and responsible international conduct. However respected for his noble intentions, the American President seemed to many to be an ineffective captive of extremists within his own party, a party traditionally associated with isolationism and with hostility to Europe.

The President had largely delegated to his Secretary of State responsibility for framing and executing American foreign policy. And Secretary Dulles, who could win no popularity contest in any Western European country, was especially distrusted in France. What was at issue was only partly a matter of policy, although French resentment at American actions, as in the Suez affair, often ran high. It was also a matter of irritation with the tone and style of the Secretary's diplomacy. "Agonizing reappraisal" and "massive retaliation" had a most unpleasant sound in French ears. Deficient in other attributes of national power, France considers diplomatic skill one of its major assets. Frenchmen tend, therefore, to be overly critical of the diplomacy of other countries, finding in their actions evidence of an inferior culture as well as unworthy motivations. They are especially suspicious of a diplomacy that appears to equate material power and wealth with moral virtue, a combination they label as a form of sanctimonious hypocrisy, absent from the diplomacy of Truman and Acheson.

While recognizing President Eisenhower as a man of peace, many French observers felt after 1953 that America's powerful military establishment was being given a potentially dangerous freedom of action.[16] Secretary Dulles also

[16] Frenchmen recalled Truman's spectacular dismissal of General Douglas MacArthur as an example of a strong President determined to keep military officers, whatever their prominence, in line.

seemed unwilling to control those in the Department of Defense advocating provocative military gestures or to dissuade elements of his party from supporting them. On the contrary, he appeared too much impressed with the alleged capacity of military power or military threats to overcome political obstacles and win diplomatic victories and too prone to adopt as infallible truths American military dogmas of dubious or transitory validity. France, a country without nuclear weapons, could hardly welcome the idea that megaton bombs have the final say on all major international issues.

Chapter Fourteen

ALGERIA, GRAVE OF THE FOURTH REPUBLIC

THE FOURTH REPUBLIC's final convulsions began when the Right overthrew Gaillard on Algeria. "It is a fact," declared Mollet, "that within less than a year, three times running, the policy desired by successive governments has been defeated because a group of 120 deputies decided to support the Communists."[1]

The Setting of the Revolt

In addition to the usual difficulties of building another coalition to replace the one just cast aside, the Center and non-Communist Left finally saw that a new approach to the Algerian problem was required. Socialist and Radical governments had, since February 1956, accepted the demands of the Right for augmented military force and a stern stand. And yet the Right had destroyed one government after another. The predicament of the "governmental parties" was highlighted by Bidault's inability to form a coalition after Gaillard's fall. He had planned to place in key positions several advocates of a "firm line" toward Algeria: Duchet as Minister of Public Works, Morice as National Defense Minister, Soustelle as Minister for Algeria, himself as Foreign Minister, if Robert Schuman refused (as he did).[2] A four-hour conclave of his party direc-

---

[1] *Le Monde*, April 23, 1958; Mollet was announcing the decision of the Socialists not to support Bidault's bid to form a government.
[2] Same.

torate, however, voted against MRP participation—the first time under the Fourth Republic a party had openly repudiated an investiture attempted by one of its own leaders. Until De Gaulle's advent, Bidault was to be a lone MRP dissident in key votes of the National Assembly.

Pleven's protracted effort to unite the internally divided groups of the Assembly behind a "Common Charter" of principles to end the crisis revealed the Socialist shift, instituted behind the scenes by Mollet. A loud Socialist minority was plumping for a government of the Left, even with Communist support. On the eve of a meeting of the Socialist national council, the *Tribune du Socialisme*, repudiated by Mollet, circulated the text of a dissident manifesto drafted by André Hauriou. In part, it declared: "A government composed of Socialists (determined to break with present policy), of Radicals of the Left, of representatives of the UDSR-RDA will be able to count on the votes of much of the MRP, and the Communists will not be able to do otherwise than to support it."[3]

Another group within the party was advocating new ceasefire overtures to the Algerian nationalists. One of its leaders, Albert Gazier, reportedly favored enlisting Tunisia's and Morocco's help in arranging a halt to hostilities. He also felt that negotiators should not a priori exclude the possibility of Algerian independence. Any French-Algerian pact should, Gazier contended, receive an international guarantee and the eventual support of Tunisia and Morocco.[4]

To gain party backing for any new policy, Mollet first had to see that Lacoste did not continue as Minister to Algeria. For this reason, and because Pleven had insisted on a postponement of wage increases, the Socialists refused to enter his government.[5] But at the same time, Mollet, who reportedly had suggested calling Pleven in the first place,[6] made it clear that he would support the UDSR leader within the National Assembly,[7] and added that the Socialist party

[3] Manifesto printed in *Express*, May 2, 1958.
[4] *Le Monde*, May 4-5, 1958.
[5] Same, May 3, 1958; *Express*, May 8, 1958.
[6] *Express*, May 8, 1958.
[7] *Le Monde*, May 4-5.

"will not support any other ministry and will vote against any government following a dangerous or adventurous policy in North Africa."[8]

Pleven's "Common Charter" was another indication of the new orientation within the Center and Left. His ten points on Algeria included, to be sure, opposition to "internationalizing the war" and to its secession, but they laid greater stress on general French-Moslem relations, special ties to Tunisia and Morocco, rapid implementation of the *loi-cadre* for Algeria, which called for equal suffrage by French and Moslems, and a new appeal for a cease-fire.[9] One reason for Pleven's ultimate failure was the belief of some leaders that the Algerian section of the "Common Charter" did not go far enough toward a "liberal" solution. They also feared that rightist parliamentary groups would accept the Charter, but then, taking advantage of its vagueness, sabotage government proposals for its implementation.[10] Pleven's patient negotiations, nevertheless, undoubtedly paved the way for the rapid investiture of Pflimlin, known as a "liberal" on Algeria, although his Cabinet and program differed little from Pleven's.[11]

Thus, by the time the revolt against the government broke out in Algiers, shifts within the Socialist, MRP, and some Center groups, had produced a new majority in the National Assembly, one favorable to scrapping the previous sterile policy and, in its place, seeking to end the conflict on the basis of close association not only with Algeria, but also with Tunisia and Morocco. Surely, this was not the least tragic element in the collapse of the Fourth Republic.

In chaotic Algiers, conspiratorial elements were busily planning a coup. Military and civil authorities ignored their

[8] Same, May 6, 1958. The additional statement was interpreted as an effort to carry Pleven to investiture even though the Socialists would not enter his government.

[9] Same, April 29 and May 3, 1958.

[10] Same, May 3, 1958.

[11] Pflimlin's Cabinet numbered 18, as compared to Pleven's 20; there was one less Independent and one less Dissident Radical. Both men had omitted from their ministries those identified with the "hard line," men such as Duchet, Chaban-Delmas, Morice, Lacoste, and Soustelle.

activities,[12] and by May 13, top-level representatives of Metropolitan France had lost control. Lacoste's weakness had been demonstrated when his orders to ban the April demonstrations were disregarded and the Algiers prefect actually congratulated the demonstrators on their performance. General Salan, military commander of the region, had on May 11 assured Pflimlin of his and General Jacques Massu's loyalty. He neglected to mention, however, that Colonel Godard effectively held the police powers presumably administered by Salan himself and that Lieutenant Colonel Trinquier actually directed the "para" units technically led by Massu.[13] Civilian and military plotters were thoroughly organized.[14] Originally they planned to act when Pflimlin was invested and Mutter designated Minister for Algeria.[15] Instead, however, the impatient plotters seized upon the occasion of a parade scheduled for May 13, honoring three victims of the FLN for their uprising. "It is no longer possible to perpetuate this paradox of monstrous absurdity," wrote Alain De Sérigny in *Écho d'Alger* on May 12, "to see the mission of forming a government given to *a* M. Pflimlin, author of a program which ends with the Mendésiste goal of abandoning Algeria; this, after the ministry of M. Félix Gaillard was overturned by a massive majority of men determined, like Lacoste, Bidault, Soustelle, Duchet, Morice, to avoid ever seeing

[12] *Express*, May 29, 1958, examines the pre-May 13 activities of one conspiratorial group, the Union Française Nord-Africaine. Official knowledge of this and other groups was demonstrated when those arrested after the attack on General Salan were released and Bourgès-Maunoury, whose Minister of National Defense was Chaban-Delmas, refused to order inquiries to proceed.

[13] Pierre Popie, a lawyer at the Algiers Court of Appeal, "How May 13 Was Prepared in Algiers," *Le Monde*, May 30, 1958.

[14] Before the May 13 coup, Colonel Barberot wrote that subversive organization had gone beyond "the anarchy of spontaneous demonstrations ... This manifestation is not a repetition [of them]. It is one of the grand maneuvers of Revolt. Such is the latest warning by the Algerian French to the Metropolitan French and to the government." ("Répétition Générale à Alger," *Express*, May 2, 1958.)

[15] Jean Daniel in *Express*, May 15, 1958.

Algeria menaced by foreign intervention in more or less open collusion with the FLN or its allies."[16]

The march on Government House offered Lacoste, then in Paris, and Massu and Salan, in Algiers, the extremely unpromising alternative of opposing the movement and being brushed aside or accepting it and being swept along on its reckless tide. Lacoste, whose maneuvers between Paris and Algiers had provoked the distrust of both the Metropolitan Socialists and the Algerian plotters, had already replied to the Vigilance Committee's demand that he repudiate his fellow Socialists by stating, "I cannot break with a party dear to my heart."[17] Massu, previously an advocate of political reform in Algeria, despite his sanction of torture tactics against the nationalists, closed his eyes, held his nose, and "jumped off the dock." Salan, his superior, watching this irrevocable step in silence,[18] then had little alternative but to place the military behind the revolt unless he wished to quit and allow the revolt to proceed without him.

The final element in the setting for May 13 was the most imponderable of all. At Colombey-les-Deux-Églises, brooded General de Gaulle, seeing a number of public and private figures, but revealing no plans. In the fifth month of 1958 the General had perhaps only one-tenth as many avowed followers as six years before. There were even fewer "Gaullists" whom he had not at some time expressly or implicitly repudiated. Against him, on the other hand, stood all the Left, almost all the Center, and a majority of the Right within the National Assembly and within the party structures outside the Assembly. He could counterbalance these formidable obstacles to his political aspirations with one great advantage that both the Paris government and the Algerian Public Safety Committee lacked: his national and international prestige. The essential element of this prestige lay in its negative character. De Gaulle was in no way in-

[16] Same, May 13, 1958.
[17] Same
[18] *L'Aurore*, May 15, 1958, reporting an interview with Massu. Massu supposedly asked Paris if he should open fire on the crowd. The purpose of this inquiry was quite clearly to embarrass the government.

volved with the disintegrating "system," nor implicated in the plots and demonstrations taking place in Algiers. The fact that both Metropolitan France and Algeria were at the outset not overtly committed to him was a factor of supreme importance in his final success.

Prerequisites for Success of the Algerian Revolt

To win Algiers had been easy for the conspirators; to win France was an entirely different matter. Several related steps had to be taken and taken swiftly if the minority movement were to impose its will.

1. *The conspiracy had to be legitimatized* This process was accomplished in stages. First, General Salan was induced to address the crowd from the balcony. Next came the announcement that General Salan "provisionally assumes, beginning today, May 14, civil and military powers to protect property and persons and the conduct of operations. The Committee of Public Safety, which has been constituted in Algiers under the pressure of events to affirm the will of the French-Moslem population to remain French, assures liaison between it and the command, which gives it orders "[19] The Pflimlin government then formally assigned to General Salan the special powers conferred on it by the overwhelming vote of the National Assembly—despite the Premier's statement on May 15 that ". . . some military chiefs—I say it with regret—have adopted an attitude of insurrection against Republican legality,"[20] and his declaration of May 17 that "the coup was minutely prepared by civilians some of whom came from the *Métropole.*"[21] Thus the Committee of Public Safety, composed, not of elected officials in Algeria, but of leaders and associates in insurrection,[22] received sanction by Salan, who in turn was expressly recognized as France's legal representative in Algeria. To obtain the Assembly's overwhelming approval—and anything less would have been too little—

[19] *Le Monde,* May 15, 1958.
[20] Same.
[21] Same, May 17, 1958.
[22] Popie, cited.

Pflimlin had to accept a unanimously endorsed commendation of the army and its leaders in Algeria.

2. *The revolutionary spirit had to be intensified.* Nightly assemblages in the Algiers forum whipped up revolutionary fervor. While the Committee of Public Safety called for more and better demonstrations. District by district, block by block, house by house, organizers drew the crowd to the forum where they were led in chants, slogans, and songs before, during, and after harangues from the balcony. Special attractions in the composition of the mob were announced daily in the papers. On May 16, for example, residents of the Casbah were in the limelight; on the seventeenth, the Haiks; on the eighteenth, Moslem women; and so forth.[23] This showmanship aroused the people, dinned appeals into their minds and hearts, provided amusement and activity, demonstrated the daily presence of political and military power, and above all gave the demonstrators a sense of immediate participation in the making of history.

3. *Political contact with the "Métropole" had to be solidified.* To replace Lacoste, who remained in Paris, the revolution needed another political leader from the *Métropole*. The Algerian dissidents had no intention of accepting Pflimlin's designated Minister for Algeria, the Independent André Mutter. A telegram to Pflimlin said:

> All measures will be taken to prevent the arrival on the soil of French Algeria of a minister charged with embarking on an Algerian policy conforming to his recently announced position. The Vigilance Committee is astonished to see an Alsatian representative envisage as a means to resolve the Algerian problem

[23] Claude Choublier, "'L'Arme Psychologique' entre les Mains des Colonels," *La Nef*, July-August 1958, p 31. This article is an interesting examination of French military conclusions concerning the uses of psychological warfare, based upon studies by nationalist movements in Indo-China, Tunisia, Morocco, and Algeria. The author quotes (p. 27) from one of the tracts produced by the Cinquième Bureau of the army· "The true democratic regime is founded on reason and discussion. But today the image replaces the concept. Appeal is made only to the effectiveness of the masses, to images. Example. United States elections no longer have anything to do with democracy."

formulas which will inevitably lead to breaking the lines with the mother country.[24]

When Pflimlin asked Bidault to undertake a special mission to Algiers, Bidault reputedly replied, "I would willingly go in the name of General de Gaulle. In your name, I would be tossed into the sea. And I cannot swim."[25] In contrast, Mutter, replying to the assaults of his fellow Independents and to the fears of his three colleagues over his remaining in the Pflimlin government, said, "I will put on my decorations. I will take the plane. I will get off in Algeria, and I will say, 'Here I am!'"[26] Mutter's willingness to take risks was not, however, matched by the government's willingness to sacrifice him as a bridge to Independent support. Nor could the government chance an open blow to its prestige at a time when Pflimlin still insisted that Salan was in control of the situation and was acting under orders from Paris. Most providentially for the revolutionaries, the impasse was broken with the arrival in Algeria on May 17 of the self-appointed spokesman for De Gaulle, Jacques Soustelle. Soustelle had been placed under "police protection" immediately after he had issued, with Bidault, Morice, and Duchet, on May 14, a proclamation approving the Algerian coup. In what must be a new low in police efficiency, his guards allowed him to escape in a laundry basket, change cars three times, cross the border into Switzerland, and take a specially chartered Swiss Balair plane to Algiers.[27]

One cannot exaggerate the importance of Soustelle's arrival. As former Minister for Algeria, the Social Republican represented a familiar contact with Paris. Only with his dramatic presence was the revolution able to consolidate two further prerequisites to ultimate triumph: involvement of the Algerian Moslems, and introduction of an overshadowing candidate for national political authority.

4. *The concept of the Algerian "problem" had to be changed.* Said Soustelle, after Frenchmen and Moslems had

[24] *Le Monde,* May 13, 1958.
[25] *Express,* May 29, 1958.
[26] Same, May 22, 1958.
[27] *Figaro,* May 19, 1958.

joined hands in the forum of May 19, singing "La Marseillaise," "All the foundations of the Algerian problem have been swept away." Such demonstrations, including the spectacle of Moslem women tearing off their veils, certainly impressed a France heretofore fed on reports of increasing hostility and terrorism by the Algerians. The success of the managers of the revolt in carrying out these "manifestations of solidarity" was undoubtedly of great influence on De Gaulle's decisions. It also weakened Pflimlin's determination to hold on. On May 23 the Premier told the French people, "Today the movements of fraternization which are taking place in Algeria have given birth to a great hope."[28]

Closer analysis, however, indicates that the foundations of the problem had merely been covered up temporarily. The Moslem demonstrations in Algiers were made possible, first, by Colonel Bigeard's effective organization of the Casbah after the February 1957 strike, and, second, by the work of pacification patiently undertaken by Jacques Chevallier, Mayor of Algiers, and the SAS, special army units established for this purpose. The "ultras" had long vilified Chevallier; in fact, his defense by Pflimlin had exacerbated the opposition of the French in Algeria to the Premier. The SAS enjoyed little support within the French military hierarchy stationed in Algeria. Outside Algiers, the Moslem population was deprived of its leadership, oppressed by the FLN, and fearful of the French.[29]

The price of buying the continuing allegiance of these three groups represented a substantial alteration in the attitudes of the extremists who had begun the movement and now must continue it. Despite initial opposition from many Algerian French,[30] the stage managers of the revolt had cast in their lot with De Gaulle by the time the Moslems began to join the French crowds. But the Moslems were cheering De Gaulle because to them he represented the

[28] *Le Monde*, May 23, 1958.
[29] Jean David reporting on the "new Algeria" created by the May 13 revolt; *Express*, May 29, 1958.
[30] On the original preferences of De Sérigny and the Union pour le Salut et le Renouveau de l'Algérie Française (USRAF), see *Express*, May 22, 1958.

promise of equality between Moslems and French. De Gaulle and equality were in turn symbolized for the moment by the single electoral college, the very issue on which the Algerian French had overthrown Bourgès-Maunoury and Gaillard. Now these same Algerian French were joining with the Moslems in cheering Soustelle's words, "All Algerians must be French, with the same rights and the same duties."[31] If a new step had indeed been taken toward an Algerian solution, it was precisely the "liberal solution" that had touched off the reactionary revolt in the first place.

5. *An alternative political solution had to be found.* The person of De Gaulle served to unite the movement in Algiers, to commit Salan irrevocably, and to start the Pflimlin government down the slippery slide to oblivion. When General Massu first telephoned the Hotel Matignon, he told Lacoste, "We have formed a Committee of Public Safety. What we wish to do is to pacify the situation without spilling blood. I have accepted the provisional presidency and I could not have done otherwise. This is not a *coup d'état;* we are here to impress on Parliament Algeria's desire to remain French. We await the formation in Paris of a government of public safety."[32] There was no mention of De Gaulle. When Salan, from the balcony, demonstrated the commitment of the military hierarchy, he spoke of military action against the Algerian nationalists. "My friends," he told the crowd, "you know that I am one of you since my son is buried in the Clos Salembier cemetery. That I will never forget. For eighteen months we have fought the *fellagh*. We will continue, and we will win. In showing the world your determination to remain French, Algeria will save France."[33] Salan concluded, "Vive la France; vive L'Algérie française!" As he started to step back, one of the leaders standing by him—some say it was the arch-conspirator Delbecque—said in a low voice, "Vive De Gaulle." Salan moved forward again and cried to the crowd, "Vive De Gaulle!"

---

[31] *Le Monde*, May 22, 1958.
[32] Jean Ferran, "La République dans l'Alarme," *Paris-Match*, May 24, 1958, p. 64.
[33] *Figaro*, May 16, 1958.

General de Gaulle responded promptly to this invocation of his name. Had he not, the revolt might well have lost momentum and shortly died. "The great hope of the civilian members of the Committee," said Massu in an interview on May 14, "was the arrival of M. Soustelle in Algiers. It was then hoped that General de Gaulle would throw off his reserve and take the head of a government of public safety."[34] Soustelle was delayed by police measures, but extra pressure on De Gaulle was not necessary. The time had come, and he was ready. At 5:00 P.M. on May 15 he delivered a short pronunciamento:

The degradation of the State inevitably entails the estrangement of associated peoples, disturbance of the army in combat, national dislocation, loss of independence. For twelve years France, pressed by problems too severe for the regime of parties, has been following a dangerous course. Once the country, in its deep difficulties, confided in me entire leadership to its health. Today, faced with new tests that arise before it, let it be known that I am prepared to assume the powers of the Republic.[35]

This was no equivocal response, nor was it an offer to throw the weight of his prestige behind the authority of the constitutional government. Here was clear willingness to be again *the* government.[36]

6. *The "Métropole" had to be threatened with a worse alternative.* Once having launched De Gaulle against Pflimlin, the Algerian Committee of Public Safety had then to threaten Pflimlin with a still more fearsome alternative. Only in this way could De Gaulle finally appear to the vast majority of French political leaders arrayed against him as the lesser of two evils. When the Algiers revolt took place, only a few politicians openly supported it: Delbecque in Algiers; Duchet, Morice, Soustelle, Bidault in Paris. Only one other important leader, Pinay, wanted Pflimlin to quit.

[34] *L'Aurore*, May 15, 1958.
[35] Same.
[36] Jean Farran of *Paris-Match*, who was in Algiers at the time, was of the opinion that De Gaulle's declaration rescued the revolters, who were hesitating over what to do next. When read to the crowd, it was taken as approval of the actions of May 13. "La République dans l'Alarme," cited, p 65.

Mollet at once agreed that he and the Socialists would join in Pflimlin's Cabinet.[37]

Against the Paris government, the rump regime in Algiers mixed open threats with mysterious messages. The Committee of Public Safety wired President Coty on May 17:

France, in your person, runs the risk today of losing its best chance if you do not respond to this fervor, formed by French and Moslems assembled under the same ideal, by accepting the arbitration of the liberator of the country in order that there may be constituted a committee of public safety headed by General de Gaulle. Any other solution will create grief, misery and despair. . . . You know our resolution is immovable and that all the forces of French Algeria will remain assembled and united until final victory.[38]

More menacing was General Salan's response on May 21 to the mob's cry of "the army to power." Calling it "this good word," Salan continued: "You will see that we are indissolubly united. We shall march together up the Champs-Élysées, and the French people will shower us with flowers."[39] To dispel any lingering doubts, De Sérigny told a press conference on the same day: "The Algerian revolution cannot be snuffed out but must be the beginning of revolution in France. There can be no compromise with Pflimlin. The Revolution [sic!] of May 13, 1958, has created national unity. De Gaulle must follow the popular will. . . . We will do everything to bring him to power."[40] A final example of the general tone of mounting threat was Massu's outburst to a London *Times* correspondent when, at the last moment, it appeared that De Gaulle might retire "to his *chagrin*." "It is up to him," said Massu, "to decide whether *we* bring him to power or not."[41]

Supporting the numerous public declarations of strength

---

[37] The vote of the Socialist directorate was 61-6, with 6 abstentions. A condition was that the government continue to be composed only of those who accepted Pleven's or Pflimlin's original program. (*Figaro*, May 15, 1958.)

[38] *Le Monde,* May 17, 1958.

[39] Same, May 21, 1958.

[40] Same.

[41] As reported by *Le Monde,* May 29, 1958; italics added.

and determination were mysterious messages from the Algiers radio: "We have received an important missive from CSP No. 6 in the SE: M. X having taken a trip, Puss in Boots will replace him. . . . Committee No. 6 asks the voice of French Algeria to speak more often and especially to unions in the *Métropole,* because all workers and laborers must know the truth. Committees of Public Safety are being formed all over the *Métropole.* Vive la France; vive l'Algérie française; vive De Gaulle, Signed, Puss in Boots."[42] "The road is good. Claude Alexandre thanks the gendarme. Jojo and Dominque want to drink the wine urgently."[43] Much more than liaison work, this was a nightly psychological war of nerves against Paris and its sleepless Premier, designed to create the impression of an irresistible movement.

7. *Success had to be built rapidly on success.* The Algerian venture had to build success on success in order to maintain the unity of the group and keep up the pressure on the Paris government. The organization of Moslem participants in demonstrations at the forum helped, as did the rapid spread of public safety committees to other Algerian cities. On May 13 Pierre Lambert, the prefect of Oran, cabled Pflimlin: "I have the honor to tell you that calm reigns throughout the Oran departments. The civil population, like the military authority, has at no moment deferred to the orders of the Algiers committee of public safety." Three days later he arrived in Paris, saying, "I was expelled from my prefecture."[44] On May 19 the local committees were grouped into an Algeria-Sahara committee, dominated by the "men of May 13" and under the official orders of General Salan.[45]

The revolt could, none the less, still be regarded as a local one. Between France and Algeria lay the Mediterranean.

---

[42] Choublier, cited, p. 33.

[43] *New York Herald Tribune* (Paris edition), May 29, 1958, reporting London reception of Radio Algiers.

[44] *Le Monde,* May 17, 1958.

[45] *Le Monde,* May 25-26, 1958, commented: "Whatever were their original intentions, M. Delbecque and Colonel Trinquier seem to have had the greatest difficulty in finding to sit beside them representatives of a Moslem elite that is none the less numerous, and whose cooperation M. Chevallier had obtained, as Mayor of Algiers."

Although the Algiers radio broadcast reported that committees were springing up all over France, Metropolitan plots remained largely underground. To break through this barrier the Algerian insurrectionists, after careful preparation, carried the revolt to Corsica. Led by paratroopers, a handful of civilians on May 24 quickly invested Ajaccio and moved on to Bastia, where it brushed aside the opposition of the prefect and the municipal council.[46]

If Paris wished now to unseat the Corsican committees, it would have to organize an expeditionary force and conduct an invasion. Of course, nothing of the sort could be undertaken. All Pflimlin could do was bring a group of deputies to the microphone in an appeal to the Corsicans for calm and respect for the law.[47] Pflimlin's loss of control was apparent when he requested the Assembly to deprive the Corsican deputy Pascal Arrighi, a participant in the coup, of his parliamentary immunity. The Premier achieved an impressive favorable vote, 428-119, but not before rightist deputy, Tixier-Vignacour had poured scorn on his puny gesture. "It is peculiar," he said, "that a government which for two weeks has not been able to form an opinion on the behavior of certain generals, has wanted to take away the parliamentary immunity of M. Arrighi. But this deputy arrived in Corsica on board a plane of the armed forces whose chief is General Salan, to whom the government says it has delegated its powers."[48]

Countermeasures to the Algerian Revolt

Against the uprising of May 13 Premier Pflimlin had several countermeasures to consider. All these possibilities were undoubtedly discussed by him and his Cabinet; some of them were attempted. All either failed outright or had only a limited success.

---

[46] Same, May 27, 1958; *Express*, May 29, 1958.
[47] Same.
[48] A general bill introduced at the same time to remove parliamentary immunity from any deputy, convicted or not, who acted against the laws of the Republic, ran into so much opposition that it was watered down to removal of legislative mandate pending legal judgment In its revised version the bill passed 395-150. (*Figaro*, May 27, 1958.)

1. *Restoration of military obedience.* Pflimlin certainly tried to bring the French military units back into the Republican fold. For this purpose he quickly and publicly delegated exceptional powers to Salan. Coty added the weight of the presidency, telling the French army in Algiers:

> Guardian of national unity, I appeal to your patriotism and your good sense not to add to the trials of the country a division between Frenchmen facing the enemy. [Meaning the Algerian nationalists, of course.] Any lack of discipline can only profit those who fight us. Chief of the armies by virtue of Article 33 of the Constitution, I order you to remain at your duties under the authority of the government of the Fourth Republic.[49]

Pflimlin's effort to enlist the Chief of Staff, General Ély, in the cause, however, resulted in the General's resignation. For some time the General, who would have reached retirement age at the end of 1958, had been unhappy over the government's policy toward the army, especially Gaillard's reduction of the military budget and disciplinary actions against two of Ély's associates.[50] After Ély's departure, the country waited for some general, any general, to speak out against the Algiers revolt. None did. Pflimlin was left with Salan, who, far from restoring military respect for the Republic, was talking of marching up the Champs-Élysées.

2. *Military pressure on Algiers.* Failure of the first countermeasure doomed the second. Of the French military establishment, totaling about one million men, slightly less than one half was in North Africa and the Overseas Territories. Sixty thousand were in West Germany and approximately 460,000 in France itself. Of the latter, 280,000 were army personnel, including recruits in training and support troops. In addition, the *gendarmerie* and Republican Guard totaled between fifty and sixty thousand.[51] Theoretically, the French government controlled more troops than the units which had broken away and joined in the May 13 revolt, but in the contest of will the numerically smaller force

[49] *Le Monde*, May 15, 1958.
[50] Same, May 18-19, 1958
[51] A study by *Le Monde* made during the crisis to answer the question, "Where Is the Metropolitan Army?" May 17, 1958.

completely dominated the larger. Even if someone could be found to order units to Algiers and command them to break up the insurrectionary movement, the result would have been civil war or, as President Coty more delicately phrased it, "division between Frenchmen facing the enemy." The rebellious military groups in Algeria and their civilian backers were prepared to threaten France with civil war, but the responsible government in Paris shrank from making a counterthreat.

3. *Removal of the causes of the revolt.* Invested as an advocate of a "liberal solution" in Algeria, Pflimlin lost no time in giving the military what Gaillard had denied them. Confronted with a revolt in Algeria which soon spread to Corsica, he took up with his Cabinet and the National Assembly plans for constitutional reform. These "contradictory" policies actually represented a deliberate attempt to undercut the appeal of the revolution and to steal De Gaulle's thunder.

A primary concern of Gaillard, both as Bourgès-Maunoury's Finance Minister and as Premier, had been to balance the budget. To accomplish this, he decided to reduce military expenditures by 80 billion francs. French commanders in Algeria feared the consequences of a reduced military effort. Pflimlin, however, on May 17 decided to release the funds after all and also to raise the period of military service to twenty-seven months.[52] It followed that military supplies and equipment for carrying on the war against the Algerian nationalists were to be made available before, not after, "republican order" had been restored.[53] The military now had what it wanted, but the gesture manifestly came too late to restore its allegiance to the Republic.

Constitutional reform also came too late. Even before his investiture, Pflimlin had announced that constitutional reform would receive a high priority under his government, indeed that he would resign when the Assembly had acted

---

[52] *Combat*, May 19, 1958.
[53] Announced by Premier Pflimlin in his address to the nation, in same.

on his proposals or on December 1, 1958, if it had not done so.[54] The Algerian revolt only somewhat delayed government action. On May 23 Pflimlin won cabinet agreement to several proposed changes. Sessions of the National Assembly would be reduced to the three months from October 1 to December 31, plus additional sittings of one month in each of the next two three-month periods. The legislature could delegate to the government power to abrogate, modify, and replace laws on the advice of the Conseil d'État, although reserving its own constitutional authority in such matters as declarations of war and states of siege, amnesty, constitutional revision, and the budget. A government would be invested at the beginning of each five-year legislative period, and it could be overthrown only by a motion of censure which carried with it the investiture of a new government. Should the Assembly name a premier who was then unable to form a government, dissolution would be automatic.[55]

On the evening of May 27 the National Assembly overwhelmingly passed these proposals, 408-165. But legislative adjournment over Whitsun weekend (May 24-25) had lost precious days.[56] Debate finally opened at 11:30 P.M. on May 27 after having been postponed several hours at Pflimlin's request. This delay provoked rumors that Pflimlin had resigned or was about to do so. The debate, consequently, dealt not with constitutional reform at all, but with whether and how Pflimlin should quit. His great majority came from the decision of the Communist party to support him, a fact with which Communist leader Jacques Duclos taunted Pflimlin: "The project can only be adopted by an absolute majority of the deputies—296 votes—thus with our votes.

---

[54] *Le Monde*, May 24, 1958

[55] Same. Pflimlin, supported by Jules Moch and Edgar Faure, had originally proposed that a government be guaranteed a life of two years, but opposition by the Garde des Sceaux and President Coty caused him to abandon the idea.

[56] Anthony Nutting, writing from New York for the Paris *Herald-Tribune* on May 29, 1958, reported that Pflimlin, after learning from French prefects that eight of ten Frenchmen favored De Gaulle, decided to push ahead with his plans for constitutional reform as rapidly as possible, but could not get the measure debated by the Assembly before the long weekend adjournment.

How simple it would all be if the project were defeated. It would be an alibi. Well, Monsieur Pflimlin, you will not have this alibi. France will know that your text was adopted but that you took flight to make way for the usurper."[57] Pflimlin did indeed formally resign the next day.

4. *Neutralization of the political alternative.* French leaders attempted to neutralize the political alternative by insisting that General de Gaulle decide either to repudiate the Algiers revolt, and thus alienate the group seeking to bring him to power, or to approve the revolt and rally the great mass of Frenchmen behind the legal government. Shortly after De Gaulle had broken silence, Guy Mollet, now Vice-President of the Council of Ministers, put several questions to him. Two were: "Do you recognize the present government as the only legitimate one?" "Do you disown the promoters of the Committees of Public Safety in Algeria?"[58] Before he saw De Gaulle on his own initiative, Pinay informed Pflimlin that his purpose would be to ask the General to use his authority to restore normal relations between Paris and Algiers. "If he refuses, De Gaulle will prove that the attraction of power comes before the national interest."[59] Pflimlin likewise requested De Gaulle to use his moral authority to gain the insurrectionists' respect for the law.[60]

Adroitly sidestepping these pitfalls, De Gaulle said on May 20, "It is profoundly normal and natural that the Algerians cry 'Vive De Gaulle' as do all Frenchmen in agony or in hope . . . [This is] the best proof that the French in Algeria want at no price to separate from the *Métropole*, for one does not cry 'Vive De Gaulle' when one is not with the nation."[61] Regarding the delicate situation in Corsica, he declared, "Any action, from whatever source it comes,

---

[57] *Le Monde*, May 29, 1958.

[58] The questions were published in *Le Populaire* (organ of the Socialist party); *Le Monde*, May 18-19, 1958.

[59] *Express*, May 29, 1958.

[60] So the Premier declared in his report to the National Assembly, May 27, *Le Monde*, May 29, 1958.

[61] *Figaro*, May 20, 1958.

which jeopardizes public order, runs the risk of the gravest consequences. While recognizing the circumstances, I could not approve it."[62] Pflimlin was forced to report to the National Assembly, "I must say that I was not able at the end of my interview to obtain the assurance that General de Gaulle would publicly and immediately take a position in favor of the maintenance of public order."[63]

In fact, the pressure was increasingly on the government, not on De Gaulle. The General's every utterance reflected his readiness to assume power. His final response to Pflimlin[64] was a public announcement at 5:00 P.M. on May 27: "Yesterday I began the process necessary to the establishment of my government."[65] Political leaders, whether they met with De Gaulle for this purpose or not, found themselves discussing, not how the General could assist Pflimlin, but how De Gaulle could peacefully and quickly assume power.

5. *Isolation of the infection.* The Paris government moved to isolate Algiers from the *Métropole* in hope that the revolt would subside. The Assembly gave Pflimlin full powers. Jules Moch, entering the Cabinet as Minister of Interior, mobilized the police, called out the Republican Guard, and deployed over 35,000 men in Paris alone.[66] Communications were cut off for a time with Algiers, and politicians suspected as incipient revolutionaries, such as Soustelle and Jean-Baptiste Biaggi, were placed under house arrest. Four Right-wing groups were ordered dissolved, and some of their members were arrested. Several violators of the decree banning demonstrations were also arrested. Moch delivered the tough radio speech expected from the man who ten years earlier had broken the Communist strikes:

The duty of all who hold any authority, the duty of all Frenchmen, of all Republicans is to show the Republic and its govern-

---

[62] *Express*, May 29, 1958. Note that De Gaulle did not say that any action jeopardizing public order had actually taken place.

[63] *Le Monde*, May 29, 1958.

[64] The Premier later told the Assembly he did not know about the statement until he read it in the papers. (*Le Monde*, May 29, 1958.)

[65] *Express*, May 29, 1958.

[66] *Le Monde*, May 17, 1958.

How simple it would all be if the project were defeated. It would be an alibi. Well, Monsieur Pflimlin, you will not have this alibi. France will know that your text was adopted but that you took flight to make way for the usurper."[57] Pflimlin did indeed formally resign the next day.

4. *Neutralization of the political alternative*. French leaders attempted to neutralize the political alternative by insisting that General de Gaulle decide either to repudiate the Algiers revolt, and thus alienate the group seeking to bring him to power, or to approve the revolt and rally the great mass of Frenchmen behind the legal government. Shortly after De Gaulle had broken silence, Guy Mollet, now Vice-President of the Council of Ministers, put several questions to him. Two were: "Do you recognize the present government as the only legitimate one?" "Do you disown the promoters of the Committees of Public Safety in Algeria?"[58] Before he saw De Gaulle on his own initiative, Pinay informed Pflimlin that his purpose would be to ask the General to use his authority to restore normal relations between Paris and Algiers. "If he refuses, De Gaulle will prove that the attraction of power comes before the national interest."[59] Pflimlin likewise requested De Gaulle to use his moral authority to gain the insurrectionists' respect for the law.[60]

Adroitly sidestepping these pitfalls, De Gaulle said on May 20, "It is profoundly normal and natural that the Algerians cry 'Vive De Gaulle' as do all Frenchmen in agony or in hope . . . [This is] the best proof that the French in Algeria want at no price to separate from the *Métropole*, for one does not cry 'Vive De Gaulle' when one is not with the nation."[61] Regarding the delicate situation in Corsica, he declared, "Any action, from whatever source it comes,

[57] *Le Monde*, May 29, 1958.
[58] The questions were published in *Le Populaire* (organ of the Socialist party), *Le Monde*, May 18-19, 1958.
[59] *Express*, May 29, 1958.
[60] So the Premier declared in his report to the National Assembly, May 27, *Le Monde*, May 29, 1958.
[61] *Figaro*, May 20, 1958.

which jeopardizes public order, runs the risk of the gravest consequences. While recognizing the circumstances, I could not approve it."[62] Pflimlin was forced to report to the National Assembly, "I must say that I was not able at the end of my interview to obtain the assurance that General de Gaulle would publicly and immediately take a position in favor of the maintenance of public order."[63]

In fact, the pressure was increasingly on the government, not on De Gaulle. The General's every utterance reflected his readiness to assume power. His final response to Pflimlin[64] was a public announcement at 5:00 P.M. on May 27: "Yesterday I began the process necessary to the establishment of my government."[65] Political leaders, whether they met with De Gaulle for this purpose or not, found themselves discussing, not how the General could assist Pflimlin, but how De Gaulle could peacefully and quickly assume power.

5. *Isolation of the infection.* The Paris government moved to isolate Algiers from the *Métropole* in hope that the revolt would subside. The Assembly gave Pflimlin full powers. Jules Moch, entering the Cabinet as Minister of Interior, mobilized the police, called out the Republican Guard, and deployed over 35,000 men in Paris alone.[66] Communications were cut off for a time with Algiers, and politicians suspected as incipient revolutionaries, such as Soustelle and Jean-Baptiste Biaggi, were placed under house arrest. Four Right-wing groups were ordered dissolved, and some of their members were arrested. Several violators of the decree banning demonstrations were also arrested. Moch delivered the tough radio speech expected from the man who ten years earlier had broken the Communist strikes:

The duty of all who hold any authority, the duty of all Frenchmen, of all Republicans is to show the Republic and its govern-

[62] *Express,* May 29, 1958. Note that De Gaulle did not say that any action jeopardizing public order had actually taken place.
[63] *Le Monde,* May 29, 1958.
[64] The Premier later told the Assembly he did not know about the statement until he read it in the papers. (*Le Monde,* May 29, 1958)
[65] *Express,* May 29, 1958
[66] *Le Monde,* May 17, 1958.

ment unlimited devotion. I expect in particular from all under my orders action without failure, strict execution of my orders. . . . The fate of the Republic is at stake. . . . No failure will be tolerated. . . . Henceforth nothing counts but the unity of the country and the safety of the democracy.[67]

Pflimlin also warned the nation that "a large majority has acted to give the government powers which it needs. We shall certainly use these powers against all who try to violate the law."[68]

Although these measures and public announcements did preserve order in France, they were not enough to isolate the infection. Severance of ties with Algiers was incompatible with delegation of power to Salan and augmentation of the military effort against the Algerian nationalists. In France the government was impotent to proceed against its real enemies. The dissolved Right-wing groups were inconsequential,[69] and the incarcerated demonstrators bore as little relationship to the actual conspirators as juvenile delinquents to members of Murder Incorporated.

After De Gaulle took power, Moch reported that the thousands of armed men he had arrayed so threateningly about Paris had been but a cardboard façade. Police morale, he said, was exceedingly low; all too often orders were not carried out. The Compagnies Républicaines de Sécurité, previously the bastion of public order, were "worn out and contaminated by long and useless stay in the capital." "The metropolitan army was almost exclusively composed of career officers and men who made common cause with their African comrades and were in a state of moral rebellion against the legitimate government." Few, if any, of the sup-

[67] *Libération*, May 19, 1958.
[68] *Combat*, May 19, 1958.
[69] The dissolved groups were the Parti Patriote Révolutionnaire, founded by Biaggi in 1957; Jeune Nation, founded in 1949 by three brothers Sidos and having a membership of about 600; Front d'Action Nationale, with only a few dozen members and whose only noticeable activity was an "open letter" to President Eisenhower protesting the sending of American arms to Tunisia; and Phalange Française, founded in 1956, whose organization "appears extremely reduced if indeed it has not completely fallen asleep." (*Le Monde*, May 17, 1958)

posed guardians of the public order would in fact have forcibly resisted a military coup.[70]

6. *Creation of a popular counterforce within France.* If the guardians of the law would not resist, could the Pflimlin government fall back on the organized weight of the people? The principal source of popular strength came from the three great trade-unions, the Communist Confédération Générale du Travail, the Socialist Force Ouvrière, and the Catholic Confédération Française des Travailleurs Chrétiens. The leaders of all three, and the affiliated parties, were at the outset against De Gaulle, against the Algiers plotters, and for Pflimlin. Two of the unions and their parties, however, feared the third union and its party more than they did De Gaulle. Thus neither the FO nor the CFTC followed the CGT in ordering a work stoppage to coincide with De Gaulle's first press conference. A generous estimate is that only 15 per cent of the workers responded to the call.

Increasingly frantic appeals by the CGT for labor unity were rebuffed. "All together, workers, democrats, republicans, as in February 1934," wrote *L'Humanité*. "Fascism shall not pass. Vive la République."[71] In bold type the paper quoted the May 18 declaration of the Communist party Political Bureau: "The French Communist party solemnly reaffirms that in the battle which has begun it has no other aims for the working class than to defend republican loyalty and to safeguard democratic and constitutional institutions."[72] "We have said it before and we repeat it: We intend to defend the liberties of the Republic and we wish to do so in company with all republicans," wrote Benoît Franchon four days later.[73] But the FO was simultaneously rejoicing that the crisis had not given the Communists an opportunity to act under the guise of anti-Fascist defense.[74] And

[70] Jules Moch, "De Gaulle d'Hier et Demain," *La Nef*, July-August 1958, pp 9-10.
[71] May 19, 1958.
[72] Same.
[73] *L'Humanité*, May 23, 1958.
[74] *Le Monde*, May 22, 1958.

when the CGT finally moved from its formally declared "state of alert,"[75] to order a twenty-four hour general strike on May 27,[76] both the FO and the CFTC central bureaus refused to participate, thus causing the Communists to cancel the strike.

Instead the CFTC ordered its affiliates "to preserve their calm and to do everything possible to avoid any failure or any policy exploiting a position which is strictly limited to the defense of the Republic and its democratic liberties, in the front rank of which is liberty of the trade-unions."[77] In a last-minute decision the non-Communist groups, forming a Republican Action and Defense Committee, organized a mammoth march of 200,000 down the Boulevard Voltaire from the Place de la Nation to the Place de la République. The Communists hooked onto the march but were allotted the tail end, on condition that they "not be noisy" and not "brandish Communist placards."[78]

This march, impressive though it was, was a far cry from united trade-union action in defense of the government. Furthermore, the game had already been lost. Two days earlier De Gaulle had laconically stated that he had started the process leading to the formation of a government, and the day after the march Pflimlin confirmed the rumors which had circulated even during the demonstration by announcing his resignation.

7. *Formation of a government of national union.* Pflimlin tried to satisfy Algiers' demand for a government of public safety and De Gaulle's advocacy of a united government by forming a cabinet of national union. Although Guy Mollet entered the coalition—bringing with him Jules Moch, Max Lejeune, and Albert Gazier—Pinay, considered the strong-

[75] *New York Herald-Tribune* (Paris edition), May 19, 1958.
[76] *L'Humanité*, May 27, 1958.
[77] *Le Monde*, May 27, 1958.
[78] *Express*, May 29, 1958. Although *Figaro*, May 29, 1958, said the march was "orchestrated by the Communists and should have been forbidden by Minister of Information Gazier," the Paris *Herald-Tribune*, May 29, 1958, substantiates the account given above; the march was "held in impressive order and no one blow was exchanged during its five and one-half hour duration."

est anti-Gaullist among the Independents, refused. To Pflimlin's repeated requests, Pinay finally reduced his answer to, "Call on Bidault."[79]

Lacoste had been mentioned as a replacement for Mutter as Minister to Algeria with the special mission of bringing the rebels back into line. Pflimlin, originally against Lacoste's participation, nearly yielded to Duchet, Pinay, Laniel, Reynaud, and members of his own Cabinet.[80] Then word reached him that the Algiers' mob had booed Lacoste's name. "What do you say now?" Pflimlin asked his tormentors.[81]

Although Pinay would not enter the government, his fellow Independent Mutter remained a member and by so doing was influential in keeping the three other Independent ministers officially involved to the very end. With a coalition stretching from the Independents to the Socialists, Pflimlin won repeated endorsements from the National Assembly. Before the government was broadened, he had been invested by a vote of 274-129, with 137 abstentions (of which 135 were Communists). His request for emergency powers was accepted by a vote of 462-112, with only 7 abstentions (the Communists were now supporting him). Another vote on special powers won him a majority of 473-93. The Assembly passed the bill permitting the government to remove a deputy's immunity by 395-150 and proceeded to apply the law to Arrighi by a vote of 428-119. Finally, the bill for constitutional reform was accepted 408-165.

Normally these majorities, without precedent in the Fourth Republic, would have been impressive signs of legislative confidence in the executive. That they failed in fact to impress was due to three main weaknesses of that majority, in addition, of course, to the successful acceleration of the Algiers revolt. First, there was the persistent uncertainty about the Right wing of Pflimlin's regime. Twenty-five Independents of ninety-one, and three Peasants of Social

[79] *Express*, May 22, 1958.
[80] But not including Mollet, who continued to oppose Lacoste.
[81] *Express*, May 22, 1958.

Action of nine, had voted for his investiture. Thirty-eight Independents supported the Premier's original request for special powers. But from that high point the Right began to slip away. When the vote on constitutional reform came, only seven Independents supported the Premier, and seventy-six voted against, as did eight Peasants of Social Action. By the margin of this loss of Independent and Peasant support Pflimlin failed to get an absolute majority, excluding the Communists.

Second, Pflimlin's refusal to accept Communist support cut the strength which he could muster in the Assembly. If De Gaulle were ruled out, the only visible alternative to Pflimlin was a Popular Front with participation by the Communists. But the majority of the National Assembly rigorously rejected this alternative, as did the Catholic and Socialist trade-unions. To the Right, which wished him to use governmental authority against the Left, Minister of the Interior Moch replied, "I have every right to congratulate myself on the fact that citizens who first wished to organize a great demonstration in the Place de la République gave it up to conform to the law and instead decided to demonstrate inside the plants, beyond public view."[82] Pflimlin went further in announcing his intention of using emergency powers against all violators of the law: "I am not thinking only of the Right-wing extremists; I do not forget that there is also on the extreme Left a peril to our liberties."[83] When he openly rejected Communist support before the vote on constitutional reform, Pflimlin was trying to prove that his was the *only* Republican government possible.

Simultaneous Negotiations of a Political Alternative

The third factor which made illusory Pflimlin's broad coalition and its massive support in the Assembly was the simultaneous negotiations behind the scenes with the alternate candidate advanced by the Algerian revolters and by the candidate himself. These negotiations destroyed any claim that Pflimlin's government, in addition to being

[82] *Le Monde*, May 22, 1958.
[83] *Combat*, May 19, 1958.

broadly based and legislatively popular, was at the same time ready to stand steadfast against all comers.

The discussions carried on with De Gaulle by politicians from outside the parties formally pledged to Pflimlin were damaging enough to the crumbling façade of the Fourth Republic. Far more destructive was the involvement of members of Pflimlin's own coalition. As previously mentioned, Mollet on May 18 had asked the General to support Pflimlin, but—and it is a large "but"—he then continued: "If you were one day requested to form a government, would you agree, like any candidate, to present yourself to the National Assembly, place before it your program, if invested, to be responsible to the sovereign Assembly; if not invested, simply to withdraw?" This, coming from Mollet, meant that one of the mainstays of the executive coalition was prepared at least to consider sacrificing it if only republican niceties were preserved. No wonder De Gaulle, at his press conference on May 19, said, "I have a great deal of respect for M. Guy Mollet," and proceeded to recall an incident that never took place: Mollet at his side when he spoke to the crowd at Arras after the Liberation.[84]

Pinay's role was equally crucial. No sooner had he, with Pflimlin's agreement, seen De Gaulle on his own responsibility than he began to insist that Pflimlin do likewise. By May 27 the contacts between De Gaulle and the political leaders had so multiplied that Pinay abruptly repudiated fellow Independent Roger Duchet's claim that "all our friends, and President Pinay himself, are now going to vote against the government." "That's political folly," answered Pinay. "We must avoid any hiatus of power."[85]

By this time, then, the Pflimlin regime was considered not an obstacle to De Gaulle, but rather a vehicle for the orderly transition necessary to prevent the accession to power of civilian and military extremists, quite possibly by a *coup d'état*. On May 27 De Gaulle announced that he had started the process of establishing his government, and the corridors of the National Assembly resounded with rumors

[84] *Figaro*, May 20, 1958.
[85] *Express*, May 29, 1958.

that Pflimlin intended to resign. Indeed, he apparently had already made his decision when the debate opened on the bill for constitutional reform.[86]

The Significance of the Information Gap

The great disparity between what a few political leaders knew about the situation and what was told to the rank and file in the parties made more difficult the smooth transfer of power. While many deputies believed Pflimlin's coalition was still fighting for its life against De Gaulle and his advocates in Algiers and the *Métropole,* actually after about May 20 the coalition was seeking a graceful exit. More concretely, few knew that Algiers had reached the point of planning an invasion of Metropolitan France if De Gaulle were not given power by a certain date.[87] It was apparently to prevent these plans from being carried out that De Gaulle publicly announced the imminent formation of his government.

The manifesto of the Socialist deputies on May 27 and the opening speeches in the National Assembly that evening strikingly illustrate this gap in information. The manifesto, adopted 112-3, with Mollet, who knew far more than he felt he could say, abstaining, declared: "1. That the duty of the legal, regularly invested government is to remain at its post as long as it has the confidence of the majority of the National Assembly; 2. That they [the Socialist deputies] will under no conditions support the candidacy of General de Gaulle, which, in the very form in which it is posed and the considerations which accompany it, is and will remain under all possibilities a defiance of republican legality."[88] When the manifesto was passed, Mollet, Pinay, and Pflimlin

---

[86] According to the Paris *Herald-Tribune,* May 29, 1958, Pflimlin met with members of his government after the constitutional reform bill had passed, in the early hours of May 28, and found that most of them wanted him to stay.

[87] A report from Algiers passed by the censor said paratroopers were standing by for a signal to land in France; same. Similar rumors concerning the imminence of landings at airfields around Paris were circulating in the capital.

[88] *Le Monde,* May 29, 1958.

himself were receiving assurances from De Gaulle on the procedures he would follow in establishing his government.

That evening former Socialist Premier Ramadier addressed Pflimlin: "It is only the National Assembly that can relieve you of this charge. . . . You do not wish to quit, Monsieur the President of the Council. You do not have the right. Even under physical constraint you would not have the right. Today is the great test; we are ready to follow you for the safety of the Republic; we will remain at your side to defend it and bring about its triumph." These passionate words aroused anguish in Bidault, who was well aware of what was going on. How ridiculous, he pointed out, to pretend that the General was forming a government without assurances by those in authority that the government would be accepted. Then, to negate the effect of Ramadier's words on Pflimlin, he recalled Mendès-France's recent observation that when France's forefathers wished to defend the Republic, they cried "Vive la nation." "Monsieur the President of the Council," Bidault went on, "you have to save the nation—the Republic too of course, but I beg you; do nothing, say nothing that could even for a moment separate the Republic from the Nation."[89]

President Coty's Role in De Gaulle's Accession

Into the breach between the deputies and their leaders stepped the President of the Republic. Coty conferred with the presidents of both legislative houses, with Mollet, Pinay, P. H. Teitgen, Auriol, and, of course, Pflimlin. He sent envoys to De Gaulle to discuss the procedures under which the General would form his government. Then, when it looked as though this effort for an orderly transfer would fail after all, he called in the political leaders once more to say that if their parties did not accept De Gaulle, his only option would be to call on Mitterand to form a Popular Front. Bringing the Communists back into positions of executive responsibility, he added, was so contrary to his conscience that he would resign and publicly inform the As-

[89] Same.

sembly of which leaders continued to oppose De Gaulle, thereby forcing France into civil war.[90]

Coty's subsequent message to Parliament carried overtones so threatening that even Bidault thought it poorly conceived:[91]

> We are now on the verge of civil war. . . . On both sides people seem ready for fratricidal combat. . . . When it comes to forming a government, as our Constitution is at present, the President of the Republic proposes and the National Assembly disposes. . . . In this time of peril for the country and the Republic I have turned to the most illustrious Frenchman, the man who in the darkest days of our history was our leader for the reconquest of liberty and who, having created national unity around himself, turned away from dictatorship to form the Republic. . . . I am asking General de Gaulle to agree to confer with the head of State and to examine with him what, within the framework of republican legality, is necessary for the formation of a government of national safety and what can then be done over the long or short range basically to reform our institutions. If the failure of my effort should make it appear that in so critical a moment I was in error, I will not fail immediately to draw the inevitable conclusions. Failing to retain henceforth the moral authority more than ever necessary to one who is commonly called the highest arbiter, I could only transfer immediately all of my functions to the President of the National Assembly in conformity with Article 41 of the Constitution.[92]

The President's message left some political groups confused and divided. Most Independents had long been ready for De Gaulle. MRP deputies had had the advantage of hearing Pflimlin state categorically, "I was convinced that in the actual circumstances, *about which I knew all the facts,* civil peace could only be preserved by the legal formation of a government headed by General de Gaulle.

---

[90] Same, also *New York Herald-Tribune* (Paris edition), May 29, 1958.

[91] So too, apparently, did André Le Troquer, President of the National Assembly, who read the address brusquely and then adjourned the Assembly Le Troquer was given such an ovation by the Communists, Socialists, the MRP, and some Center groups that "one would have thought one was at the palace of kings at the end of a hard-fought presidential election." (*Le Monde*, May 31, 1958.)

[92] *Combat*, May 30, 1958

... The choice was henceforth between a military coup and De Gaulle."[93] Even so, some, including Robert Schuman, still demanded further guarantees. The Radicals as usual did not know what to do. Pierre Clostermann, a supporter of De Gaulle, tried to manipulate his group into accepting the General by suggesting that Mendès-France, at one time friendly to De Gaulle but now an opponent of his investiture, see the General and ask for assurances on procedure to satisfy the Radicals. Mendès, of course, refused. Most difficult of all was the position of the Socialists, twenty of whom were adamantly against De Gaulle, twenty for him, and the rest (fifty-five) still waiting for guarantees, including concrete statements on defense of the Republic and on Algeria. In a meeting of the Action Committee for Republican Defense, called by a group of Socialists, Mitterand of the UDSR said the only course was to appeal to a widely respected man, such as Naegelen, Ramadier, or Schuman.[94] Even as he spoke De Gaulle was forming his Cabinet and drafting his investiture speech to be delivered to the National Assembly.

Terms on Which De Gaulle Came to Power

The result of this highly confused race against time—this effort to get De Gaulle to protect the "system" against the plotters who wanted him to destroy it—was a compromise. De Gaulle abandoned some of his original demands in order to get what he wanted: power through peaceful means. Leading politicians of the Fourth Republic surrendered the Republic to De Gaulle in order to avoid possible civil war and preserve for themselves a place in the new scheme of things.

At his press conference of May 19 De Gaulle said, "It is certain that if De Gaulle were led to assume—to see himself delegated—[an important modification!] exceptional powers for an exceptional task in an exceptional moment, it is evident that this cannot be done by following customary rites and procedures—so customary that everyone has gone

[93] *Le Monde*, May 31, 1958.
[94] Same.

beyond them—and it is necessary to adopt an equally exceptional procedure."[95] While there was considerable question as to just what the General had in mind (it may be that at this early stage he did not know exactly himself), possibly he envisaged a sort of pre-investiture by the National Assembly, convened to approve his program. This idea was, however, dropped.[96]

Instead, De Gaulle adapted himself to the selection procedures laid down by President Coty. Although Coty, following the resignation of Premier Pflimlin, approached De Gaulle through intermediaries and requested him to form a government, there were irregular features to this "regular" process: prior announcement by De Gaulle that *he* was setting the train in motion; the President's inviting De Gaulle before other possible candidates had been canvassed; and the semisecrecy surrounding the President's overtures. While De Gaulle abandoned his original plan of having his program read for him before the National Assembly in his absence, he showed his contempt for the "system" by leaving immediately after his brief statement, forcing the deputies to address their remarks to an empty bench.

De Gaulle's final concession to the "system" served to appease political leaders and groups more concerned over the manner in which the General took control than over what he would do with his powers. The new Premier's investiture address had requested "full powers" for six months and, in effect, a mandate to remake the constitution. But he obtained these exceptional rights by the normal parliamentary means of submitting bills to the Assembly, having them considered and reported by appropriate committees, debated and passed by the legislative branches.

Possibly these concessions to the institutions and procedures of the Fourth Republic were greater than De Gaulle had first expected would be necessary. Whether or not the

---

[95] *Figaro*, May 20, 1958.
[96] At one time De Gaulle apparently also wished to be called formally by all "national" parties, which would thereby assure a commitment to vote in the Assembly for his investiture. (*Express*, May 29, 1958.)

General was irked by the constitutional niceties, he soon had in his hands the full authority he demanded. On this, the essential point, he made no compromise. He at no time alienated the Algiers revolters by repudiating them, although he did administer a gentle tap on the wrist for their activities in Corsica. On June 4 he said in the Algiers forum: "I have understood you. I know what happened here. I see what you wanted to do. I see that the road you have opened is the road to renewal and brotherhood."[97] If he did not accept the pre-May 13 demand of the "ultras" for full integration of Algeria into France, neither did he concede autonomy to the Algerian nationalists. His deliberate ambiguity reserved his full freedom of maneuver.

From the political leaders in France he had won the right to name nonpoliticians to his Cabinet. Besides such party men as Pinay, Mollet, and Pflimlin—eleven in all—there were five "technicians": two ambassadors, two civil servants, and André Malraux. These five held such important ministries as Armed Forces (Pierre Guillaumat), Foreign Affairs (Maurice Couve de Murville), and Interior (Émile Pelletier).[98]

On June 4, when he went to Algiers, De Gaulle was to all intents and purposes dictator of France. The National Assembly had ended its session. De Gaulle could issue decrees as he saw fit, without restraint, covering the full range of economic, social, and foreign affairs. He could draft an entirely different constitution, with the advice but without the consent of a few political leaders named to help arrange the formal interment of the Fourth Republic.

What was the nature of the final legislative opposition to De Gaulle's accession to power? The General had naturally wished for an overwhelmingly favorable vote on his investiture, and his consultation with party leaders was partly directed to that end. President Coty's pressure on

[97] *Le Monde*, June 6, 1958

[98] De Gaulle's original government was published June 2, 1958, in the *Journal Officiel*; *Figaro*, June 3, 1958. The men of Algiers, however, were annoyed that eleven products of the defunct "system" were retained by the General.

Assembly groups had the same objective, although possibly Coty's manner in using the presidential office had the reverse effect. Certainly the information gap between leaders and ordinary deputies made it difficult for the former to convince the latter that De Gaulle was the only solution. (This was especially true of the Socialists, who proved so rebellious that for a brief time Mollet resigned as their Secretary-General.)

The Assembly put De Gaulle into office by a vote of 329 to 224, with 32 abstentions. Groups within the Assembly divided three ways. Those predominantly favorable to De Gaulle, giving him 42 per cent of the Assembly vote, were the Rassemblement des Gauches Républicains, the Gauche Démocratique, the MRP, the Social Republicans, the Independents, the Peasants, and the UFF. Two parties, representing 25 per cent of the Assembly, were almost unanimously opposed—the Communists and the Progressives. The rest, 31 per cent were on the fence: Socialists, Radicals, UDSR-RDA, Regroupement Africain, and unlisted deputies who, together, voted 85 to 72, with 24 abstentions.

De Gaulle's support, thus, came mostly from the Center and Right. All the Communists, all the Progressives, and 54 per cent of the Socialists voted against him or abstained. Surely this was impressive opposition, considering the threat of military action against the previous government, the undoubted personal prestige enjoyed by General de Gaulle, the concessions he had made to parliamentary *amour-propre,* and the stand of President Coty, who left the deputies with no practical alternative to accepting De Gaulle.

Part Three

FOUNDATIONS AND PROSPECTS OF DE GAULLE'S FIFTH REPUBLIC

Chapter Fifteen

THE CONSTITUTION OF THE FIFTH REPUBLIC

WHEN DE GAULLE took office as Premier, the oft-predicted "crisis of the regime" had lasted almost two months. Policy, foreign and domestic alike, had necessarily marked time while Pleven struggled long and arduously to bring democratic factions to agree and Pflimlin strove, first, to defend the Republic and, then, to bring about a smooth transition in executive responsibility which would spare the nation a *coup d'état* or civil war. Once in power, De Gaulle was confronted with a triple task: starting up the wheels of government again, breaking with the "immobilist" past by providing definite direction to the machine, and settling the particular problems which had caused the revolt. In this undertaking he followed in part the precedent set by previous premiers through securing from the Assembly special powers for a limited period—in De Gaulle's case for six months—and covering three areas: Algeria, domestic affairs, and constitutional reform. But the new Premier did not stop there. He also demanded that the deputies act swiftly and then go home, leaving him and his Cabinet free to act without the continuous harassment of the executive which had been so typical of the Fourth Republic.

De Gaulle and his ministers short-circuited the pressures normally exerted between legislative sessions by Assembly committees through the simple expedient of refusing to discuss anything with them. For example, after De Gaulle had agreed to regroup all French troops in Tunisia at the

Bizerte naval base prior to their evacuation, he granted Chairman Pierre Montel of the Defense Committee an audience lasting exactly three minutes.[1] Later, during the Near East crisis, the Communists agitated for a special session of the Assembly. To forestall this maneuver the Foreign Affairs Committee, by a unanimous vote, requested Foreign Minister Couve de Murville to appear before it and discuss France's position. He refused to do so.[2]

Foundations of Constitutional Change

One emergency measure which De Gaulle demanded of the legislature was the abrogation of Article 90 of the constitution of the Fourth Republic on the procedure for amending the constitution. It was not so much that Article 90 was impossible to operate; rather, De Gaulle wished to take the entire process of revision out of the hands of the legislature.[3] Instead, he proposed simply that "the Government of the Republic shall draw up a constitutional bill."

In requesting the Assembly to abdicate its power of amendment, the new Premier gave some assurances that the new constitution would be a democratic one and that the legislature would remain a basic political institution. "Universal suffrage alone is the source of power; it is from universal suffrage *or* from bodies elected thereby that the legislative power and the executive power are derived."[4] "The government must be responsible to the Parliament," and "the judicial authority must remain independent so as to enable it to ensure respect for the basic freedoms as defined

[1] *New York Times*, June 20, 1958.
[2] Same, July 27, 1958.
[3] Article 90 provided that a resolution clearly stating the purpose of the revision must first be passed by an absolute majority of the members of the Assembly. If within three months the Senate had not adopted the same resolution by an absolute majority, the resolution was once more to be put to the Assembly Only after these two hurdles had been surmounted could a textual revision be elaborated within the Assembly and passed by both legislative branches as an ordinary bill. Moreover, unless the Assembly accepted the text by a two-thirds majority or unless both houses passed it by a three-fifths majority, a popular referendum was required.
[4] Italics added; the choice of a conjunctive is significant, as will be shown later.

by the preamble to the constitution of 1946 and by the Declaration of the Rights of Man to which it refers."[5] At odds with the principle of executive responsibility to the legislature, however, was the statement that "the executive power and the legislative power must be separate and apart so that the Government and the Parliament can, each for its own part and on its own responsibility, assume its full powers."[6] Finally, following the precedent of the 1946 constitution, De Gaulle declared his intention to "organize the relations of the Republic with the peoples associated with it" as part of the new political structure.[7]

In his second appearance before the Assembly De Gaulle, with suavity and deference, had done much to remove the bitter taste left in the mouths of the deputies by the curt manner in which he had presented his statement of investiture and by his disdainful withdrawal before the debate began. The conciliatory bearing and his proffered guarantees, however, were not enough to eliminate the Assembly's ingrained suspicion of executive authority. Its Committee on Universal Suffrage, to which the Constitutional Reform Bill was referred, elected a hostile rapporteur, Radical Socialist Albert de Bailliencourt, 25-19. None the less the measure itself passed the Assembly by a vote of 329-224, with 70 abstentions. By comparison with the vote on his investiture, De Gaulle picked up 16 of the 21 additional affirmative votes from deputies within the UDSR-RDA and the Regroupement Africain who had previously abstained.[8] The changed attitude within the Regroupement Africain undoubtedly stemmed from De Gaulle's appointment of Houphouet-Boigny as Minister of State; this was viewed as a token of his determination to replace the French Union by an entirely new Franco-African Community.

---

[5] These assurances were contained in "Principles" 1, 3, and 4 of De Gaulle's speech of June 1.

[6] "Principle" 2.

[7] "Principle" 5. For the French text and an English translation of the Constitutional Reform Law adopted by the National Assembly on June 3, 1958, see *Current History*, August 1958, p. 116

[8] *Le Monde*, June 3, 4, 1958.

De Gaulle and his advisers were now free to draft their constitution. Their aim was to create a strong state, as De Gaulle had so often demanded since his abrupt resignation on January 20, 1946.

> The crisis was inevitable, because for twelve years the party system, insecurely based on a deeply divided people, in the midst of a terribly dangerous world, showed itself totally unfit to insure the conduct of affairs. [To be sure,] those who held positions of power under the Fourth Republic were able people, honest, and patriotic. But as they never represented anything but small factions, those who governed did not identify themselves with the general interest. Moreover, divided among themselves, . . . struggling against the encroachments of the parliamentary Assembly from which they received their mandates, subject to the demands of the parties they represented, they were doomed to live for a few months or a few weeks, faced with huge problems which they could not possibly solve. [To replace this tragically incompetent system,] it is my task, together with my government, to propose to our people *new* institutions that will establish for the Republic an authority strong enough, stable enough, effective enough, to be responsible for its destiny.[9]

The type of men who had brought De Gaulle to power re-enforced the Premier's determination. A strong state was what they wanted; for that they had made the Revolution of May 13. Unless De Gaulle could quickly present his draft constitution to this end, France ran the risk of another revolt, this time, in all probability not restricted to Algeria and Corsica. A more constructive role was played by those supporters who, like Michel Debré, had for years been considering what new structure should take the place of the Fourth Republic. The essential issue was what kind of strength to create and how to do the job.

The answer to the "how" was provided by the abrogation of Article 90. De Gaulle and his advisers would draft the new constitution themselves. They were under no obligation to accept the suggestions of the consultative committee, composed of seventeen members of the Assembly, twelve

---

[9] Address to the Nation, June 13, 1958; translation, *Current History*, August 1958, pp. 119-120.

Senators, and twelve persons co-opted from outside the legislature. None the less, as will be seen, the committee did introduce some significant changes into the final version of the constitution.

De Gaulle's conviction that no basic reform could emerge from legislative initiative and debate had been reinforced by the history of the constitutional amendments which had been promulgated on December 7, 1954. Four years of maneuvering among the National Assembly, Senate, and Council of Ministers had left the basic relationships among these three institutions almost unchanged, except for restoring to the upper house a greater share in the legislative process, more like its role under the Third Republic.[10]

Some of the 1954 revisions had altered slightly the workings of the Assembly. To restrict the influence of the Communists, its officers no longer would necessarily be chosen on the basis of proportional representation.[11] Parliamentary immunity, though still surrounded by safeguards, was somewhat restricted during periods when the legislature was not in session.[12] It was made harder for the deputies to force the calling of a special session of the Assembly, since a majority, instead of one-third petition, was required.[13] In theory, dissolution of the legislature was made more likely; henceforth a government which had been defeated on a vote of confidence would not have to quit if it dismissed the legislature but would continue to serve until the new one had been elected and had convened. A government which was defeated on a motion of censure would lose only its premier and minister of the interior, who would be replaced by the president of the Assembly and his appointee.[14] A premier could be invested by a simple majority; more important, he no longer had to seek investiture twice—once for himself and his program, and again for his govern-

---

[10] Marcel Plaisant, "La Révision Laborieuse," *Revue des Deux Mondes*, February 15, 1953, p. 605
[11] Article 11.
[12] Article 12.
[13] Article 12.
[14] Article 52.

ment.¹⁵ This change no doubt made it easier for would-be premiers to gain acceptance by the Assembly, but neither it nor the increased attractiveness of dissolution added notably to executive stability between 1954 and 1958.

This picayune tinkering with the constitutional machinery was so obviously unsatisfactory that all groups felt compelled to fight the election of 1956 on the issue of constitutional reform. Not until the last weeks of the Fourth Republic, however, did the Assembly's Committee on Universal Suffrage report its recommendations. It proposed to place on the Assembly the burden of defying the government; a motion of confidence would have to be coupled with a resolution setting forth an alternative program. Deputies would then be required to choose between the two resolutions; they could not abstain from voting.¹⁶ The immediate peril to the Fourth Republic impelled Premier Pflimlin to urge the Assembly to adopt these changes, along with others designed to shorten legislative sessions and to facilitate the granting of decree powers to the government. But by then the Fourth Republic was beyond saving.

The history of constitutional reform had conclusively demonstrated the futility of asking the members of the Assembly to strengthen the executive at their own expense, or to promote executive stability when, as Alfred Pose pointed out, "their desire for power naturally inclines our deputies toward a regime which opens to them a ministerial career and in any event assures them of a wide area of influence on the government."¹⁷ Various political groups inevitably judged the merit of proposed changes by calculating their effect on their own fortunes. Radical-Socialists, Independents, and Gaullists were all for enlarging the competence of the Senate, in which they were proportionately stronger than in the Assembly. The MRP and the Communists fa-

---

¹⁵ Article 45.
¹⁶ *Le Monde*, April 8, 1958.
¹⁷ Alfred Pose, "Un Gouvernement Stable," pt. 2, *Revue des Deux Mondes*, February 1, 1953, p. 195.

vored maintaining the predominance of the Assembly, where they were stronger.[18]

Agonies of calculation became most acute when the system of electing members of the Assembly was up for discussion. Any deputy or any group could probably have produced a workable constitution, but, confronting other deputies and other groups, each was apt to conclude that little or no change was possible. Some, including the MRP, even decided that the 1946 constitution was not such a bad document after all, given the will to make it work. But the will was stifled by the "system" which the constitution had produced. It was to break this pattern that De Gaulle entrusted the task of constitutional reform to his own advisers within the executive branch.

The first issue which De Gaulle faced was whether to revise the constitution of the Fourth Republic or to scrap it altogether. His choice of the second course involved more than a deep-seated hostility toward the Fourth Republic. Born of revulsion against defeat, against the suicide of the Third Republic, against Pétain's authoritarian regime, the Fourth Republic had defined democracy as popular sovereignty expressed by the electorate through an all-powerful legislature, and the popular will as proportional representation controlled by disciplined parties. The trouble was that the Fourth Republic, designed to correct past mistakes, could not cope with the new problems. Anarchy, not Vichyite authoritarianism, now became the more evident danger. The Soviet Union, not Germany, soon stood forth as the real external threat. The Republic underrated the seriousness of France's economic problems, and it failed to muster the degree of unity needed to solve them.

The failure of the Fourth Republic to reform itself in time provided a strong argument for framing a brand new constitution. Another was the absence of popular support for the Fourth Republic. Thanks in considerable part to

---

[18] Roy Pierce, "Constitutional Revision in France," *Journal of Politics*, May 1955, pp. 221-248.

De Gaulle's opposition, the second constitution of 1946 had been accepted by only a plurality, not a majority, of the French voters. By May 1958, only the Communists still defended the twin columns of the Fourth Republic: a dominant National Assembly, and an election system based on proportional representation. Internal cleavages within Socialist and MRP ranks, and the conflict between the two parties, prevented them from presenting a common program of reform and taking the burden of constitutional defense away from the Communists.

As De Gaulle and his advisers saw it, even if the Fourth Republic could be strengthened, its effectiveness would still be undercut by association of the Republic, in the popular mind, with weakness at home and retreat abroad. More important than constitutional norms was the creation of a *mystique,* an aura of vitality and competence. If Frenchmen came to believe that their country was going to be strong, they would make it strong. In the creation of this *mystique* the figure of De Gaulle was crucial. He alone was not associated in popular thinking with the failures of the previous years, despite his important part in determining the structure and operation of the Fourth Republic.[19]

The Constitution of the Fifth Republic

In examining the main provisions of the new constitution, it must be borne in mind that literally all the structural innovations introduced, or even discussed, had previously been advanced by someone at some time. Most of them had been debated over and over again. Perhaps the average French voter understood better than the experts that all constitutional norms contain evil as well as good and that

[19] First, by calling for the election of a Constituent Assembly just after the war instead of presenting a draft constitution to the electorate; second, by establishing proportional representation as the basis for that election; third, by failing to understand, while head of the provisional government, the necessity for prompt, effective action in the economic sphere, fourth, by resigning precipitously instead of continuing to lend to the still inchoate political process the strength of his name and reputation.

the balance between them will be determined by the men charged with putting them into effect.

Possibly the foremost decision which confronted De Gaulle and his advisers concerned the separation of the executive and legislative branches. In his report of 1956 to the Committee of Studies for the Republic, Georges Vidal had proposed the adoption of a presidential system,[20] an idea which had received support from the well-known, liberal political scientist Maurice Duverger.[21] Proposals for a milder executive-legislative separation included the establishment for the executive of a fixed term, which would be renewable.[22] In his Bayeux address of June 16, 1946, De Gaulle had espoused the idea without committing himself to any particular method. ". . . All principles and all experience," he said, "demand that the public power, legislative, executive, judicial, be clearly separated and strongly balanced and that there be established above political circumstances a national arbitration which can assure continuity amid various combinations."[23]

The constitution of the Fifth Republic has indeed moved toward the separation of powers, but not to the point of instituting a presidential system. "The functions of members of the Government," reads Article 23, "shall be incompatible with the exercise of any parliamentary mandate. . . ."[24] The advisory committee, which objected strenuously to this clause, recommended by a vote of 13-11 a substitute: "The ministers can have no political functions concurrently with that of government. They cannot be members of a political party. For the duration of their

[20] For a summary of his recommendations, see François Goguel, "Vers une Nouvelle Orientation de la Révision Constitutionnelle?" *Revue Française de Science Politique*, July-September 1956, pp. 493, 499-501.

[21] *Le Monde*, April 12, 13, May 18, June 12, 1956.

[22] Albert de Bailliencourt, "Mane, Thecel, Phares—L'Assemblée et ses Problèmes," *Revue Politique et Parlementaire*, November 1957, p. 198.

[23] *La France Sera la France* (Paris, Rassemblement du Peuple Français, 1952), p. 36.

[24] Translation by Ambassade de France, Service de Presse et d'Information, French Affairs no. 66 (New York, September 1958). Quotations from the constitution follow this translation unless otherwise noted.

ministerial functions, they are placed on leave from their respective Assemblies."[25] De Gaulle rejected this *in toto*.

Under the Fifth Republic, the Premier and his Cabinet are linked closely to the President, whose powers have been greatly enlarged. The President is no longer elected by the legislature. This function has been transferred to a special college, which, in addition to members of Parliament and representatives of Overseas Territories, includes mayors and municipal councilors. The idea of direct election was reportedly dropped without serious discussion.[26] By gaining approval for the multiple representation of larger communes, the advisory committee succeeded in counteracting somewhat the overweighting of rural areas. With its membership increased to more than 70,000,[27] the college can never meet in one place, much less deliberate or act on its own.

Elected for seven years, the President appoints the Premier and then, on proposal of the Premier, the members of the government.[28] Within fifteen days the President may request Parliament to reconsider any bill or part of a bill passed by it, a request which it may not reject.[29] After consultation with the Premier and the Presidents of the Assemblies (implying that the President may override the wishes of the Premier and the Assemblies), the President may dissolve the National Assembly.[30]

Finally, but by no means least in importance, Article 16 empowers the President, in cases of grave national peril, "to take the measures required by those circumstances after official consultation with the Premier and the Presidents

---

[25] *Le Monde*, August 15-16, 1958. Members of the government are given access to both chambers (Article 31), and in case they do not choose to appear frequently, the right of interpellation has been added, one session a week being set aside for this purpose. (Article 48, Paragraph 2.)

[26] *Le Monde*, July 30, 1958.

[27] Article 6 sets forth the program for representation in the college.

[28] Article 8. "To him the mission of naming the ministers and first of all, naturally, the Premier," De Gaulle had proposed at Bayeux (*La France Sera la France*, cited, p. 38.)

[29] Article 9.

[30] Article 12.

of the Assemblies, as well as with the Constitutional Council." This provision, perhaps the most criticized feature of the constitution,[81] seems to leave the door open, for a presidential coup, especially when combined with his right of dissolution. The advisory committee pressed hard for a provision that the President must seek approval of the Constitutional Council before arrogating to himself emergency powers,[32] but De Gaulle refused to yield.[33] Some, but by no means all, objections to Article 16 were removed by the addition of two short paragraphs: "Parliament shall meet by right. The National Assembly may not be dissolved during the exercise of exceptional powers."

Two other aspects of the constitution have strengthened the separation of the executive from the legislative branch. In addition to the ban on holding positions in the legislature, the Premier and the members of his government are not required to seek investiture for themselves or their program from the legislature.[34] In addition, Article 38 permits the government to obtain from the legislature the right, for a limited but unspecified time, to issue ordinances on matters ordinarily within the scope of legislation.[35] Although these ordinances are to be voided if a bill for their ratification is not submitted before the expiration of the time limit, no parliamentary approval is required during the period of their exercise. Any acceptance or condemnation by the legislature can only be *ex post facto*.

In its relation to the Assembly, the position of the government is far stronger than under the Fourth Republic. Writing in 1955, Michel Debré had likened the government's role in the Assembly of the Fourth Republic to that of an interested spectator whose interference astonished and annoyed the deputies; legislative monopoly of the agenda gave added power to already overbearing special in-

[81] *New York Times,* August 2, 1958.
[32] Same, August 15, 1958
[33] *Le Monde,* August 15-16, 1958
[34] Although Premier Debré did so, thereby possibly establishing a precedent.
[35] This provision was clearly in line with efforts made by Pflimlin and his predecessors.

terests.³⁶ Article 48 of the new constitution provides that on the agenda of both houses priority shall be given to bills introduced or accepted by the government. This control is strengthened by Article 42, which provides that a government text is to be debated in the chamber in which it has been introduced. Taken together, these two articles are certain to reduce the initiative of deputies in law making.³⁷ Such, at least, was the experience of the first session of the new Assembly in 1959.

The constitution has further added to the authority of the executive by empowering it to intervene in conflicts between the two legislative houses. Under Article 45 the government may convene a committee of both houses in the event of their failing to adopt a common text after two readings (or after one reading on bills considered urgent by the government). If the committee agrees on a text, the bill goes back to both houses for passage but may not be altered without government approval. If the committee fails to agree, or if both houses do not accept the committee's text, the government may then, as under the system adopted in 1954, require the Assembly to choose definitively one of the following: the committee's text, if there is one; the latest version passed by the Assembly; or that version as modified by the Senate.

Before the draft constitution was made public, it was uncertain how far the Premier and his advisers intended to go toward establishing a corporate state. At Bayeux, De Gaulle had said, "It will be normal to introduce there [the Senate] in addition [to political figures indirectly elected] representatives of economic, family, and intellectual organizations to interpret within the State the voice of the great activities of the country."³⁸ In his view, the Economic Coun-

---

³⁶ Michel Debré, "Trois Caractéristiques du Système Parlementaire Français," *Revue Française de Science Politique*, January-March 1955, pp. 29, 33.

³⁷ Under the Fourth Republic, between a quarter and a third of French laws were initiated within the Assembly, rather than by the executive, as compared to 10 per cent in Great Britain between 1948 and 1952. See François Goguel, "Les Méthodes du Travail Parlementaire," *Revue Française de Science Politique*, October-December 1954, p. 681.

³⁸ *La France Sera la France*, cited, p. 37.

cil established by the Fourth Republic was too limited in its powers and too remote from the process of decision-making. Few Frenchmen, however, supported the corporate idea. The minimal part actually played by the Economic Council in legislation was a strong argument for not increasing the power of social and economic groups to affect political institutions. In this respect, the new constitution has not departed greatly from its predecessor. Under Article 24, the Senate is elected indirectly, on the basis of "territorial units of the Republic." The unforeseen result was to create a Senate at least verbally more intransigent than the Assembly because prominent figures of the Fourth Republic, defeated in the election, found safe berths and another oratorical platform in the Senate. Frenchmen living "outside France" are also to be represented in the Senate. Instead of being represented in the Senate, special groups are to participate in the work of the Economic and Social Council, which replaces the Economic Council.[39] The Council may, but need not, be consulted on matters within its undefined range of interest. It may, but need not, be called upon for its opinion on proposed legislation, ordinances, and decrees. The stature, if not the influence, of the Council is increased by allowing its opinions on draft bills to be presented directly to parliamentary assemblies.[40]

Of key importance in legislative-executive relations are motions of censure and confidence. The new constitution follows past proposals in placing on the Assembly the responsibility for overthrowing a government, not on the government for winning a vote of confidence. If the government chooses to stake its life on a particular text, that text will be considered adopted unless a motion of censure is filed within twenty-four hours. Motions of censure are difficult to enter—they require the signature of at least one-tenth of the Assembly's membership—and are even harder to pass. A delay of forty-eight hours must intervene before the voting. Then, when the votes are tabulated, only those

[39] The change of title implies a broader base for the Council, but its exact composition, says the Constitution, is to be fixed by an organic law.
[40] Articles 69-71.

favoring censure (no abstention is permitted) are tallied, and the motion loses unless it receives an absolute majority of the Assembly's membership.[41] Bloc-voting has been eliminated, and irresponsible decision reduced, by the provision that only under exceptional circumstances and by an organic law may proxy-voting take place, and, even then, "no member may hold more than one proxy."[42] Motions of censure are likely to be rare, since the same members may not introduce a second during the same session, if the first has failed, unless the government decides to ask for a vote of confidence on a particular measure. During the first session of the Assembly the government beat back an effort to introduce a technique of informal censure by holding a vote after interpellation.

Legislative harassment of the executive is further reduced by continuation of the trend toward shorter regular sessions and fewer provisions for emergency meetings. From a normal sitting of over nine months in the early years of the Fourth Republic, the Assembly is now to meet for less than six.[43] To convene a special session requires a request of the Premier or an initiative by a majority of the members of the Assembly. Special sessions are limited to an agenda presented by the government, which the deputies may discuss for not more than twelve days. Until a month has elapsed, only the Premier may request another session.[44]

Two other features—dissolution and referendum—demonstrate the efforts of the framers of the constitution to shift the balance of power toward the executive. Both involve delicate issues, since they are deeply entrenched in the French conception of popular democracy. Because of the National Assembly's prestige as the representative of the people, there was strong opposition to granting the executive the right to dissolve the legislature. Dissolution, an anonymous Socialist and one-time premier is quoted as saying, "is not adapted to our constitutional norms and in

[41] Article 49.
[42] Article 27.
[43] Previous proposals had recommended seven.
[44] Article 29.

our country remains infected with the idea of personal power."[45] The single, unhappy experience of the Third Republic with dissolution had led the Constituent Assembly of 1946, in its first and abortive postwar constitution, to locate the right of dissolution in the Assembly itself, acting by a two-thirds vote. The second draft, which became the constitution of the Fourth Republic, returned this power to the executive, but under conditions which invited that branch to conspire with the legislature to avoid invoking it.[46] Not until Premier Faure's dissolution of the Assembly in 1955 was the long-standing psychological barrier actually broken by the executive.[47]

This precedent encouraged constitutional revisionists to propose that dissolution be made easier or even automatic. Just before he retired to make way for De Gaulle, Pflimlin gained Assembly approval for a new extension of the right of dissolution. The Assembly could be dismissed if, after overthrowing a government, it did not accept the premier-designate or he failed to form a cabinet.[48]

A consistent advocate of increased executive power, Paul Reynaud had favored automatic dissolution,[49] and continued to propound this idea as chairman of the advisory committee on the new constitution. However, at the urging of others of its members, including Teitgen and Coste-Floret, the committee plumped overwhelmingly for a different proposal, advanced by De Gaulle and his advisers. Its most notable feature was to cut the traditional link between dissolution and motions of censure. This was consistent with De Gaulle's insistence on denying to members

[45] Quoted by Pose, cited, p. 401.
[46] The Assembly could be dissolved after eighteen months of its term if a government were twice forced out of office by the defeat of a motion of confidence or the passage of a motion of censure Upon dissolution, it will be remembered, the government members automatically lost their cabinet offices.
[47] Faure's decision to dissolve the Assembly was made easier by the constitutional reforms of 1954, which eliminated the requirement that the executive be replaced whenever the Assembly was dissolved.
[48] *Figaro*, May 22, 1958.
[49] Paul Reynaud, "De Gaulle et ses Problèmes," *Revue de Paris*, July 1958, pp 9-11.

of the legislature the right to designate the Premier or even to serve in his government while holding their seats. Dissolution now becomes the sole prerogative of the President of the Republic; before taking this step, he must consult the Premier and the presidents of the legislative branches, but is not bound by their advice. The only restriction on the President is that he cannot dissolve the legislature twice within a single year.[50] He can, however, use the right of dissolution to strengthen a government already in power, to help it, through new elections, to change the political complexion of the Assembly, and to bring important issues before the people.

Regular use of the referendum had long been advocated in France. It had been proposed for the Third Republic by André Tardieu, and some constitutional experts still preferred it to dissolution.[51] It was a basic element in the Gaullist conception of governing according to the popular will.[52] Naturally enough, therefore, this power has been granted to the President in the new constitution, although the conditions under which he can exercise it are left broad and imprecise. By proposal of the government or by a joint motion of the two legislative chambers, the President can submit to a referendum "any bill dealing with the organization of the public powers, entailing approval of a Community [linking France to overseas territories] agreement, or providing for authorization to ratify a treaty that, without being contrary to the Constitution, might affect the functioning of the institutions."[53] A bill accepted by the people through a referendum must be promptly promulgated as law.

In seeking to reduce the power of the National Assembly, the reformers could not avoid coming to grips with one of the thorniest of constitutional questions: the system of elections. The problem was to find a single method which

[50] Article 12.
[51] Louis Rougier, *La France à la Recherche d'une Constitution* (Paris. Sirey, 1952), p. 168 ff.
[52] See, for example, Marcel Waline, *Les Partis contre la République* (Paris: Rousseau, 1948), pt. 2, p. 112.
[53] Article 11.

major groups would accept. Significantly, De Gaulle, though an advocate of the referendum, rejected the pleas of the advisory committee that, after the referendum on the constitution, a second vote be held to ascertain the wishes of the people concerning the new electoral system.[54] Instead, he used his grant of full powers to impose a solution.

Behind many lofty disquisitions on the sanctity of the democratic process, the actual choice among election systems in France has always been determined by the interests of competing political parties and by the relative value the various parties have attached to building strong party organizations. The collapse of the Third Republic, in addition to discrediting the Right, had also undermined the prewar electoral system, which was held responsible for turning the Chamber of Deputies into an heterogeneous agglomeration of undisciplined groups. In 1946, after nine years without an election, the leaders of the Resistance, in agreement with De Gaulle, chose a system of proportional representation and blocked lists within multiple-constituency districts[55] The natural consequence was that the Constituent and first National Assemblies came under the domination of the three disciplined parties of the Resistance—the Communists, the Socialists, and the Mouvement Républicain Populaire.[56]

Between 1946 and 1951 two major and related developments served to discredit, in its turn, the blocked-list, proportional-representation system. The onset of the cold war put an end to cooperation among the Socialists, MRP, and Communists. At the same time, the rehabilitation of the

---

[54] *Le Monde*, August 15-16, 1958

[55] Proportional representation had been accepted by the Chamber of Deputies in 1939, but the Third Republic fell before the Senate acted, François Goguel, *France under the Fourth Republic* (Ithaca, N Y. Cornell University Press, 1952), p 60. "Blocked lists" meant that voters chose slates rather than candidates, who were seated in the order in which they appeared on the lists of their parties.

Peter Campbell, *French Electoral Systems and Elections* (London, Faber,

[56] In the balloting for the First Assembly, voters were permitted to indicate preferences on party lists, but the order of election would be changed only if a majority of lists were altered, which did not occur. 1958), p. 111.

Center and Right soon returned to the political spectrum the Radicals and the Independents, traditionally fragmented groups whose historic roots were firmly planted in the Third Republic. These two groups proceeded to attack the existing electoral system on the grounds that proportional representation had not produced stable government, being a device for legislative, not executive, dominance and that it favored the Communist party.

By 1951 non-Communists were prepared to adopt measures which would reduce Communist representation and strengthen the precarious tenure of "third-force" governments. But, also, the Center parties wanted to avoid benefiting the massive Rassemblement du Peuple Français— De Gaulle's RPF—which, after its sweeping successes in the municipal elections of October 1947, threatened to engulf the newly restored Republic. While Radicals, Socialists, and MRP seemed doomed to work together in executive coalitions, each party was naturally eager to improve its own electoral position against the other two.

Out of these calculations emerged an electoral law which, while producing the results intended, was so obviously partisan in its inspiration that it further increased popular distrust of political institutions. In the first election under the 1951 law, the Communist party lost seventy-one seats that it would have won under the previous system, and the RPF lost twenty-six.[57] The election could be credited with an additional success: the supposedly monolithic RPF quickly broke apart on the issue of how long it should wait for the collapse of a regime which had shown itself adept at minimizing the effects of the Rally's own popularity. On the other hand, even with Gaullist splinter participation, governments continued as unstable as ever, and the National Assembly was even more disorganized.

After 1951 new divisive issues within the Socialist, MRP, and Radical ranks caused members of the Assembly to fear that party alliances in the next election would be less consistent and more difficult than before. Hence the electoral

[57] Same, p. 122.

system was again brought forward for revision, with growing legislative support for single-member constituencies and a two-stage ballot. Edgar Faure's dissolution of the Assembly, however, prevented the adoption of such a plan, and the authority of the national directorates over their parties remained unimpaired.

The experience with previous election systems made De Gaulle's choice an easy one. The new method must both reduce the power of the Assembly and work against the Communists. Proportional representation, multiple-member constituencies, and blocked lists all added to Communist membership in the Assembly. The system of lists, furthermore, solidified party control, and while alliances could be made within the framework of a single round of voting, they did not commit parties or deputies to any post-election course of action or, indeed, to any agreement on national or local policy. The answer, therefore, lay in setting up single-member constituencies and two-stage balloting. On the first ballot candidates garnering a majority of the votes were to be declared elected; on the second a plurality would suffice.[58]

The Inner Meaning of the New Constitution

In March 1958, Michel Debré issued one of his many calls for "the arbitration of a true chief of government, without hate, without personal interest, a chief who will be able to re-establish the affairs of France in liberty, in legality —an arbiter who will not be a partisan, not even the partisan of the angry men, except that his policy will, like their anger, arise from a steadfast desire to serve the honor and grandeur of France."[59] The constitution of the Fifth Republic in whose drafting Debré played a leading part, has as its prime aim a government founded on the general will, not on a precarious balance among conflicting forces. The President of the Republic is the one to define this general will. He is not its representative, since the people is not to

[58] The total number of deputies was reduced from 544 to 466.
[59] "Les Raisons de la Colère," *Le Monde*, March 8, 1958.

participate directly in electing him. Selected by the lesser governors, not by the governed, the President, in communion with himself, is to divine what the people would choose as the best policy for France, if it were competent—as it presumably is not—to penetrate the complexities of foreign and domestic affairs.

Inherent in this conception is the judgment that party structures and party doctrines have failed in their dual task. Doctrines had become increasingly abstract, increasingly meaningless in defining the issues before the country. They had ceased to provide the foundation for genuine choices by the electorate. Instead, they had deepened conflicts among forces which ought somehow to have been brought to compromise their aims. The Fifth Republic now asks the voters to ballot, not on doctrines, but on men, leaving those elected free to subordinate local demands to the common weal.

To this view of the function of the electorate the new emphasis on the referendum offers only an apparent exception. True, it may require the people to voice its opinion on a specific issue of national policy, but the matters appropriate to a referendum will in practice be selected by the executive; otherwise, if the executive had the required majority in the parliament, it would secure approval of its proposals without submitting them to a referendum. Moreover, in a referendum the electorate will not actually be able to select one among several alternatives. It can only divide into two factions—or three, counting the abstainers; in other words it can indicate only the degree of consensus on a proposed course of action, without recording multiple shades of its preference among multiple possibilities.

In one important respect, however, the Fifth Republic does not rely on the general national will. Divisions among Frenchmen had made the Fourth Republic a weak instrument of government, faithful mirror of those divisions. Now the French people, by another in a long series of somersaults, has repudiated this system, for which it felt no special attachment, in favor of a new experiment with strong government. But, once established, the Fifth Republic, like all political institutions, seeking self-perpetuation, is attempting to avert a new change of mind. Against any temptation to fickleness there stands a whole array of political institutions, only one of which is directly elected and that by a method best calculated to prevent control by disciplined parties. As a further safeguard against change, Article 4 of the constitution states that political parties "must respect the principles of national sovereignty and of democracy." The French Communist party has been declared by its critics to meet neither criterion, but the question of who can or will rule the Communist party beyond the pale remains unspecified.

To establish a government expressing the abstract "national will" transcending all conflicting forces the Fifth Republic has deliberately weakened parliamentary democracy, without substituting for it a clear separation of powers. As a result, a great deal will depend on the personality and behavior of the President of the Republic, on his ability to exercise a charismatic leadership. De Gaulle will serve for seven years, longer if re-elected. In this office he has the power to bring the Fifth Republic to life by the meaning he infuses into the articles of the constitution. Much like Konrad Adenauer in the German Federal Republic, De Gaulle *is* the Fifth Republic, the guarantor "of what liberty we may hope to preserve."[60] Small wonder that he so frequently slips from the first person singular to the impersonal third person. De Gaulle is an institution, as he has long been keenly aware.

The structure of the French State has been strengthened so as to subordinate special interests to the national welfare. The new effectiveness of the state means, however, that these interests will redouble their efforts to influence or control its actions. The difficulties of this have perhaps been increased, but the rewards for success are also far greater. The presidency, because of the method of selection, seems destined to remain a stronghold of conservatism, but the power of the office and the huge size of the body which selects its incumbent make it inevitable that, after De Gaulle

[60] André Siegfried, quoted in the *New York Times*, September 9, 1958.

steps down, all the great political movements in France will mobilize their forces to capture the citadel.

Another arena of struggle may involve the Premier and the Cabinet. While the President seeks to make them executors of his policies, the National Assembly will doubtless strive to recapture some measure of its former influence over the executive. Remaining fragmented, the Assembly may again seek to turn the Cabinet into a coalition reflecting legislative groupings, in place of the unified instrument desired by the President. The new Assembly, like its predecessors under the Third and Fourth Republics, may become an arena of conflict among many special interests. Conservative forces, historically in close alliance with private pressure groups, can be expected, under the new electoral system, to increase their power in both the Assembly and the Senate. Finally, the constitutional relationship of the new Economic and Social Council to both legislative and executive branches may encourage special interests to use this channel to influence national policy.

The Constitutional Referendum and the Parties

As expected, Communists, still fighting the May revolution, opposed the new constitution adamantly. Equally predictable was the favorable attitude of the MRP and the Right, the only prominent defector being Pierre Poujade. Lively intra-party battles took place within Radical and Socialist ranks. Before their party congress, held early in September, Socialist deputies had voted 56-4 for a manifesto declaring that the constitution "contains grave dangers for the Republic."[61] At the congress four attitudes were made evident. Some members opposed the constitution and announced their intention of campaigning against it; some opposed it but were prepared to follow the majority in the name of party discipline; some were unenthusiastic and fearful but felt that acceptance was now the only practical choice; and a few were enthusiastic.[62]

[61] *New York Times*, August 6, 1958.
[62] *Le Monde*, September 14-15, 1958.

The first group was epitomized by Félix Gouin, President of the Constituent Assembly and De Gaulle's successor as Premier under the Fourth Republic. "This is," Gouin announced, "without doubt the last time I shall speak in a Socialist congress";[63] soon afterwards he addressed a Communist rally at Marseilles [64] Édouard Depreux told the congress that he and his followers would remain loyal to Léon Blum and to the May 27 vote of the Socialist deputies against De Gaulle's accession to power.[65]

One of those willing to abide by the party's decision to support the draft constitution was Albert Gazier who, as Pflimlin's Minister of Information, had been responsible for press censorship in the latter days of May. Although he decided to follow the majority in accepting the constitution, he recognized that such a course would legalize the revolt of May 13 and would constitute a victory for all those rightist forces which had made it impossible for the Fourth Republic to govern.[66] Old-time Socialist Paul Ramadier also had grave reservations; he singled out as particularly objectionable Article 16, which permitted the President to assume special powers in an emergency.

Former Premier Guy Mollet led the fight for the constitution. His role in De Gaulle's accession to power, in June, and his immediate entry into the General's Cabinet had alienated so many leading Socialists that he seemed certain to be ousted as Secretary-General. However, between then and the meeting of the congress, his position had been greatly strengthened. His principal rival, Gaston Defferre, had abandoned his opposition to De Gaulle and announced that he would support the constitution in the hope that the Fifth Republic would continue the liberal colonial policy which he had carried out as Minister of Overseas Territories

[63] Same.
[64] *New York Times*, September 21, 1958.
[65] *Le Monde*, September 14-15, 1958, the first reference was to Blum's statement that De Gaulle's address at Bayeux, June 16, 1946, posed the danger of a new Boulanger.
[66] *Le Monde*, September 13, 1958.

in 1956.[67] At the congress in September, over 80 per cent of the delegates—3,146 to 598, with 136 abstentions—accepted Mollet's report in favor of the new constitution.[68]

The Radical party congress also had no real enthusiasm for the constitution. Félix Gaillard, leader of the group which was prepared to accept it, labeled it "a text which can lead to a permanent conflict between the [executive and legislative] powers." Lucien Degoutte called it a "bad job." Maurice Faure declared, "It is impossible to deny that the constitution shows the effects of the Orleanist concept which presided over its first drafting."[69]

One of the few Radicals who went beyond criticism of the constitution to attack De Gaulle in person was Mendès-France. "Democracy exists only if the organizers of power are elected by the people," he declared at a press conference on September 5. ". . . Let us not renounce this principle. If we do, we will aggravate the division between the institutions and the country."[70] At the Radical party congress he called the proposed assembly a "fifth wheel" in a "strange constitution," under which power did not rest with the people, but with the President, the Premier, the Senate, and the Constitutional Committee. "They tell us General De Gaulle is not a dictator. He has said himself that one does not begin a career as dictator at sixty-seven. Please excuse me, but one does not choose a constitution according to the age of a leader."[71]

Mendès advanced an alternative to the referendum, which De Gaulle and his advisers were turning into a test of the General's personal popularity—the election, in November, of a constituent assembly by majority vote within

---

[67] *New York Times*, September 6, 1958. According to Alexander Werth, De Gaulle told Defferre that only a large favorable vote on the constitution would make it possible for him to put the army and the *colons* in their place and negotiate an Algerian peace with the nationalists. (Alexander Werth, "Anatomy of a Ballot," *Nation*, October 11, 1958, p. 210)

[68] *Le Monde*, September 13, 1958; the vote, of course, should not be taken as an indication of the full measure of latent opposition even within the congress.

[69] Same, September 14-15, 1958.

[70] Same, September 7-8, 1958

[71] Same, September 14-15, 1958.

the *arrondissements*, with a mandate to draft within one month a constitution containing certain principles, such as the right of dissolution. Simultaneously a conference of the territories of the French Union would be called to decide on the structure of a new Community, and the search for an Algerian settlement would be renewed, with the participation of genuine spokesmen of Algerian nationalism and with the cooperation of Moroccan and Tunisian authorities.[72] By this time, however, few Frenchmen favored a plan which would prolong the constitutional hiatus, if only for two months. Most agreed with René Pleven that it was vital to get a legitimate government established quickly so that France would no longer be the only major country in the world ruled by decree.[73]

The lack of an attractive alternative was only one of many obstacles confronting the opponents of the constitution. As in May, the role of the Communists as De Gaulle's most vociferous opponents made it virtually impossible for other groups to join them in a united front. The Union of Democratic Forces, grouping some Socialists and Radicals, was little more than a grandiose label for a collection of unrelated, individual campaigns. Rather surprisingly, in Toulouse, Bourgès-Maunoury campaigned actively against the constitution, aided by fellow Radical Jean Baylet's *Dépêche du Midi*.[74] Daladier once more tried to live up to his nickname of "bull of the Vaucluse," and Mendès-France did his best to influence the voters of Louviers. Individual opponents were aided by the teachers' union and by sections of the Force Ouvrière and Christian Federation of Trade-Unions, although the national directorates of the two non-Communist labor federations did not explicitly sanction these and other local actions.

Isolated voices of opposition were almost drowned out in the sea of unofficial and official propaganda. Against a few journals such as *Esprit, Express,* and *France-Observa-*

[72] Same, September 7-8, 1958.
[73] Pleven, in his journal, *Petit Bleu des Côtes-du-Nord*, cited in *Le Monde*, September 14-15, 1958.
[74] *New York Times*, September 18, 1958.

teur was arrayed the entire Paris press[75] (except, of course, *L'Humanité*). Under Jacques Soustelle's skillful direction, the government radio and television stressed the theme of national salvation and unity rather than a sober exposition of the constitution's terms. In all, opposition groups received five minutes in which to argue their uncoordinated points of view.[76] Posters favorable to the constitution, printed at government expense, blanketed the country, while prefects were instructed to remove unfavorable stickers, also at government expense.[77]

The real candidate was De Gaulle, not the constitution, just as Mendès-France had foreseen. Against his towering figure, clothed in the majesty of dictatorial power, against the carefully cultivated *mystique* which continued to surround him, no individual, no combination of individuals, could stand. The Fourth Republic had made pygmies of them all. De Gaulle told the voters that the constitution was less important than the way its powers would be used,[78] and the people, inured to constitutions and politicians, either believed him or feared to reject him. The favorable vote on the constitution surpassed even Soustelle's prediction of 65 per cent.[79] Actually, in the *Métropole* 79.25 per cent, or 17.7 million, voted "oui," and only 20.75 per cent, or 4.6 million, "non."[80]

The result of the referendum was widely interpreted as a major defeat for both the Communists and those non-Communists who had actively campaigned against the constitution. Certainly the Communists suffered a severe set-

---

[75] Even Hubert Beuve-Méry declared his intention of voting "oui," not so much for the constitution as for political institutions as such, and for De Gaulle, who alone could tell the army that victory cannot be won by war "without mercy and without end." (*Le Monde*, September 25, 1958). He stated, however, that *Le Monde's* staff was divided on this question.

[76] Werth, cited, p. 210.

[77] *Le Monde*, September 23, 1958.

[78] In his tour of Rennes, Bordeaux, Strasbourg, and Lille, September 20-23.

[79] *The Economist*, October 4, 1958, p. 15.

[80] *New York Times*, September 30, 1958. Bas-Rhin in strongly Catholic Alsace yielded the highest percentage of favorable votes—93.4—while Corrège in central France had the lowest—64. (*The Economist*, October 4, 1958, p. 15.)

back. In the famous "Red Belt" around Paris, for example, the number of "non" ballots was markedly less than the Communist total in the Assembly elections of 1956. Even if all the negative votes were credited to the Communists—manifestly not the case—the total was about a million less than they had received two years earlier.

Early in October, at a meeting of the Communist Central Committee, Marcel Servin and Maurice Thorez attributed the Communist losses and De Gaulle's victory to a series of unfortunate circumstances. First was the "shameful surrender" of Mollet, Gaillard, and Pflimlin to "the 'ultras' of Algiers."[81] Another was the disunity of the forces opposed to the constitution. "Is this the end?" asked Thorez. "Are we going on all alone and in disarray?"[82] Many voted yes "to bring an end, so they thought, to all that had burdened them and the country for ten years."[83] Moreover, a part of the working class "has still not thrown off completely the aftereffects of colonialist ideology. It must not be forgotten that colonial surplus profit has been and remains one of the bases of social democracy."[84] Finally, Algerian nationalist terrorism in the *Métropole* had backfired.[85] "If the FLN thinks to alert opinion, it is deceiving itself. . . . Far from gaining sympathy, it loses it."[86]

In the face of the debacle, what should the Communist party do next? In discussing this, Servin and Thorez showed some significant differences in approach. Servin argued for a relatively mild and flexible approach, appealing to non-Communists and straying party followers. "It would," he said, "be dangerous for the future to regard as negligible the 'nons' coming from democrats, socialists, radicals, and, of lesser importance, from Christians. . . . We must . . . speak, demonstrate, explain in convincing language . . .

---

[81] *Le Monde*, October 7, 1958
[82] Same, October 11, 1958.
[83] Servin, *Le Monde*, October 8, 1958
[84] Thorez, *Le Monde*, October 11, 1958.
[85] While neither Servin nor Thorez mentioned it, the reaction had fallen chiefly on the Communist party, which was the only political group to condone FLN tactics.
[86] Thorez, *Le Monde*, October 11, 1958.

and not rub them the wrong way."[87] Thorez took a stronger line. He urged the other groups of the Left to unite with the party on the Communists' own terms. "Those who lack firmness, the snivelers, will say, 'It's the line, it's the leadership which is at fault.' They will propose another policy, another party. Must I repeat that the party's policy is right and that a fraction of our electorate could abandon us without this being a black mark against the party and its line?" As for the election campaign, "the tactics of the party should be to develop the Communist program on the first balloting and to do everything possible on the second to rally the republican forces against reaction."[88]

While neither Thorez nor Servin mentioned it, the French Communists were not getting much aid or comfort from Moscow. The attraction of communism for Frenchmen had been weakened by Russian actions in Hungary and by the Kremlin's alternate wooing and rejection of Tito, toward whom Thorez had long advocated a harsh line. All through the months of De Gaulle's rise to power Khrushchev had kept silent. Some observers even concluded that Moscow had issued orders to the French Communists to avoid extreme measures, such as rioting or industrial sabotage.[89] Once he had become Premier, De Gaulle appeared at least tolerable to Khrushchev, as evidenced by the active correspondence between them on the subject of a summit conference. Even the threat, contained in Article 4 of the constitution, to the legality of the French Communist party had provoked no response from Moscow. "The Russians had better watch their step," so Cyrus Sulzberger quoted sources in the party's Central Committee in Paris. "They are foolish if they reckon that we will forever follow them blindly. Many of us are getting fed up."[90]

In the case of individual non-Communist opponents of the constitution, the results of the referendum were not so clear-cut. Mendès-France saw his stronghold of Louviers

---

[87] *Le Monde*, October 7, 1958.
[88] Same, October 11, 1958.
[89] Cyrus Sulzberger, *New York Times*, July 2, 1958.
[90] *New York Times*, July 2, 1958.

pile up a pro-constitution vote of 69 per cent. Bourgès-Maunoury lost Montastruc by 821 to 105. In Toulouse, where the plotters of May 13 had been more active than in any other metropolitan area, 74 per cent voted for the constitution.[91] Nièvre repudiated Mitterand by 94,808 to 31,994 [92] On the Right, Pierre Poujade lost his home town of St. Ceré by 1,292 to 543.[93] Yet, if non-Communists were as unsuccessful as the Communists in opposing the constitution, they none the less had some hope for a better outcome in the forthcoming elections to the Assembly. Indeed, with the exception of Bourgès-Maunoury, prominent individuals for the most part succeeded in holding below the national average the local majorities favorable to the constitution. Viewing their effect on the voters, they could still hope to retain their seats in the new Assembly under an electoral system which placed a premium on local popularity and in a campaign which might for the first time bring to light the latent dissensions among the supporters of the new constitution.

[91] Same, September 29, 1958.
[92] Georges Szard, "Et Maintenant?" *La Nef*, October 1958, p. 6.
[93] *New York Times*, September 29, 1958.

Chapter Sixteen

POLITICS AND PARTIES UNDER THE FIFTH REPUBLIC

IN ESTABLISHING the institutions of the Fifth Republic, De Gaulle adhered to a rigid schedule. No sooner was the constitution drafted than he began the referendum campaign in France and in the overseas territories. Two months after the acceptance of the constitution, he held legislative elections in the *Métropole* and in Algeria. Although warned of the consequences of balloting in Algeria under wartime conditions, De Gaulle refused a postponement because that would have meant postponing the re-establishment of constitutional government in France. Ahead lay the election of a president of the republic, organization of the new Assembly, selection of the Senate's membership, formation by the president of his government, and his presentation of it to the legislature. De Gaulle wished to complete all these steps by the end of January so that the executive, under his direction, could then have three months of unobstructed activity before the Assembly met for its first regular session.

Electoral Problems and Party Disputes

Holding elections for the National Assembly on the heels of the referendum posed serious problems for the various political parties and groups. In effect, the elections were a continuation of the referendum; from one to the other, there was no time for the tides of public opinion to change. There was no real opportunity to present any new issues, any questions other than the one on which the referendum had been fought: Does France accept or repudiate De Gaulle? There was no time to heal the many conflicts, naturally bitter, often personal, over the events of May and over the constitution. While most political leaders professed to believe the new mode of election was an improvement over proportional representation,[1] its provision for 465 single-member constituencies made it difficult to decide what issues would appeal to voters whose opinions, apart from their feelings toward De Gaulle, remained largely unknown.

The elections in the *Métropole,* as in Algeria, took place under crisis conditions. De Gaulle still wielded full powers without effective legal or constitutional controls. On October 8, 1958, the *Journal Officiel* published three ordinances permitting the Minister of the Interior to order the detention in jail or "in a locality specially designated" of "persons considered dangerous to the public security" by reason of "material aid, direct or indirect," given to the Algerian nationalists. "This text," concluded the liberal Vigilance Committee of Republican Jurists, "establishes in France the concentration-camp system." While the ordinances also provided for a commission of verification, its decisions, as the jurists pointed out, "have no executory force: the Minister [of the Interior] is free to follow or disregard the advice of the commission. Thus on the very morrow of the promulgation of the constitution, the government nullifies the principle embodied in Article 66 of this constitution; that 'no one may be arbitrarily detained,' by depriving the 'judicial authority' of its constitutional role as 'guardian of individual liberty.' "[2]

The emergency measures took on added significance when the rejection of De Gaulle's overtures by the Algerian nationalists made it apparent that the war was going to continue. While obviously aimed at the nationalists' under-

[1] Interesting exceptions were reported to be Jacques Soustelle and Georges Bidault Bidault was said to have asked the MRP directorate why it had so meekly abandoned its traditional support for the blocked list and proportional representation; *Le Monde,* October 8, 1958.

[2] *Le Monde,* October 10, 1958.

cover apparatus in France, the ordinances marked a continuation of the climate of crisis which had marked the last months of the Fourth Republic and the first months of De Gaulle's regime. Moreover, the government persisted in its practice of censorship, with recurrent seizures of newspapers and other periodicals.[3]

As the campaign got under way, it became clear that the voters were apathetic. Having voted once for De Gaulle, they saw little reason to ballot again for the reconstruction of a parliamentary system which, they had been told, was responsible for their domestic difficulties, for the prolongation of the Algerian war, for the low regard with which France was regarded by other countries. They regarded the elections as a formality, a bewildering interference with their daily affairs.

These circumstances tended to re-enforce the continued divisions in the ranks of the Socialists, the Mouvement Républicain Populaire, the Radical Socialists, and the Union Démocratique et Sociale de la Résistance. The Socialist congress in September had been followed by a split, despite Mollet's success in gaining majority endorsement for his support of De Gaulle and the referendum, and Édouard Depreux now broke away, with a number of dissidents, to form an "Autonomous Socialist party, SFIO." Admitting that the group had "neither a centime, nor a headquarters, nor a typewriter," Depreux announced that eventually "we intend to become a large, a very large party of true Socialist unity." "The real lines of demarcation," he continued, "run through the very heart of political parties, all of which are undergoing a crisis."[4]

Within the MRP the dramatic debate over Bidault's bid to succeeed Gaillard as Premier had reflected a long-standing conflict between party workers—the *militants*— who wished it to continue its support for the liberal principles on which it had been founded, and those, including many

[3] An issue of *Look* containing an article entitled, "Jacques Soustelle: Most Dangerous Man in Europe," was barred from France.
[4] *Le Monde's* "Tribune Électorale," a column opened before the election to statements by leaders of all political groups, November 14, 1958.

parliamentarians, who had accepted the rightist drift of the party as shown by its colonial policy and its participation in increasingly conservative coalitions. Led by Bidault, some of those whose political sympathy lay with the Right formed a Catholic Center group to fight the election. This group at once entered into negotiations for the joint endorsement of candidates with the Independents, the Right-wing Radicals and the "Gaullist-Gaullist" Union pour la Nouvelle République.

Dissension was nothing new to the Radicals. The division between the followers of Edgar Faure and the Mendésistes had been a prominent feature of the 1956 electoral battle. Thereafter the fight had been intensified by André Morice's opposition to Mendès-France's efforts to remake the Radical party in his own image. The Radicals were now theoretically headed by Félix Gaillard, but the Right or Morice fringe, still estranged, conducted a separate electoral campaign under the label of "Republican Center." Supporters of Mendès-France retained the Radical label only because Gaillard did not choose, at least for the time being, to raise the question of their simultaneous membership in the Union des Forces Démocratiques. His silence permitted Mendès-France to announce that some twenty candidates would be presented by the dissident group, which would continue within the Radical ranks "to play the minority game without abandoning its ideas." Concluded *Le Monde* prophetically, "Thus there remain a strange and fictitious 'unity' and coherence. In truth the Radical party is very sick."[5]

While the Socialists, Radicals, and MRP remained largely under the control of middle-of-the-road leadership, François Mitterand, advocate of a liberal solution in Algeria and determined opponent of both De Gaulle and his constitution, kept a firm grip on the Union Démocratique et Socialiste de la Résistance. The Mitterand majority condemned those who wished to follow Pleven and Eugène Claudius-Petit in breaking away from the party: their "persistent

[5] *Le Monde*, October 21, 1958.

opportunism over recent years partly explains the discredit attached to parliamentary institutions [a discredit] which led to the fall of the Fourth Republic."[6] Mitterand himself was one of the few Assembly candidates to campaign vigorously against the new leadership of France.

The Right, on the other hand, presented a greater semblance of cohesion than under the Fourth Republic. The Independents congratulated themselves on their rise to prominence, which they attributed "quite simply" to the fact that they "were the first—as far back as ten years ago—to rise up against the omnipotence of a single Assembly; to condemn governmental instability and impotence; to advocate and pursue unceasingly the reform of a constitution for which they had not voted and which, for a long time, they were the only ones to condemn."[7] The Independents took credit for economic solvency under Pinay and also for the initiative along with Bidault and Soustelle, in bringing De Gaulle to power without a civil war. From this record and the Gaullist tide they expected to benefit fully, but their rewards would be all the more bountiful if they could reach some agreement with Bidault and Morice and, above all, with Soustelle and the Union pour la Nouvelle République.

But here was a problem. The Union pour la Nouvelle République, the "wolf turned shepherd,"[8] had risen quickly after the May revolt, building an organization devoted to "pure" Gaullism. In October the UNR announced that it had decided not to endorse candidates in districts where De Gaulle's ministers were running. At the same time it made overtures to the "national parties" (meaning the Independents, the Christian Democrats, the Center Republicans, and Morice's Radicals), to forestall a destructive competition among Gaullists. However, it proved impossible to organize a grand alliance of the Right.

At least three reasons lay behind this failure. Some of the UNR directorate wished to preserve the façade of the Union as a Center group and therefore opposed any move

[6] Same, October 17, 1958.
[7] Roger Duchet in "Tribune Électorale," cited, November 18, 1958.
[8] Maurice Duverger in *Le Monde*, October 4, 1958.

which, by pre-electoral endorsements or alliances, would confine itself to the Right. In this, it was reported, Edmond Michelet, Jacques Chaban-Delmas, and Michel Debré were actively supported by De Gaulle.[9] A second factor was the jostling for position within the UNR itself. Some of its leaders felt that Soustelle had jumped the gun in forming the new organization without adequate consultation. They also believed that the Minister of Information was using his official position to unfair advantage, converting the UNR into a personal instrument for the attainment of power.[10] The internal struggle heightened as the pre-election mood of the country became evident. While not predicting the landslide that actually occurred, the UNR calculated that it would be the principal winner at the polls. Since other sections of the Right were viewed as weaker elements, endorsement of non-UNR candidates before the first balloting might deprive the UNR of some of its potential strength in the Assembly. Far from holding back its own nominations of candidates, the UNR went out to do battle with all comers, including the Independents and the smaller groups of the Right.

The varied reactions of the political groupings to the electoral situation blurred the lines which normally divided the three major political orientations. On one extreme, isolated and ostracized, were the Communists, marked by the method of election for a severe blow, if not for practical extinction as a force within the Assembly. The Communist party was doggedly running candidates in each district, although it had few illusions over the outcome. Early in the campaign the party's Central Committee announced that "on the second balloting we will do everything we can to rally the Republican forces against reaction and against those who, like Guy Mollet, are associated with it and share the responsibility for power and for the present difficulties."[11]

[9] *New York Times,* October 31, 1958.

[10] *Le Monde,* October 18, October 31, 1958. The split was so serious that at one time both antagonists, Soustelle and Michelet, were reportedly on the verge of resigning.

[11] *Le Monde,* October 24, 1958.

Mollet defined the Socialists' position as in the center of the Left, ready to make alliances with all other "anti-Fascists." This definition of a non-Communist, non-Right position resembled the clarion calls to opportunism in the name of principle which had characterized Socialist campaigns in the recent past. The same could be said of the electoral claims of the Center-Right. "In the competition which is beginning," said Duchet, "the Independents ask the electorate to make an unequivocal choice between the two orientations which are offered to our country: a 'dirigist policy' desired by the Socialists and a liberal policy advocated by the Independents."[12]

Unfortunately for the Independents, the UNR was simultaneously trying to force its way between the Socialists and the Independents, pushing the latter away from "liberalism" to a simpler, more lonely position on the far Right. ". . . We believe," said Roger Frey, "in the necessity of being the indispensable link between Right and Left, the meeting place of ideas and of men. . . . It would be an error to believe that the collision of the Right against the Left is desirable in such a country as ours."[13]

To this claim the Republican Center could only counter that it proposed to play in Parliament the same role as the middle class in the national society,[14] presumably as a conduit and channel of communication between upper and lower groups.

Gaullism and the Elections

All the talk of "reaction," "anti-fascism," or "liberalism" as distinctions between the various political movements merely added to the miasma of Gaullism which already hung so heavily over the country. Almost all groups wanted to campaign as Gaullists. "The Left with De Gaulle!" proclaimed Jean-Claude Servan-Schreiber, of the Center of Republican Reform; "[Its] candidates are loyal to General de Gaulle and faithful to the spirit of dynamic and con-

[12] Duchet, in "Tribune Électorale," cited, November 18, 1958.
[13] Frey, in same, November 21, 1958.
[14] Bernard Lafay in same, November, 1958.

tinuous renewal which is the characteristic of the true men of the Left." "This double qualification contains no internal contradiction."[15] Equally positive was the UNR, self-styled "party of fidelity." Even Maurice Thorez, while he could hardly invoke the name of De Gaulle, wrote his piece for *Le Monde's* "Tribune Électorale"[16] without once mentioning the General. Devoting all his allotted space to a plea for peace in Algeria, Thorez found therein "the prerequisite of all policy seeking to guarantee the restoration of the Republic and the grandeur of France." (At least the General had no patent on grandeur.)

The desire to appropriate De Gaulle's name did not fully account for the vacuous irrelevancy of party statements. Central party control over candidates had been weakened by the new electoral system. Local issues, it was thought, would play a prominent part in the campaign. Any attempt by central organizations to prescribe substantive positions merely invited the candidates to evade them or go down in defeat. The obvious apathy of the electorate toward the election in general, and toward make-up of the future Assembly in particular, led to still further concentration on local issues. Finally, the future of all political parties, the very existence of some, rested so heavily on the standing of their candidates at the end of the first balloting that the individual nominee was considered the best if not the sole judge of the stress he should lay on "national themes," such as Algeria, economic progress, and political renovation.

De Gaulle himself refused to endorse any political group. At a press conference on October 23, he said:

Everyone understands—I allow myself a personal word or two —everybody understands that I do not wish, that I cannot take any direct part in this contest. The mission with which the country has entrusted me prevents me from taking sides. Thus I shall not do so on behalf of anyone, even of those who always have shown a friendly loyalty to me through all vicissitudes. Of course, I shall not disapprove if groups or candidates of all

[15] Jean-Claude Servan-Schreiber, in same, November 19, 1958.
[16] November 16-17, 1958.

shades of opinion make known their support of the action of Charles de Gaulle. Besides, others will not fail to make known their opposition, utilizing that freedom that they accuse me of wishing to destroy. This impartiality compels me to make it very clear that my name, even in the form of an adjective, must not be used in the title of any group or in the slogan of any candidate.[17]

The effect of the Premier's words was to encourage the proliferation of candidates running for office under labels unfamiliar to the voters.

By avoiding commitment on specific questions of national policy De Gaulle reinforced his position above partisan conflict; at the same time he made it difficult for candidates to follow his professed wishes and discover the feelings of the voters. "General de Gaulle's policy being in large measure unforeseen and secret and apparently capable of change during this campaign," wrote a keen observer, "none of those who use the [Gaullist] label wish to appear disavowed if tomorrow De Gaulle pronounces an unexpected speech or takes an unforeseen decision, entailing for example genuine negotiations over Algeria, or on the contrary turns toward war 'to the bitter end.' Thence the vagueness, thence the frequent resort to the same formulas as those employed by the General, formulas whose elliptical, mysterious, ambivalent nature will allow a candidate to say in the future, whatever may occur, that he was 'on that side' ('dans la ligne')."[18]

While some French commentators may have been quite correct in concluding that, unlike 1951 and 1956, there were no real *issues* in the elections of 1958,[19] none the less they reflected nuances which were of great importance to the future of the Fifth Republic. One concerned Algeria. Right-wing groups—Independents, UNR, and Republican Center—consistently referred to it as "French Algeria."

[17] Ambassade de France, Service de Presse et d'Information, *Speeches and Press Conferences*, no. 119 (New York, October 1958), p. 2.
[18] Claude Bourdet of the Union de la Gauche Socialiste, one of the formations in the Union des Forces Démocratiques, "Tribune Électorale," cited, November 20, 1958.
[19] See, for example Jacques Fauvet in *Le Monde*, November 20, 1958.

The non-Communist Left could not reply with a tag of equal brevity and emotional appeal, but they did have the advantage of standing closer to De Gaulle's own statements on economic assistance (the "Constantine Program") and recognition of Algeria's "personality."

On domestic economic policy, the Left answered the Right's advocacy of national progress based on "liberalism" and "anti-Socialism" by removing the capital "S" and emphasizing the need for social progress and social justice. The two Socialist groups (the Union de la Gauche Socialiste and the Parti Socialiste Autonome) dedicated themselves "to defining the new paths of socialism in a country economically advanced, as is France," wrote Claude Bourdet.[20]

While local candidates vied in attacking, retrospectively or prospectively, legislative control of the executive and all political groups placed some emphasis on "renovation" through presentation of "new" candidates for the Assembly; there were some differences both in the extent to which the candidates were really new and in the type of candidates. Of 336 endorsed by the UNR, its leaders proudly told the press, only sixteen were former deputies, eight former senators, and seven representatives to the French Union. "The men whom the Center of Republican Reform presents to the Metropolitan voters . . . are new men for the most part," wrote Jean-Claude Servan-Schreiber. Not being able to claim the same degree of amateurism, the traditional parties advanced three types of counter-argument. Theirs, said the MRP, was a party of program, not just of "notables." The Independents pointed to their candidates as men of proven experience, whose previous protests against the abuses of the Fourth Republic now deserved support by the voters. Finally, many groups of both Left and Right fought the UNR with the argument that their candidates, whether new or old, were at least bona fide residents of their districts, not "foreigners."[21]

[20] "Tribune Électorale," cited.
[21] The various party positions on their candidates are outlined in "Tribune Électorale," cited.

Especially irritating to the Right was the presence of some twenty military candidates, of whom fourteen, including the most famous of the lot—"old leather-nose" Thomazo—were specifically endorsed by the UNR. "Whether one wishes it or not," said Independent Roger Duchet, "these colonels are candidates of division."[22]

Results of the Elections

Since government regulations permitted only those parties presenting at least seventy-five candidates to have any time on the national radio network or in the local districts,[23] a great flood of candidates was expected. The actual number, however, totaled just under 3,000, an average of about six contestants per district. This was approximately 2,000 fewer candidates than in 1956 or in 1936, the last time the single-member constituency form of election had been employed. Reflecting the emphasis on new faces, the average age of the candidates was only fifty, as compared to sixty-two in the last election to the National Assembly under the Fourth Republic. The withdrawal of over 70 former deputies and the competition for single seats among over 100 others made it certain that there would be a substantial percentage of political tyros in the next Assembly.

The results of the first balloting, held on November 23, 1958, appear in different lights, depending on whether they

[22] *Le Monde*, November 14, 1958. While many political groups set forth their positions on the perennial state-church issue, particularly as it concerned public support of private religious schools, there did not appear to be much real difference among them. All were for religious harmony. Several wanted the question removed from partisan politics by agreement among the leading parties. Groups associated with the Catholic side took care to point out that their candidates and supporters included nonpracticing Catholics, while those which had in the past stood for the lay state and against the grant of public funds to Catholic schools stated with equal care that their groups were open to adherents of all faiths or none. This circumspection did not prevent the issue from reappearing during the session of the Assembly. See, for example, Bernard Lafay, Maurice-René Simonnet, Félix Gaillard in "Tribune Électorale," cited, and Guy Mollet's statement on the eve of the election, *Le Monde*, November 22, 1958.

[23] Five minutes were provided on the national network and an equal period in the local districts.

are viewed in terms of percentages of the popular vote, shifts in the bases of party strength, or relative positions for the second and decisive round. Scanning the figures in the table below, one is struck by the high degree of stability in the broad "tendencies" of political opinion, notwithstanding the great upheaval which had taken place since the previous May.

PERCENTAGE OF POPULAR VOTE, BY PARTIES[24]

Political Groups	1951	1956	1958
Communist	25.4%	25.7%	18.9%
Socialist	14.3	14.8	15.5
Other Left	.2	2.0	1.4
Radicals and Center Left	9.8	13.3	11.5
UNR and "Gaullists"[a]	21.5	4.4	17.6
MRP[b]	12.3	11.0	11.6
Moderates	13.5	14.3	19.9
Extreme Right[c]	—	13.1	3.3

[a] RPF in 1951, Social Republicans in 1956
[b] MRP and Christian Democracy in 1958
[c] Poujadistes

Although the Communists drew a considerably smaller vote than in 1951 or 1956, they were still, next to the "Moderates," the strongest group in the political spectrum. The 4 million "Moderate" votes were divided among several factions, of which the largest, the Independents, received 2.8 million, or 13.7 per cent. The Gaullist UNR ranked third, but fell 500,000 votes (3.9 percentage points) short of the showing made by De Gaulle's own Rassemblement du Peuple Français in 1951. The abrupt decline of Poujade's know-nothing union had been anticipated in view of the competition by the UNR and some Moderates for extreme Right votes, the overshadowing, perhaps temporary, of the tax-revolt issue out of which the movement had grown, and the conflict between Poujade and many of his followers over whether or not to oppose General de Gaulle and his constitution. Apart from these exceptions, the results of the election show that little change in voting patterns had actually occurred as compared to either

[24] Based on tables in *Le Monde*, November 25, 1958.

1956 or 1951. It should be noted, however, that the figures for the Radicals and the MRP are deceptive, since both were badly split during the election.

A different pattern, of greater importance for the second balloting, emerges from the geographical shifts in party strength. The Communists lost ground generally throughout the country. In 1956 they had received at least one-third of the votes in 11 Departments, and at least one-fourth in 41 of them. In 1958 there were only 4 in which they had one-third and 12 in which they had one quarter of the votes. Their losses were most substantial in Corsica, in the two southwestern Departments of Lot and Lot-et-Garonne, in the Departments of Savoy, adjacent to Italy, and Moselle, next to Germany, and in the west-central Department of Deux Sèvres. In the Paris region they dropped between 5 and 8 per cent, while still holding over one quarter of the votes. Benefiting from the weakness of the Communists and the divisions among the Radicals, especially in southwest France, in most French Departments the Socialists maintained their popular support at approximately the same level as in 1956. Left-wing groups opposing both the Socialists and the Right—the Autonomous Socialists, the Union de la Gauche Socialiste, and the Center of Republican Reform—had no success. On the other hand, the Right-wing (Morice) Radicals and the Pleven-Claudius-Petit version of the UDSR, grouped in the Republican Center, fared somewhat better, Pleven being one of the few to win a majority on the first round.

Since only 39 candidates were elected by an outright majority on November 23, despite predictions of as many as 60 to 80, the question of relative strength became of crucial importance in deciding whether to maintain or yield this or that candidacy and, if the decision was to withdraw, then for whose benefit. The second balloting, it was certain, would distort the results of the first; the only question was, how much distortion would result. Two factors made the bargaining difficult. The Communists had said they would yield for the second balloting only to adamant opponents of De Gaulle, but it was precisely these anti-Gaullists, who, under whatever labels they chose to run, had suffered the greatest reverses on November 23.[25] Where the Communists kept their candidates in the field, they added, on balance, to the chances for rightist victory on the second round.[26]

But what kind of Right would ultimately win? The November 23 results could only whet the UNR's appetite. Despite a percentage of the popular vote smaller than that of the Moderates, the proliferation of Moderate lists had placed many of their candidates in a relatively weaker position compared with those endorsed by the UNR. The campaign to bestow upon the UNR the dual label of a Center group and of the group most loyal to De Gaulle seemed to have paid off amply, despite the political commotion this decision had caused behind the scenes. Therefore, in general, UNR candidates stayed in the race, the party's justification being that there was no danger of a Communist victory.[27]

Thrown together before the elections by their common opposition to the Communists and the Right, the regular Socialists and Radicals frequently yielded to each other for the second balloting. Much less common were agreements between Socialists and MRP.

The results of the second round surpassed even the most optimistic hopes of the UNR. Having looked forward originally to winning between 140 and 165 seats, then after the first ballot to 170, the Union actually garnered 188-56 more than the second largest group, the Moderates. Other parties were left far behind; the two Catholic groups won only 57, and the Socialists 40.

---

[25] Thereby dashing their post-referendum optimism See above, Chapter 15, p 379

[26] The Communists deviated from their principle of withdrawal only in the Nord Department, where they considered the defeat of Léon Delbecque of such importance that they yielded to a Socialist candidate despite his having favored the constitution in the recent referendum.

[27] Much publicity was given to a few UNR cessions in favor of Socialists—Guy Mollet in Arras, Lacoste in Dordogne, and Tarrazzi in Marseilles, and a few Independents were given UNR support, particularly in the Paris area.

COMPOSITION OF THE NATIONAL ASSEMBLY, ELECTIONS
OF 1956 AND 1958[28]

Group	Number of Seats	
	Old Assembly	New Assembly
UNR	13[a]	188
Moderates	107	132
Catholics	71	57[b]
Socialists	91	40
Radicals and Center Left	77	35
Communists	140[c]	10
Poujadists	30[d]	1
Total	529	463

[a] Social Republicans
[b] MRP and Christian Democracy
[c] Including Progressives
[d] After the mandate of some had been removed

De Gaulle's popularity and the introduction of single-member constituencies had had disastrous effects for the parties of the Left. Socialists, with 15.4 per cent of the vote, received 8.6 per cent of the seats. Communists with 20.1 per cent—200,000 *more* votes than the UNR—got exactly 10 seats or about one-twentieth of those won by the group of Gaullist purity.[29] Clinging to the UNR skyrocket ("planet or meteor?" asked Jacques Fauvet),[30] the Moderates also picked up more seats than their percentage of popular votes would have given them under nation-wide proportional representation.

One of the most striking results of the two-stage election was the political carnage among prominent figures whose names were associated with the Fourth Republic. Although in the second balloting Mollet held on to one of the 40 Socialist seats with UNR backing, his defeated party members included Defferre, Ramadier, Lacoste, Pinaud, Le Troquer, and Gazier. Félix Gaillard could still lead the pitifully small band of Radicals. He would have André

[28] Based on figures in *New York Times*, December 1, 1958
[29] "This is perhaps a normal consequence of a majority electoral system," wrote Pierre Viansson-Ponte in *Le Monde* before the final balloting; "it is none the less shocking." (*Le Monde*, November 29, 1958)
[30] Same, November 27, 1958.

Marie at his side, but not Edgar Faure or important Radicals of the Left as Mendès-France, Bourgès-Maunoury, and that perennial symbol of classical Radicalism, Édouard Daladier. Rather surprisingly, the leader of the Right-wing Radicals, André Morice, was also defeated. While Pinay and Reynaud won easily, Joseph Laniel, whose government had represented the full bloom of *immobilisme*, was defeated. The two Catholic groups returned to the Assembly Bidault, Pflimlin, and Schuman, but Teitgen, who had served in many coalitions after Liberation, withdrew after the first balloting. The ten Communists elected did not include such familiar names as Jacques Duclos and Jeannette Vermeersch. Altogether, six former premiers were defeated. Only 146 members of the previous National Assembly, under 30 per cent, would be present when the 465 deputies of the new Assembly convened. Some of those who were beaten subsequently returned to Paris to take up positions in the Senate.

These wholesale changes demonstrated the futility, under the single-member system, of relying on local notables to capture votes. The UNR had invaded many fiefs dominated by politicians well known both locally and nationally, and had defeated them. In the absence of national issues it was not, as it turned out, local reputations or parochial interests which determined the results. The electorate usually preferred a newcomer wrapped in the Gaullist mantle to a familiar figure draped in the tattered remnants of the Fourth Republic. By his oft-repeated determination to remain above party—hence above parliamentary divisions— De Gaulle had succeeded in creating a Parliament dominated by nonparliamentarians or even antiparliamentarians. Because the Fourth Republic had been repeatedly equated with parliamentary rule, the emphasis in 1958 was on destroying the old institutions, even more than on building new ones, unless De Gaulle himself be viewed as an institution.[31] However, the revolution against the political customs of the Fourth Republic did not redound to the

[31] Same, November 22, 1958.

benefit of the military candidates. In the competition to flog the dead Fourth Republic, prominent rightists, like Chaban-Delmas and Delbecque, were able to win out over most of the military officers, with the prominent exception of Colonel Thomazo.

The virtual elimination of the Communists would have improved the positions of the Socialists and other groups of the non-Communist Left had they held on to their numerical strength in the Assembly. But in addition to seeing their representation cut to less than half, they were no longer an effective political force; as Mendés-France said, they were "atomized." Having destroyed the Communists as a parliamentary factor, the Right could now concentrate its fire on the Socialists and others of the Center-Left. The Left, particularly the Socialist party, was thus confronted with a difficult decision. It could, on the one hand, attempt to rally behind it all the scattered groups of opposition to the Right, to the UNR, in a word, to Gaullist rule. This was precisely what the Autonomous Socialists and the Union of Left Socialists had advocated in the election, only to suffer political annihilation. Given the reduced power and prestige of the Assembly, the prospect was slight that opposition to De Gaulle would sooner or later attract a large portion of the working class, unless De Gaulle's leadership faltered or the country blundered into a series of castastrophes. On the contrary, as time passed, the power of the Right was more likely to serve as a magnet attracting fragments of the Center-Left, which had traditionally placed ministerial responsibility before doctrinal consistency.

The second alternative open to the Center-Left was scarcely more attractive. It might, for example, take a strong stand against the Right, including the UNR, while also attempting to distinguish between De Gaulle and the party which now dominated the Assembly. This approach would be consistent with Mollet's previous course of action. "While admiring him for the great services he has rendered the country," Mollet declared, "I had, as a democrat, a number of suspicions about the General, whom I did not know personally. But I hoped that, if we remained at his side, he would restore democracy instead of burying it."[32]

Under this tactic, however, the Center-Left would run a serious political risk. Suppose that the French public refused to draw any distinction between President de Gaulle and his followers in the government and in the Assembly. Suppose particularly that they would constantly point to their faithful acceptance of De Gaulle's wishes. Under these circumstances, the attempt to blend support for De Gaulle with opposition to the UNR in the Assembly would catch the Socialists in a crossfire: from those who wanted the non-Communist Left to move all the way to Gaullism, and from those who, now practically without legislative representation, hoped for strong, determined, independent leadership.[33]

The successful UNR also had its problems. It claimed to be a Center grouping. However, Soustelle, its most powerful figure, had his base clearly on the Right, as had been demonstrated in the pre-election conflicts over the endorsement of Right or Center candidates. Furthermore, the Union still claimed it was not a party and would not be forced to become one until the play of the National Assembly began in earnest. For the time being, it was a broad movement, whose leaders did not see eye to eye on strategy or program and whose membership in the Assembly was composed largely of neophytes or political nonentities. When or if the UNR actually did install itself in the parliamentary Center, it would be staking out a traditionally weak position in which, like other Center groups in the past, it might well be divided in its operations even though preserving a semblance of organizational unity. Centrifugal tendencies would be increased by the size and inexperience of the group. The separation of executive and legislative branches under the Fifth Republic would increase the chances of discord within the UNR, since Soustelle, the embodiment of its success, would

[32] Same
[33] Future Socialist tactics were much argued after the election, but the majority agreed with Mollet that a decision should not be made until the normal operation of French institutions had begun.

make his home in the cabinet. Some of the faithful would find themselves deprived of ministerial plums; there were just too few of them to pass around among the many whose only claim to office was their faith in De Gaulle. Because the UNR, though by far the largest group in the Assembly, fell some 45 votes short of a majority, some rewards of office would also have to be reserved, to the "ultra" bloc elected from Algeria.[34]

This is not to say that very many members of the UNR would gravitate toward the Left or even the Center. Rather, they might feel the allure of the Independents, who, more experienced in the distinctions between pre-election behavior and post-election actions, would tend, as before, to form cross-party ties within the Assembly on specific issues. The electoral competition gratuitously provided them by the UNR leadership would only add zest to their activity. Traditionally disorganized themselves, the Independents would not be able to provide unity within the Assembly; rather would they be instigators of further fragmentation.

Another notable upshot of the election was to weaken the bonds which held together the various elements of each of the parties. This was, of course, one objective of De Gaulle and his advisers in devising both the constitution and the electoral system. Old doctrines and old leaderships had been repudiated, alienated or decimated. Even the Radicals, who had stated with traditional and delightful candor that they had no internal party unity but were just individuals, fared badly. And only by abandoning any pretense at Socialist doctrine did Guy Mollet succeed, at least temporarily, in keeping some control over his diminished band. The elections had completed the destruction of that coherence of parties of which the founders of the Fourth Republic had been so proud (and which the enemies of the Fourth Republic detested for that very reason). Perhaps new unifying ties could now be forged, better adapted to the conditions and problems which confronted the Fifth Republic. Party groupings, even party organizations, have demonstrated an unex-

[34] The course elections took in Algeria is discussed in Chapter 18.

pected capacity for survival. On the other hand, the dominance of a leader who does not believe in "factions," and whose "system" has been built of both old and new materials, may well delay for an extended period the reappearance of any vital or viable political formations.

Options for De Gaulle

De Gaulle naturally had wanted a strong representation of his supporters in the National Assembly. He got his wish, pressed down and running over.[85] The General's problem then became how to govern France in circumstances where the Gaullists were too Gaullist, perhaps not loyal enough to the new De Gaulle. The new President had his choice of several courses of action which he could employ singly or in combination. A logical procedure would be to use his personal prestige and the authority of his office, to escape the embrace of his friends as well as the attacks of his enemies. The enhanced power of the presidency would make this possible. De Gaulle could seek deliberately to increase the distance between the presidency and the Cabinet. He could attempt to enforce on his Cabinet the function of carrying out rather than of making policy.[86] Even in the execution of his policy the President could by-pass the Cabinet, employing instead the administrative apparatus which in France had long played a key role in attaining or blocking goals set by the executive. Under this two-way pressure, the Cabinet might become more pliable to De Gaulle's influence. Its responsiveness would be further increased if rifts within the UNR should widen into actual cleavages and if the Premier recruited into his Cabinet representatives of other Right or even Center and Center-Left parties.

Such a course would put in the foreground the authoritarian elements in the Fifth Republic. On the other hand,

[85] An analysis of the first balloting by André Chênebenoît in *Le Monde*, November 25, 1958, was entitled, "When the Bride is too Beautiful."

[86] An important effort in this direction was De Gaulle's long press conference of March 25, 1959, during which he clearly identified himself as responsible for French policies, foreign and domestic.

it might move the Premier and the Cabinet closer to the National Assembly, in search of ways to increase their voice in national policy. Even under De Gaulle, the National Assembly is likely to try to increase its influence or even its control over the Cabinet, as was shown in the rules of procedure originally proposed. Joining of forces by Cabinet and Assembly to enhance the power of each might lessen the effects of divisions within the huge bloc of the UNR. Chief victor in the election, supported by the die-hard bloc from Algeria, and certain of substantial representation in the Cabinet, the UNR might be able to prevent the President from pursuing an independent policy over a protracted period. Notwithstanding constitutional provisions, in a struggle between the President and the Cabinet, it is possible that the latter might ultimately come out on top. In this, the unforeseeable factors of De Gaulle's age and health are relevant.

A second course open to De Gaulle, one consistent with his past behavior, his personality, his age, and probably with his conception of the presidency, would be to continue as the aloof exponent of lofty national themes. Since 1940 the public had looked to De Gaulle to express all-encompassing French aspirations. The images of De Gaulle and "Marianne" had, if possible, become even more closely merged as the result of the campaign. Emphasis on abstractions like "renovation" and "grandeur" enhanced the prestige, and therefore the political power, of the President.

Abstractions often contain or conceal certain dangers. As friends and critics alike were quick to point out before and after June 1958, De Gaulle deliberately delayed in defining specific measures for France, either in Algeria or in its foreign policy. Many problems pressed for decision, and continuing postponement would be increasingly difficult. Once De Gaulle had stated his intentions on controversial subjects, he risked losing his above-the-battle aura. He might indeed become the captive of those Right-wing groups, especially in the UNR, which in his name had been busy assigning concrete meaning to national aspirations: as, for example, French Algeria (integration), military power (perhaps militarism), economic "liberalism" (conservatism), and economic protectionism (within the Common Market). "With the best intentions in the world," wrote André Chênebenoît, "France runs the risk of being dragged into a crisis of nationalism such as it has not known, even under rightist majorities, for more than a century."[87]

That De Gaulle would thus bow to the extreme Right was possible. But it seemed more likely that he would accept the necessity for making urgent and difficult decisions and "descend" into the embattled arena of policy. He would then have to bring to bear the full authority of his office and his person to impose on the Right solutions which he felt met the realities and needs of France best, as in the case of Algeria. At the same time he might bolster up the Right by satisfying it on other issues, such as nuclear power and economic policy, which involved less risk to the national position.

The ultimate success of De Gaulle's political system will depend not only on strengthening the capacity of France to make decisions but also on enlarging the limits of tolerance. If stable institutions of government have really been erected, they will gather strength from widening the permitted area of dissent. Recurrent experiences with authoritarian rule have amply demonstrated the ability of French democracy to survive many experiments. Weakened in the last years of the Fourth Republic, its foundations were temporarily buried by the crisis of May 1958 and its aftermath. If the democratic tradition should be persistently flouted, however, a counterattack might sweep the Fifth Republic into the discard along with other authoritarian experiments. Elements powerful within the Fifth Republic have proposed regressive policies in Algerian, European, and domestic affairs—policies which are beyond France's long-term capacities, which would disrupt the country's internal unity and damage its newly won international prestige. On the other hand, by giving more latitude to democratic and progressive forces in France, De Gaulle can channel them toward the

[87] Same.

changes necessary to make the Fifth Republic more than a transitory constitutional phenomenon. There were many who hoped General de Gaulle would recognize the need to protect the right of opposition and dissent as the very life blood of a Western society, of which France is a pivotal member.

Chapter Seventeen

ECONOMIC AND SOCIAL PROBLEMS OF THE FIFTH REPUBLIC

DE GAULLE'S GOVERNMENT inherited the critical economic and social problems which the Fourth Republic had left unsolved. France's position was further weakened by the hiatus of power which lasted for seven weeks between the fall of Gaillard and the entry of General de Gaulle. That conditions in June were not worse than they were was a tribute to the basic soundness of the French economy. The price of gold had risen in the two months, but gold sales had not increased proportionately. There had been little panic-buying in the stores. The internal price level remained fairly stable, although the foreign-trade deficit, growing every month, reached 30 billion francs in May, the highest since April 1957.[1] Postponed national decisions included promulgation of the 1958 budget, still incomplete five months after the beginning of the fiscal year; flotation of the public loan planned by Gaillard; and satisfaction of wage demands, particularly in the nationalized electric and gas industries.

Emergency Economic Measures

De Gaulle's pattern of action was determined by the need to cope with the immediate emergency while at the same time planning long-range reforms to strengthen the economy. In his investiture address, though in all probability

[1] *Le Monde*, June 1-2, 1958, *New York Times*, June 13, 21, 1958.

referring to political institutions, the new Premier used words applicable to economic and social affairs as well: ". . . What good would be a temporary remedy, a remedy of sorts, for a disastrous state of affairs unless we decided to eradicate the deep-seated cause of our troubles? This cause —the Assembly knows and the nation is convinced of it—is the confusion and, by the same token, the helplessness of constituted authority." To restore authority De Gaulle asked for full powers. To restore confidence in that authority he appointed Antoine Pinay Minister of Finance and Economic Affairs. The Independent leader had played an important role in De Gaulle's return, and in the public mind his 1952 government was still associated with one of the few postwar periods of price stability. A small industrialist and one-time deputy to Pétain's National Council, Pinay enjoyed the confidence of French producers despite his policy, as premier, of exhorting businessmen to lower prices.

The national loan put Pinay's and De Gaulle's prestige to an immediate test. Launched on June 13, the loan was pegged to gold and carried an interest rate of 3.5 per cent, tax free. As was customary, holders of older government bonds could convert them to the new issue.[2] Within a week Pinay could acclaim the loan's success. Ninety-eight per cent of the subscriptions were in cash; 34 tons of gold (80 billion francs) had been brought out of hiding to bolster reserves and help meet foreign-trade deficits.

Coincident with preparations for the loan, Pinay took drastic action to balance foreign-trade accounts. Requests for import licenses were examined "one by one," and the OEEC was notified that France intended to reduce its imports for the second third of 1958 by 100 billion francs.[3] The effects of the restrictions were quickly felt. French exports in August covered 78 per cent of imports, in September

[2] The government reportedly considered terms less favorable than those planned by Gaillard but decided the psychological requirement of an overwhelming public response was too important to take the risk.

[3] *Le Monde*, June 1-2, 1958.

80 per cent.[4] By that time the government felt confident that the immediate crisis in the balance of payments had been surmounted.

In an effort to maintain price stability, the government persuaded manufacturers to lower their prices by 3 to 5 per cent on various consumers' items, such as nylon goods and electrical household appliances. Farmers were next in line. In 1957 the government, bowing to agricultural pressure, had announced that suggested prices would be established annually, in light of contemporary conditions and price objectives for 1961. Now, when the proposed prices for 1959 were published in the *Journal Officiel* in October 1958, agricultural organizations protested vigorously, asserting that in most instances prices were appreciably lower than those they had recommended. They added the familiar complaint that sacrifices exacted from farmers were not reflected in lower retail prices paid by consumers, but merely enlarged the profits of middlemen.[5]

De Gaulle's government rapidly completed the missing portions of the budget by decree. Pending more complete fiscal measures, it imposed emergency taxes to hold the 1958 deficit near the level promised when France obtained its foreign loan late in 1957. Some old targets—gasoline and luxury items, including yachts, race horses, high-rent apartments, phonograph records, and distilled spirits—were hit again. In addition levies were raised on corporate profits and business transactions.

The "Truth and Austerity" Program of December 1958

These and other stop-gap measures enabled De Gaulle's government to concentrate on creating new political institutions and gaining popular acceptance for them. But economic reforms as radical as the political changes could no longer be held in abeyance. Shortly after becoming Finance Minister, Pinay asked his friend and fellow Independent Jacques Rueff to study France's financial position, and later

[4] Same, October 22, 1958.
[5] Same, October 16, 18, 1958.

requested him to submit recommendations for action. A member of the Court of Justice of the Coal-Steel Community and widely known as an advocate of conservative fiscal policies, Rueff had assisted Premiers Poincaré and Laval in their financial reorganizations and had served as a prewar adviser to the governments of Bulgaria and Greece. For his new assignment Rueff assembled a small group whose most prominent members held orthodox economic views compatible with his own.

The Rueff Report was prepared in great secrecy and then subjected to close scrutiny by the government. Announcing the results of its deliberations to the nation, De Gaulle said, on December 28, 1958:

We have adopted and shall put into effect tomorrow a complete program of financial, economic, and social measures that places the nation on a foundation of truth and austerity, which is the only foundation on which it can build its prosperity. I make no secret of the fact that for some time our country will be put to the test, but the recovery at which we are aiming is such that it can repay us for everything.

The measures which he then summarized emerged in the next weeks as a veritable flood of ordinances. They had reached a total of more than 250 before Debré, early in February 1959, brought a sigh of relief from the public with his announcement that no further steps were contemplated in the next two months.[6]

De Gaulle's "New Look" economic program had four parts. (1) Quantitative restrictions were removed on 90 per cent of French imports from OEEC countries (based on 1948 levels). (2) The franc was devalued by 17.55 per cent (to 493.7 per dollar) and made convertible when held by people living abroad. (3) Taxes were raised on corporate profits from 42 to 50 per cent; on tobacco, alcohol, wine, and distilled spirits by between 20 and 100 per cent. Reform, simplification, and reimposition of taxes resulted in higher levies on a variety of raw materials and manufactured products, including coal, gas and electricity, and household ap-

[6] Same, February 4, 1959

pliances. (4) Taxes on personal incomes at all levels were raised, and attempts were made to stiffen enforcement by comparing declared incomes with "exterior signs of wealth." The additional yield from increased taxes was estimated at 313 billion francs.

To cut down national expenditures, a number of subsidies were abolished or reduced. War veterans under sixty-five, and less than 50 per cent disabled, lost their pensions. Medical insurance and reimbursement for expenditures for medicines were cut. Price supports for bread, rice, chocolate, preserves, and noodles were eliminated, as was the Paris milk subsidy. State aid to the railroads, the coal and electric industries, and the Paris Métro system was reduced or ended. In this manner about 250 billion francs were cut from the budget. The saving, however, was offset by an increase of 245 billions in state investments.[7]

Criticism of the new austerity program centered both on procedure and on content. Decrees were promulgated so fast that the newspapers, let alone the general public, could not keep pace. UDSR leader René Pleven complained that, "In giving the government the right to promulgate the budget for 1959 and to legislate for several months, the people have not freed the Council of Ministers of the obligation of informing them, of telling them the reasons for its decisions and its choices. . . ."[8] Is this the way, asked André Chênebenoît in *Le Monde,* to gain the public acceptance which is necessary for the success of the new program?

The main complaint was based on the belief that the brunt of the new economic program would fall on consumers in general, and particularly on the lowest income groups: salaried employees, laborers, and farmers. Consumers' incomes, it was estimated, would be reduced by 95 billion francs, and retail prices would rise by about 265 billion. These changes, taken together, implied a reduction

[7] *New York Times,* December 29, 1958, and *New York Herald-Tribune* (Paris edition), January 15, 1959, provided concise summaries of the economic measures and their estimated effect on the 1959 budget.
[8] *Le Monde,* January 11-12, 1959.

in over-all consumption by about 2.3 per cent. But this was not all. A third category of measures, including added charges for energy resources, postal rates, transport, social welfare, and imports, would raise costs of production between 450-500 billion francs, causing consumption to fall in the long run by another 1.3 to 2 per cent.[9] Frenchmen with the lowest incomes would naturally suffer most from increased prices. While the minimum wage was raised (government employees were given an extra 4 per cent), the gain would not be enough to offset the rising cost of living. Critics claimed that changes in the tax structure would reduce the total burden on industrialists, despite the increase in taxes on corporate profits, while farmers would have to pay an extra 30 to 100 billion francs.[10]

The diminished and divided Left could hardly be happy about the economic measures of the De Gaulle-Debré government. "Often it has been said and repeated that this severity was courageous," wrote Mendès-France. "It would have been more courageous if the severity had not been reserved for the weak alone. . . . The measures which have just been taken in the economic, financial, and social fields are, in their perfect consistency, the most reactionary that the French people have had to undergo since the Laval government of 1935."[11]

In the cabinet deliberations which preceded the public announcement of De Gaulle's economic program, both Mollet and Pflimlin had argued against the recommendations of the Rueff Report. For Pflimlin the pill was not too bitter, despite the added burdens laid on families and farmers. While protesting, the MRP leader remained in De Gaulle's Cabinet, and his party did not oppose participation in Debré's government. However, De Gaulle's conception of austerity was more than Mollet could swallow.

---

[9] See analysis of Gilbert Mathieu, *Le Monde*, January 18-19, 1959.

[10] *Express*, January 1, 1959; *Le Monde*, January 7, 1959. The point is not the accuracy or inaccuracy of the analyses, rather the composition of the critical groups.

[11] *Cahiers de la République*, January-February 1959, pp. 5, 3.

Having helped negotiate the accession of De Gaulle, having beaten back Socialist criticism of his participation in the government, Mollet now boggled at the economic corollary of Right-wing politics. He resigned on December 27, 1958, but, by agreeing not to publicize the fact until Debré had been designated Premier, he negated any effect his last-minute gesture might have had. At the Socialist congress in January 1959, which voted an extensive denunciation of the economic program, Mollet, under heavy attack, declared his willingness to leave the party direction to someone else, provided no common front was made with the Communists and Socialist policy (whatever that was) remained the same. At the annual congress in July economic issues were subordinated to criticism of France's Algerian policy, a shift in targets which may have aided Mollet's reelection to the party's executive committee, albeit by a diminished majority.

Overt labor opposition was limited by a number of factors. Leveling off of production was causing fear of unemployment, or at least of a shortened work week. Direct action in the form of strikes might be dangerously ineffective, whereas quiet negotiations with employers might produce improved wage and hour agreements. There was also the traditional tendency of the workers to seek security rather than economic gains. This frame of mind made it difficult for their leaders to arouse local unions before the full impact of the new program was felt in higher prices and a reduced standard of living. Even then, there was doubt as to the efficacy of techniques available. Neither the Force Ouvrière nor the Christian trade-unions wanted to leave the field wide-open for the Communist CGT to monopolize; on the other hand, they did not want to ally themselves openly, on the national level, with the Communists. Political action, for the time being, seemed equally fruitless; the new regime enjoyed far greater powers than had the Fourth Republic and was confronted with practically no opposition in the National Assembly. This was amply demonstrated when railroad workers in June,

1959 called off their strike after Debré's government prepared to draft the strikers.

De Gaulle had planned his austerity program to prove that, with the proper policies energetically and consistently enforced, France could continue to fight the war in Algeria, embark on an ambitious program of assistance to that territory, discharge its other heavy economic responsibilities overseas, submit to international competition within the Common Market, and resume its rapid progress in productivity, all without bankrupting the country or destroying popular support for his regime. His success depended on his winning several bets. One was that the general price rise would be slow in coming and when it had run its course would not exceed 5 to 7 per cent.[12] Another was that, with exports stimulated and imports discouraged by currency devaluation, the foreign-trade accounts would be balanced, and would stay balanced. A third was that the upward movement of national production would be quickly renewed as the result of increased investments by the state, by private funds in France, by French funds repatriated after their flight from the franc, and by foreign capital.

Two implicit assumptions made the odds more favorable. De Gaulle counted on his great prestige to bring most Frenchmen to accept the sacrifices imposed on them, and on the power of the government to overcome any efforts at disruption. Besides, there was always the chance that peace might suddenly come in Algeria, through victory or negotiation, setting free the major part of the 900 billion francs which France was spending each year on military operations there.

Unfinished Economic Business

Comprehensive as were the decrees issued in December 1958 and January 1959, they could be regarded as only the prelude to reform of French economic institutions. Although no legislative action took place before the National

[12] In mid-1959 it was estimated that internal French prices had risen about 4 per cent over-all.

Assembly adjourned in the summer of 1959, a beginning had been made on tax reform with recommendations by a committee for governmental action. The heart of the matter was how to deal with the habitual deceptions of the French taxpayer. The experts, said Giscard d'Estaing, Secretary of State for Finance, would have to take into account the social and psychological characteristics peculiar to France in the choice of a system which would insure both justice and simplicity.[13] A tax system which was just because it prevented evasion was not likely to be simple, while one which was both simple and effectively enforced might handicap economic expansion.

Expanded production depended in part on renewed efforts to decentralize and coordinate economic activity. While there was an increasing number of regional programs, their effective implementation depended on devolving on regional authorities responsibilities long scattered among executive agencies in Paris. Moreover, coordination of regional plans was still needed to provide an internally consistent basis for national action. Through division of authority, emphasizing greater autonomy of various French regions in planning and executing economic programs, great political benefits might ultimately accrue as more French citizens became involved in the creation and operation of local agencies responsive to local needs.[14]

A related aspect of economic coordination involved setting up some formal association among private groups to develop a broad consensus in support of national policy. Abandoning his early ideas of a parliamentary body organized along corporate lines, De Gaulle viewed the new Economic and Social Council as at least partially filling this need. The President of the old Economic Council, Émile Roche, wrote that politics must have the "means to control economics without in any way running the risk of obstructing its development. The primary principle is

[13] *Le Monde*, February 11, 1959.
[14] The importance of local political action has previously been stressed. See p. 134.

therefore that economics shall not constitute a power [in itself]. The only power is political power. But economic forces exist, and their increasing pressure carries the danger that political power may become only an illusion, either because it neglects those forces, not perceiving that left to themselves they soon make of events a blind, disorganized, cruel game, or because it leaves to technocrats not responsible to the people the job of directing them."[15]

When out of power, De Gaulle had urged closer relations between management and labor, discouraged neither by the failures encountered in this area by the Fourth Republic nor by the hostility of workers and coolness of employers to the idea.[16] Almost overlooked in the austerity decrees was one establishing norms for management-labor contracts, both industry-wide and on an individual-plant basis. Such agreements, limited on the employee side to "representative" (i.e., non-Communist) unions, could provide for fringe benefits in the form of stock, bonuses for unusually high productivity, or profit-sharing. Incentive to profit-sharing was provided through tax favors to both employers and workers.

Also on the roster of unfinished business was an attack on France's archaic system of wholesale and retail distribution. Between producers and consumers stretched a long line of middlemen—processors, transporters, and shopkeepers—always prepared to band together to gain protection under the Fourth Republic and ready to resist openly when that protection was not granted. If the austerity program of the Fifth Republic were to succeed, prices had to be kept down. The principal weapon against inflation was fiscal policy. But something could be accomplished by the reform of distribution practices. In imposing price ceilings, the government could give encouragement to the more efficient

[15] Émile Roche, "Le Conseil Économique Français," *Revue Politique et Parlementaire*, August-September 1958, p. 163.
[16] Excerpts from De Gaulle's speeches on this subject may be found in *La France Sera la France* (Paris: Rassemblement du Peuple Français, 1952), pp. 120-134.

processing and marketing enterprises. The fire which in August 1959 broke out in Les Halles of Paris was a providential assistance to government efforts to destroy this uneconomic, monopolistic, anachronistic network. If it succeeded, the government would demonstrate that, while imposing heavy sacrifices on the French people, it was attempting to ensure that they need not be needlessly burdensome.

Programs of Economic Expansion

At the same time that the government was requiring the French people to consume less, it hoped they would produce more. To that end, as has been noted, it increased state investments, even though the probable consequence was increased budgetary deficits. On February 3, 1959, the Economic and Social Council overwhelmingly approved the Third Four-Year Plan of Modernization and Equipment to cover the years 1958 through 1961. Its terms were almost identical with those set a year earlier, except for the addition of a section based on the Constantine program for Algerian development. In the Council, representatives of the CGT and CFTC opposed the plan, claiming that it was based on two false assumptions—that there would be no economic recession and that military costs would be reduced to 1954 levels. In the end, however, both organizations, together with representatives of independent unions, abstained from voting, leaving the agricultural interests as the only opposition of record.[17]

The Third Plan envisaged national production rising by 1961 to levels 25 per cent above 1956—20 per cent in the case of agriculture, 30 to 35 per cent in industry. To promote this expansion, state investments in the following

[17] *Le Monde*, January 30, February 5, 1957. "Don't say the plan must be modified," pleaded Étienne Hirsch to the labor representatives. "Say rather the plan should be applied through compatible government policy." Hirsch was succeeded as Director of the Plan by Pierre Massé, previously associated with the Monnet Plan, the direction of the nationalized electrical industry, and the committee planning the utilization of the gas of the Lacq area.

amounts would be needed: 4,135 billions in 1959; 4,370 in 1960; and 4,570 in 1961. Of the 17,018 billion total for the four years 1958 through 1961, 3,420 billions would go to housing, 2,470 to sources of energy, 1,870 to agriculture and fishing, 1,490 to processing industries. Of all the production goals, those for energy sources were probably crucial. For coal the objective was 62 million tons in 1961, 65 million in 1965, as compared to 58 million produced in 1956. By 1961, it was hoped that refineries would be handling 43 million tons of oil, 54 millions in 1965. Gas production, including 20 million cubic meters from Lacq in 1961, should be 30 million in 1965, triple the 1956 output. Electrical production by 1965 should be enough to satisfy the estimated domestic needs of 104 billion kilowatts.[18]

Ambitious as was the projected expansion of energy sources, there was a strong possibility that it was not ambitious enough, considering probable increases in French population and in national income. Paul Maquenne, for example, has forecast not a diminishing but an expanding deficit in the production of energy:

FRANCE'S PROJECTED ENERGY NEEDS IN 1961, 1965, AND 1975[19]

	1961	1965	1975
(Figures in millions of tons of coal equivalent)			
Estimated Consumption	144	155[a]	220
Estimated Production	87.7	105.2	158
Deficit	56.3	49.8[a]	62

[a] An alternate forecast was for 171 million tons in 1965, which would increase the energy deficit to 65.8.

While each source of energy had its own problems, their common denominator was the need for greater capital investment. With regard to coal the depressing prospect was that additional funds were destined to produce a declining yield per franc. The hopes that Saharan oil, added to existing resources, would satisfy 90 per cent of domestic oil requirements by 1965 appeared to depend on achieving a

[18] *Le Monde*, January 30, 1959.
[19] Paul Maquenne, "Le Problème Énergétique Français dans le Cadre du Marché Commun," *Revue Politique et Parlementaire*, August-September 1958, p. 111.

level of investment even higher than the 604 billion francs projected in the Third Plan. The estimated cost of the Lacq gas program, only one of several regional plans, was 115 billion francs, including housing construction as well as pipelines to Lyons and thence to Paris.[20]

In electric power the need for additional investment was equally acute. France has long been electricity-poor. Its per capita consumption lags behind that of Norway, Belgium, Germany, Great Britain, and Switzerland. This was one reason why France so readily accepted membership in Euratom. But atomic power in substantial quantities is still far off. By 1965 a mere 5 per cent of French electric current is expected to come from atomic plants, and the rapid expansion planned for the ensuing decade would raise the percentage to only 25 per cent. Thus even in 1975 France would still be relying mostly on "conventional" sources of electricity. Annual investments of 191 billion francs for power production under traditional methods are regarded by Maquenne as far below the level required to meet French needs; the billion francs planned for annual investment in atomic energy through 1961 are also inadequate.[21]

Forecasts of capital requirements matched against estimated state investment reinforce the conclusion that the economic fortunes of the Fifth Republic depend on its ability to convince investors of various types—Frenchmen, private foreign groups, and foreign governments—that the often promised national rejuvenation is finally at hand. Upon this conviction depends French and foreign willingness to bridge the gap between the demand for capital and the supply now available. De Gaulle and Debré have deliberately framed their economic program to appeal to financial interests in France and abroad. Prosperity at the top will eventually, it is hoped, "trickle down" to the masses at the bottom. While waiting, the lower groups may reflect on the meaning of "grandeur," for which they had placidly witnessed the destruction of the Fourth Republic.

[20] Same, pp. 107-161; André Blanchard, "Le Gaz du Lacq," *France-Amérique*, nos. 7-9, 1958, pp. 94-95.
[21] Maquenne, cited, pp. 140, 151, 137, 139, 142.

Social Issues Facing the Fifth Republic

Frenchmen may also ponder the social implications of economic choices which have been made for them by their new leader. If they did not like "truth and austerity," the chances are they will not care for Gaullist social policies either. In neither case will they have at hand effective devices to secure modifications. It is true that the Cabinet's recognition of their social implications watered down somewhat the pristine purity of the Rueff Committee's original recommendations before they emerged as individual decrees. Notable among the deviations were the retention of some price controls, the maintenance of old-age assistance levels, and an advance in civil-service salaries. After the flood of decrees had ceased, some further modifications were made. Taxpayers were assured that the club labeled "external signs of wealth" would not be wielded as vigorously as had at first appeared. Previous levels for social security contributions were reinstated so that modern concerns paying higher wages would not be further penalized, as against those paying low wages. Some increases were made in allotments to lowest-income families and rebates in purchases of medicines. All these amendments were modest and, with the possible exception of continuing some of the price controls, they did not basically alter the orthodox philosophy which so strongly underlay the work of the Rueff Committee.

More important in the field of social relations is De Gaulle's decision to hold down wages by eliminating any legal connection between them and the cost of living. Unless employers connive with workers to raise real wages through extra hours or special benefits, or unless unions can somehow change governmental policy, workers are likely to see their standard of living fall further and faster than that of other groups. They may then recall the way in which latter-day governments of the Fourth Republic manipulated the official price index so that automatic pay rises could be avoided, and they will certainly regret their self-denial in postponing wage demands during the last weeks of the Fourth Republic and again during the first weeks of De Gaulle's regime. In the face of mounting local foci of resentment, Catholic and Socialist national federations may be unable, even if they so wish, to continue holding back their members from direct action. Ultimately the effects of an increasing gap between wages and prices may go beyond isolated strikes, social unrest, and growing attraction to Communist-dominated unionism. Having taken away with one hand, the government will be under heavy pressure to give back with the other, in the form of more social assistance to working families, for whom such aid provides a substantial portion, sometimes even the bulk, of their income.

Labor-management relations encompass more than pay scales. In 1958 a survey found that the worker was inclined to relate his wages to his social position: "Many of the men we interviewed look upon the 'collective promotion' of French workers as a battle in which wage demands are only one stepping-stone on the path to a much broader goal: the conquest of equal rights and equal consideration for everyone." Workers, the survey concluded, want most of all to be understood; labor-management relations must therefore be viewed as one aspect of human relations.[22]

To reduce social tensions, De Gaulle has counted heavily on his plan for labor-management "association." It is unlikely, however, that any sudden change will occur in the mutually hostile attitudes of workers and employers. More pressure is needed if employers are to modify their frequently antediluvian labor practices. Instruments for state action are available, but have been rusting away from disuse. Although in France the state has always played a large part in what passes for collective bargaining, it has neglected the social in favor of the legal implications of its role. The large investment of state funds in French industries may make possible a more effective national code of fair-employment standards. Moreover, official recognition

[22] Georges Rotvand, "What the French Worker Thinks Today," *Réalités*, October 1958, pp. 15-19.

and endorsement can be accorded to progressive elements in employers' organizations. Such gestures may have more than a propaganda value, for De Gaulle's economic policy greatly increases the potential influence of the modern industrial Right.

Housing is another problem in the field of human relations which was left unsolved by the Fourth Republic. The living quarters of Algerian workers at a site four miles from Paris, appropriately named Bidonville ("tin can town"), have been described as follows: "Roofs leak, there are no windows, few stores. Baking is done on a fire of twigs built on the earth or stone floor. Bidonville has no streets and is devoid of sanitary provisions. Virtually all the children and adults have tuberculosis and suffer from malnutrition."[23] Algerians, to be sure, represent an oppressed class, in the sub-basement of the social and economic scale. But their housing conditions have attracted scarcely any notice in France because they differ only in degree from those of Parisians living in squalor within sight of newly built and partially empty luxury apartments.

Pierre Sudreau, Minister of Construction in De Gaulle's and Debré's governments, has stated the Fifth Republic's housing goals in these terms: "I hope eventually to make it possible for a French workman without capital to buy his own home. At that moment the problem of communism will be settled in France."[24] But the 1959 budget did not provide housing funds sufficient to compensate for anticipated increases in costs of current programs, let alone, to progress toward satisfying future French needs. In fact, Sudreau lowered his sights significantly in February 1959, when he announced an increase in government loans *so that the existing, inadequate level of building activity would not decline.* He insisted that more attention should be paid to the upkeep of the "13 million dwellings existing in France. Why continue to build 300,000 dwellings an-

[23] Mrs. Lenore Sorin, Associate Executive Director of the Foster Parent Plan, quoted in *New York Times,* June 15, 1958.
[24] *New York Times,* October 26, 1958.

nually if at the same time we allow our patrimony to deteriorate, to be destroyed?"[25]

The answer is that private funds are lacking to prevent the deterioration of existing housing accommodations, except those occupied by a few well-to-do families. In order to carry through an adequate housing program, the government's efforts must go beyond the provision of capital funds. Additional measures should include the assignment to regional authorities of responsibility for supervising housing design and construction, a responsibility now centralized—or ossified—in Paris. Construction of luxury apartments could be further discouraged by increasing taxes, already high, on this type of housing. Building codes, antiquated and ineffective, could be redrawn to give tenants better value for their money. Special incentives could be offered to manufacturers of standardized building materials. Industries could receive more encouragement and certainly more supervision in housing programs for their employees. If some, or all, of these steps were successful, then rent ceilings could be raised commensurate with improvements in existing structures. Finally, as part of any housing reform, the government should cease to wink at open collusion between owner and tenant in evading present laws.

French housing cannot quickly be made adequate in either quantity or quality. Even optimists have pushed forward to the year 2000 the date on which Frenchmen may finally be housed in acceptable conditions. Fortunately for De Gaulle's government, his countrymen are accustomed to grandiose promises followed by meager performance and accept miserable physical surroundings as a permanent feature of their daily lives. Prompt and total solutions are not expected. If the Fifth Republic can produce evidence—thus far lacking—that it is determined to make real progress in housing, it may offset somewhat the other effects of its economic policies on low-income groups. As Sudreau suggested, communism appeals most strongly to those who have no real stake in the fortunes of France.

[25] *Le Monde,* February 7, 1959.

The postwar years had witnessed no fewer than six reports on the reform of French education before the Gaullist program appeared at the end of 1958. In striking contrast to the economic innovations, it was so modest, when it appeared, as to be labeled by the opposition *Express* "the illusion of reform."[26] Its principal features are not scheduled to take effect until 1960. Compulsory education is to be extended to age sixteen (instead of seventeen or eighteen as some previous studies had advocated), and this change is only to be enforced after 1966. The heart of the reform is the postponement from eleven to thirteen of the age at which a child must choose between a terminal course of study and a curriculum leading to a higher education. During these two years students' aptitudes are to be tested and parents advised on the type of education their children should subsequently pursue. As earlier reports have pointed out, this postponement will remove two obstacles to broadening the educational base: the inadequate background of many children when the age of "decision" is reached, and the tendency of parents to cut off their children's education at too early an age in order to add their wages to the family budget.

The government's prompt adoption of the new educational reform program was partly motivated by the fact that, at least until 1967, it will add little to the cost of state aid to education. Still left untouched is the need for more classrooms, more teachers, and more equipment. So long as the postwar baby boom continues, the pressure on educational facilities at all levels will persist. Teaching standards and equipment in the provinces have deteriorated since World War II, while the concentration of population in Paris and its suburbs has raised the cost of education and increased the number of pupils per teacher.[27] This deplorable condition, as exemplified in the Catholic Schools, was in large part responsible for the reinjection into French

[26] *Express*, January 1, 1959.
[27] *Le Monde*, February 4, 1959, reporting Institut National de la Statistique et des Études Économiques, *Coût et Développement de l'Enseignement en France.*

politics in 1959 of the question of greater state assistance to religious schools.

Higher education in France has failed to provide the amount and range of scientific and technical training needed in a modernized, industrial economy. "Two years are required for a French research organization to adapt itself to a new scientific event," reported the Mouvement National pour le Développement Scientifique (MNDS), created in 1957 by professors of the faculties of science.[28] "Scientific research in France," wrote Henri Laugier one-time director of the Centre National de la Recherche Scientifique, "suffers from two maladies: an insufficiency of available funds . . . and a complete anarchy of structures."[29]

Remedies for high costs and backward methods can be found if the central government will relax its paralyzing hold on education. While continuing to set national standards for educational performance and assuming the major financial burden, Paris might still permit more initiative and entrust more responsibility to local authorities and directly to the educational institutions. Under central supervision, but not dictation, curricula at various levels could be revised and coordinated. Faculties of science and engineering, if granted the autonomy recommended by MNDS, could solicit private funds and purchase needed equipment directly. The devolution of educational responsibility would seem a logical accompaniment to efforts to create administrative, economic, and political vitality within the various regions of France.

Asked by Georges Rotvand and his fellow interviewers to name the most shocking injustice in French society, workers pointed to the "impossibility for a French worker to educate his children according to their abilities."[30] Faith in the future of a nation includes belief that succeeding generations will have a chance to move upward in the social, as well as the economic scale. The aim of educational and other social, economic, and political reforms, declares

[28] *Le Monde*, October 18, 1958.
[29] Same, October 19-20, 1958.
[30] Rotvand, cited, p. 17.

Georges Lavau, is "to break the profoundly authoritarian, Napoleonic, Louis-Quatorzième nature of French society . . . to develop national unity by breaking open cultural and social compartments and to take from central political organizations—notably the government—control of the means of education and information of the citizens."[31]

The Fifth Republic's approach to France's economic and social problems is no less important than its political orientation. Both are cut from the same semiauthoritarian pattern. Both rest heavily on the support accorded by a greatly augmented Right, on divisions and uncertainties within the shrunken Left, and on the initial personal popularity of General de Gaulle among almost all Frenchmen. While it has been relatively easy to promulgate economic decrees designed to restore fiscal solvency, it is not going to be so simple to bring into continuing harmony entrenched and conflicting social and economic groups. To do this, more than special powers and charismatic leadership will be required. What is needed is to instil in Frenchmen a confidence that the new regime, given time, can cope with situations which were beyond the desire or capacity of the Fourth Republic to handle, a confidence that the objectives sought will strengthen social justice at home as well as build national power sufficient to command respect abroad.

---

[31] Georges Lavau, "La Réforme des Institutions," *Esprit*, September 1958, p. 239.

Chapter Eighteen

ALGERIA: PROBLEMS AND PROSPECTS

ALGERIA HOLDS the key to the success of the French Community, indeed to France's own future. From Algeria the band of civilian and military conspirators opened the route to power for General de Gaulle. Yet, in assuming power De Gaulle succeeded for a time in making a dangerously hardened situation somewhat more malleable. Temporarily bitter contestants drew together in support of the new leader, united by the prospect of his being able to find a solution to the tragic conflict.

Prerequisites to an Algerian Solution

After as before De Gaulle's coming to power, there was, however, no agreement on the nature of a possible settlement. As a result, De Gaulle's purpose, necessarily, was to maneuver each of the divergent groups into a position where it would eventually accept a solution proposed by him. This meant that he could not reveal his plans too far in advance. He had to remain vague and uncommitted so that each group could read into his pronouncements its own ideas. Vagueness was no substitute for decision, but it could buy the time to perform certain tasks prerequisite to a settlement. First, the Committees of Public Safety, nuclei of defiance, had to be both weakened and committed to De Gaulle's path. Second, the French army in Algeria had to be returned to its professional role. Third, Algerians, both Moslems and Europeans, had to endorse the Fifth

Republic. Fourth, the political and military directorates of the Algerian nationalist movement had to be neutralized if they could not be won over. Fifth, Bourguiba's government in Tunisia had to be extricated from its involvement with the nationalist Algerian military effort, if not from the political future of Algeria, as yet undefined. Sixth, within Metropolitan France De Gaulle had to renew his authority by winning popular support for his Fifth Republic.

The General found an early opportunity to begin the separation of the army in Algeria from civilian agitators when, on June 10, 1958, he received a lengthy telegram drafted by the Algeria-Sahara Committee of Public Safety and transmitted by General Salan. The Committee, jointly headed by General Massu and Sid Cara, declared itself for integration with France—hardly a surprise. It then openly demanded for the first time the abrogation of the *loi-cadre*, passed but never implemented by the Fourth Republic. Thus the groups represented by the Committee returned to their prerevolt opposition to a single electoral college for Algeria and also to any administrative autonomy for sections of Algeria. Through its bald assertions the telegram attempted to identify De Gaulle with this position: the members of the Committee "are happy to have been able to obtain the promise of total, unreserved integration of Algeria with the *Métropole*." The second theme of the telegram was the familiar attack on political parties: "Instruments of particular interest, [they are] factors of division and . . . it is vital that they disappear if all Frenchmen are to be united and regrouped around the living realities of general interest, which are the family environment, the profession, the commune, the province, and the country."[1]

De Gaulle could not ignore this double-barreled attack, the group which had started it, or General Salan, who had abetted it. The Premier had been most careful *not* to take a stand for integration, and had made no "promise." Moreover, he had already accomplished the not-inconsiderable

---

[1] The full text of the telegram in *Le Monde*, June 11, 1958.

feat of winning most political groups within France to his cause—their representatives sat in his Cabinet. Unless he now wished to become a revolutionary leader, he could not force the parties to "disappear" in favor of a monolithic movement reminiscent of fascism.

Two days after the dispatch of the telegram De Gaulle called Salan and the Committee to order. His reply read:

On the subject of the offensive and untimely incident caused by the peremptory motion of the Algiers Committee of Public Safety,[2] I remind you [Salan] that this Committee has no other right and no other role than to express *under your control* the opinion of its members. The regular authority, and first of all yourself, should not be a party to any matter which this Committee or any other *political* organization may express or demand. Moreover, there is reason to make interested persons understand that the national task I have undertaken with my government demands calmness of spirit and open and reasoned support of all those who wish to aid me in preserving national unity, integrity, and independence.[3]

De Gaulle's firm answer permitted him to continue his effort to subdue the more intractable elements among the Europeans in Algeria. Between June 12 and September 29, when the referendum was held, he accomplished much in this direction. On June 20 only Salan's personal intervention prevented the Committee from sending another telegram defying De Gaulle. In August De Gaulle was received coolly in Algiers because of what he had said in Brazzaville about the right of overseas areas to change their status within the French Commonwealth. But by September the Committee was in almost total eclipse, its proposals for mass demonstrations vetoed by the army; and the referendum showed that it could not compete with De Gaulle for popular favor. When the Premier spoke at Constantine after the referendum, his reference to Algeria's "personality" so angered the members of the local Committee of Public Safety that they left midway through the speech, vainly seeking permission from the parent committee to

[2] It was actually the coordinating Committee for all Algeria and Sahara.
[3] *Le Monde*, June 12, 1958; italics added.

organize demonstrations. The audience's disapproval was limited to keeping silent when De Gaulle, as was his custom, ended his speech with "La Marseillaise." He sang the stirring anthem all alone, "with a firm voice—the lonely, somewhat paunchy, tremendously impressive figure of an elderly man in a beige uniform."[4]

De Gaulle re-established control of the army through several devices. He restored the funds cut from the military budget by the Fourth Republic.[5] Military allegiance to civilian authority was emphasized by his reappointing General Ély as Chief of Staff. Some of the military extremists were brought back to the *Métropole,* when possible to responsible positions, so that no one could claim they were being punished.[6] General Salan himself was ultimately assigned to the post of Inspector-General of the Armed Forces. De Gaulle issued orders to Algiers that no army officers were to assume the normally civilian jobs of prefects. The army's duty, he said, was the same as before May 13: to maintain order and defend Moslem groups against nationalist terror.[7]

In addition, the army was to help run the referendum, assuring conditions of safety and freedom for the voters. It was only logical, therefore, that when this task had been accomplished and when the Committees of Public Safety had been deprived, partly through the army's efforts, of the possibility of openly opposing De Gaulle, the military should be told to divorce itself from the Committees. "The moment has come," said De Gaulle, on October 9, ". . . when military personnel should cease to be part of any organization of a political character, whatever may be the reasons which, in the circumstances which Algeria has experienced since the month of May, exceptionally motivated

---

[4] *New York Times,* October 4, 1958.

[5] Pflimlin's government had announced the restoration during the May crisis, but it was then too late to reverse the trend.

[6] For example, General Edmond Johaux, head of the air force in Algeria, was made air force Chief of Staff in Paris.

[7] De Gaulle chose an army outpost in nationalist territory, Sidi-bel-Abbès, to make a clear statement of the army's mission. *New York Times,* July 3, 1958.

their participation. Henceforth, nothing can justify their membership in such formations. I order that they withdraw without delay."[8]

Another of De Gaulle's tasks was to lead the Europeans in Algeria gradually toward a settlement which might prove acceptable to the Moslems. While vague on the final relationship, he was specific on two points, both basic in the "liberal" approach to Algeria, against which the May revolt had taken place. First, all residents of Algeria would vote together in the September referendum and in the subsequent elections to the National Assembly. Second, Algeria would not in fact be "integrated" as a province of France, but would be endowed with a "personality" of its own—that is, with some measure of self-government. During his first trip to Algiers, when he voiced approval of the revolt, De Gaulle added: "Frenchmen all together, in one and the same electoral college. . . . For these ten million Frenchmen their vote will count the same as all others. They will have to designate, to elect—I repeat, in a single electoral college—their representatives to the public powers as all other Frenchmen will do. With these elected representatives we will see what remains to be done."[9]

By avoiding use of the word "integration," De Gaulle left the way open for some other form of Franco-Algerian association. The implication of the omission was not lost on European extremists, who feared that the Premier would use the results of the referendum to move further in the direction of liberalism. Their apprehensions were realized when at Constantine, less than a week after the referendum, he outlined his program for Algeria. Most of the speech was an appeal for continued Moslem support, but toward the end of the address he said: "The future of Algeria will in any event—because of the nature of things—be built on a double foundation: her personality and her close solidarity with Metropolitan France."[10] In this one sentence the Eu-

[8] *Le Monde*, October 14, 1958.
[9] Translation from *Current History*, August 1958, p. 117.
[10] Ambassade de France, Service de Presse et d'Information, *Speeches and Press Conferences*, no. 117 (New York, October 1958), p. 2.

ropeans could not fail to read the rejection of integration. The way in which he ended the speech lent weight to their fears: "Long live the Republic! Long live Algeria *and* long live France!" This in place of their familiar formula, "Long live France; long live French Algeria."

While maneuvering to overcome the resistance of the Europeans to a liberal solution, De Gaulle sought from the Moslems a firm commitment to association with France through accepting the constitution of the Fifth Republic. To this end Moslems had to be induced to register, to stand for office, and to vote, and nationalist military and political organizations had to be prevented from interfering with this process. Special attention was devoted to the Moslem women, who had never voted in their lives. For their benefit propaganda films showed the glittering aspects of modern life which would be theirs if they voted "oui."

Algerian nationalists did all they could to keep Moslems away from the polls. Reprisals were threatened for "traitors" who voted. To provide a counterattraction for Moslem allegiance, the political apparatus in Cairo set up a provisional government of the Republic of Algeria.[11] At the same time the nationalists launched a military offensive from the area of the Tunisian border, which resulted only in crossing the mountainous, relatively depopulated region between the border and the "Morice Line" of electrified barbed wire.[12]

When these efforts failed to block the referendum, the nationalists, just before the voting, reversed their position, telling the Moslems that if they felt compelled to vote by the presence of French troops, they would in fact suffer no reprisals. In the referendum 75 per cent of those eligible

[11] This step had been under active consideration by Moroccans, Tunisians, and Algerians ever since the Tangier conference in April. Both of Algeria's neighbors had been hesitant to approve the move because of the effect it might have on their own relations with France. In the end it was the United Arab Republic, which had no affection for either the Moroccan or the Tunisian governments, which allowed the Algerians to proceed.

[12] The French had removed many of the former residents to interior "security zones."

registered; 80 per cent of the registrants voted, and 96.7 per cent of them voted "oui."[13] This appearance of Moslem support encouraged De Gaulle to schedule elections to the National Assembly in Algeria at the same time as in Metropolitan France and to announce that two-thirds of the Algerian representatives would be Moslems. His most important response to the referendum was a five-year plan, announced at Constantine, to give Algeria "its share in what modern civilization can and must bring to men in terms of well-being and dignity." Included in the plan was the allotment of over 600,000 acres to Moslem farmers, housing for a million people, "regular" employment of 400,000 "new" workers, enrollment of two-thirds of the girls and boys in school within five years, their complete enrollment within eight years.[14]

To cut through Tunisia's connections with the Algerian war, De Gaulle moved quickly to settle the issues arising out of the French attack on Sakiet in the preceding February, and on June 13 diplomatic contact was restored. The agreement which was reached only four days later between the two countries was more favorable to Tunisia than the suggestions made in April by the Anglo-American good offices mission, since there was no provision for international inspection of the Tunisian-Algerian border. France agreed to withdraw its garrisons from all parts of Tunisia, concentrating them in the Bizerte base, and to evacuate them by October 1. De Gaulle's government recognized Tunisian sovereignty over Bizerte and undertook to negotiate the terms of its "temporary" status. Tunisia in return removed its barricades, which had fenced off the French communities since Sakiet, and gave France permission to construct a pipeline from the Saharan oil field of Edjelé to El Skhira, near Gabès. The agreement raised prospects

[13] Ambassade de France, Service de Presse et d'Information, French Affairs no. 71 (New York, October 1958), p. 2. In Algeria, as in Metropolitan France, nationalist activities may actually have increased the percentage favorable to the constitution.
[14] *Speeches and Press Conferences*, cited, pp. 1, 2.

for Tunisia moving closer to France and away from the Algerian nationalists.[15]

Fading Chances for Settlement

The referendum represented a high-water mark in De Gaulle's efforts to reach a solution of the Algerian problem. It was followed by many setbacks and a year later the impasse appeared as formidable as it had a year before. The turn for the worse was marked by a growing rigidity on the part of all the major participants, except possibly De Gaulle. The political and military organizations of the FLN, their position apparently more unified than at any time since May, turned away from direct negotiations with France. European extremists in Algeria dominated the November elections to the National Assembly. Bourguiba, despairing of a "liberal" settlement, once more abandoned the policy of conciliation with France.

The approach to direct negotiations between France and the Algerian "government" was marked by false moves on both sides. Apparently the FLN had hoped for French overtures as soon as the referendum was over. But De Gaulle's Constantine speech, which so shocked the Europeans of Algeria, was almost equally disappointing to the nationalists. Instead of proposing a meeting, De Gaulle merely told the nationalists, "Stop this absurd fighting, and you will at once see a new blossoming of hope over all the land of Algeria."[16] In the ensuing two weeks Ferhat Abbas, the head of the nationalist political organization, and Mohammed Yazid, Minister of Information and observer at the United Nations, issued repeated calls to De Gaulle. Denying previous reports, each claimed that recognition of Algerian independence was not a prerequisite to negotiation. At the same time Abbas clearly suggested that independence was the logical outcome. As reported in the

---

[15] Algerian nationalists denounced the agreement as a violation of the Tunisian-Moroccan-Algerian understanding that no settlement would be made with France until Algeria was free.

[16] *Speeches and Press Conferences*, cited, p. 3. The nationalist reaction is reported in *New York Times*, October 4, 1958.

West Berlin newspaper *Der Tag*, he said, "I know De Gaulle.... I know he is a great patriot and a man of good will.... He has promised independence to the Africans. For what reason should the Algerian population be treated worse? We are not the enemies of France. We wish, on the contrary, to cooperate with the French on the basis of new relations *when we have obtained independence.*"[17]

De Gaulle's gesture toward negotiation, when it finally came, at his press conference of October 23, 1958, took the form of an attempt to split the Algerian military bands from the nationalists' political apparatus. Of the army, he said, "Wherever they are organized for combat, their leaders need only enter into contact with the French command. The old warrior's procedure, long used when one wanted to silence the guns, was to wave the white flag of truce." To the nationalists these words suggested, not the cease-fire which they wanted, but a surrender. As for what De Gaulle called the Algerian "external organization," he proposed that its delegates come to France under guarantee of safety and freedom to depart. (He said nothing about the five nationalist leaders abducted from a French-piloted Moroccan plane in 1956 and still held in a Paris prison.) What concessions could these delegates expect? De Gaulle's answer was clear: none. "Opening fire does not give a man the right to determine the [political] destiny" of Algeria. Algeria's future would be determined in the various elections—legislative, municipal, and senatorial—then scheduled for November 1958 and March and April 1959.[18] What De Gaulle demanded was capitulation by the Algerian political leadership, as well as the surrender of nationalist fighting units.

In taking a hard stand De Gaulle was encouraged by the success of the referendum, the failure of the nationalist military offensive, and the cool attitude other governments were showing toward the Algerian nationalist leadership.

[17] As quoted in *Le Monde*, October 15, 1958; italics added.
[18] Ambassade de France, Service de Presse et d'Information, *Speeches and Press Conferences*, no. 119 (New York, October 1958), pp. 4-5.

However, his attitude now solidified the nationalist groups in equal intransigence, since moderate elements now had no place to turn. Reverting to an earlier position, Algerian leaders announced that any talks with France must examine the entire question of Algeria's political status. Abbas, regarded as a moderate, declared angrily that the "Algerian ministers will not journey to Paris with a rope around their necks. The army of liberation is not ready to hoist the white flag."[19] In New York, Yazid redoubled his efforts to bring about intervention by the United Nations. Secretary-General Hammarskjöld was reminded of the resolution of the 1957 General Assembly and was asked to use his influence with France. The Afro-Asian bloc was inspired to prepare a new series of accusations and recommendations for the current meeting of the General Assembly.

Western governments were simultaneously threatened and wooed by the nationalists. Already concerned over the possibility of Communist meddling in Algeria, they were kept informed of Peiping's agreement to supply arms as an indication of the determination of the nationalists to seek support wherever the prospects looked promising. In Algeria French prisoners were periodically released to lend support to the contention that the nationalists were in fact a legitimate government formally at war with France and, like most non-Communist governments, recognizing the International Red Cross Convention.

De Gaulle had won a great numerical victory in the referendum, but the factors which had produced the "oui" vote in Algeria were such that he could not use it to prepare the way for an Algerian settlement. Civil and military officers surrounded the referendum with a climate which permitted voters no real option. Because France was still at war in Algeria, freedom of speech and assembly was as little tolerated in September as in May. Transported to polling places in military vehicles, Moslems voted amidst signs of French power. Yet, any genuine fraternization had long since ended. Europeans and Moslems were as far apart as before the uprising. Asked how they would vote, individual

[19] *Le Monde*, November 2-3, 1958.

Moslems replied, "Algeria is going to vote 'oui' by an overwhelming majority, when each family carries the grief or the wound of one of its members seized, disappeared, killed, or tortured." Or, "we are too poor and too ignorant to understand these things. The lieutenant says that things will be good and our condition improved." Or, "I will vote "yes" because then my son will soon come home."[20] Above all, they voted for De Gaulle because they still believed he might bring them peace after four years of suffering at the hands of both belligerents.

Even in the referendum, less than three-fifths of the eligible Moslem voters cast "yes" ballots[21] a sombre omen of what was to come. Although De Gaulle had promised that Moslems would constitute two-thirds of the Algerian representation in the new National Assembly, to be elected in November, the possibility of his negotiating directly with the nationalists meant that pro-French Moslem candidates might later find themselves out on a limb, hated by the nationalists and abandoned by the French. De Gaulle's invitation to the nationalists on October 23 did nothing to clarify the prospects. Moslems who might have become candidates to the Assembly feared that they would be abandoned by France in a direct Franco-FLN settlement. On the other hand, after the nationalists rejected De Gaulle's overture, nearly all Moslems still hesitated to become candidates alongside Europeans for fear of nationalist retaliation. Genuine representatives of Moslem attitudes remained aloof, leaving the field to the "béni-oui-ouis" or "tame" Moslems so identified with Europeans that no camouflage was possible.

De Gaulle still sought to preserve the integrity of the elections. To ensure selection of the promised number of Moslems without identifying each candidate closely with a specific electoral district, he ordered the balloting to be carried out by regional lists, not individual candidates as in Metropolitan France. He publicly instructed General

---

[20] "Lettres d'un Français d'Algérie," *La Nef*, October 1958, pp. 23-25.
[21] Ambassade de France, Service de Presse et d'Information. French Affairs no 71, cited, p 2.

Salan that he wished the elections to be truly competitive, and he forbade civilian and military employees of the government who had served in Algeria within the past year to present themselves as candidates.[22] Freedom of expression for candidates and journals was to be protected,[23] and a control commission was to supervise the counting of ballots, as had been done in conducting the referendum.

Notwithstanding these efforts, most European "moderates" were driven to abandon any attempt to compose lists of candidates, and the European integrationists were left in control of the elections. In ten out of eighteen districts there was no real electoral competition at all. The actual struggle took place within European organizations. Here the "ultra-extremists" wanted to defy De Gaulle openly, whereas the "intransigents," who also favored integration, felt that De Gaulle, voluntarily or involuntarily, could be brought to accept this objective. The Algeria-Sahara Committee of Public Safety was finally able to agree on a list of candidates just before the deadline for filing. The success of the integrationists in avoiding an open conflict in their ranks made it even more difficult to persuade Moslems to appear on joint lists with European "liberals." The Committee attained another major objective when Algeria was once more divorced from the political currents of Metropolitan France. True, on orders from the Socialist party headquarters in Paris, which hoped to gain votes by posing as De Gaulle's firm support on the Left, Socialist lists were drawn up in Algeria, but other Algerian lists bore no relation at all to traditional French parties. French conservatives like Duchet were regarded as dangerous leftists in Algeria; Algerian candidates called "moderates" would have been on the extreme Right in France proper. De Gaulle's efforts had not ended the isolation of Moslems from Europeans, or of Algeria from the *Métropole*.

[22] The result was that several officers returned to run in Metropolitan districts.

[23] Of course, as Algerian authorities themselves pointed out, it would be practically impossible to guarantee anything at all to those advocating freedom for Algeria.

Boycotted by many disillusioned Moslems who had voted in the referendum, the elections produced sixty-seven representatives, most of whom held such extreme views that they seemed destined to cause as much trouble for the Fifth Republic as they had for the Fourth. Henceforth De Gaulle would face even more vociferous opposition to his policies in Algeria and to his plans for economic reform. Allegedly speaking for Africa within the Assembly, the die-hard representatives of European supremacy in Algeria would exert a strong pull on members of the Gaullist Union pour la Nouvelle République, perhaps driving some of its neophyte members toward the classical conservatism of the Independents and Bidault's Catholic group, while others might turn to a new version of authoritarianism in their insistence on making Algeria as "French" as the rest of France.

The record was somewhat better in the Senatorial elections of May 1959. More actual competition took place, more Moslems appeared to be willing candidates, above all most "ultra-ultras" were defeated. However, the real meaning of this result was that all parties to the conflict had resigned themselves to the fact that De Gaulle would not be able to bring a quick peace to Algeria.

Prospects for a solution in Algeria were further dimmed by events in Tunisia. As the months passed without a glimmer of a solution, Bourguiba's own position once more seemed in danger, as it had in early 1958. Internal unrest forced him to tighten his grip on the country and renew his quarrels with Nasser and the Arab League. Again he turned to the West for arms, threatening, when he met with delays, to buy them from the Communist bloc. This pressure brought a new small shipment from the United States and Great Britain. The Anglo-American action and the American statement that "we have never proceeded on the basis that we needed anyone's permission to sell arms to a sovereign government"[24]—a statement designed to assuage Tunisian susceptibilities—produced new friction between France and the United States.

[24] *New York Times,* November 14, 1958.

Direct Franco-Tunisian relations worsened on the same issues which had embittered the Sakiet affair: the permeable Algerian-Tunisian border and the status of Frenchmen within Tunisia. French military action against the nationalists led to new charges of their violating the border. The two countries remained at odds over the number of French troops which could be stationed at Bizerte and how long they would remain. Bourguiba linked the future of the base to the "liberation of the entire Maghreb"[25] and demanded that the French either begin training Tunisians to take over the base or withdraw altogether.[26] He labeled French landholders alien exploiters and warned of expropriation. This pronouncement, in turn, reinforced the determination of the Europeans in Algeria to resist any settlement which might subject them to rule by the Moslem majority.

By mid-1959 any easy optimism about De Gaulle's ability to bring contending groups together and to reach a settlement had all but vanished. At the same time, no party or combination of parties to the conflict seemingly possessed the ability to impose its will on the others. While the French army controlled most areas at most times and launched a highly publicized drive to clear the nationalists from their mountain strongholds, it still was unable to force the nationalists to capitulate. Nor could the latter, despite the assistance they were receiving from outside, wrest Algeria from the French. European extremists had recaptured political control in Algeria but were unable to win over either the Moslem majority or, so far, the new French leadership in Paris. Once more the conflict had spread to the international sphere. The Arab League, Tunisia, Morocco, the United Nations, and France's Western allies were all involved, directly or indirectly, and Communist China had declared its support for the Nationalists. But outsiders appeared to be unable or unwilling to tip the scales in favor of either contestant.

De Gaulle was hemmed in between advocates of dia-

---

[25] In an interview in *Le Monde*, October 30, 1958.
[26] *New York Times*, June 19, 1959.

metrically opposed solutions. The policy of integration, wrote Marshal Juin, must be revived as the goal of French action in Algeria.[27] An English observer urged the unification of Algeria, Morocco, and Tunisia. "Maghreb unity," he wrote, "is not merely an aspiration, but a fact. . . . An independent Morocco and Tunisia and an Algeria integrated with France make about as much sense, politically, as an 'independent' Scotland and Wales and an England integrated with Germany would have in 1940."[28] But a prominent French writer concluded "that the area (*pays*) has never known its own autonomy, that it has never been capable by itself, in spite of the numerous opportunities granted it, of substituting itself for a decadent invader in order to establish a semblance of organization, and that the only 'unity' it has ever known is that of the authority of its successive overlords."[29] In the circumstances, De Gaulle could only play for time, hoping that his supply of that precious commodity would prove greater than that vouchsafed to the Fourth Republic. "Our problem," he said in December 1958 on his fourth visit to Algeria since the preceding June, "is above all a human problem—to give each Algerian his liberty, his well-being, and his dignity." After this has been accomplished, through the five-year program outlined at Constantine, "the personality of Algeria and the nature of the things that tie her to France will reveal themselves more clearly" and "the so-called political solution will appear."[30]

Meanwhile De Gaulle was faced with the task of breaking up the still threatening combination of army and civilians, in other words, of completing the work begun in June. More was involved than shifting a few officers and drafting a few directives. In Algeria an effective civilian system had to be constituted in place of the military ad-

[27] Marshal Alphonse P. Juin, "Algérie, 1958," *Revue Politique et Parlementaire*, August-September 1958, pp. 169-170.
[28] Thomas Hodgkin, "Battle for the Maghreb," *Political Quarterly*, October 1958, pp. 349, 351.
[29] Raymond Veillas, "Réalité et Fiction en Afrique du Nord," *France-Amerique*, nos. 7-9, 1958, p. 51
[30] *New York Times*, December 8, 1958.

ministration, one which would respect the authority of Paris. In addition, the French military command had to be brought to full acceptance of its role as an agent for carrying out national policy as formulated by President de Gaulle and his government, whatever that policy might be. The armed forces must confirm their allegiance to political institutions, not merely to individuals whose objectives seemed to coincide with their own.

Conclusions for American Policy

Delay in reaching a settlement in Algeria could only mean a continuing dilemma for the United States. So long as the conflict continued, the United States would be criticized by all for its aloofness, real or presumed. The French government of Michel Debré would make of American behavior in the United Nations a test of American attitude toward the Fifth Republic. Behind Debré's increasing promises, French integrationists would claim that the goal of the United States was to promote the independence of unviable territories throughout Africa so that its business interests could penetrate them, to France's detriment. At the same time exponents of North African freedom would complain that pretended American neutrality was a cover for continued aid to French colonialism. "American policy has been subject to ambiguities," said Bourguiba; "while Soviet intervention in Hungary is strongly criticized, France is supplied with airplanes and bombs for use in Algeria. . . . The United States must put an end to such ambivalence and must no longer support . . . France in its actions in Algeria. . . ."[31]

Continued American aloofness can be justified only on the ground that any possible move would make matters more difficult for the West and better for the Communists.

---

[31] Radio broadcast, July 25, 1958, printed as "We Chose the West" in *Orbis*, Fall 1958, p. 318. The title correctly reflected the tenor of the broadcast Bourguiba, while urging on the United States, a stronger policy was simultaneously saying, "I cannot . . . take refuge in the old Arab proverb that 'my enemy's enemy is my friend.' I cannot bring myself to ask help from Russia against France or Great Britain for the mere sake of revenge and without thinking of the consequences" (p. 316).

In the case of Algeria, however, inaction may be the worst policy of all. If the United States believes that the repression of nationalist movements is in the long run dangerous and futile, it should support the essential ingredients of De Gaulle's initially stated policy. Large-scale assistance to the Algerian Moslems' development of local autonomy, negotiation of a cease-fire, may not produce the permanently stable subordination of Algeria to France envisaged by De Gaulle. But if the end result is, instead, the effective independence of all North African areas, the chances of these new countries voluntarily associating themselves with the West will be greatly enhanced by a prompt American endorsement of a "liberal" solution to the present impasse.

Chapter Nineteen

EMERGENCE OF THE FRENCH COMMUNITY

AFTER IMPLEMENTING through decrees the *loi-cadre* of 1956, the Fourth Republic failed to complete the job of colonial reform. It did not replace the French Union with a new structure appropriate to the new responsibilities which had now been assumed by the individual overseas territories. Indeed it became clear that the Fourth Republic had gone about as far as it could in reshaping Metropolitan-colonial relations, given the conflicts within the legislative and executive branches, and the contradictory pressures from outside. It was therefore incumbent upon General de Gaulle to convince the African elites that he was about to succeed, and succeed promptly, where the Fourth Republic had failed. He started with the prestige accruing to the "man of Brazzaville." His continuing concern for African development was indicated by his appointing as Minister of State Félix Houphouet-Boigny, an African leader who advocated the permanent and direct association of each of the territories with France, *on an individual basis*, as opposed to either a transitional relationship or African federations which would then enter as units into equal relationship to France.

Drafting and Acceptance of the Community

The necessity of gaining a quick commitment by France's African areas, before the situation could deteriorate further, was one additional reason for having the Cabinet draw up the new constitution instead of entrusting this task to the Assembly. The same urgency lay behind De Gaulle's gamble of incorporating the arrangements for the French Community in his new constitution and allowing the residents of the colonies to participate in the constitutional referendum at the same time and under the same conditions as citizens living in France.

The new constitution establishes an Executive Council and a Senate. The President of France presides over the Council, which also includes the French Premier, the heads of government of the member states and "ministers responsible for the common affairs of the Community."[1] The Senate is to have representatives from the French and other legislatures in a number "determined according to [each state's] population and the responsibilities it assumes in the Community." The Senate is to "deliberate" on Community economic and financial matters, "examine" international agreements involving the Community, and "make executory decisions" if authorized to do so by the various legislatures.[2] Because a relationship which is in rapid evolution could not be completely spelled out in such a short time,[3] the constitution provided that future organic laws would determine the organization and procedure of the Executive Council, and the composition and rules of the Senate and also of the Court of Arbitration, which is to rule on legal disputes arising among the members On two highly important points, however—a change of status of the members and the powers reserved to the Community—the constitution is explicit. A change in the status of a member of the Community may be requested either by a territory, through action taken by its legislature, and confirmed by a referendum, or by the French Republic. The "modalities" of the change were then to be determined "by an agreement approved by the Parliament of the Republic and by the legislative assembly concerned."[4] Presumably

[1] Article 82.
[2] Article 83
[3] That it was not left even more vague was due to the Consultative Committee.
[4] Article 86.

the French Parliament could not refuse to accede to a request which complied with the prescribed conditions, but the nature of the new status would largely be determined by the agreement finally negotiated with the member's legislature.

Powers explicitly reserved to the Community under Article 78 were those retained by France under the 1956 *loi-cadre*. Now, however, they were divided into two categories; one group of powers were presumably to be held by the Community as long as it endured, the others were to be retained by it "except by special agreement" to the contrary. Foreign policy, defense, the monetary system, common economic and financial policy, and policy on "strategic" raw materials (undefined) were placed in the first classification; justice, higher education, transport, and telecommunications in the second.

No sooner was the constitutional draft completed than De Gaulle threw the full weight of his prestige into the battle of the referendum by touring Africa from Madagascar to Senegal. In addition to small Communist formations, organized opposition to the Community came from sections of the Parti du Regroupement Africain, with which local parties and the African Socialist Movement were affiliated. At its congress held at Cotonou in July, the PRA had called for "*immediate* independence, a federal African nation, *then* multinational confederation with France."[5] The Secretary-General of the party, Djibo Bakary, Premier of Niger, campaigned against the constitution, declaring, "We are not afraid of the economic consequences of independence."[6] At De Gaulle's first stop the Congress for Madagascan Independence fomented a mass demonstration against the Community. In Senegal on the other side of Africa the local branch of the PRA, allegedly supported by Communist sympathizers, organized large demonstrations in favor of immediate freedom. Anticipating this reception, two Senegalese leaders friendly to De Gaulle, Léopold Senghor and Mamadou Dia, discreetly

[5] *New York Times*, August 31, 1958; italics added.
[6] Same, August 12, 1958.

stayed in France, later indicating their "respect for the former chief of Free France, who incarnates the honor and dignity of the French people."[7]

In his travels De Gaulle attempted to show that African independence could be attained within the Community as well as outside. He awoke memories of his wartime liberal view of the French empire by selecting Brazzaville as the site for his most important speech. The provisions of Article 78, enumerating the powers reserved for the Community, were not, he declared, as rigid as the constitutional text implied. It was "natural and legitimate for the African people to reach a political level at which they would have entire responsibility for their external affairs and decide on their own governments." "Economic, political, cultural, and defense communities" could then emerge from association of independent states with France. Earlier, at Tananarive, in Madagascar, De Gaulle had pointed out that Article 86 permitted secession at any time.

While attempting to prove that there was a place for African nationalism inside the Community, De Gaulle warned France's overseas citizens that they would vote *non* "at their own risk and peril." France, said Houphouet-Boigny, would not hesitate to draw the necessary conclusions from such an act. The issue for the territories, said De Gaulle in Madagascar, was between joining a "federal" community under French leadership and "separating their destiny completely from that of France."[8]

When it came to balloting, only the people of Sekou Touré's French Guinea indicated their desire for immediate separation from France. Previously a prominent figure in the pro-French Rassemblement Démocratique Africain, Touré had broken with the party and with Houphouet-Boigny on the issue of the constitution. That his opposition could produce a negative majority of 97 per cent (almost 575,000 *non* votes) was a striking demonstration of his hold on Guinea. Elsewhere the result was quite different.

[7] Same, August 31, 1958.
[8] Same, August 26, 1958.

RETURNS OF THE CONSTITUTIONAL REFERENDUM
IN THE VARIOUS TERRITORIES[9]

	For	Against	Majority Per Cent For
Senegal	772,058	21,540	97
Sudan	490,679	10,349	98
Guinea	15,551	573,470	..*
Ivory Coast	1,553,705	197	99
Dahomey	399,442	9,289	98
Niger	214,840	59,856	78
Mauritania	192,444	13,080	94
Upper Volta	768,639	6,822	99
Gabon	137,650	11,376	92
Ubangi-Shari	452,230	4,808	99
Middle Congo	296,359	1,361	99
Tchad	182,028	1,734	99
Madagascar	1,178,595	332,294	77

* Majority per cent *against*, 97% in Guinea.

Except in Guinea, the referendum represented an impressive victory for De Gaulle. But this generalization needs qualification. In most of the territories, established party leaders were able to deliver virtually all the vote. The sole exception in French West and Equatorial Africa was Niger, where, despite the opposition of local leaderships, the electorate approved the constitution by a large majority. Elsewhere the position of the "older" African elites, those which had emerged soon after World War II, was strengthened at the expense of the more impatient, nationalistic elements. This older elite lost little time in consolidating its victory. In Niger, the Premier and his Cabinet were forced to resign. Meeting just after the referendum, Houphouet-Boigny's Rassemblement Démocratique Africain voted to expel Touré and his Guinea section. De Gaulle's Minister of State took this occasion to emphasize his own interpretation of the Community as a permanent institution in which territories would be associated as separate political entities. "Those who have entered the Community with the inten-

[9] Same, September 30, 1958.

tion of withdrawing tomorrow are not with us," he declared.[10]

In voting for the Community the territories were, as it quickly became clear, *voting for national freedom*. Though the established elites emerged on top, they did so only by espousing the cause of African nationalism. Said Léopold Senghor of Senegal: "For us the Community is only an avenue and a means to prepare ourselves for independence in the manner of the British dependencies. Beyond nominal independence—which is easy to obtain—it is actual independence which we wish to realize."[11] Serou Apithy, head of the Dahomey government, declared that his country was seeking the "economic and social development which will permit it one day to become an associated, independent state," and assured Touré of Dahomey's continued friendship.[12]

The Problem of Guinea

The concept of the Community as a vehicle for the eventual attainment of independence made France's relations most difficult with Guinea, the one territory which had voted against joining it. If Guinea were immediately recognized as independent and likewise continued to receive French economic and administrative assistance, several other territories might conclude that there was no advantage to remaining in the Community. Therefore, even before the final vote was tabulated, Guinea was informed that it could "no longer normally expect to receive the aid either of the administration of the French state or of its development funds."[13] About a week later the French Ministry for Overseas Territories stated that France would be in no hurry to recognize the new state:

If the actual situation created by the vote of last September 28 in Guinea is in no way contested, and if the government of

[10] *Le Monde*, October 12-13, 1958.
[11] Same, October 2, 1958.
[12] Same, October 2, 1958; *New York Times*, October 3, 1958.
[13] *New York Times*, September 30, 1958.

Guinea is free in its policies, it does not follow that the final regulation of legal relations between the French government and the government of Guinea can take place before the intentions and the concrete and practical possibilities of the latter are known and before the French government has the opportunity to consult the Community, certain members of which have already manifested a concern to be asked to express their advice.[14]

This roundabout statement seemingly indicated the French government's doubts over Guinea's ability to survive as an independent state. At his press conference of October 23, De Gaulle made this clear. ". . . For us," he said, "Guinea is in a state of flux, and we do not know where it is headed. We shall see how it develops and what it will do under its present government, both with regard to its leanings and its foreign associations and from the point of view of its ability to form a State, if it succeeds in establishing one. We shall establish our relations with Guinea on the basis of what happens in these different fields. We shall do so without bitterness, but without any certainty—I must admit—that what is today can remain tomorrow." When Guinea requested membership in the United Nations, France tried unsuccessfully to delay the vote, arguing that until February 4, 1959, other French territories still had the right to change their status and might in theory reverse their decision to join the Community.

In his contest with France Touré was not without weapons of his own. Within Guinea, he was clearly in control.[15] Speaking to the Parti Démocratique de Guinée, he warned his listeners to "beware of all the world, including Sekou Touré," to be on the look-out for adversaries of Guinean independence. "France had the guillotine, Guinea will have the stake," he declared. He went on to denounce the laziness of those who spent their days on porches and

[14] *Le Monde,* October 8, 1958.
[15] Touré appointed as Secretary of Telecommunications Abdoulaye Diallo, formerly vice-president of the Communist-led World Federation of Trade Unions, who had been expelled from the French Sudan for having campaigned against the constitution.

verandas. "We will be the first African government to install forced labor [an exaggeration]. We are not afraid to pronounce the term, for this labor will not be for the benefit of President Sekou Touré or any individual, but for the profit of the people."[16] So strong was his position that Touré was able to strip tribal chieftains of their power and to subordinate administrative officials to his direction.

From his entrenched position in Guinea Touré was able to go beyond mere correctness in his relations with France to a positive demonstration of friendship. "You know," he told *Le Monde,* "that we have taken our decision with the conviction that it represents not only the interest of Guinea, but the best opportunity for French interests in this country."[17] Although France delayed its recognition, Touré announced that "the Republic of Guinea and its government, desirous of maintaining and reinforcing the bases of Franco-Guinean friendship and cooperation, are certain that no one will support with more authority than will General de Gaulle any action directed toward this end."[18]

Whatever his official attitude, De Gaulle could hardly remain indifferent to France's stake in Guinea. In the nine years after 1948 about 78 million dollars of French public funds had been invested there. Private French capital had been associated with British, Canadian, Swiss and American interests in developing Guinea's resources, notably its rich bauxite reserves. Guinea is a poor country, its principal exports, in addition to bauxite, being bananas, pineapples, citrus fruits, and green coffee. If Touré was to be successful in obtaining substantial outside assistance, it was hardly in France's interest for other governments and their citizens to monopolize the role of Guinea's benefactors.

Perhaps with these advantages in mind, other countries were less reluctant than France to recognize Touré's regime. The Soviet Union was one of the first to extend recognition, at the same time offering economic and technical assistance and advisers. Touré declined to reveal the full contents of

[16] *Le Monde,* November 7, 1958.
[17] Same, October 2, 1958.
[18] Same, October 28, 1958.

the Russian communication, though disavowing any intention of indulging in international blackmail. Still, Soviet initiative may well have spurred the Western powers, particularly the United States and Great Britain, to recognize the new state and, in the case of the United States, to assistance programs of its own. After waiting a decent interval out of regard for French sensibilities, both countries recognized Guinea—Great Britain on November 2, the United States a day later. By that time no fewer than twenty-seven states had taken the step, including France's NATO allies, Italy and West Germany. As a result, when Guinea applied for membership in the United Nations, its claim to be a recognized member of the international community was well established.

Part of Touré's strength in his contest with France lay in his espousal of African unity. While opposed to membership in the French Community, he was anxious for Guinea to be associated with other African states, French or British, inside or outside the Community and Commonwealth. He proclaimed African unity the goal of all political movements, even though their leaders might take different roads. Suiting action to words, he and Prime Minister Kwame Nkrumah of Ghana announced a "confederation" of their two states, which, they declared, was designed to be the "nucleus of a union of West African states." Touré openly solicited support and membership by other territories. In fact, however, the Guinea-Ghana "union" or "confederacy" was scarcely more than a statement of intent. Like the French Community, no one could predict what course its development would take. There was, however, no doubting the powerful attraction exerted on French territories by the underlying idea of African federation.

New Threats to the Community

A double challenge had been posed to the Community ever since African leaders began to ask for a wider devolution of powers than that envisaged in the *loi-cadre* of 1955. De Gaulle's constitution permits the autonomous states which make up the Community to choose independence at any time. By implication, if not by intention, it places no barriers to their forming close ties among themselves. Only if African leaders become convinced that these principles are permanent features of French policy will they be able to persuade their peoples of the other advantages of permanent association with the *Métropole*. There are three obstacles to the emergence of this looser type of organization. One is the view that the Community entails a permanent membership by individual territories or states possessing limited powers to control their own affairs. De Gaulle continued to balance statements that the African territories could leave the Community at any time with explicit denials that the Community would evolve into a French counterpart to the British Commonwealth.[19] So strong was the African current toward federation, of which the Mali grouping of West African States was an example, that even Houphouet-Boigny was moved to announce a customs union for the area.[20]

A second obstacle lies in the commitment of some French representatives to the idea of grouping the various territories in two organizations: French West Africa and French Equatorial Africa. These units, which might at one time have become the basis for a purely French federation within Africa, by the end of 1958 had fallen behind the march of events. Some form of association among French territories in some status short of national autonomy might have been possible under the regime of the *loi-cadre*; it was no longer possible under the Community, which they had entered as autonomous states. Moreover, French West and Equatorial Africa symbolized both the division and the organization of Africa which had been dictated by the accidents of colonial conquest. With independence achieved or imminent for Ghana and Guinea, for Nigeria, Togo, and the Cameroons, many African leaders were professing to discover as many ties with new states emerging from a different

[19] *New York Times*, July 8, 1959, reporting De Gaulle's speech to the Executive Council of the Community
[20] Same, June 7, 1959.

colonial rule as with those which had been conquered by the same European overlord.

A third and final obstacle to the development of the Community lies in its need of financial resources. If France does not find the wherewithal, in addition to meeting many other claims, to satisfy the demands of the now-autonomous African territories, the new states will look outside the Community to see whether independent African nations are faring better. They may even conclude that some sacrifice of economic aid is worthwhile if they can thereby throw off an association which reminds them of their recent colonial status.

This has been hinted rather broadly by Léopold Senghor, president of the Parti du Regroupement Africain and a rival of Houphouet-Boigny:

> It is not our intention to spend our time talking about independence. We will remain in the Community if we can give to it the dynamic interpretation which springs from the constitution. The latter envisages, in effect, the possibility of the transfer of powers which have been assigned to the Community, which means that the States will proceed progressively toward real independence.

Senghor added that "the formation of primary federations [is] the essential condition if the States of Africa are to attain real independence. . . . Territories . . . can thus develop federations which are economically sound and which in the future can do without the aid of FIDES."[21]

Centrifugal forces at work in the Community have been stimulated by recent events in Togo and the Cameroons, United Nations trust territories whose evolution had influenced developments within the French colonies before and after the passage of the *loi-cadre*. Once the referendum on the constitution had been held, both Togo and the Cameroons moved quickly to put an end to the French trusteeship. In October 1958, Sylvanus Olympio, Premier of Togo, and Ahmadou Ahidjo, Premier of the Cameroons, jour-

---

[21] "Fonds d'Investissement pour le Développement des Territoires d'Outre-mer," *Le Monde*, November 7, 1958.

neyed to Paris to enlist French support for their independence. While Olympio found Bernard Cornut-Gentile, Minister of Overseas France, annoyed by the promptness with which the request was presented, the French representative at the United Nations supported the termination in 1960 of trusteeship status for both territories.[22] Once on their own, both states would be free to join with other African territories in new associations. The Premier of the French Cameroons, concerned over the attraction of Ghana, has indicated that he will explore the possibility of federating his country with the smaller Cameroon territory under British trusteeship. On the other hand, the Premier of Togo has expressed the hope that the Ghana-Guinea union will eventually be expanded to embrace other West African states, including his own.

France, therefore, faces the danger that its Community may turn out to be an ephemeral organization, bridging the transition of its territories to independence and then vanishing. Conversely, it is possible that, if France is quickly to adopt substantive policies to give real meaning to the nationalist slogans of "independence" and "unity," it can counteract the attraction which is exerted on members of the Community by former French and British territories from outside it. The institutions of the Community can be made to serve as centers for planning, coordinating, and implementing projects for economic and administrative development. No barriers need be raised to cooperative arrangements among member states, or to cooperation between them and others outside the Community. Indeed, member states could be actively encouraged to initiate, individually or collectively, long-range programs of this kind. The Community could then determine priorities among projects in the light of the resources available.

While the cost to France of adequate overseas development would be very high, substantial economies would result from increased cooperation among the members of the Community. For example, the Community could organ-

[22] After that date France would continue to sit on the Trusteeship Council, but as a nonadministering power.

ize a corps of experts in administrative and technical assistance. The principle of self-help, demonstrated to be of major importance in assistance to underdeveloped areas, could be applied by including in the corps of experts an increasing number of people from the African members; they would then be able to apply to the problems of other member states the experience they had gained at home.

In considering the prospects for economic development two new factors merit special mention: the European Common Market and the resources of the Sahara. In the recent past the Common Market was publicly advocated in France as a means of keeping African territories French, while the vast reservoir of oil in the Sahara desert was regarded as a solution to France's energy requirements. Now that the French territories have become autonomous, both objectives need redefining so as to stress African, as well as Metropolitan, interests. The two are incompatible only if France insists on making them so. If the countries in the Common Market can reach agreement with members of the OEEC and GATT, the economic horizons of France's African areas would broaden. The former French territories would not then be dependent exclusively on the Six, particularly France and West Germany, and the larger association would facilitate reaching agreements with African areas excluded from the Common Market. At the same time the Community could be strengthened by charging it with responsibility for promoting trade between French territories and a wider Europe.

The Organisation Commune des Régions Sahariennes (OCRS), it will be remembered, includes representatives of neighboring French African states. If the authority of the French Minister for the Sahara comes to be shared with the Community, possibly through establishing direct ties between the OCRS and the Community, the exploitation of the Sahara can become a force for strengthening and perpetuating the Community. France would get the oil it needed, and the resources of the other member states would be systematically explored and developed for their benefit.

Administrative planning by the Community should take account of the aims of its African states. It would be useful to announce time tables for the transfer to Africans of specified positions in local governing bodies and to set up programs to train Africans to fill them. At the same time France should steadily reduce the number and authority of its civil servants overseas, perhaps transferring to the Community responsibility for their supervision. Many Africans are aware of the difficulties of manning the apparatus of an independent nation. And in accepting the Community they recognized that they were not ready to go their own way, that they lacked both experience and trained personnel. The assumption of the training function by the Community would accustom African leaders to cooperate within the Community, demonstrating the advantages of membership during the transition to self-government. Equally important, the leaders so trained would be better able to hold their own in relations with states, such as Nigeria and Ghana, outside the Community. They do not want France to slam and lock the door between them and the rest of Africa outside the Community. Neither do they want to be swallowed by expansionist forces exploiting the attractive slogan of African unity.

Relations between the Community and Guinea, Togo, and the Cameroons may prove a test case. Sooner or later France will be forced to accept cooperation between members of the Community and Guinea, and after 1960 the same will be true of its two former trust territories. French, African, European, and other Western interests have combined in a policy aimed at developing viable regimes friendly to the West—if not party to Western alliances, at least resistant to either Communist or Arab influences. There may be some reason to fear that too close an association by them with Guinea may draw some African states away from the Community. But it is possible also that a strengthened Community will attract independent nations to it through specific cooperative arrangements. In this way the Community may become a middle ground, offering an attractive alternative to African "balkanization," on the one hand, and to absorption into one or more autocratic African states on the other.

Article 78 of the constitution gives the Community jurisdiction over a number of matters. This represents a step away from the centralization of authority typical of the *loi-cadre*. The constitution, moreover, outlines the possibility of transferring to the member states the responsibility for certain of these matters. In his African tour De Gaulle indicated that more authority might in time be entrusted to the new states. At the meeting of the Executive Council in July, 1959 it was announced that African states would have their own officials attached to French embassies abroad.[23] There is, in fact, no good reason why the Community cannot serve, in all areas enumerated by Article 78, as a planning and coordinating body, even after the member states have assumed control over their domestic affairs. States seeking a larger degree of African unity would then find that their membership in the Community enhances their influence in African councils as well as their weight in outside groupings, such as the Afro-Asian bloc, and in the United Nations. Likewise France would gain in prestige throughout the non-Communist world as the leader of a developing system of increasingly independent states.

The task for France is to keep the initiative by staying ahead of the pressure of events. To a certain extent this was accomplished by the *loi-cadre;* more effective has been the establishment of the Community. Other demands for self-government had been met in France's initial agreements with Tunisia and Morocco. Now the Community may provide a channel for influencing the course of relations with those two countries. In their first steps both wished to remain independent, but, despite continuing friction, they still favored close ties with France. Their attitude then was close to that of most of the sub-Saharan territories today. They wanted the assistance which France could provide, the contacts with other African states, with

[23] *New York Times*, July 8, 1959.

Europe, and with the West which could be facilitated by a continuing connection with France. The growing role of the United States, which France came to resent in Tunisia and Morocco, developed in part from France's own failure to provide them with the aid it had promised in the conventions which accompanied the granting of independence.

One link in the chain of Franco-African association remains unforged. Cooperation among African states, between those states and France, between North and sub-Saharan African countries, and between North African nations and France might make faster progress if the three components of the Maghreb—Morocco, Tunisia, and Algeria—could be brought into a closer relationship. In this matter the war in Algeria is critical. If France should somehow succeed into returning Algeria to the status of a conquered territory, the initial and temporary effect might be to strengthen the Community. But sooner or later this success would compromise France's larger aims. The Eur-Africa on which France builds such high hopes would eventually be torn apart between Frenchmen still struggling to keep "French Africa" French and despairing African nationalists demanding complete separation from a country seemingly incapable of voluntarily abandoning anachronistic habits of colonial rule.

Chapter Twenty

THE IMPLICATIONS OF GRANDEUR

"THIS GENERATION of Americans," said President Roosevelt in accepting his party's nomination for a second term, "has a rendez-vous with destiny." "The destiny of France," said President de Gaulle in his 1959 inaugural address, "these words bring to mind the heritage of the past, the duties of the present, and the hopes of the future." Both Presidents were appealing to the sense of unity and purpose of their countrymen whose affairs they were directing in exceptional circumstances and with exceptional powers. But the student of the Fifth Republic, looking behind the clarion calls to greatness, must seek the meaning of these noble phrases. Since at the time of this writing the historical record of De Gaulle's France contains only a preface and a few pages of the initial chapter, the examination of its foreign policy must be fragmentary, the conclusions tentative.

The Common Market

De Gaulle, while a staunch exponent of French nationalism, has moved with care and finesse in dealing with international affairs. He revealed the outlines of his policy and his conception of France's proper role through his approach to the complex, and interrelated problems of the Common Market and the North Atlantic Treaty Organization. When he took power, protracted negotiations over the Free Trade Area and Common Market were approaching an impasse. French negotiators suspected that the

British were up to their old game of destroying "Europe," seeking through the device of the Free Trade Area to deprive cooperation among the Six of any real meaning. Well aware of being the weakest partner of the new group, France could be accused of once more attempting to alleviate its own domestic difficulties by claiming a special position within a discriminatory European organization. Wearying of concessions seemingly solicited without end, some of France's partners might be drawn toward the far looser form of cooperation advanced by Great Britain. Most disastrous would be the defection of West Germany, on whose diplomatic, economic, and military support France had leaned heavily since 1955.

Unity among the members of the Common Market in further negotiations with countries of the Free Trade Area depended on French action. And vigorous measures had to be taken at home if France was to enter the Common Market on time and with a leading role. Successive internal political tests between June and December 1958 had shown that De Gaulle was indeed master of France, able to use to the utmost the exceptional powers which the Fourth Republic, expiring, had placed in his hands. French industrial leaders feared the new competition within the Common Market, but they were more alarmed at the risks which the larger, looser Free Trade Area seemed to hold in store for them. De Gaulle could count, so he was told, on support by business interests for a decision to launch the Common Market, even at considerable sacrifices, if only to avoid the greater hazard posed by the Free Trade Area. Furthermore, while Great Britain had discounted the chances that a Common Market Treaty would actually emerge, it, along with the United States, West Germany, and France's other allies, was so relieved at De Gaulle's success in arresting French decline without a civil war that it agreed to join the others in helping him solve the financial and economic problems he had inherited.

De Gaulle acted with firmness and imagination. As late as mid-December, it had been widely assumed that France could not follow its Common Market partners in removing quotas from 90 per cent of its 1948 imports. With no advance warning, even to French representatives, however, the Premier announced that this was precisely what France would do. The ground was thereby cut from under the British position that the Common Market represented a double discrimination by France. Simultaneously with the relaxation of quotas the franc was revalued and France joined with other European nations, including Great Britain and West Germany, in making its currency convertible when held by foreign individuals and concerns. The unusual feature of these currency reforms was that they were taken after international consultation and agreement. This revived harmony was reflected in the credits made available to France, by British, German, and American banks. In turn, the strengthened convertibility, supported by these credits, enabled the member nations to replace the European Payments Union with the European Monetary Union, which had been set up in August 1955 for just this eventuality. France had reportedly been pushed by Britain into adopting this limited convertibility even though it much preferred the assistance it had so often derived from membership in the European Payments Union to the clearing requirements of the new Monetary Union.[1] However that may be, the new financial policies eased the tension between France and Great Britain, dispelled any immediate danger of a trade war, and at the same time strengthened the bonds between France and its five Common Market partners.

In November 1958, Reginald Maudling broke off negotiations between the Free Trade Area and Common Market after Jacques Soustelle had stated flatly that France would not accept Britain's version of the Free Trade Area. One month later the rift deepened when Sir David Eccles, President of Britain's Board of Trade, accused France of excessive discrimination against other OEEC countries and threatened trade reprisals. However, as the Common Market went into effect on January 1, 1959, the Six extended to outside countries the 10 per cent tariff cuts they were grant-

[1] *New York Times*, January 3, 1959.

ing to each other. With this concession the Six felt in a stronger position to defend their decision that the 20 per cent increase in import quotas, equal to 3 per cent of each nation's production of the commodity involved, would not automatically be extended to countries outside the Common Market. But in this continuing discrimination, also, the way was paved for eventual compromises which might satisfy Great Britain and its European associates. Studies had shown that the two countries most affected by the 3 per cent rule were France and Great Britain, but that only a few products, such as automobiles and aluminum, were at issue. France had all along taken the position that the two economic arrangements might be reconciled by preserving the Common Market and making commodity-by-commodity agreements between its members and outside countries. In January 1959, representatives of the Six agreed on this procedure. A requisite to satisfactory compromise, however, was determination among the "Outer Seven" of the arrangement they wished to substitute for the defunct Free Trade Area. Extended talks in the spring and summer of 1959 revealed little agreement apart from the conclusion that the negotiators did not like the Common Market and still hoped its development would be toward a looser, more comprehensive trading system.

Franco-German Relations

Reinforcement of Franco-German cooperation was the subject of the meetings between French and German officials, including an exchange of visits between De Gaulle and Adenauer. In their discussions, the Common Market was related to a more fundamental question. Given De Gaulle's emphasis on nationalism and grandeur, would the cooperation between the two countries, so marked a feature of the past three years, still be possible and, if so, on what basis? There were grounds for apprehension on both sides. West Germany feared that the new France would retreat from the commitment to Western European cooperation, for which Chancellor Adenauer has become by all odds the most prominent spokesman. On the other hand,

France feared that Adenauer, because of this very prominence, would only reluctantly accept as an equal a revitalized nation dominated by one man.

Possible clashes of two strong personalities were avoided by the recognition of common interests. When France abandoned its claim to preferred treatment, West Germany agreed to support France and the Common Market in future discussions with Great Britain over the Free Trade Area. This meant in effect unifying German policy; while Adenauer had been backing the Common Market, his Finance Minister Ludwig Erhard had made no secret of his sympathy for the Free Trade Area. After the Franco-German consultations, the Chancellor told Erhard to step back into line. Adenauer's subsequent decision to remain as Chancellor, depriving Erhard of his golden opportunity, was ascribed in France to a desire to strengthen the Common Market and forge a lasting entente with France.[2] With harmony between the two leading powers of the Six publicly reaffirmed, there was no longer a possibility that, as the British had hoped, the other four members would break away.

In turn, De Gaulle took pains to strengthen Adenauer's position by his clear and consistent support of the Western position in Berlin. West Germany was extremely sensitive to any signs that Great Britain and the United States were willing even to discuss the Berlin issue with the Soviet Union, or to make any contacts with East Germany. Macmillan's government in England appeared rather more flexible than the West Germans might have wished, and some remarks by Secretary Dulles aroused nervous flutterings in Bonn. By contrast, "what has impressed the directors of the Federal Republic is the desire of the French government to keep a cool head during this affair and, while waiting to learn the true intentions of the Kremlin, to refrain from any gesture which might needlessly increase the existing tension."[3] De Gaulle's undeviating support

[2] Such was the opinion of André François-Poncet, writing in *Figaro*, June 6, 1959.
[3] *Le Monde*, November 28, 1958.

meant all the more to West Germany when contrasted with the vacillation of some of the governments of the Fourth Republic.

The agreement between France and Germany on the Common Market and the Berlin crisis seemed to indicate an internationalist orientation in De Gaulle's policy. Not so other aspects of Franco-German discussions. Despite arrangements to develop jointly a medium-range military transport plane,[4] in military affairs the two countries appeared to drift apart. While the Fourth Republic had left the door open to cooperation on atomic matters with both Germany and Italy, De Gaulle's views were fundamentally nationalistic. Adenauer could only hope that France's self-restraint and its limited supply of nuclear weapons would for a long time restrain it from any precipitous action.[5]

On questions of conventional armament it was Germany which proved uncooperative. In May 1959 Germany and Great Britain announced plans looking toward "a standardized family of light-tracked military vehicles."[6]

Adenauer was the best "European" still in office in Western Europe. De Gaulle, on the other hand, had consistently opposed any form of supranational political federation. That France would persist in the course which it had followed ever since the demise of the European Defense Community Treaty was evident from the discussions between the two leaders and their representatives. The communiqué issued at Colombey-les-Deux-Églises after the first meeting between De Gaulle and Adenauer spoke of "organized" cooperation but added that it should "extend to

[4] *New York Times*, January 29, 1959.

[5] This subtle, perhaps temporary change in the military climate had potentially profound implications for regional organizations such as Western European Union.

[6] *New York Times*, May 16, 1959. The announcement followed British protests that the United States was seeking to monopolize military production in Europe. An example, as damaging to the French as any long-range German-British agreement would be, was the German decision to adopt the American F-104 over the French Mirage-III, although the latter was advertised as built in Europe for European tasks. Whatever their internal squabbles, Anglo-American policy, the French saw, was still firmly behind West Germany's reviving military power.

the greatest possible number of European states."[7] In the stress on *states* and on *number* Adenauer and De Gaulle by implication were ruling out a merger of sovereignty among the Six.

The international congress of European federalists, held in January 1959 under the chairmanship of Robert Schuman, supplied an opportunity for re-emphasizing the limits of France's "European" policy. After the congress had adopted a resolution urging the creation of a popularly elected European parliament and an international executive to direct all existing and contemplated European organizations, a message from Finance Minister Pinay emphasized the gap between the federalists and their governments. The leader of the Independents had in the past been sympathetic to the idea of European federation. Now that he was a key figure in the new French nationalism, his attitude was a very different one.

I wish, [he wrote] that you would not search for this or that ideal political statute which would, after all, prove to be premature. You are doing very useful work in examining the ways in which commercial, tariff, and economic policies envisaged by the Common Market lead to the confrontation, then to the coordination, of national policies in social, fiscal, and juridical fields; how the progressive development of a homogeneous international economic territory implies the harmonization of the commercial policies of the member states, the permanent linking of their diplomatic and defensive efforts; finally, how, without pointing to the setting up of vast federal structures, European international institutions can be established, and how they can be related to national institutions and to existing European institutions.[8]

Pinay's message reveals a dilemma of French policy in the area of European cooperation. It is true, the Coal-Steel, Common Market, and Euratom communities are limited in respect to membership, substance, and organization. It is equally true that the French architects of the

[7] *New York Times*, September 14, 1958.
[8] *Le Monde*, January 11-12, 1959.

Common Market and Euratom, unlike the creators of the Coal and Steel Community, did not envisage the goal of an eventual political federation. Yet all three communities, to be successful, had to grow. As they grew, they would progressively assume supervision over so much that hitherto had been subject to national control that a partial merger of sovereignty would inevitably result.[9] Did this mean that the Fifth Republic would become increasingly enmeshed in the type of political federation rejected by De Gaulle and repeatedly denounced by Premier Michel Debré? On the other hand, if French leadership limited the relationship among the partners to "cooperation," would this not lead sooner or later to the stunting and even the virtual dissolution of the three communities? In short, it appeared possible that De Gaulle had started in one direction, but still had in mind the opposite destination. If the time came when the Fifth Republic concluded that membership in the Six was compromising its sovereignty, then it would logically turn toward Great Britain and Britain's continental associates, and away from West Germany, Italy, and Benelux.

When the process of reconciling the Europe of the Six with the Europe of the "Non-Six" reached its decisive stage, French leaders would be swayed by their estimate of their country's intrinsic strength. If they were certain of its economic and political power, they would seek to expand their horizons from the "little Europe" to the larger world beyond. If they were uncertain or were opposed by substantial sections of French opinion, they might well retreat to the safer confines of the Common Market.

France and NATO

In September 1958 De Gaulle addressed letters, the exact texts of which were not made public, to Macmillan and Dulles, giving them the benefit of his unsolicited opinion

---

[9] Statements by the directors of the three Communities during their visit to Washington in June, 1959 recognized this eventuality (*New York Times*, June 10, 1959).

as to the proper role of France in the North Atlantic Treaty Organization.[10] Under the Fourth Republic, successive governments had complained over the refusal of Great Britain and the United States to accord France its rightful position of equality with them. This underrating of France, said critics of the Fourth Republic, was inevitable so long as France was weak. Therefore a change in its position in NATO would constitute an international recognition that the new Republic had effectively mobilized the country's great power potential.

De Gaulle raised three specific and related points, all of which had been presented previously by France and other countries both in NATO councils and in extra-NATO diplomatic exchanges. De Gaulle first protested that while NATO had fifteen members, the important decisions were taken for the most part either by the United States alone or by the Anglo-American partnership. He did not suggest that the two countries should bring to the full NATO Council issues which they were inclined to settle between themselves; instead, he urged that the two-power conclave should become a triumvirate. This proposal for a "political directorate" came directly out of De Gaulle's resentment at the decision of the United States and Great Britain to take concerted action in Lebanon and Jordan, during the Near Eastern crisis of 1958, without consulting him. The two big powers had, he felt, left France to tag along behind, holding their coats, so to speak, while they prepared to fight. French indignation was increased by the belief that the crises in Jordan and Lebanon had their roots in the mishandling of the Suez affair in 1956. At that time France and Great Britain had initiated military action, only to be frustrated by the United States. The ensuing two years, however, had produced a basic change in alliances, to the exclusion of France. Evidence was found in the "climate" of the NATO military Standing Group in Washington. After the Suez affair, good relations had been restored fairly rap-

[10] *Le Monde*, October 29, 1958, puts the date of the letters as September 24.

idly between Americans and British in the Group, but not between representatives of those countries and the French.

De Gaulle urged that the three-power directorate not be restricted to the area covered by the North Atlantic Treaty. This was consistent with the General's view of NATO. As a military security system it had helped to maintain the freedom of Western Europe. But now Soviet advances in other areas, and in nonmilitary fields, were threatening to encircle and isolate the West. France, of course, was not alone in recognizing this danger. The United States, and to a lesser extent Great Britain, were already reacting to the Soviet menace outside Europe. But—and this was the trouble—they were doing so without allowing France to participate in their decisions. Unlike other unconsulted members of NATO, France, in De Gaulle's opinion, was a world power, by right of its interests, its responsibilities, and its influence. He insisted, therefore, that global Western statecraft should have a tripartite foundation.

Like Fourth Republic governments, De Gaulle complained also that France had been denied its fair share of important positions in the NATO command structure. Believing that the future of NATO would be determined outside the continent, including areas where French interests were crucial, he sought to reinforce French claims to a leading role in Africa. After all, France was responsible for the defense of the African members of the French Community, and this defense was important to all of the West, which was threatened by the "balkanization" of Africa. The original NATO concept had recognized the significance of Algeria to the security of Europe, and especially to the Mediterranean area. But this did not go far enough. A North-South NATO axis should be added, stretching to the limits of the Community. Although NATO members should assist France in discharging its military commitments, there was, in De Gaulle's view, no implication that responsibility for command should be shared. Presumably France would retain leadership and control of the Community in Africa, while through France the Community would be brought within the protective framework of the North Atlantic Alliance.

De Gaulle's ideas were aired at the December 1958 meeting of the NATO Council. They were also discussed desultorily over a period of months by an informal Franco-Anglo-American Committee in Washington. Pending some agreement, De Gaulle made it clear that NATO could expect little from France. There would be no missile bases on French soil, no unified air defense, and the French Mediterranean fleet would in war and peace be exclusively under French direction.

Reluctantly General Norstad began to relocate NATO planes, formerly based in France, in West Germany and Great Britain. The SHAPE commander was only too well aware that while some concessions might be made to obtain France's military cooperation, there were serious obstacles to granting De Gaulle all he wanted. Other European countries, especially West Germany and Italy, would most certainly object to a three-power political directorate. Once the principle of a political hierarchy was admitted, it would be impossible to find any criterion for limiting its membership. Large nations would expect to be admitted as a matter of right; yet in some issues small nations had a crucial interest. Formal differentiation of status might endanger those advances which had been made since 1956 in strengthening the processes of political consultation within NATO.

In its search for a tripartite global strategy, France, feeling left on the outside looking in, may have exaggerated the degree of consensus which actually prevailed between the United States and Great Britain. Moreover, even a formal acceptance of France's demands might prove meaningless, since Britain and the United States had commitments which France could not share. As for Africa, so long as the war continued in Algeria, France's ability to maintain its position on that continent remained in doubt. The French Community had established a new relationship with French African territories, but it still remained to be seen whether the Community was to be a permanent institution or only a new phase in French retreat which had been going on for almost two decades. Premature support of France's military ambitions, inside or outside NATO, might produce the opposite effect from that intended. It might stimulate unrest in some countries of the French Community if their leaders came to feel that it was impeding their legitimate development toward independence. American and British policies, founded on recognition of new sovereign states as they emerged, provided one possible way of keeping Africa free from Communist subversion, and there was no assurance that France's alternate approach would succeed as well.

To France's allies, in short, it appeared that De Gaulle's proposals assumed the existence of a strong France, whereas in reality he had made only a start in correcting some of its weaknesses. The dilemma was similar to that posed by France's relation to the Common Market. In a period of its greatest weakness and of the greatest evident external threat, France had agreed that NATO should be a closely integrated military organization. Now that the threat had diminished, French leadership openly questioned the wisdom of military integration. Under such direction would not France's growing power prove disruptive? Increased military strength depended on two developments: an end to the war in Algeria, and production of an atomic bomb followed by the acquisition of a modest nuclear capability. If De Gaulle could accomplish both these feats, he could argue convincingly that NATO should become what he had originally wanted—a traditional military alliance among national states. In such an alliance, De Gaulle might achieve his basic aim for France, national grandeur. Arrangements for missile bases could then be made between the states directly concerned, with only limited participation by NATO as such. The nonsensical talk about a NATO stockpile of atomic weapons would cease; there would be no NATO-American control over nuclear warheads.[11] Cooperation among Western states would continue, but each nation

[11] This issue arose in part from French fears that in a crisis precipitate American action would produce nuclear war in Europe.

would have exclusive jurisdiction over its own military establishment and exclusive control of its own weapons.

France, Eastern Europe, and the Soviet Union

With regard to the Common Market, West Germany, and NATO, De Gaulle's initial moves were quite clear. On the other hand, the Fifth Republic's policies toward Eastern Europe and the Soviet Union remained obscure. De Gaulle held that the errors of Western statecraft, to which a weak France had subscribed, had made possible the expansion of Soviet control over a large part of Europe. While Western Europe had been saved, the upshot had been a highly dangerous East-West confrontation in the heart of the continent. The West had compounded its error by surrendering to the Soviet Union the initiative outside Europe, aiding Soviet penetration by its colonial policies. In this situation France had two contributions to offer, one stemming from its history and geographic position, the other from its special understanding of Russia.

France had an historic interest in the countries of Eastern Europe, an interest not shared by the United States or Britain. As a continental country its definition of "Europe" went beyond that area still free from the Soviet grasp. The communiqué issued after the first De Gaulle-Adenauer meeting spoke of their wish that Franco-German cooperation "extend to the greatest possible number of European states."[12] The makers of U.S. policy had at one time flirted with something called "liberation." This was a dangerous word. Its use could only increase Russian determination to cling to all aspects of control over Eastern Europe in the face of what it regarded as a direct threat to Soviet security. To impart a renewed meaning to "Europe," political leaders would first have to find out how far the Soviet Union would go in permitting expanded contacts between Eastern European states and the non-Communist world. Because of its geographic position and

[12] *New York Times*, September 15, 1958.

because in the Soviet view it did not pose anything like the same threat as the United States, France was the only nation which could undertake this mission.

Within non-NATO Europe French ties had traditionally been close with Rumania, Czechoslovakia, Poland, and Yugoslavia. Rumania was now tightly held within the Soviet orbit, and the Czech Communist apparatus seemed especially devoted to Moscow. Poland and Yugoslavia offered more attractive prospects. De Gaulle had become acquainted with Poland during a tour of duty after World War I. A long history had demonstrated the capacity of Polish nationalism to survive conquest and even partition, but Western policy had not explored fully the possibilities of cultural and economic ties with Wladyslaw Gomulka's regime. Lying between East Germany and the Soviet Union, Poland posed a potentially difficult problem for the Russians. Support for East Germany ran the risk of alienating Poland. On the other hand, if Russian security considerations dictated strong connections with Poland, difficulties might arise with the East German puppet government.

After it appeared that Tito's break with Moscow was more than a family spat, the Fourth Republic discovered the value of its traditional friendship with Yugoslavia. Now the Fifth Republic might see some advantage in sponsoring closer Yugoslav connections with European organizations, as well as bilateral agreements with Western European countries, particularly Italy. A rehabilitated Yugoslavia, for one thing, might embarrass the French Communist party, perhaps the most Stalinist among the larger Communist parties anywhere in the world.

If French efforts should fail, the existing impasse in Europe would not thereby be made worse. On the other hand, French initiatives, if successful might represent progress toward two important goals. They could make possible more meaningful discussions of European problems with the Soviet Union. The objective would not be to destroy Soviet influence in Eastern Europe, but rather to lessen the fear, held by both East and West, that war—sooner or later involving the use of nuclear weapons—might break out by accident. A second goal would be to build up Western contacts with Eastern Europe to the point where the Soviet Union would recognize that only a settlement halfway satisfactory to the West could preserve Russian security requirements in the area.

Granted that French views of Eastern Europe were fragmentary, tentative, and initially unreciprocated, they were none the less related to what appeared to be the early Gaullist conception of the Soviet Union. The threat to the West, according to this interpretation, arose not so much from the inflexible determination of international communism to dominate the world as from the unusually potent combination of techniques and power available to the rulers of the Russian state. France had had considerable experience in dealing with Russia as, under various regimes and in various eras, it pushed forward its frontiers. In the present plight of East-West relations propaganda forensics in the United Nations availed nothing, while negotiations on disarmament were either futile or dangerous. Soviet leaders must be convinced that their government, like other Russian governments in the past, was a member of the international community and as such shared an interest in and responsibility for the preservation of peace. So long as each side thought the other was aiming at exclusive control over particular areas, a contest for spheres of influence all over the world would inevitably occur, a battle difficult, as postwar events had shown, to restrict to nonmilitary levels. Any specific agreements which could be reached limiting the degree of influence sought and the techniques employed would reduce the insecurity felt by all members of the family of nations.

France could also, De Gaulle felt, test this hypothesis and its acceptability to the new rulers of the Soviet Union over the arc of Asia stretching along the southern border of the Soviet Union. Here, as in Eastern Europe, American and British blunders had caused irreparable damage to the West. Belated efforts to compensate for their mistakes through the creation of exclusive anti-Soviet systems of defense had only made a bad situation worse; they had invited, indeed forced, the Soviet Union to increase its pressure. But France was not a member or a supporter of the ill-begotten Baghdad Pact. Hence, it could take the lead in discovering whether the Soviet Union would be interested in diplomatic agreements, designed to limit the range of controversy. Since it had been demonstrated time and time again that Western "containment" did not actually contain, any progress toward a modus vivendi in the Near East, South Asia, and the Far East would cost the West little. If both the West and East could be convinced that the battle for the allegiance of these areas should be fought out by nonmilitary measures, the prospects for competitive but at least peaceful coexistence would be greatly enhanced.

Techniques of a Gaullist Foreign Policy

The instrumentalities employed by a large, influential nation in advancing its foreign objectives must necessarily vary widely over time and space. Since policy choices are conditioned by domestic capacities, as well as by the leaders' conceptions of the international environment, it follows that no dramatic alteration in techniques and no radical shift in priority of their use was to be expected at once in the foreign policy of the Fifth Republic. Like the British Labor party, which for all its hue and cry before the elections of 1945, had in most respects carried forward a Churchillian policy, De Gaulle also concluded that a continuation of the Fourth Republic's foreign policy was inevitable and even desirable. De Gaulle's early moves allayed the fear, arising from his denunciations of the previous regime and its policies, that he would alter rapidly and drastically the international relationships which had evolved since World War II. The same might be said for Premier Michel Debré, chosen over Soustelle because his intransigent nationalism was tempered by constant fidelity to Charles de Gaulle.

French leaders had long placed a premium on diplomacy as an instrument of policy, believing that in this field they were clearly superior to the United States and Great Britain. The Fourth Republic had used diplomacy to compensate for national weaknesses; the Fifth Republic now sought in it evidence of newly found strength. De Gaulle's appointment, renewed by Debré, of career diplomat Maurice Couve de Murville as Foreign Minister implied a determination to call the tune himself and to enlist the best musicians to orchestrate it. This emphasis on diplomacy would logically mean development of efficient administration and personnel in the Foreign Office and energetic extension of postwar efforts to improve the recruitment and training of foreign service officers. They might, however, expect to enjoy less freedom of action than had diplomatic representatives and missions under the Fourth Republic.

French concentration on cultural relations may be explained in part by lack of more forceful means of influencing other states. The significance for the cold war of historic ties with nations in Eastern Europe and the Near East may well have been exaggerated. However, for a Gaullist policy aiming at recovering as much as possible of France's former position in the world, cultural contacts could certainly serve as a useful opening wedge. Here again a lesson might be drawn from the experience of the United States and Great Britain. Both countries were suffering in their relations with non-European nationalist leaders the consequences of too heavy reliance on military and economic forms of influence.

In the field of technical assistance, France placed a premium on the training of experts to advise young countries concerning administrative organization and economic development. The creation of the French Community gave the Fifth Republic an opportunity to push ahead with programs whose example could be helpful to other underdeveloped countries. Such programs in time might become the best means of preserving French influence among the new African elites. They might also serve to introduce French products and French capital into the independent nations of the Near East, Asia, and Latin America.

For domestic as well as international reasons De Gaulle gave special attention to the military ingredient of French statecraft. The alienation of the military hierarchy from French political life could be cured by endowing the armed forces with added prestige, through modernizing them, establishing improved coordination, and centralizing control over them directly in the office of the president. Recovering its sense of mission, a revitalized French army could regard itself as a symbol of the national grandeur sought by De Gaulle for the Fifth Republic. This, however, did not mean that the direct use of military power, except in Algeria, would receive a higher priority among the instruments of French statecraft. De Gaulle's conception of the international environment, and of the requirements of a successful European policy, pointed in the contrary direction. This was the basis for the decrees of January 1959, which reflected both domestic considerations and De Gaulle's consistent views on military organization. Under these decrees, the core of the armed forces will be the professional soldiers—the elite—who furnish direction and purpose to the conscripts and to the reservists. The professionals are to carry out the "normal" missions of the armed forces; the conscripts augment the professionals, while the reservists are to be available for emergencies at home or abroad. In line with this concept, it seems probable that France will continue to press for a redefinition of NATO strategy and requirements, insisting on strengthening firepower and mobility and placing less emphasis on continuously mobilized manpower. While armed forces in being may symbolize grandeur, the potency of the new nationalism depends on a speedy resumption of domestic economic progress. For this, a larger, better trained, better educated labor force is required, but this goal would remain a mirage under a system of wholesale conscription and extended military service.

Chapter Twenty-One

AMERICAN POLICY AND DE GAULLE'S REPUBLIC

DE GAULLE'S ACCESSION to power and his initial policies have added few new issues to Franco-American relations, nor have they solved many of the old ones. However, the prospect of greater political stability than France has known for several decades provides a useful opportunity to review and reappraise United States policies toward its traditional ally. Sudden shifts are unlikely, especially since France is but one element in the complex international environment in which American diplomacy operates. How, then, does the role of the Fifth Republic compare with that of the Fourth?

Domestic Pressures and the Policy of Grandeur

Since World War II the United States has sought to help France recover its social, economic, and political health. To this end it contributed large sums to the Fourth Republic, plus emergency financial support to meet recurrent crises. The major purpose of this aid was to enable France to attain the position within the Western coalition desired by Washington and claimed by Paris. In practice, however, France did not attain the position of a great power. Confronting the persistent gap between French aspirations and French capacities, the United States was forced to base certain aspects of its policy on the conclusion that France was in fact weak, whatever its potential strength might be. It was, therefore, scarcely surprising that frustrations and irritations beset their relationship. As Americans saw it, their assistance had failed to produce solid results in France comparable to the progress shown by West Germany and Britain. For French leaders could not use the political system of the Fourth Republic to impose unity and a spirit of sacrifice on the French people. Policies, directed in practice, if not in theory, toward appeasing particular social and economic groups, failed to mobilize power to strengthen France's influence abroad. Always aware of American aid, Frenchmen regarded as inconsistent and humiliating many American actions which derived from French weaknesses. French leaders also believed that the United States underestimated the difficulties which the Fourth Republic encountered after World War II and failed to appreciate sufficiently the progress being achieved in the teeth of adverse circumstances.

Because it wants France to resume its position as a great power and has consistently underrated the obstacles to this goal, the United States has tended to exaggerate the prospects for immediate improvement created by the many superficial political and economic changes within France since World War II. A new French leader now claims for France a new unity and a new power. He has taken dramatic and far-reaching steps toward this end. Every social, economic, and political group has felt the impact of De Gaulle's leadership. But the pervasiveness of his reforms, his determination to achieve great-power status for his country, combined with American eagerness for a dynamic France, may cause the United States again to underestimate the limitations which still affect French power and policies.

The Fourth Republic, which sought to placate each conflicting domestic interest, ended by alienating practically all of them. The Fifth Republic has called on all its citizens to accept sacrifices for the unity, grandeur, and ultimate prosperity of France. Clearly, however, some groups are being asked to sacrifice more than others. De Gaulle's austerity ordinances of December 1958 have borne especially hard on labor, agricultural interests, low-income families, students, and those seeking reasonably priced housing. Time must elapse before isolated protests can turn into collective action, still longer before they have an impact on the government. For the present De Gaulle's personal popularity has thinned the ranks of those groups that traditionally oppose conservative economic and social policies. The new political institutions seem well designed to render surviving opposition ineffective, especially since the general atmosphere remains hostile to anything reminiscent of the Fourth Republic.

Over the longer run, however, the United States must expect a weakening of this emergency-born French unity. Most Frenchmen voted for a leader who would endow their country with international prestige, but in doing so they assumed he would reach the goal without sacrificing the economic progress and social benefits which had marked the last years of the Fourth Republic. They chose, in other words, the best of both possible worlds. Their disillusionment would thus be all the greater if neither objective were attained. In December 1958, the government abruptly announced that domestic consumption would be limited so that France could carry out all of its international responsibilities. The impact of this bad news on a people long accustomed to finding satisfaction in their daily life would sharpen as the full effect of the austerity measures made itself felt. If they saw with their own eyes that these sacrifices were not in vain, the French people would find the new spirit of self-denial less burdensome. That is the crucial question. Can De Gaulle in fact establish for Frenchmen the enhanced international position he has promised them? Such gains, if they come at all, will undoubtedly come slowly and erratically.

While the Fifth Republic possesses greatly increased capacity for executive decision, its focus is one man, a man who is sixty-eight years old. During the first months of De Gaulle's reign, he made crucial judgments covering the entire range of national policy. The installation of Debré as Premier and the character of his Cabinet served to preserve De Gaulle's all-powerful role. Any lapse in the

President's vigor or vision would at once decrease the effectiveness of every facet of the Fifth Republic. A decline or end of strong personal leadership would bring on a scramble for position and power matching in confusion that of the declining Fourth Republic. Even assuming De Gaulle's continued health and energy, the inevitably increasing opposition to the domestic implications of a policy of grandeur can still bring important political changes. Seeing himself as the embodiment of the general will, De Gaulle would be confronted with a serious dilemma, should his countrymen make their choice for easy domestic life over the rigors required by a policy of international prestige. In that situation, would the authoritarian elements already built into the political structure harden into a firm and dictatorial control over France's future? Any movement in this direction would add to popular opposition. But De Gaulle had stated, and his people have believed, that he has no dictatorial ambitions, however much he has wished to resume national leadership. Hence his decision might well be, rather, for concessions to enlarge the basis of his domestic support.

Whatever the future response of the Fifth Republic to domestic pressures, it will be difficult, if not impossible, for the new regime to pursue indefinitely a policy of grandeur. Over the long haul, it may well be unable to discharge all the international responsibilities it has assumed. In each of these two areas of action goals may have to be modified in order to achieve a closer balance than that now evident between domestic and international objectives. A more dubious but still tenable conclusion is that eventually the priority of domestic ends may be reasserted, again relegating to secondary importance the effort to enhance France's international status.

These possibilities bear directly on American policy at two levels. In day-to-day diplomatic contacts, the many irritations which beset Franco-American negotiations arise from the fact that only one man, overburdened with responsibilities in diverse fields and keenly aware of the necessity for prompt international recognition of France's increased stature, can speak for France. On the level of high policy, American statecraft will have to tread a cautious path between either accepting at face value the international role claimed by Gaullist France or overhastily denying that role because of the annoying intransigence of its representatives. Equally important, the United States must not be excessively optimistic over the Fifth Republic's continuing ability to solve its domestic social and economic problems while holding onto the allegiance of the overwhelming majorty of the French people.

Military Prestige

The success of the Fifth Republic in raising its international prestige depends to a considerable extent on its ability to develop an atomic arsenal of its own. Accepting his predecessors' view that great-power status requires a nuclear capability, De Gaulle has decided to press forward with an atomic program despite the added budgetary strain. His approach to Western European problems also relies on France's developing atomic weapons independently, not as part of any Western cooperative organization such as the Western European Union. Finally, domestic considerations have not been absent from this decision. Frenchmen might more willingly accept protracted sacrifices if France becomes, through its own efforts, the fourth member of the prestige-laden nuclear club. For the military high command, which seeks to reorganize the national defense establishment so that France can accomplish its military missions overseas, in Western Europe, and at home, the nuclear program is especially important. The addition of nuclear weapons to conventional armaments will, it hopes, provide the required flexibility and firepower without the use of mass manpower. Furthermore, military leaders could conceivably accept compromises in Algeria more gracefully if they were negotiated in a context of world power, unlike the series of military retreats which have been forced on the armed services by the political authorities since World War II. The prospect of developing an array of nuclear weapons, thereby restoring to France the central place in the defense of Europe that it yielded in 1940 and has not recaptured, would offset any implication of a new defeat in case a compromise settlement was reached in Algeria.

However, the Fifth Republic's preoccupation with the development of atomic weapons contains two serious dangers. Since 1957 French leaders have been hinting that France stands on the very threshold of the nuclear age. They have, in effect, invited Frenchmen and leaders of other countries to make the possession of atomic weapons a test of French vigor, but the essence of the test lies in France's ability to pass it quickly. Given the inevitable economic and political obstacles to atomic production, will a delay lead both Frenchmen and foreigners to ask whether the new grandeur is not in fact a new form of self-delusion? This danger has mounted since the government, unable to turn into reality the rumor that it would explode its own atomic weapon in 1958, announced that in all probability it would not do so before mid-1960. This is a long time to wait; many things may change in the meantime, at home and on the international scene, to thwart these plans.

A second danger lies in overestimating the value of basic knowledge of nuclear military technology. Already French experience has shown that having this knowledge is a far cry from being able to put it to use. It is equally obvious that the explosion of one nuclear devise, possibly an obsolescent one, does not prove that a nuclear capability has been achieved. If after one experiment France persists in building a national atomic stockpile, it will find, as have the United States and Britain, that nuclear weapons comprise a bewildering assortment potentially applicable to innumerable situations, all requiring difficult choices, all costing money. Since in all probability France cannot afford to match the British arsenal, let alone the American weapons systems, it may, after long travail, have to settle for far less than its allies possess.

What course will France select? The development of smaller-yield weapons would result in more individual units per billion of new francs, and would also accord with the various missions chartered for the French military establishment. However, French leaders may reject this choice as bringing insufficient national prestige and independence of policy. Should the Fifth Republic instead opt for higher-yield weapons and their accompanying delivery systems, it would again be hobbled by the disparity between the logical roles of its military establishment and its capabilities. Because many of these military missions are related to France's geographical position in Europe and within the Western alliance, this disparity might well mean that France also would fail to increase markedly its degree of independence.

The United States and the Nuclear Problem

With these French problems the United States is necessarily concerned. What American statecraft requires is an atomic policy taken in full recognition of its probable consequences. One choice is for the United States to continue on its present course, leaving France to proceed with its own nuclear program, as best it may. Then, when France has finally exploded its atomic weapon, the United States will have to decide how much to assist, and try to influence French nuclear development. Or the United States, together with Great Britain, can use to the full the year or so which remains before France becomes the fourth nuclear power, to try for an agreement with the Soviet Union on an acceptable system of limitation and inspection. France, which has repeatedly stated its view that bans on nuclear tests are undesirable and limitations on atomic stockpiles meaningless without a comprehensive enforceable inspection system (a position once taken by the United States also) has threatened to walk out of any summit conference that undertakes to discuss the subject of nuclear arms control.

American policies have in the past assumed that an unsupervised spread of nuclear capability is dangerous and should be impeded if it cannot actually be prevented. On the other hand, new policies might be based on the belief that an expansion of nuclear capabilities is either inevitable or desirable or both. If such a conclusion were reached, the United States, after removing legal barriers already partially breached, could actively assist France in technological and financial contributions to accelerate France's first atomic test without compromising the independence of the endeavor. On this basis, the United States would thereafter help France acquire the types of atomic weapons it needs and can afford to produce. In doing this it would also recognize the independence of France's power of decision. At the same time, either by contributing to national development efforts or by directly transferring its own nuclear weapons, America could assist others of its allies wishing to follow this path, thus ensuring that France would not become, or at least long remain, the only atomic power in Western Europe. Also the responsibilities of the North Atlantic Treaty Organization could be extended to the control of national nuclear armaments, carrying one step forward NATO's present role concerning nuclear warheads assigned by the United States to Western defense.

While the Fifth Republic has indicated it would welcome American assistance in building its own nuclear potential, it would probably object to any general forced-draft spread of nuclear technology under American auspices Its objective is to be the third and preferably the last member of an exclusive Western power elite, not just the first of a number of smaller nuclear powers. Because France objects to the present arrangement, whereby atomic weapons are held in U.S. custody, though within the framework of the NATO command, it will not agree readily to a collective supervision to include European armaments, either directly by NATO or through Western European Union. In the Gaullist view too much authority is already vested in organizations dominated by the Anglo-American partnership. Only a French-British-American partnership, with other members in a clearly subordinate status, would satisfy the prestige requirements of the Fifth Republic.

If the United States chooses to place its bets on the emergence of a strong France and to minimize the obstacles in that path and the adverse complications which may follow, it would logically give the Fifth Republic substantial and exclusive nuclear assistance on French terms. Such a single-track approach, however, does not seem consistent with the past behavior of the United States or with its commitments to its other allies, nor would the present prospects of the French power under the Fifth Republic justify putting so many nuclear eggs in one basket. For one thing, an exclusive policy in this field would entail a great many risks, risks which a more realistic policy would seek to spread as widely as possible. One of the hazards is inherent in the scattering of nuclear weapons about the world. From the American point of view, the slower the spread of these weapons, the greater the chances for it to take place without causing an explosion into military conflict. It is also doubtful that the French people understand and are prepared to pay all the costs of the independent development of nuclear weapons. And is it safe to assume that the positions which the Fifth Republic will take in Europe, Africa, and Asia, and toward the Soviet Union will always be in full accord with American objectives? Caution is suggested by the unpredictability of a system where power is concentrated in few hands, but operations not yet systematized.

At the risk of incurring extreme dissatisfaction on the part of France, American policy might best follow its present course of doing what it has to do in the nuclear field only when it has to and for as great a return as it can exact. This policy allows France to proceed with its atomic development unaided, while Washington continues to explore the prospects for an international agreement with the Soviet Union on the regulation of nuclear weapons. Since France cannot have even a modest nuclear arsenal for some time, the United States can publicly discount the importance of testing one nuclear device, while urging France to seek an international role more compatible with the attainment of its domestic, economic, and social goals. As part of this policy the United States could place greater emphasis than at present on NATO as the international guardian of European security and hence the logical custodian of a substantial portion of European nuclear weapons. By the time French nuclear capability becomes effective, technological developments may again have lessened American military dependence on Western Europe. Then France and Germany, both endowed with substantial independent military power, would have a greater feeling that NATO was fundamentally a European organization for European ends, responsive to their own and their partners' view of European requirements and less a tail to the American kite.

America, France, and Europe

The establishment of the Fifth Republic, France's entry into the Common Market, the formal beginning of Euratom, and continuing discussions of possible changes in the North Atlantic Treaty Organization are forcing the United States to re-examine its policies toward Western Europe as a whole. After World War II the cold war dictated an American policy resting on a partnership with Great Britain, economic aid to Western Europe, recovery of West Germany, promotion of the "unity" of Europe, and a substantial American military "presence" on the continent. From this policy emerged NATO, the subsidiary Western European Union, the OEEC, the Council of Europe, the Coal-Steel Community, and now the Economic Community and Euratom. The last two were put into operation at what may be the end of an era. To its determined aloofness from supranational agreements among the Six, Britain has added a defense strategy which has reduced its contributions to continental defense, despite the implications of its membership in Western European Union. The creation of a substantial West German army, now well under way, is bound to give Bonn a stronger voice, and perhaps a more independent one, in the affairs of Europe, especially if there is a change in the political direction of German policy. Above all, the new Fifth French Republic is emphasizing in domestic affairs national strength, and in international affairs, interstate cooperation rather than integration. One can add to this list of changes the economic recovery of Western Europe and the new emphasis by the post-Stalin Soviet leadership on building its influence in non-European areas. Despite the deliberately provoked Berlin crisis, these changes have generally downgraded the expectation that the Soviet Union intends in the foreseeable future to attack Western Europe. All these factors argue against making any new sacrifices of national sovereignties in order to build an organized supranational unity in Western Europe in the next few years. What should American policy do to meet these changes?

Under the Fifth as under the Fourth Republic, France has resented the Anglo-American partnership. Clearly, the French believe that wherever and whenever Britain or the United States is forced to choose between the other partner and France, it is France that is rejected. This feeling is partly a psychological reaction to France's awareness of its own weakness. Therefore, while insisting on full equality with the two great Western powers as a matter of right, France has not really believed that its claims would be acknowledged. For their part, both the United States and Great Britain see themselves and each other as world powers, but consider France primarily a continental country. De Gaulle's determination to restore France's national power and press a foreign policy of nationalism and grandeur raises the question of how far and in what areas American policy can be accommodated to his claims.

Few Americans would suggest abandoning the Anglo-American partnership. The Suez invasion and the Formosa Strait crisis provided severe tests of the relationship. They also demonstrated its durability, the strong concern of leaders in both countries to avert any permanent estrangement. At the same time, however, in its global strategy, the United States does not and cannot rely exclusively on its cooperation with Britain, for Britain's power, like that of France, has declined throughout the world and this trend is still proceeding. Postwar British policies, taking this shift into account, have leaned toward maintaining a prosperous, if less influential, nation. Hence

British leadership, whether Conservative or Labor, cannot accept *in toto* the American interpretation of the extent of sacrifices required by international developments. As only one member of a Commonwealth rapidly becoming ever more diversified in its composition and international outlook, Great Britain cannot afford to follow any single rigid approach to world problems, let alone one completely congruent with that of the United States. Only through flexibility can Britain hope to avoid repudiation by certain Commonwealth countries and consequent dissolution of the last important element which lends plausibility to British claims to be a world power.

Neither the United States nor Great Britain regards their partnership as an exclusive, immutable corporation. There are, therefore, certain concessions that can be made to satisfy French demands, without altering the basic Anglo-American relationship. One is for the United States to take a firmer position on the future relations between the Common Market and the wider Free Trade Area. The Common Market has been launched, and France has made considerable sacrifices to join it. It is in American as well as French interest that the venture succeed, even if it falls short of fully integrating the economies of the Six. On the other hand, the Free Trade Area was essentially a makeshift arrangement, patched up by Britain in hasty reaction to the Common Market. Months of negotiations were required before Great Britain was convinced that the Six could not be separated and that France in particular could not be isolated. American support could accelerate the process of adjustment by both sides, at the same time rescuing Great Britain from the consequences of its most un-English idea of what constitutes diplomatic effectiveness. More important, it would show French leadership that the United States did not in practice support Great Britain in all things at the expense of France. That demonstration would be all the more valuable, since American statecraft could not so easily accept the French viewpoint on other questions, notably nuclear and colonial matters.

Concerning NATO some concessions to French demands

are also plausible. There is no reason for the United States to go along with France in establishing a French-British-American political directorate within the Organization. Objections of other members to French proposals of this sort are legitimate. Moreover, this does not appear to be an unalterable objective of Gaullist policy. What De Gaulle seeks is a more responsible position for France within the Organization and entry into a world-wide diplomatic triumvirate transcending the confines of the alliance. And on these points certain concessions might well be made. French military representatives can be given more and better posts within the command structure. The appointment of a Frenchman to succeed General Norstad as Supreme Commander can be seriously considered. Responsibility within the European theater can be more generously apportioned, even to the extent of setting up a joint Franco-German command over NATO forces in Germany. The same can be done within the Mediterranean, recognizing the logic of the French contention that arrangements based on the situation existing before 1956 are long overdue for revision. In the air staffs of Supreme Headquarters suitable acknowledgment can be made of the progress made by French aviation. While supporting these structural modifications, the United States should make greater efforts to reserve for European arms in general and French arms in particular an adequate place in equipping NATO defense forces.

A wider diffusion of national responsibilities within NATO would be in line with the probable evolution of the Organization in the next few years. Given the elaboration of the European Communities, NATO is highly unlikely to assume a direct role in economic affairs. Nor is it likely to become a channel for establishing unified positions among the Western powers on problems outside the NATO geographic area. Finally, within the NATO area the process of formal political consultation has apparently progressed about as far as it can. Whatever may be its contribution to Western diplomacy, the Organization as such will not become the principal decision-making body for resolving problems which arise among its members. In short, NATO can be expected to remain primarily and essentially a military organization. International developments strongly indicate that within the Western alliance system the emphasis will shift from an Organization pooling national capacities to a cooperative arrangement among individual members. This trend should not alarm the United States. To attempt to tighten the bonds between members artificially might do more harm than good. The United States, after all, originally favored building up the unity of Western Europe and making NATO a closely knit organization as a means, not an end—a means for European survival when Europe was weak economically and militarily. If the European members of NATO are determined to emphasize allied cooperation on a national basis rather than supranational integration, and if they can thereby, with the aid of the United States, continue to preserve the freedom of Western Europe, the initial objective sought by all, including the United States, will be attained.

Africa and the French Community

Next to the creation of the Fifth Republic itself, De Gaulle's most striking achievement in 1958 was the establishment of the French Community, which represents a logical and considerable advance over the policies initiated in 1955 by the Fourth Republic. Although the Community was intended to be a finished structure, many factors continue to prevent any stable relationship between France and Africa. The Algerian war is still unsettled—De Gaulle's most evident failure. The emerging forces below the Sahara that led France to establish the Community probably will not remain satisfied indefinitely with an institution within which France controls their economic, military, and regional development. While France can do a great deal for its former colonial territories in improving their standards of living and diversifying their economies, its efforts will probably be insufficient to satisfy the rising expectations of the future African elites and their newly self-conscious African supporters. France has not yet been able to arrest the drive of nationalism throughout French Africa, and despite its recent sweeping concessions, may not be able to stop it short of a complete break in political ties to Paris.

American policy still reflects the tradition of the past century, that major responsibility for Africa has been held by the colonial powers of Western Europe, France included. However, continued American aloofness may lead to conflicts both with France and with emergent groups of North and sub-Saharan Africa. The present degree of American identification with France has tended to alienate African nationalists without completely satisfying the French. Inevitably pressures for a more active policy have been growing apace.

The leaders of Tunisia and Morocco are determined to gain real independence for their countries, and their response to De Gaulle's devaluation of the currency makes it uncertain how long they will choose to remain within the franc zone. American assistance to France to enable it in turn to fulfill its long-standing commitments to aid the two countries is justifiable only if the United States simultaneously develops strong separate ties with both. So far, three factors have handicapped American policy in its direct relations with Tunisia and Morocco. First, there has been France's continued economic, military, and political predominance. Now, however, with the French withdrawing steadily from their previous positions, France may soon carry no greater influence than other nations in its erstwhile protectorates. Second, the West in general and the United States in particular have had an important military interest in Morocco and Tunisia as part of the Western system of defense against Soviet aggression. It is now unlikely that these two countries will permit the United States or other Western nations to maintain unilateral control over military installations for very long. An attempt to hang on to them against the expressed will of the local leaders would only impair the effectiveness of the bases. Fortunately, the availability of American-built facilities in Spain and prospective developments in military technology forecast the time when North African bases will be less crucial to Western defense. Morocco and Tunisia are prepared to accept a period of transition from external to national control, provided it is explicit and brief. They also want economic and military assistance for a far longer period and in greater quantities than France is able to provide. This situation presents the United States with another opportunity to frame its own policy in North Africa.

The third factor that has inhibited a separate American approach to Tunisia and Morocco is Algeria. De Gaulle wishes to end the war, to develop an Algerian "personality," and to embark on a large-scale program of economic and social development. If he succeeds, his policies will produce an Algeria evolving toward autonomy and possibly full self-determination. Algeria's contacts with its neighbors, already numerous, will become more substantial with the passage of time. The longer De Gaulle has to wait for the French extremists to concur with his views, however, the greater the price France will have to pay for peace. Americans, as well as Algerians, Moroccans, and Tunisians, also have an interest in seeing the present conflict ended. While the United States cannot publicly espouse Algerian autonomy, American diplomacy, using various available leverages, may be able to do much to bring it about. If successful in its efforts, the United States would strengthen greatly its relations with the three countries of the Maghreb; continued aloofness, on the other hand, might be a prime cause of repudiation of the West throughout Africa. Equally important, a settlement in Algeria based on real autonomy will reinforce the stability of the Fifth Republic militarily, economically, and even politically, once the Right-wing extremists are permanently curbed.

If the French Community survives at all, it will be as a grouping of independent states. The chances of this are jeopardized by the French belief that the Franco-African relationship has evolved as far as can be permitted and that any further devolution of responsibility—particularly in the area of military defense—is inadmissible. Another obstacle is France's view of the Community as excluding any idea of an African federation. If these attitudes remain unchanged, the Community may very well become an area of conflict, with the risk of an ultimate dissolution of the various territories to France. While the United States has an interest in seeing the Community succeed, American policy must not ignore the possibilities of a serious deterioration. In these circumstances, a bifurcated approach seems called for: through private and governmental channels Americans can work with France to make the Community an instrument for the progress of African areas; at the same time the United States should make it clear that it is not opposed to national independence for African peoples within or outside the Community, or to cooperative, even federative, relationships among African territories.

The loss of French Africa would be a calamity for France. Perhaps De Gaulle's Fifth Republic could not survive such a catastrophe. On the other hand, an Africa independent of French political influence would not constitute an equivalent disaster for the United States. The United States would suffer a major defeat only if the peoples of Africa turned actively against the West, as the Soviet Union fervently hopes and expects they will. A policy whose only political alternatives for Africa are the maintenance of its connection with France or its complete alienation from the West would face diplomatic bankruptcy. France has long suspected that the United States is not dedicated to the preservation of French interests in Africa. This suspicion is justified. The United States may sympathize with France's difficulties and hope French interests will not suffer in the new evolution, but it cannot make French goals the mainspring of its relations with Africa. If Franco-American cooperation in this area is to continue, it is primarily French, not American, policy, which must make most of the adaptations demanded by African nationalism.

France in the World

By the tests of military and economic strength and political influence France is not a world power. Although still a Eurafrican power, it will be less and less so in the years to come. Fundamentally, France is a continental European power; its future as a nation will depend on whether it recognizes that role and how it plays it. Its contributions to the maintenance of freedom and security in the crucial area of Western Europe will depend, in turn, on how well it builds up its domestic strength and how realistically it redefines its international ambitions and commitments. Events since World War II have made France's transition to a new position in the world especially painful and disorderly. A nation which has been as strong and as influential as France cannot be expected to relish its reduced circumstances. Willingly or not, France has been following the path previously traced by other European countries—Holland, Sweden, Spain, Portugal, and Italy. Viewed in the perspective of relative international prestige and power, this path leads unevenly but inexorably downward. Yet, in terms of material and cultural satisfactions for the French people, the path may in fact lead upward.

Some see De Gaulle's republic as a convulsion, a rebellion against France's diminished stature in world politics, but this notion is in part fallacious. Actually, only a very small percentage of French society was so unwilling to accept the change, that it threatened a civil war against a republic which seemed lacking in the means or the desire to reverse the decline. De Gaulle and his Fifth Republic, though dedicated to the nationalism and grandeur demanded by this small group, do not depend on the revolutionists for their survival. Rather does their success rest on the ability of French leadership to strike a new balance between power and responsibility. Naturally, De Gaulle has begun by claiming to increase French power and to exercise French responsibilities unaltered. Over the next few years, however, this posture can scarcely be maintained. It is doubtful that the French people, who until recently have not had to face up to the hard choice between sacrifice and prestige, will accept for the long run the summons to a grandeur that is in fact beyond their resources. The ultimate function of the Fifth Republic may well be to supervise a smoother and more effective transition from a world-wide to a European role.

If Gaullist France does, in practice, regardless of its officially proclaimed goals, carry out this transition, it will merit the continuing sympathy and support of the United States. A primarily European France, strong and responsible, must be a primary objective of American statecraft. Such a France is uniquely equipped to fill the power vacuum that has menaced Europe's future since World War II. A Western Europe without France's contribution can dissolve in chaos. A Western Europe in which France plays a leading role is indispensable to the strength and vitality of the free world.

BIBLIOGRAPHICAL NOTE

THERE ARE a number of studies in English of the political operations of the Fourth Republic, among the best of which is Philip Williams' *Politics in Post-War France: Parties and the Constitution in the Fourth Republic* (New York Longmans, 1958). Catherine Gavin's *Liberated France* (New York: St. Martin's Press, 1955) traces the development of French foreign policy, while David Schoenbrun's *As France Goes* (New York: Harper, 1957) reveals the insights of long acquaintance with French problems. Herbert Luethy's *France against Herself* (New York. Praeger, 1955) and Alexander Werth's *France, 1940-1955* (New York. Holt, 1956) follow the decline of the Fourth Republic into *immobilisme;* Luethy pinned major hope on Pierre Mendès-France, while Werth devoted more attention to the interaction of foreign and domestic policy. *The House without Windows: France Selects a President*, by Constantin Melnik and Nathan Leites (Evanston, Ill.: Row, 1958), and Leites's *On the Game of Politics in France* (Stanford, Calif.: Stanford University Press, 1958) offer penetrating analyses of party politics in the last years of the Fourth Republic. Useful studies of French politics have been presented by David Thomson, *Democracy in France: The Third and Fourth Republics* (3rd ed , London: Oxford, 1958), Owen R. Taylor, *The Fourth Republic of France: Constitution and Political Parties* (London: Oxford, for the Royal Institute of International Affairs, 1951), and Dorothy M. Pickles, *French Politics: The First Years of the Fourth Republic* (London: Oxford, for the Royal Institute of International Affairs, 1953).

Among French self-examinations, Emmanuel Berl's *La France Irréelle* (Paris: Grasset, 1957) and Jacques Fauvet's *La France Déchirée* (Paris: Fayard, 1957) deserve attention, as do the criticisms leveled against "the system" by Jean Maze in *Le Système, 1943-1951* (Paris: Ségur, 1951), by Michel Debré in *La*

Mort de L'État Républicain (Paris: Gallimard, 1947) and *La République et Son Pouvoir* (Paris: Nagel, 1950), and by Louis Vallon in *Le Dilemme Français* (Paris: Denoël, 1951). A reader of De Gaulle's war memoirs, *Call to Honour, 1940-1942* (New York· Viking, 1955) and *Unity, 1942-1944* (New York: Simon and Schuster, 1959) will not miss the many indications of the French leader's personality and attitude. De Gaulle's major speeches delivered before 1951 have been collected under the title *La France Sera la France* (speeches collected by Le Rassemblement du Peuple Français in 1952).

Most useful among studies in English of the French economy are Warren C. Baum, *The French Economy and the State* (Princeton: Princeton University Press, 1958) and J. S. G. Wilson, *French Banking Structure and Credit Policy* (Cambridge: Harvard University Press, 1957). Recent French studies include Jean-Marcel Jeanneney, *Forces et Faiblesses de L'Économie Française* (Paris: Colin, 1956), and Jean Chardonnet, *L'Économie Française* (Paris: Dalloz, 1958). More specialized works are Henry W. Ehrmann, *Organized Business in France* (Princeton: Princeton University Press, 1957) and Mario Einaudi, Maurice Byé, and Ernesto Rossi, *Nationalization in France and Italy* (Ithaca, N.Y.: Cornell University Press, 1955).

While satisfactory studies of French society in its development since 1945 are lacking, some of the gaps are filled by Rhoda B. Métraux and Margaret Mead in *Themes in French Culture* (Stanford, Calif.: Stanford University Press, 1954), by Hadley Cantril and David Rodnick, *On Understanding the French Left* (Princeton· Institute for International Social Research, 1956), and by Albert Pasquier, *Les Doctrines Sociales en France* (Paris: Librairie Générale de Droit et de Jurisprudence, 1950). *The Culture of France in Our Time*, edited by Julian Park (Ithaca, N.Y.· Cornell University Press, 1954), contains separate sections on art and literature, as well as an examination of French education by Mr. Park. Under the editorship of Alfred Sauvy, the journal *Population* has explored the social and economic implications of France's rapidly increasing population. Valuable regional studies include Laurence W. Wylie, *Village in the Vaucluse* (Cambridge: Harvard University Press, 1957), and Charles Bettelheim and Suzanne Frère, *Auxerre en 1950, une Ville Française Moyenne* (Paris: Colin, 1950). The link between social and economic groupings on the one hand and political behavior on the other greatly preoccupies French writers, foremost of whom is François Goguel, with his study of the *Géographie des Élections Françaises de 1870 à 1951* (Paris: Colin, 1951). For indications of the nature of the French military establishment as a social group, one can usefully follow articles in *Revue de Défense Nationale* which resumed publication in July 1945. The journal *Esprit* devoted its issue of May 1950 to "Armée Française?," but the military commentator of *Le Monde*, Jean Planchais, is one of the few to attempt a volume on the subject of *Le Malaise de l'Armée* (Paris: Plon, 1958). Edward L. Katzenbach, Jr., "The French Army," *Yale Review* (Summer 1956), pp. 498-513, is a pioneering effort in English.

The development of postwar policies toward Africa has been treated succinctly but thoroughly by P.-F. Gonidec in *L'Évolution des Territoires d'Outre-Mer depuis 1946* (Paris: Pichon, 1958), while Pierre Moussa, *Les Chances Économiques de la Communauté Franco-Africaine* (Paris: Colin, 1957) makes clear the economic stake which France has in its African territories. Indispensable to an understanding of the Algerian problem is Germaine Tillion, *Algeria: The Realities* (New York. Knopf, 1958), Jean-Jacques Servan-Schreiber, *Lieutenant in Algeria* (Tr. by Ronald Matthews, New York: Knopf, 1957), and Henri Alleg, *The Question* (New York: Braziller, 1958), the latter supplemented in its English edition by a self-revealing introduction by Jean-Paul Sartre.

General studies of French foreign policy, in French or English, are few. The author's *Weaknesses in French Foreign Policy-Making* (Memorandum No. 5. Princeton: Center of International Studies, Princeton University, 1954) and *France: Keystone of Western Defense* (Garden City, N.Y.: Doubleday, 1954) are short studies, as is *La Politique Étrangère et ses Fondements*, prepared by the Association Française de Science Politique (Paris: Colin, 1954). Noteworthy journal articles include Alfred Cobban, "Security and Sovereignty in French Foreign Policy," *International Journal* (Summer 1953), pp. 172-180; J.-B. Duroselle, "The Crisis in French Foreign Policy," *Review of Politics* (October 1954), pp. 412-437; the same author's "L'Élaboration de la Politique Étrangère Française," *Revue Française de Science Politique* (July-September 1956), pp. 508-525, as well as his larger and more general work, *Histoire Diplomatique de 1919 à nos Jours* (Paris: Dalloz, 1953). Edgar S. Furniss, Jr., "The Twilight of French Foreign Policy,"

Yale Review (Autumn 1954), pp. 64-80, and Daniel Lerner and Raymond Aron, editors, *France Defeats EDC* (New York: Praeger, 1957), are concerned, respectively with the unfolding course and the implications of France's most traumatic experience since World War II.

France's developing role in Western Europe must be followed in treatises devoted to various European institutions. A. H. Robertson, *The Council of Europe: Its Structure, Functions, and Achievements* (New York: Praeger, 1957), gives an excellent analysis of that organization. Derek Bok has summarized *The First Three Years of the Schuman Plan* (Princeton: Princeton University Press, 1955); Fred H. Sanderson gives a useful survey in "The Five-Year Experience of the European Coal and Steel Community," *International Organization* (Spring 1958), pp. 193-200. William Diebold, Jr., has given an authoritative analysis in *The Schuman Plan* (New York: Praeger, for the Council on Foreign Relations, 1959). The evolution of Euratom and the Common Market are traced in a special issue of the *Chronique de Politique Étrangère* (July-November 1957), pp. 409-918. Ben T. Moore has considered *Euratom: The American Interest in the European Atomic Energy Community* (New York: Twentieth Century Fund, 1958), and Miriam Camps has written a most informative memorandum on *The European Common Market and Free Trade Area* (Memorandum No. 15, Princeton: Center of International Studies, Princeton University, 1957). A later pamphlet by Mrs. Camps clarifies the various positions taken by the participants in *The Free Trade Area Negotiations* (Memorandum No. 18, Princeton: Center of International Studies, Princeton University, 1959). Those interested in the complex problems arising from the efforts at political and economic unity in Western Europe should not neglect the articles in the *European Yearbook* (4 volumes covering the years 1953 to 1956-57, The Hague: Nijhoff, 1955-1958).

Indications of France's role in and attitudes toward NATO may be found in Ben T. Moore, *NATO and the Future of Europe* (New York: Harper, for the Council on Foreign Relations, 1958), a volume which covers a wider field than its title indicates; also in Gardner Patterson and Edgar S. Furniss, Jr., *NATO: A Critical Appraisal* (Princeton: International Finance Section, Princeton University, 1957), which reports the discussions of a conference of representatives from all the

NATO countries. A critical and challenging examination of NATO's military posture has been given by Marshal Alphonse P. Juin and Henri Massis in *The Choice before Europe* (London: Eyre, 1958). Foremost among journal articles are those by Jules S. Moch and General Pierre Gallois, "Les Conséquences Stratégiques et Politiques des Armes Nouvelles," *Politique Étrangère*, No. 2, 1958, pp. 149-180, by Maurice Duverger, "Neuf Thèses sur l'Alliance Atlantique," *La Nef* (December 1957), pp. 15-21; by Edgar S. Furniss, Jr., "France, NATO and European Security," *International Organization* (November 1956), pp. 544-558; and by Arnold Wolfers, "Europe and the NATO Shield," *International Organization* (Autumn 1958), pp. 425-439.

Four items specifically concerned with Franco-American relations merit special mention. Donald C. McKay, *The United States and France* (Cambridge: Harvard University Press, 1951) is a fairly general treatment. Raymond Aron and August Heckscher, *Diversity of Worlds* (New York: Reynal, 1957), reporting a Franco-American conference, is also an illuminating dialogue between the two authors. Maurice Honoré is not so much interested in better relations with the United States as the title indicates: "Pour des Relations Meilleures avec les États-Unis," *Revue Politique et Parlementaire* (December 1952), pp. 380-394, while Raymond Cartier is not as negative as is suggested in the title of his article, "Pourquoi les Américains Sont-ils Détestés dans le Monde Entier?," *Paris-Match*, March 24, 1953. A later, well-focused discussion of the United States from the French viewpoint is Joseph E. Baker, "How the French See America," *Yale Review* (Winter 1958), pp. 239-253.

INDEX

Abbas, Ferhat, 197, 430-32
Acheson, Dean, 45, 48, 75, 86, 63-64, 315
Action Committee for a United Europe, 252
Action Committee for Republican Defense, 345
Action Républicaine et Sociale (ARS), 88
Act of Chapultepec, 35
Adenauer, Konrad, 26, 47, 76, 84, 103, 108, 296; *see also* Germany
  and France, 50-51, 275, 459-62, 468
  and NATO, 75
  and the Saar, 46, 68
  a symbol, 371
Administration, French governmental, 128-31, 133-34, 238-40
Africa, 7, 279-80, 298-99, 309; *see also* Algeria, Morocco, Overseas Territories, Tunisia
Africa, sub-Saharan, 179-95, 193-95, 216; *see also* Overseas Territories, French Community, French Union
African Convention, 188
African Socialist Movement, 188, 442
Afro-Asian bloc, 309
Agony of Indo-China, The (Navarre), 175
Ahidjo, Ahmadou, 450-51
Aid, economic
  French to Algeria, 207-09
  French to Morocco, 234
  French to Tunisia, 221
  U.S. to France, 22-23, 160, 173, 304-07, 474-75
  U.S. to Morocco, 234-35
  U S. to Spain, 71

Aid, military
  U.S. to Europe, 34-35, 58-59
  U.S. to France, 71, 161-62
  U S. to Tunisia, 222
Ailleret, Charles, 285
Ajaccio, 330
Alabama, 308
Albord, Tony, 171, 178
Alcoholism, 148-49
Algeria, 117-18, 121, 180, 186, 212, 214-15
  and Black Africa, 192
  censorship affecting, 170-215
  "Common Charter," 319
  conspiracy in, 319-40
  and De Gaulle, 380-82, 423-39
  economic aspects of, 156-58, 194, 206-09, 212-13, 258
  and Egypt, 217-18
  elections in, 209, 388-89, 433-35
  and Fourth Republic, 196-218, 241, 317-48
  and Great Britain, 216-17
  military in, 167-72, 176-78, 204-05, 210-14, 318, 331-32
  and Morocco, 192, 205-06, 216-17, 229-35, 318-19
  and NATO, 37, 197, 276, 289
  oil in, 199-202
  and political parties, 119, 157, 301
  ratissage and torture in, 170, 211, 214, 321
  and Soviet Union, 216-17
  and Tunisia, 192, 205-06, 216-17, 219-29, 318-19, 428-30, 435-37
  and UN, 198-99, 209, 246, 432
  and U.S., 216-17, 301, 310-11, 438-39, 489
Algeria, Republic of, 428
Algiers, 5, 197, 319, 325, 329
Alleg, Henri, 211, 215

INDEX

Allied Control Council for Germany, 7, 15
Alphand, Hervé, 226
Alsace-Moselle Canals, 272
Anglo-American Good-Offices Mission, 226-29, 302, 429
Anglo-American partnership, 247-48, 464-67, 484-85
Anglo-French Union, 4
Anti-Americanism in France, 301-03
Anticolonialism, American, 307-11
Apithy, Serou, 445
Arabia, 199
Arab League, 20, 218, 231, 435
Arab nationalists, 222, 231, 304; see also Algeria, Egypt, Morocco, Tunisia
Argentina, 35
Armand, Louis, 263n
Armengaud, André, 267, 307
Arms to Tunisia, 222-23, 248, 302, 435
Army-Youth Committee, 171
Aron, Raymond, 283, 312 quoted
Arras, 341
Arrighi, Pascal, 330, 339
Article 90, 352-55
Asia, 298-99
Atomic weapons, 250, 264-66, 314, 480-83
and France, 249-50, 284-90, 478-83
and NATO, 248-49
Auriol, Vincent, 44, 62, 70, 127, 343
Austria, 32, 95-96, 261, 287

Baghdad Pact, 218, 471
Bailliencourt, Albert de, 353
Bakary, Djibo, 442
Bamako, 191
Bandung Conference, 180
Bank of France, 156
Bantus, 308
Barangé law, 142
Barberot, Colonel, 320n
Bases
French in Tunisia, 220, 225-26, 228
North African, 488-89
U.S. in France, 162, 293
U.S. in Italy, 274
U.S. in Morocco, 233-34
U.S. in Spain, 71
Bastia, 330

Bastid, Paul, 86
Bayet, Jean, 141-42 quoted, 375
Bayeux address, 359, 362
Beeley, Harold, 227-28
Bekkai, Embarek, 230
Belgian Congo, 186
Belgium, 55, 57, 222, 232, 279
economic aspects of, 152, 155
Benelux, 27, 28, 57, 99, see also Belgium, Luxembourg, Netherlands
Ben Guerir, 233
Ben Gurion, David, 218
Bénouville, Guillain de, 178
Berlin, 37, 45, 95, 104, 460, 484
Bermuda meeting, 95, 247-48
Beuve-Méry, Hubert, 376n
Bevin, Ernest, 26-29
Bey of Tunis, 229
Biaggi, Jean Baptiste, 335
Bidault, Georges, 26-27, 98n, 327, 381n
and Algeria, 320, 324, 435
and De Gaulle, 384
on European affairs, 11-12, 46, 90, 269
fall of government, 54
as foreign minister, 9, 95, 237
on Germany, 14-18, 45, 63
and Indo-China, 97
at London meeting, 39-40
and Near East, 20
at Paris Peace Conference, 10-11
and party, 118, 317, 382-83, 395
and Pflimlin, 343
and secret agreement with Italy, 37
and U.S aid, 34
Bidonville, 418
Big Five, 6
Big Four, 11
Big Three, 4, 6-9, 13, 24, 290
Bigeard, Colonel, 325
Billères, René, 117, 143
Billotte, Pierre, 62
Bizerte, 220, 225-28, 352, 429, 436
"Black Commandos," 205
Bloch-Lainé, Françoise, 145
Blum, Léon, 18, 22, 28, 373
Bollardière, Jacques Marie Roch Paris de, 214
Bonn, 270, 483
Bonnefous, 28, 31, 52, 120

Boulanger, Georges E., 136, 178
Boulhaut, 233
Bourdet, Claude, 388-89 quoted
Bourgès-Manoury, Maurice, 116-17, 126, 395
  and Algeria, 158, 209-10, 326
  and atom weapons, 266
  and constitution, 375, 379
  and European Common Market, 258
  and tax reform, 156-57
Bourguiba, Habib, 221-24, 226-29, 424
  and Algeria, 206, 218, 430, 435-36
Boyd Orr, John, 86
Brady, Thomas F., 228 quoted
Brazzaville, 184, 425, 440, 443
Briand, Aristide, 29-30
Brindillac, Charles, 134
British Commonwealth, 28, 70, 102, 180, 193, 260, 281, 449, 485
Brussels, 67, 269-70
Brussels Pact, 26, 33-37, 39, 99, 103-06
  and NATO, 100, 103
Buchalet, Georges, 223
Bulgaria, 10, 21, 406
Bundestag, 68
Burma, 310
Byrnes, James F., 16-17

Cabinet, ministerial, 129-30
Cairo, 217-18, 222, 428
Caltex, 200
Cambodia, 293
Cameroons, the, 180, 186-87, 190, 195, 449-51, 453
Canada, 35-36, 63, 198
Cantril, Hadley, 147-49
"Capital of Europe," 269-70
Cara, Sid, 424
Carthage Declaration, 219
Cartier, Raymond, 307-08 quoted
Catholics, 99, 142, 268
Censorship, 382n; *see also* Algeria
Censure and confidence, motions of, 363-64
Center-Left, the, 396-97
Center of Republican Reform, 386, 392
Central Europe, 3-4, 21-22, 296, 468-71
Ceuta, 231

Chaban-Delmas, Jacques, 212, 385, 396
Chapultepec, Act of, 35
Chênebenoît, André, 401 quoted, 407
Chevallier, Jacques, 325
China, Communist, 246, 312, 436
Christian Democrats (German), 57
Churchill, Winston, 4, 28, 45, 62-63, 95, 471
Clappier, Bernard, 161
Claudius-Petit, Eugène, 383
Clay, Lucius D., 44n
Clostermann, Pierre, 345
Cocatre-Zilgien, André, 134
Colombey-les-Deux-Églises, 321, 461
Combaux, E., 281-82 quoted, 283, 386-87
Commissioners for West and Equatorial Africa, 187
Committee of Ministers, 30, 69, 238, 294
Committee of National Defense, 175
Committee of Public Safety, 321-23, 326-29, 423-26, 434
Committee on Universal Suffrage, 353, 356
Constituent Assembly, 8-9
Communist party, 7-8, 23, 30, 117, 121
  and Africa, 182, 215, 231, 301, 442
  and atomic weapons, 283
  and constitution, 356-58, 372, 376-77
  economic influence of, 128
  in elections, 116, 385, 391-92, 394
  and European cooperation, 66, 72, 99, 259
  and Fifth Republic, 370-71
  and Germany, 14
  in government, 11, 26, 72-74, 137, 292, 317, 368
  and government officials, 240, 241, 333, 337, 340, 343-44, 348
  and Indo-China, 83
  and the military, 172
  and Near East crisis, 352
  and neutrality, 244-45
  in Resistance, 4, 367
  and Socialists, 318
Compagnies Républicaines de Sécurité, 336
Conakry, 185

Confédération Française des Travailleurs Chrétiens, 337-38, 375, 413
Confédération Générale du Travail (CGT), 23, 146, 337-38, 409, 413
Congress for Madagascan Independence, 442
Congress of European Unity, 28
Connally, Tom, 35
Conseil d'État, 134
Conservative party, 52, 82, 485
Constantine, 389, 413, 425, 427-30, 485
Constitution
  Fifth Republic, 352-79
  Fourth Republic, 31-32
  German, West, 44
  West European, 8
Constitutional referendum, 443-44
Constitutional reform, 332-34, 352-58
Consultative Assembly, 27-30, 46-49, 52, 62, 69
Convention on Relations between the Three Powers and the Federal Republic of Germany, 76-77
Cornut-Gentille, Bernard, 451
Corsica, 330, 334-35, 347
Coste-Floret, Alfred, 7n, 267-68, 365
Cot, Pierre, 32, 240
Cotonou congress, 442
Coty, René, 126-27, 328, 331-32, 343-48
Coudenhove-Kalergi, Richard N. von, 270
Council of Europe, 27, 29-33, 53, 57, 69, 268-69
  defects of, 58, 79
  and ECSC, 56
  and European Political Community, 92
  and France, 45-46
  and Germany, 32-33, 45, 49
  and Great Britain, 46, 67
  and the Saar, 32, 47
Council of Foreign Ministers, 10, 16, 19
Council of Ministers, 69, 238, 294
Council of the French Union, 181
Council of the Republic, 62, 108-09, 242-43

Couve de Murville, Maurice, 240, 347, 352, 472
Crises, governmental in France, 124-28, 300
Crozier, Michel, 148 quoted
Czechoslovakia, 21-22, 27, 37, 469

Dahomey, 185, 188, 444-45
Dakar, 185
Daladier, Édouard, 66, 99, 375, 395
Danube, 22
David, Marcel, 257
Debré, Michel, 84 quoted, 361, 408, 438, 463
  and De Gaulle, 354, 369, 385
  and economy, 406, 415
  and premiership, 471-72, 476
Defense, national, and Council of Europe, 32-33
Defferre, Gaston, 181, 373-74, 394
Degoutte, Lucien, 374
Dehler, Thomas, 100 quoted
Delbecque, Léon, 212, 326, 396
Democratic party (US), 299
Denmark, 29, 267, 279
Dépêche du Midi, 375
Depreux, Édouard, 373, 382
Dia, Mamadou, 442-43
Diallo, Abdoulaye, 446n
Dienbienphu, 96-97
Disarmament, 313-14
Dissolution and referendum in Fifth Republic constitution, 364-67
Duchet, Roger, 117, 317, 339, 341
  and Algeria, 320, 324, 327, 434
  quoted on elections, 386, 390
Duclos, Jacques, 333-34 quoted, 395
Duhamel, Jacques, 52n
Dulles, John Foster, 100-02, 234, 301-02, 304, 463-64
  French opinion of, 315-16
  and Germany, 460
  and Tunisia, 226
Dumesnil de Malicourt, René, 214
Dunkirk Treaty, 11, 21
Duverger, Maurice, 54 quoted, 61-62, 87-88, 215, 359

Eastern Europe, 12, 468-71
East-West talks, 85-86, 95
Eccles, David, 458
Écho d'Alger, 320

École Nationale d'Administration, 142-44, 238
École Polytechnique, 167
Economic and Social Council, 411, 413
Economic Cooperation Act, 43, 53, 253
Economic Council, 133, 144
Economic recovery, European, 43
Economic union, 51; *see also* Schuman Plan
Economist, The, 162, 267
Economy, French, 22-23, 151-64, 193-95, 221-22, 403-15
    Fourth Republic, 61, 252-54, 292, 304-07
Eden, Anthony, 5, 34, 100-02, 261
Edjelé, 199, 429
Education, 141-45, 420-22
Egypt, 202, 217-18, 232, 240, 264, 309
Eisenhower, Dwight D., 71, 234, 247-48, 307, 315
Elections in Fifth Republic, 366-69, 380-99, 428-29
Electric power, 415
El Glaoui, 229
El Skhira, 429
Ély, Paul, 176-77 quoted, 331, 426
Erhard, Ludwig, 460
Esprit, 375
Estaing, Giscard d', 411
Etzel, Franz, 263n
Euratom, 251, 262-66, 294, 297
    and France, 114, 242, 462-63
Europe, defense of, 27, 34-37, 58-61, 70-71, 77, *see also* EDC, NATO
European army, 63; *see also* EDC, NATO
European Coal and Steel Community (ECSC), 27, 100, 106, 252-53, 294
    defects of, 79
    establishment of, 55
    and "Europe," 56, 75-76, 92, 164, 264
    and France, 55, 153, 239, 272, 462-63
    and Germany, 65, 67, 68, 94
    and Great Britain, 54
European Common Market, 251-62, 264, 294, 297, 305
    and France, 114, 163-64, 242, 259-62, 452, 456-59, 462-63
    and Great Britain, 253-54, 260-62; *see also* Free Trade Area
    and French Overseas Territories, 195, 254
    and U S., 485
European Defense Community (EDC), 27, 67-70, 212, 237, 294
    and ECSC, 75-76
    failure of, 63, 251, 271-72, 300
    and France, 77-100, 105, 123, 216, 240
    and Germany, 84
    and Great Britain, 75, 78, 82-83, 89-90, 102
    and NATO, 77, 84
    Treaty negotiations, 71-100
    and U.S , 100-01
European Investment Fund, 258
European Monetary Union, 458
European Nuclear Energy Agency, 263
European Payments Union, 157, 458
European Political Community, 27, 92-95, 98, 294
European political cooperation, 266-75
European Recovery Program, 23, 58n, 100, 161
European union, 24-59, 253, *see also* Euratom, European Coal and Steel Community; European Common Market; European Defense Community, European Political Community, NATO; Western European Union
European Unity, 54
Exercise "Foudre," 275
Executive functions
    in Fifth Republic, 361-62, 369-70, 441
    in Fourth, 120-24
Express, 215, 375, 420

Faure, Edgar, 114, 117, 257, 383, 395
    and dissolution of National Assembly, 115, 365, 369
    in government, 73, 74, 88, 108, 236

INDEX 503

Faure, Jacques, 213-14
Faure, Maurice, 117-18, 374 quoted
Fauvet, Jacques, 394 quoted
Federalists, European Congress of, 462
Fifth Republic, 351-52, 423-39, 445-48, 457-58, 492; see also Fourth Republic, France, Gaulle, Charles de
  and atomic weapons, 478-88
  constitution of, 354-79
  and East Europe, 468-71
  economy of, 403-15
  education in, 420-22
  elections in, 366-69, 380-402, 428-29
  and European cooperation, 456-59, 462-68
  foreign policy of, 456-92
  and Germany, 459-63
  housing program of, 418-19
  and military in, 426-27, 473
  parties in, 380-402
  social issues in, 416-22
  and Soviet Union, 357, 468-71
  and U.S., 435, 474-90
Finland, 10
Fonds d'Investissement et de Développement Économique et Social (FIDES), 193-94
Fonds d'Investissement pour le Développement des Territoires d'Outre-mer, 450
Force Ouvrière, 337-38, 375, 409
Foreign Affairs Commission, 23
Foreign Affairs Committee, 9, 29, 31-32, 38, 44, 242
Foreign Ministry, 239
Foreign policy, French, 22-59, 236-50, 291-316, 456-92
Formosa, 312, 484
Fourth Republic, 131, 138, 177, 249-50; see also Fifth Republic, France
  and Algeria, 196-218, 317-48
  constitution of, 31-32, 332-34
  crises, governmental in, 124-28, 300
  economic aspects of, 51-52, 61, 97, 114, 137-38, 151-64, 252-54, 292, 304-07
  education in, 141-45

  elections in, 114-16, 188
  and European cooperation, 24-59, 114, 216, 259-62, 276-90
  the executive in, 120-27
  foreign policy, 22-59, 236-50
  and Germany, 13-19, 39-46, 59, 74-75, 107-08, 176, 251-52, 270-75, 296
  and Great Britain, 274, 297
  and great-power status, 246-50
  housing program in, 139-41
  and Italy, 36, 252, 273-74
  and the military, 61, 165-78
  and Morocco, 229-35
  public opinion in, 145-46, 243-46
  and the Saar, 46-50, 81
  social dissatisfaction in, 145-50
  and Soviet Union, 85, 95-96, 295-96, 313-14
  taxation in, 150-51
  and Tunisia, 302
  and UN, 180, 186, 246-47
  and U.S., 86-87, 291-316
Franc, devaluation of, 163, 406
France, 3-13, 20-23; see also Fifth Republic, Fourth Republic; Third Republic
  and Central Europe, 3, 21-22
  and Germany, 3-5, 23, 25
  and Great Britain, 3, 4, 7, 9, 11, 20-21
  and NATO, 37-39, 248
  and the Saar, 13, 23, 25
  and Soviet Union, 8, 9, 10, 20-21, 37, 66-67
  and UN, 5-6, 20-21, 197-99
  and U.S., 7, 9
France-Observateur, 375-76
Franchon, Benoît, 337
Frandon, René, 214
Free Democratic party (German), 100
Free Trade Area, 260-62, 305, 456-57, 485; see also ECSC
French Atomic Energy Commission, 283
French Community, 440-55, 472, 489-90
French Equatorial Africa, 108, 185, 192, 449
French Guiana, 258
French Union, 83, 89, 181, 307, 353
  inadequacies of, 182-83, 192, 440

French West Africa, 185, 188, 192, 449
Frey, Roger, 386
Front d'Action Nationale, 336n
Front de la Libération Nationale Algérienne (FLN), 22, 217-18, 224-25, 320-25, 377, 430-33
Functional integration, 52, 57n

Gabès, 225, 228
Gabon, 186, 188, 194-95, 444
Gafsa, 225, 228
Gaillard, Félix, 157-58, 249-50 quoted, 374, 383
 and Algeria, 210, 332, 336, 377
 fall of government, 119, 270, 317, 320, 403
 in government, 116, 124, 126-27, 382, 394
 and Tunisia, 222-24, 226-29, 241-44, 302
Gallois, P. M , 286
Gasperi, Alcide de, 26
Gauche Démocratique, 348
Gaulle, Charles de, 114, 135, 239, 299, 324, 341; *see also* Fifth Republic
 accession of, 262, 321-22, 341-42, 345-48, 351
 and Algeria, 325-29, 334-35, 380-82
 and budget, 158
 in exile, 4-5, 196-97
 and Indo-China, 83
 and NATO, 464-65
 program of, 345-48, 351-52, 380
 and provisional government, 3, 7, 8
 and RPF, 113, *see also* RPF
 on Rhine, 14-15
 as symbol, 13, 358, 371, 400
 and trade-unions, 337
Gaullism, 386-90
Gaullists, 73-74, 88, 99, 116, 119, 321
 and European cooperation, 66, 72, 84, 93, 259
Gazier, Albert, 318, 338, 373, 394
General Agreement on Tariffs and Trade (GATT), 260-61, 305, 452

General Assembly, 197-98, 210, 432; *see also* United Nations
General Society to Promote the Development of Commerce and Industry in France, 259
Geneva conference, 96, 277, 296, 312
Géraud, André, 80 quoted
Gerbet, Pierre, 267
Germany, 6, 9, 45, 99, 141
 economic aspects of, 16, 150, 152-53, 155, 271
 and ECSC, 55, 57, 94
 and European cooperation, 47, 49, 72-99, 103-05, 258
 and France, 3-5, 13-19, 23, 25, 39-46, 74, 176, 251-52, 270-75, 295-96, 459-62
 and Great Britain, 13-14, 18-19, 25, 41, 43
 and NATO, 75, 107, 271, 279, 289-90, 292, 304
 occupation of, 7, 67-68
 rearmament of, 50, 59, 61-68, 71, 85, 87, 108, 250, 265
 and the Saar, 46-50, 94-95, 272
 and Soviet Union, 13-14, 16-17, 19, 45, 76
 and UN, 76-77, 104
 and U.S., 13-15, 18-19, 25, 41, 43
Ghana, 180, 190, 448-49, 451, 453
Gibraltar, 231
Giordani, Francesco, 263n
Giraud, Émile, 23 quoted
Giroud, Françoise, 215-16 quoted
Godard, General, 320
Gold Coast, 180
Gomulka, Wladyslaw, 469
Gouin, Félix, 373 quoted
Great Britain, 6, 9, 11, 101-02, 140-41
 and Africa, 180, 186, 194, 216-17, 447-48
 economic aspects of, 150, 152-53, 155
 and European cooperation, 46, 53-54, 77, 253-54, 260-63, 281-90
 and EDC, 75, 78, 82-83, 89-90, 102
 and European unity, 28-30, 59, 93, 483-84

INDEX 505

Great Britain (Cont.)
  and France, 3-4, 7, 9, 11, 20-21, 274, 297, 457-58
  and Germany, 13, 14, 18-19, 25, 41, 43, 63, 66
  and UN, 10, 20, 177, 247
Great-power status, French attitude toward, 4-8, 246-50
Greece, 11, 30, 279, 406
Grosser, Alfred, 301
Grumbach, Salomon, 9-10 quoted
Guadeloupe, 258
Guillaumat, Pierre, 347
Guinea, 185, 188-89, 194, 443-48, 453; see also French Community, French Union, Overseas Territories

Hague, The, 28, 270
Halles, les, 413
Hammarskjöld, Dag, 247, 432
Hassi Massaoud, 199
Hauriou, André, 318
Herriot, Édouard, 28, 44, 99, 117
High Authority (ECSC), 55-56
Hirsch, Étienne, 413n
Hirsch Plan, 152
Hitler, Adolf, 3-5, 13
Ho Chi Minh, 83
Hodgkin, Thomas, 437 quoted
Hoffman, Paul, 43, 53
Hoffmann, Johannes, 81, 94, 271-72
Hoover, Herbert, 71
Honoré, Maurice, 86-87 quoted
Houphouet-Boigny, Félix, 180-81, 188, 201, 443-44, 449
  appointment of, 353, 440
Housing, 139-41, 418-19
Hull, Cordell, 299
Humanité, L', 95, 337, 376
Hungary, 21, 312, 378, 438

Ibadan congress, 310n
Iceland, 30, 36
Ifni, 230-31
Immobilisme, 113-64, 236-50, 301
Imperial preference, 261
Independents party, 88, 117, 122, 157, 340
  and Algeria, 324, 435
  and De Gaulle, 338, 344, 348
  and elections, 383, 389, 391
  and European unity, 93, 258, 462
  and Fifth Republic, 384, 356
  in government, 368
  and Mollet, 240-41
India, 197
Indo-China, 97
  defeat in, 175, 180, 237, 309
  economic aspects of war in, 156, 173
  and military, 166-67, 169-70, 172
  and NATO, 276
  and U.S., 83-84, 293
  war in, 20, 71, 75, 83, 87, 96, 162, 176, 203, 211
Indonesia, 310
Inter-American Treaty of Reciprocal Assistance, 35
International Monetary Fund, 157, 162
International Red Cross Convention, 432
Iran, 10, 21, 309
Ireland, 10, 29, 33
Israel, 218, 240
Istiqlal party, 229-30, 232
Italy, 6, 10, 27, 29, 57, 491
  and atomic weapons, 250
  economic aspects of, 150, 155
  and European cooperation, 37, 55, 57, 100, 103, 279
  and France, 36, 252, 273-74
  and Germany, 99
  and housing, 141
  and North Africa, 222, 232
  and Yugoslavia, 469
Ivory Coast, 108, 185, 189, 444

Japan, 6
Jeanneney, Jean-Marcel, 145
Jeune Nation, 336n
Jordan, 231, 464
Journal Officiel, 381, 405
Juin, Alphonse, 437

Khrushchev, Nikita S., 296, 378
Kinitra, 233
Korea, war in, 57, 59-60, 62, 69, 71, 85, 96, 176, 292
  economic aspects of, 155, 160

Labor party, 52-54, 67, 69, 82, 471, 485

Labor-management, 412, 417-18
Lacoste, Robert, 210, 320-21, 323, 326, 394
 and Algeria, 118, 204, 206, 213, 339
 and coalition, 119
 and Mollet, 318
 quoted, 178
Lacq, 414-15
Lambert, Pierre, 329
Lamine-Gueye, 188
Langevin Commission on Education, 141
Laniel, Joseph, 88-89, 96-97, 183, 257, 339
 in government, 91, 95, 120-21, 125, 395
Laos, 293
Larminat, Edgard de, 78-79
Laugier, Henri, 421 quoted
Laurens, Camille, 257
Laval, Pierre, 406
Lavau, Georges, 422 quoted
Lawrence, W. H., 203 quoted
Lebanon, 20-21, 231-32, 464
Lejeune, Max, 338
LeRoy, François, 6 quoted
Liberia, 186, 197
Libya, 36-37, 186, 197, 222
Lie, Trygve, 10
Lieutenant in Algeria (Servan-Schreiber, J.-J.), 211
Lisbon, 75
Lloyd, Selwyn, 261-62
Locarno Treaty, 104
Loi-cadre
 and Algeria, 209-319, 424
 and French Community, 442, 448-50, 454
 and Overseas Territories, 181-82, 185-86, 188-89, 192, 194, 440
 system of, 129
London, 4, 43, 100-02, 105, 107
London Council of Foreign Ministers, 6, 7, 15
Louviers, 378-79
Luxembourg, 55, 57, 269-70

"McCarthyism," 315
McCloy, John J., 48, 50, 62
Mackay Protocol, 269
Macmahon, M. E. P. de, 114-15

Macmillan, Harold, 247-48, 460, 463-64
Madagascar, 186-87, 190-91, 229, 444
Maghreb, 192, 436-37, 455
Mali grouping, 449
Manne, Georges R., 177 quoted
Maquenne, Paul, 414-15
Marchand, Jean, 197 quoted, 307-08, 310
Marie, André, 27, 395
Marshall, George C., 11, 34
Marshall Plan, 12, 28, 35, 58, 297
 and France, 11, 51, 152, 161, 292, 304
 and Germany, 25, 45
 and Great Britain, 11, 53
Martinique, 258
Massigli, René, 130 quoted, 193
Massu, Jacques, 320-21, 326-28, 424
Maudling, Reginald, 458
Mauriac, François, 87 quoted
Mauritania, 185, 194, 201, 444
Maurras, Charles, 241
Mayer, Daniel, 119
Mayer, René, 81, 88-91, 92n, 95, 120-21, 156
Médecin, Jean, 257
Mediterranean, 486
Medjez-el-Bab, 225
Mendès-France, Pierre, 118, 215, 241, 343, 396
 and Brussels Pact, 103, 105, 251
 and East-West talks, 109
 and European Common Market, 255-58
 and EDC, 78, 97-99
 and Fifth Republic, 345, 374, 378-79, 408
 in government, 88, 96-97, 107, 113-14, 122-23, 127, 236, 243, 297, 395
 and Indo-China, 176, 237, 239
 on North Africa, 108, 114, 197, 212, 219
 and Paris Accords, 108
 and party, 116-17
 and reform, 135, 149
Mendésistes, 117-18, 320, 383
Messina conference, 255
Michelet, Edmond, 385
Middle Congo, 186, 188, 195, 444
Middle East, 202, 297

Milice, 166
Military, 165-78, 426, 473
  and Algeria, 167, 169-72, 176-78, 211-14, 331-32, 423
  and expenditures, 8, 61, 156, 172-74
  and Indo-China, 166-67, 170, 172
  and NATO, 175, 177
  and Suez, 177
Minerals, in Africa, 194-95
Ministry of National Defense, 213
Mississippi, 308
Mitterand, François, 212, 343, 345, 379, 383-84
Moch, Jules, 61, 64-66, 73, 313, 338
  Minister of Interior, 128, 335-36, 340
Mohammed V, 234
Moktar, 226
Mollet, Guy, 142, 157, 247, 265-66, 317-19
  and Algeria, 118, 209-10, 212, 377
  and De Gaulle, 334, 341-42, 344, 347-48, 373, 382, 396-97, 408
  and European cooperation, 82*n*, 93, 181, 255, 268
  in government, 116, 125-26, 237, 240-41, 243, 385-86, 394, 398, 409
  and Paris Accords, 107
  and Pflimlin, 328, 338
  and Pleven, 73
  and SFIO, 119, 318
  and Tunisia, 221-22
  quoted, 265
Molotov, Vyacheslav, 7, 11, 16
Monde, Le, 61-62, 215, 383, 387, 407, 417
Monnet, Jean, 55, 98-99, 106-07, 239, 252
Monnet Plan, 22, 51, 128, 152-53
Montastruc, 379
Montel, Pierre, 352
Montgomery, Bernard, 39
Morgenthau Plan, 14
Morice, André, 117, 317, 383-84
  and Algeria, 320, 324, 327
  in government, 157, 209, 395
  "Line," 428
Morocco, 180, 192, 198, 202, 241
  and Algeria, 205-06, 216-17, 232, 318-19
  and Fourth Republic, 114, 229-35
  independence of, 194
  and Tunisia, 222
  and U.S., 488-89
Morocco, Southern Protectorate of, 231
Moscow, 19, 85, 378
Moslems, 180, 197, 208, 319, 325-26, 427-35; *see also* Algeria, Morocco, Tunisia
Moulay ben Arafa, 229
Mouvement National pour le Développement Scientifique, 421
Mouvement Républicain Populaire (MRP), 8-9, 25, 64, 96-97, 116-17, 382-83
  and Algeria, 319
  and Bidault, 317
  and European cooperation, 73, 100, 258
  and De Gaulle, 344-45, 348, 356-58, 372, 382, 389, 392
  in government, 14, 18, 122, 137, 237
  and Mollet, 240-41
  and Paris Accords, 107
  in Resistance, 367
  and Socialists, 142
Murphy, Robert, 227-28
Mutter, André, 229, 320, 323-24, 339
Mutual Assistance Program, 161
Mutual Defense Assistance Bill, 39
Mutual Security Act, 253, 292

Naegelin, Marcel-Edmond, 202, quoted, 345
Napoleon, 136, 177
Nasser, Gamal Abdel, 177, 217-18, 222, 277, 435
National Assembly, 12, 18, 26, 28-32, 121, 124-25
  and Algeria, 198, 210, 322
  and budget, 157-58, 172
  and De Gaulle, 345-48
  dissolution of, 115
  and elections, 380-84
  and European cooperation, 45-46, 65-66, 72-73, 257-58
  and EDC, 77-100, 123
  and ECSC, 55
  and Germany, 40, 42-43

and NATO, 38
and Overseas Territories, 181, 183, 187, 192
and Pflimlin, 339
and Suez, 240
National Bank of Commerce and Industry, 163-64
Nationalist movements, French-U.S. conflict over, 307-11
National School of Administration, 131
National Solidarity Fund, 207
Navarre, Henri, 175 quoted
Near East, 20, 160, 287, 299, 309; see also Suez
crisis in, 352
and France, 20-21, 218
Neo-Destour party, 229
Netherlands, the, 155, 491
and European cooperation, 55, 93, 256, 258-59, 279
New York Times, 203, 226, 228
Nièvre, 379
Niger, 185, 188, 201, 444
Nigeria, 180, 449, 453
Nigeria, British, 190
Nixon, Richard M., 235
Nkrumah, Kwame, 448
Norstad, Lauris, 282, 466, 486
North Atlantic Treaty Organization (NATO), 27, 31-32, 58, 61, 172
and Algeria, 37, 197
and Brussels alliance, 57, 100, 103
Council, 60, 63-64, 66, 71-72, 74, 102, 248-49
and EDC, 77, 84, 97
and France, 37-39, 248, 276-90, 463-68
and Germany, 50, 75, 271, 304
and Italy, 37
and Korea, 292
Pact, 30, 34, 241
and Soviet Union, 96
and UN, 290
and U.S., 70, 162, 248, 464-67, 485-87
and WEU, 275
Norway, 29, 141, 198, 261, 279
Nouasseur, 233
Nuclear tests, French view on, 314; see also Atomic weapons

Observateur, 215
Occupation, of Germany, 67, 154
Oil, 160, 195-96, 414-15, 429
in Sahara, 199-202, 311, 452
and the Suez crisis, 241, 264
Olympio, Sylvanus, 181*n*, 450-51
Oran, 217, 329
Organisation Commune des Régions Sahariennes (OCRS), 201, 452
Organization for European Economic Cooperation (OEEC), 31-32, 53, 298, 404, 452
and Euratom, 263
and European Common Market, 260, 305
and France, 159, 406
and Germany, 47
and Great Britain, 458
Overseas Territories, 114, 121, 179-95, 209, 235
and European Common Market, 254, 257-60

Pacific war, 6
Palais Rose, 67-68
Pan-European Union, 269
Paris, 6, 10, 12, 105, 269-70
Paris Accords, 106-07, 176, 271, 296
Paris-Match, 308
Parodi, Alexandre, 10
Parti Africain de l'Indépendance, 191
Parti Démocratique de Guinée, 446
Parti du Regroupement Africain, 188-89, 442, 450
Parties, in Fifth Republic, 372-75, 380-402
Parti Patriote Révolutionnaire, 336*n*
Parti Socialiste Autonome, 389, 392
Pay-scale controls, 416-17
Peasants and Social Action, 339-40, 348
Peiping, 432
Pelletier, Émile, 347
Perón, Juan, 35
Perrin, Joseph, 189 quoted
Pétain, Henri, 128, 141, 166, 357, 404
Petersberg agreements, 47-48

Petit Bleu des Côtes du Nord, Le, 66-67
Petkov, Nikola, 10
Pezet, Ernest, 247
Pflimlin, Pierre, 157-60, 322, 356, 365, 395
  and Algeria, 229, 323-43, 377
  and De Gaulle, 347, 351, 408
  in government, 119, 125, 270, 319-20
Phalange Française, 336n
Philip, André, 63, 82 quoted, 119
Phillippeville, 160
Piatier, André, 163 quoted
Pinay, Antoine, 109, 117, 121, 343, 462
  and economy, 122, 156, 158, 384, 404-05
  and European Common Market, 257
  and De Gaulle, 334, 347
  in government, 88, 125-26, 243, 395
  and Pflimlin, 327, 339-42
Pineau, Christian, 198, 210, 255, 394
  Plan, 279
  quoted, 312, 314
Planchais, Jean, 282 quoted
Pleven, René, 61, 85, 171, 318, 383
  and "Common Charter," 319
  in crisis, 126, 270
  and De Gaulle, 351, 375, 407
  and EDC, 78
  and Germany, 62, 65
  in government, 54, 70, 73, 88, 392
  Plan, 62-73, 75, 108
Poincaré, Raymond, 406
Poland, 17, 21, 469
Political Committee, 198
Political unity, European, 27-33, 267; *see also* European Political Community
Popular Front, 117, 310, 343
Port Lyautey, 233
Portugal, 10, 32, 36, 186, 491
Pose, Alfred, 356 quoted
Potsdam conference, 6-7, 15-16
Poujade, Pierre, 114-15, 151, 372, 378, 390-91
Poujadistes, 215, 240, 259

Premier, role of, in foreign policy, 336-37
President of the Republic, role of, in crisis, 125-26
Protocol, French tripartite, 8-9
Progressive party, 30, 32, 240, 348
Provisional government, French, 3-8
Public opinion, 72-73, 145-46, 243-46, 268

Quai d'Orsay, 237
Question, La (Alleg), 211, 215
Queuille, Henri, 34 quoted, 37, 73

Radical party, 26, 73, 113, 115-18, 142, 318
  and Algeria, 317
  and atomic weapons, 266
  and constitution, 372, 374-75
  and De Gaulle, 345, 348
  and European cooperation, 99, 258
  in government, 64, 108, 368, 392
  and Mendès-France, 96, 122
Radical-Socialist party, 114, 124, 157, 356, 382
Ramadier, Paul, 11-12, 28, 343, 345, 375, 394
Rapacki Plan, 296
Rassemblement Démocratique Africain (RDA), 180, 188, 191, 443-44
Rassemblement des Gauches Républicaines, 120, 348
Rassemblement du Peuple Français (RPF), 26n, 83, 113, 117, 244-45, 368, 391
Recession, U S., 294
Regroupement Africain, 348, 353
Remada, 228
Republican Action and Defense Committee, 338
Republican party, 299
Resistance, 4, 367
Réunion, 258
Reynaud, Paul, 28, 31, 54 quoted, 257, 339
  on Germany, 63, 108
  in government, 127, 365, 395
Rhineland, 13-15, 17, 19, 46
Richard, Max, 271 quoted

Right, the, in Fifth Republic, 384, 393-94
Rio de Janeiro conference, 35
Roche, Émile, 411-12 quoted
Rodnick, David, 147-49
Rome, 72, 270
Roosevelt, Franklin D., 5, 234, 299, 456 quoted
Rotvand, Georges, 421
Rueff, Jacques, 405-06
Rueff report, 408, 416
Ruhr, 13, 15-17, 19, 39-47, 54
Rumania, 469

Saar, 271-72
  and "Europe," 32, 47, 54, 92-94, 105-06
  and France, 13, 17, 19, 23, 25, 46-50, 81
  and Germany, 46-50, 68, 94-95, 272
Sahara, 160, 180, 231, 452; see also Organisation Commune des Régions Sahariennes
  oil in, 196, 199-202
St Ceré, 379
St. Cyr, 166-67
Sakiet-Sidi-Youssef, bombing of, 203-04, 206, 220-21, 224-26, 242, 302, 429
Salan, Raoul, 203, 320-31, 336, 424-26, 433-34
San Francisco conference, 5, 14
Sartre, Jean-Paul, 212 quoted
Saudi Arabia, 197, 231
Sbeitla, 226
Scandinavia, 36, 46, 69
Schneiter, Pierre, 18
Schuman, Robert, 26-27, 37, 86, 345
  and EDC, 90, 254
  and European cooperation, 53, 68-69, 269, 462
  as foreign minister, 64, 237, 317
  and French empire, 83
  on Germany, 38, 345
  in government, 42, 70, 395
  Plan, 45, 50-58, 82
  quoted, 41, 307
Second Modernization Plan, 153, 161

Section Française de l'Internationale Ouvrière (SFIO) see Socialist party
Security Council, 225-27; see also United Nations
Seekt, Heinrich von, 80
Senegal, 180, 183, 185, 188, 442, 444
Senghor, Léopold, 180-81, 188, 442-43, 445
  quoted, 183-84, 450
Separation of powers in Fifth Republic constitution, 359-61
Sérigny, Alain de, 320 quoted, 328
Servan-Schreiber, Jean-Claude, 386-87 quoted, 389
Servan-Schreiber, Jean-Jacques, 205, 211, 215
Servin, Marcel, 377-78
Sfax, 225, 228
Sidi Slimane, 233
Siegfried, André, 9 quoted, 24-25
Six, the, 55
Social Democratic party (German), 57, 69, 296
Socialist party, 8-9, 26, 64, 117, 358
  and Africa, 181, 188
  and Algeria, 119, 215, 317, 319, 321
  and atomic weapons, 283
  and De Gaulle, 342-43, 345, 348, 372, 434
  and economic questions, 157, 258
  and elections, 382, 386, 392, 394
  and EDC, 82, 88, 99
  and European unity, 92-93, 252, 268
  and Germany, 14, 296
  in government, 74, 118, 122, 137
  and Mollet, 318
  and MRP, 142
  and Pflimlin, 328, 339
  and Pleven, 73
  in Resistance, 367
Social Republican party, 116, 126, 348
Somaliland, 36-37
Sorin, Lenore, 418 quoted
Souk-el-Arba, 226
Soustelle, Jacques, 73, 126, 376, 458, 471
  and Algeria, 212, 317, 320, 327
  arrest of, 335

Soustelle, Jacques (Cont)
  and De Gaulle, 324, 384
  and Germany, 108
  and UNR, 385, 397
Soviet Union, 4, 152, 177, 246, 447-48
  East-West talks, 92, 109
  and Europe, West, 11-12, 58, 268, 484
  and France, 7-9, 20-21, 27, 37, 66-67, 85, 295-96
  and Germany, 7, 13-14, 16-17, 19, 45, 76, 313-14, 357, 468-71
  and Great Britain, 9
  and housing, 141
  and Near East, 309
  and North Africa, 180, 216-17
  and NATO, 276, 286
  and Potsdam conference, 6
  and UN, 10
  and U.S., 12, 295-96, 482
Spaak, Paul-Henri, 26-27, 69-70, 258
Spain, 62, 71, 186, 231, 491
Sputnik I, 294-95
Stalin, Joseph, 7, 95, 296
Standard Oil, 200
Standing Group, 280; see also NATO
Statute of Europe, 29-31
Strasbourg, 30, 55, 70, 269-70
Strategic Air Command (SAC), 233, 282, 287-88, 304
Stuttgart, 16
Sudan, 185-86, 188, 201, 444
Sudreau, Pierre, 418 quoted
Suez crisis, 160, 199, 240-41, 247-48, 484
  and oil, 264
  and military, 177-78
  and Nasser, 217-18
  and NATO, 276-77
  and U.S., 307, 309, 464-65
Sultan of Morocco, 234
Sulzberger, Cyrus, 378 quoted
Supreme Allied Command, Europe (SACEUR), 101-03, 282
Supreme Headquarters, Allied Powers in Europe (SHAPE), 71, 282, 466
Sweden, 29, 33, 141, 261, 491
Switzerland, 32, 141, 261, 324
Syria, 20-21, 231

Taft, Robert A., 71
Tag, Der, 431
Tananarive, 443
Tangier, 230
Tardieu, André 366
Taxation, 150-51, 406-07, 410-11
Tchad, 186, 188, 201, 444
Teitgen, P. H., 343, 365, 395
Third Force, 24-26, 267-28
Third Four-Year Plan of Modernization and Equipment, 413-14
Third Republic, 8
Thomazo, Colonel, 396
Thorez, Maurice, 377-78, 387
Tillion, Germaine, 202-03 quoted, 208-09 quoted, 309-10
Times (London), 6-7
Tito, Josip, 378, 469
Togo, 180-81, 186-87, 190, 449-51, 453
Torture, in Algeria, 170, 211, 214, 321
Toulouse, 379
Touré, Sekou, 181n, 443-44, 446-48
Trade, foreign, of France, 158-64, 305-07
Trade-unions, 337-38, 340
Transjordan, 10
Tribune du Socialisme, 119, 318
Trieste, 10-11
Trinquier, Colonel, 320
Tripartite government, in France, 8-9, 14
Troquer, André Le, 344n, 394
Truman, Harry S., 11, 38, 71, 314-15
Truman Doctrine, 35
Trusteeship Council, 180, see also UN
"Truth and Austerity" program, 405-08
Tunis, 222, 225
Tunisia, 192, 202, 241-42, 298
  and Algeria, 205-06, 216-17, 219-29, 318-19, 428-30, 435-37
  and Anglo-American Good-Offices Mission, 226-29
  economic aspects of, 194, 221-22
  and France, 114, 302, 351-52
  independence of, 180, 219-21
  and Mendès-France, 97, 108, 176
  and Morocco, 222, 231

and UN, 225-26
and U.S., 488-89
Turkey, 30, 279

Ubangi-Shari, 186, 444
UDSR-RDA (Rassemblement Démocratique Africain), 318, 348, 353
Union Démocratique et Socialiste de la Résistance (UDSR), 64, 126, 345, 382-84, 392
Union de Défense des Commerçants et Artisans (UDCA), 151
Union de la Gauche Socialiste, 389, 392
Union des Forces Démocratiques (UFD), 375, 383
Union des Populations du Cameroun, 190
Union et Fraternité Française (UFF), 114, 348
Union of Soviet Socialist Republics, see Soviet Union
Union pour la Nouvelle République (UNR), 383-400, 435
United Arab Republic, 428n, see also Egypt; Nasser
United Nations, 5-6, 10, 36-37, 77-78, 247
  and Algeria, 209, 432
  and France, 5-6, 10, 20-21, 180, 186, 197-99, 241, 246-47, 454
  and Germany, 76-77, 104
  and Guinea, 446-48
  and NATO, 286
  and San Francisco conference, 5-6
  and Tunisia, 225-26
United Nations Disarmament Commission, 313
United States, 483-87
  and Algeria, 198, 216-17, 301, 310-11, 438-39, 489
  and Brussels Pact, 36
  economic aspects of, 150, 152
  and Euratom, 263-64
  and Europe, defense of, 34-37, 63, 77, 100-01
  and European Common Market, 485
  and European unity, 12, 45, 253
  and France, 7, 9, 86-87, 291-316, 435, 474-90
  and Free Trade Area, 485
  and French Community, 489-90
  and Germany, 13-19, 25, 41, 43, 65-66, 71, 85, 87
  and Guinea, 447-48
  and Indo-China, 83-84
  and Morocco, 488-89
  and NATO, 70, 279, 281-90, 485-87
  and Near East, 20
  and Potsdam conference, 6
  and the Saar, 17
  and Schuman Plan, 53
  and Suez, 177, 301
  and Soviet Union, 295-96, 482
  and Tunisia, 488-89
  and UN, 10, 247
Upper Volta, 185, 188-89, 444

Vandenberg, Arthur H., 35-36
Van Naters, Marinus Van der Goes, 272
Veillas, Raymond, 437 quoted
Vermeersch, Jeannette, 395
Vernant, Jacques, 288
Vichy, 13, 128, 141, 166, 357
Vidal, Georges, 359
Viet-Nam, 83, see also Indo-China
Vigilance Committee, 321

Washington, 109, 263, 466
Weimar Republic, 129
Western European Union (WEU), 13n, 35, 106, 266, 273-75, 294
  and Germany, 251, 273
  and NATO, 275, 278
Weygand, Maxime, 80
World Economic Congress, 85-86
World War I, 166-67
World War II, 166

Yalta conference, 5, 15
Yazid, Mohammed, 430, 432
Youssef, Sidi Mohammed ben, 229
Yugoslavia, 217, 287, 469

Zeller, General, 177-78

CPSIA information can be obtained
at www.ICGtesting.com
Printed in the USA
BVHW050409310522
638430BV00022B/240